ORDER OF
BATTLE

ALLIED GROUND FORCES OF OPERATION DESERT STORM

THOMAS D. DINACKUS

Hellgate Press
Central Point, Oregon

Published by Hellgate Press/PSI Research
© 2000 by Thomas D. Dinackus

Cover Designer: Steven Burns

Please direct any comments, questions, or suggestions regarding this book to:
        Hellgate Press/PSI Research
        Editorial Department
        P.O. Box 3727
        Central Point, Oregon 97502-0032
        (541) 479-9464
        (541) 476-1479 fax
        info@psi-research.com e-mail

Library of Congress Cataloging-in-Publication Data
Dinackus, Thomas D.
    Order of battle : allied ground forces of Operation Desert
Storm / Thomas D. Dinackus. – – 1st ed.
    p. cm.
Includes bibliographical references and index.
ISBN 1-55571-493-5 (paper)
1. Persian Gulf War, 1991. I. Title.
DS79.72 .D54 1999
956.7044'2 – – ddc21   99–29407
                                    CIP

Printed and bound in the United States of America

First Edition 10 9 8 7 6 5 4 3 2 1
Printed on recycled paper when available

This order of battle is dedicated to all of the soldiers, sailors, airmen, Marines, and coast guardsmen who served in Operation Desert Storm, and to the families and friends who waited for them patiently while they served. All Americans owe these patriots a special debt of gratitude.

About The Author

Thomas D. Dinackus served on active duty with the U.S. Army for four years. He entered on active duty as a cavalry officer after graduating *cum laude* from Dickinson College in 1979 with a B.A. in history. Tom graduated from the Armor Officer Basic Course at Fort Knox, Kentucky, and then served in the 2nd Squadron, 3rd Armored Cavalry Regiment at Fort Bliss, Texas. He served initially as an armored cavalry platoon leader in E Troop, then as the Squadron S-3 Air, and finally as executive officer of G Troop. Tom left active duty as a captain in 1983 and then served four years in the Army Reserve.

Today Tom is a trial attorney with the Department of Justice. He resides in the Washington, DC, area, with his wife Lisa and son Jeffrey. In his spare time, he pursues military history and collects military insignia. Tom has had numerous military history articles published in various periodicals, including *The Trading Post, Armor, Infantry, AFV News, AFV G-2,* and *IPMS Journal.* He is also the author of *The Thin Green Line: U.S. Army Order of Battle 1997,* published by H.J. Saunders U.S. Military Insignia, Inc., in 1998.

Contents

Charts

Part 1: The Allied Coalition

Part 2: The U.S. Army

Part 3: The U.S. Marine Corps

Part 4: Allied and Coalition Units

Part 5: Analysis of Units Deployed

Appendices

Bibliography

Index

Introduction

Desert Storm was one of the largest military operations since the end of the Second World War, and the only post-World War Two operation conducted by the United States that was dominated by armored forces. I have long been interested in order of battle, and as a former cavalry officer who served in the 3rd Armored Cavalry Regiment in the early 1980s, my primary interest is armor and cavalry units.

Accordingly, I began to gather order of battle information shortly after Operation Desert Shield began. I soon decided that, in light of the important role they played, Marine Corps, allied, and coalition units should also be included.

Unfortunately, the Army has not published an order of battle for Desert Storm and most probably will not do so in the foreseeable future. The Army has published three detailed histories of Desert Storm, but none contains even a basic order of battle.[1] The Army is reportedly working on a detailed order of battle for Desert Storm, however it is unclear when this will be completed. In light of the fact that the last war for which the Army published a detailed order of battle was World War One, and the post-Cold War down-sized Army's lack of resources, it is doubtful the Army will publish a comprehensive Desert Storm order of battle any time soon.

---

[1] These are: BG Robert H. Scales, Jr., et al., _Certain Victory: The United States Army in the Gulf War_ (Washington, DC: Office of the Chief of Staff, U.S. Army, 1993); Frank N. Schubert, et al., _The Whirlwind War: The United States Army in Operations Desert Shield and Desert Storm_ (Washington, DC: Center of Military History, 1995); and COL Richard Swain, _Lucky War - Third Army in Desert Storm_ (Fort Leavenworth, KS: U.S. Army Command & General Staff College Press, 1994). The Army attempted to list all of the units that are entitled to campaign participation credit for Desert Storm in General Order No. 7, April 2, 1993, but this document contains a significant number of errors and provides no information concerning the assignment or role of the units listed.

Order of Battle

The official Department of Defense account of the Gulf War, *Conduct of the Persian Gulf War: Final Report To Congress* (Washington, DC: Government Printing Office, 1992), includes some order of battle information, but only at the highest levels. For example, it lists divisions but not the units assigned to the divisions. While the Marine Corps has included order of battle information in the interim histories it has published on Desert Storm, the information in these histories is neither comprehensive nor completely accurate. The Marine Corps reportedly intends to include a detailed order of battle in its official history of Desert Storm, but this will probably not be published for at least several years.

This Project: Purpose & Methodology

In the charts that comprise this order of battle, I have attempted to list and record the assignments of: (1) all combat arms units, down to the smallest TOE element; and (2) all major non-combat arms units. While I would have liked to list each unit that deployed, that would have dramatically expanded the size and price of this order of battle, and the time needed to complete this project.

With regard to non-combat arms units, I have listed all units commanded by full colonels and above. I also listed the 5th Special Operations Support Command, despite the fact it was commanded by a lieutenant colonel, because this unit was authorized a full colonel and because of the widespread interest in special operations units.

One of the things that convinced me to pursue this project was that the popular press — and even many specialized sources that should have gotten it right — committed numerous order of battle errors. For example, it was widely reported that III Corps Artillery deployed from Fort Sill, Oklahoma, to the KTO. This is incorrect. What actually happened is that two of the three field artillery brigades that were normally assigned to III Corps Artillery — the 75th and 212th — were relieved from this assignment, deployed to the Gulf, and were then assigned to other commands. Both were initially assigned to XVIII Airborne Corps Artillery, but the 75th was later reassigned to VII Corps Artillery and fought with VII Corps during the ground war.

How To Use This Book

This order of battle consists of introductory materials (an introduction, this section on how to use this book, notes, abbreviations, a list of military installations, and several maps); the text; 38 charts organized into five parts; six appendices; an index; and a bibliography.

The **Notes** section, which begins at page xv, provides background information, followed by a list of **Abbreviations** and a list of **Military Installations**. The **maps** provide a basic overview of the ground war. The **text** provides a basic narrative with regard to the ground war and certain specific topics.

The **charts** are organized into five parts. **Part 1** consists of one chart, **Chart 1,** which portrays the overall organization of the Allied coalition that prosecuted Desert Storm. **Part 2,** which consists of 15 charts, **Charts 2-15,** presents detailed information on the U.S. Army units that served in Desert Storm. **Part 3,** which consists of 12 charts, **Charts 16-26,** presents detailed information on the U.S. Marine Corps units that served in Desert Storm. **Part 4,** which consists of three charts, **Charts 27-29,** presents detailed information on the British, French, and Arab-Islamic army units that served in Desert Storm. **Part 5,** which consists of seven charts, **Charts 30-36,** analyzes the units that served in Desert Storm comparing, for example, the U.S. Army's and U.S. Marine Corps' contribution to Desert Storm, and Desert Storm to the United States' other post-World War Two combat contingencies (Korea, Vietnam, Grenada, and Panama).

The six **appendices** address collateral issues. **Appendix A** provides basic information on how ground combat units are organized and other basic background information about ground combat units. **Appendix B** provides basic information on the hierarchy of officers' ranks. **Appendix C** provides basic information on the hierarchy of ground units. **Appendix D** provides information on how U.S. Army units were organized during Desert Storm. **Appendix E** provides information on how U.S. Marine Corps units were organized during Desert Storm. Finally, **Appendix F** contains color illustrations of selected unit insignia and medals from Operation Desert Storm.

Parts 2 and **3** employ a similar organization for, respectively, the U.S. Army and Marine Corps. In each section, the first several charts present all of the major units that served in Desert Storm, first by unit type (**Chart 2** for the Army and **Chart 16** for the Marine Corps) and then as organized for combat (**Chart 3** for the Army and **Charts 17** and **18** for the Marine Corps). **Chart 17** covers those Marine units that served under Marine Corps control in the I Marine Expeditionary Force, while **Chart 18** covers those Marine units that served under the command of the U.S. Navy.

The next charts present detailed information on the combat arms units that served in Desert Storm. For the Army, this information is presented in six charts. **Chart 4** covers the majority of Army units, those that served in Kuwait/Iraq under Army command as part of Third Army, the senior Army headquarters in the Gulf. **Charts 5-8** cover the remaining Army units. **Chart 5** covers those Army units that served under Marine Corps command in I MEF, **Chart 6** covers those Army special operations units that served in CENTCOM's Special Operations Command, **Chart 7** covers those Army units that served in Turkey with Joint Task Force Proven Force, and **Chart 8** covers those Army units that served in Israel with Task Force Patriot Defender. Finally, **Chart 4A** provides detailed task organization information for those Army heavy maneuver battalions that served in the Gulf with Third Army or I MEF.

For the Marines Corps, this information is presented in **Charts 19** and **20.** **Chart 19** covers the majority of Marine Corps units, those that served in the KTO under either Marine Corps or Navy control. **Chart 20** covers those Marine units that served in the Mediterranean during Desert Storm.

The next charts serve as cross-referencing and finding aids. These charts list all Army **(Chart 9)** and Marine Corps **(Chart 21)** combat units by unit type (e.g., tank battalions), showing the major command (e.g., division) to which each unit was assigned.

The next charts list selected reserve component units that were mobilized for Desert Storm, including units that were mobilized but did not deploy to the KTO. **Chart 10** covers Army units and **Chart 22** addresses Marine Corps units.

The next charts list the major combat arms units and senior tactical headquarters that were active outside the KTO during Desert Storm. In order to place the Gulf War in perspective, it is necessary to consider the units that were active outside the Gulf during the war. **Chart 11** addresses this for Army units and **Chart 23** covers Marine Corps units.

The major pieces of equipment used in Desert Storm are covered in **Chart 13** (Army) and **Chart 24** (Marine Corps). For each weapon system, its pre- and post-Desert Storm history is included.

The campaigns and unit awards awarded for Desert Storm are also addressed. **Chart 14** addresses Army units and **Chart 25** covers Marine Corps units. These charts also address the criteria, and other background information, for these campaigns and awards.

Post-Desert Storm developments, such as the inactivation and relocation of units that served in Desert Storm, are addressed in **Chart 15** (Army) and **Chart 26** (Marine Corps).

Finally, two charts address service-specific issues. **Chart 12** addresses the Army's Weapon Systems Replacement Operations and Squad/Crew/Team units, while **Chart 18A** addresses the Navy ships on which Marine Corps units were embarked, in the KTO or the Mediterranean, during Desert Storm.[2]

Part 4 contains detailed information on the British, French, and Arab-Islamic ground units involved in Desert Storm. Each country is addressed by a single chart which includes (1) a detailed list of the units that were deployed, as task organized for combat; (2) information on the major weapon systems employed; (3) information on how selected units were organized and equipped, and (4) other selected information. **Chart 27** addresses British units, **Chart 28** addresses French units, and **Chart 29** addresses Arab-Islamic units.

Part 5 contains seven charts that compare Desert Storm to other conflicts or analyze various aspects of Desert Storm. **Chart 30** compares the ground combat units deployed for Desert Storm with those deployed for the other significant post-World War II conflicts that involved ground units, Korea, Vietnam, Grenada, and Panama. **Chart 31** compares the major Army combat units deployed for Desert Storm with those that were not deployed, while **Chart 32** performs this same analysis for the Marine Corps. **Chart 33** addresses the Army and Marine Corps combat arms units that deployed for Desert Storm (to the KTO, Turkey, Israel, or the Mediterranean) showing, for example, how many Army versus Marine Corps tank battalions deployed and how many Army tank battalions were equipped with the 105mm-armed M1 Main Battle Tank, as opposed to the 120mm-armed M1A1 Main Battle Tank. **Chart 34** addresses selected Army, Marine Corps, British, and French combat units that served in the KTO, comparing the numbers and types of units that were assigned to the four major commands that controlled ground combat units (the Army's VII and XVIII Airborne Corps, the Marines' I MEF, and the Navy's NAVCENT). This chart shows how decisive combat power was weighted toward the Army's VII Corps. **Chart 35** addresses selected Marine Corps combat units that served in the KTO, comparing the numbers and types of units that served on land with I MEF, with those that were afloat in the Persian Gulf with NAVCENT. Finally, **Chart 36** compares selected ground combat units that were contributed by the major Allied participants in Operation Desert Storm.

---

[2] Additional information on the U.S. Navy amphibious ships that supported the Marines appears in **Charts 18** and **20.**

A detailed **Index** at the back of this order of battle can also be used to locate specific information. As explained at the beginning of the index, it is organized by major topic.

Sources & Credits

This order of battle was prepared using unclassified or declassified information that is available to the public, including after action reports and other documents on file at: (1) the Army's Center of Military History, Washington, DC; (2) the Army's Military History Institute, Carlisle, PA; (3) the library of the U.S. Army War College, Carlisle, PA; (4) the Marine Corps Historical Center, Washington, DC; and (5) the Library of Congress, Washington, DC. In addition, I obtained many documents through the Freedom of Information Act. Finally, several people provided assistance with some of the specific aspects of this project.

A special thanks to Maj John Quinn, USMC, whose mastery of the Marine Corps' Desert Storm order of battle, and commitment to documenting the Corps' service in the Gulf, is second to none. Many thanks to LTC W. Richard Clifton, U.S. Army (Ret.), the Assistant S-3 of the 1st Brigade, 24th Infantry Division(Mech) during Desert Storm, for providing information on the 24th Mech, the units that supported it during Desert Storm, and its WSRO units; Gordon Rottman, a retired Vietnam veteran and military historian who specializes in order of battle, who provided information on British and French units and answered some of the more obscure questions I had on U.S. Army units; David C. Isby, who provided iinformation on French units; and Geoff Barker, who answered many questions with regard to special operations forces, which were one of the tougher nuts to crack. Thanks also to John Huffman, U.S. Army Retired, who provided information on the ADA units that participated in Desert Storm; CPT Earl E. Atwood, Jr., U.S. Army, who provided information on the 1st Brigade, 2nd Armored Division; CPT Gary A. Francis, U.S. Army, who provided information on the 210th Field Artillery Brigade; LTC Larry Haub, Oklahoma Army National Guard, who provided information on the 1st Bn(MLRS), 158th Field Artillery; LTC Leonid E. Krondratiuk of the National Guard Bureau, who provided additional information on the 1st Bn, 158th Field Artillery; LTC Philip K. Schenck, U.S. Army Reserve, who provided information on the 173rd Medical Group; and SSG Tom Baxter, CPT Bill Becker, CPT Norman H. Fuss III, MAJ John T. Hansen, 1SG Michael R. Laney, and CPT Michael W. Milner, who provided information on WSRO units. Finally, I owe my wife, Lisa, a huge debt of gratitude for her patience while I completed this project.

I have made every effort to ensure this order of battle is as accurate and complete as possible. Nevertheless, with a project of this magnitude, and with some sources still classified or otherwise not readily available, some errors are inevitable. While many people assisted me with this project, I bear sole responsibility for any errors that may be present in the final product.

Notes

➢ All times and dates used in this order of battle are the local time/date. U.S. Eastern Standard Time was eight hours earlier than the KTO. This creates confusion as to, for example, when Desert Storm began. The first shots were fired, in the KTO, at 0237 hours on 17 Jan 91. This was, however, 1837 hours on 16 Jan 91, Eastern Standard Time. Similarly, the ground war began on the morning of 24 Feb 91 (the evening of 23 Feb 91, Eastern Standard Time) and ended four days later, at 0800 hours on 28 Feb 91 (midnight on 27 Feb 91, Eastern Standard Time).

➢ Unless indicated otherwise, the information in this order of battle is correct as of the ground war, 24-28 Feb 91.

➢ In this order of battle I generally use each unit's "official" designation, notwithstanding that many units were typically referred to using a colloquial designation. For example, the 475th Quartermaster Group(Petroleum) was generally referred to as the "475th Petroleum Group" or "475th POL Group."

➢ Throughout this order of battle, all units are active component unless indicated otherwise:

> "ARNG" = Army National Guard
> "USAR" = U.S. Army Reserve
> "USMCR" = U.S. Marine Corps Reserve

➢ In Charts 4-8, 17-19, and 28, units that served during ODS with a unit to which they were not normally assigned have their former parent unit indicated in brackets, e.g.: [Fr. 11 ADA Bde]. When a unit served during ODS with a unit to which it was not normally assigned, but I do not know its previous assignment, this fact is indicated: [Fr. _____?]. Information on pre-ODS assignments was difficult to obtain for British and Arab units, hence this information does not appear on Charts 27 and 29. However, the "Notes" section of Chart 27 contains some of this information at pages 27-7 and 27-8.

Order of Battle

➢ Reserve units are frequently located in more than one state; when one state is listed, it is the location of the unit's headquarters.

➢ Throughout this order of battle, U.S. Army groups are identified as Active Army, Army National Guard, or Army Reserve based on their peacetime organization. During Desert Storm, however, the three components were intermixed, so all or most groups (with the exception of special forces groups) included elements from all three components. Also, in some cases, such as the 265th Eng Gp [GA ARNG], only the group headquarters was mobilized, and hence identifying this unit as "GA ARNG" could be considered a little misleading. Nonetheless, in the interest of simplicity, I have adopted this approach.

➢ Information contained in parentheses "( )" is part of the unit's designation, while information contained in brackets "[ ]" is parenthetical information added by me, that is not part of the designation.

➢ For selected units, the primary weapon system is indicated in parenthesis "( )" or brackets "[ ]". For some units, such as U.S. Army field artillery and air defense artillery units, the weapon system is really part of the unit's designation; for example, the full designation of an ADA battalion equipped with the Patriot missile would be, e.g.: "1st Bn(Patriot), 43rd ADA". For these units, the weapon system is indicated within parenthesis. For other units, such as armor battalions, the type of weapon system is not part of the designation. For these units, the weapon system is indicated within brackets, e.g.: "1st Bn, 37th Armor [M1A1HA]".

Abbreviations

(A)	Armor
AADCOM	Army Air Defense Command
AAslt	Air Assault
AAV	Assault Amphibious Vehicle (USMC)
Abn	Airborne
ACE	Armd Combat Earthmover [or] Air Combat Element (USMC)
ACR	Armored Cavalry Regiment
AD	Armored Division
ADA	Air Defense Artillery
AE	Aerial Exploitation
AH	Attack Helicopter
Ambl	Airmobile
AMC	Army Medical Center

Amphib	Amphibian (USMC)
AO	Area of Operations
APC	Armored Personnel Carrier
ARCENT	Army Element, CENTCOM
ARCOM	Army Reserve Command
Armd	Armored
ARNG	Army National Guard
Arty	Artillery
A/S	Avenger/Stinger
Aslt	Assault
AT	Antitank
ATACMS	Army Tactical Missile System
ATC	Air Traffic Control
Atk	Attack
AVCRAD	Aviation Classification Repair Activity Depot
AVLB	Armored Vehicle Launching Bridge
Avn	Aviation
BCD	Battlefield Coordination Detachment
BDA	Bomb Damage Assessment
Bde	Brigade
BFV	Bradley Fighting Vehicle
BG	Brigadier (one star) General (U.S. Army)
BGen	Brigadier (one star) General (USMC)
Bn	Battalion
BP	Battle Position
BSSG	Brigade Service Support Group (USMC)
Btry	Battery
Btrys	Batteries
CA	Civil Affairs
CAG	Civil Affairs Group (USMC)
Cav	Cavalry
Cbt	Combat
CCATF	Combined Civil Affairs TF
CE	Command Element (USMC)
CENTAF	Air Force Element, CENTCOM
CENTCOM	U.S. Central Command
CEWI	Combat Electronic Warfare Intelligence
CFV	Cavalry Fighting Vehicle
CG	Commanding General
Chap	Chaparral
CIC	Criminal Investigation Command

CID	Criminal Investigation Division
Cmd	Command
Co	Company
COL	Colonel (full colonel) (U.S. Army)
Col	Colonel (full colonel) (USMC)
Construc	Construction
CONUS	Continental United States
COSCOM	Corps Support Command
Cp	Camp
CP	Command Post
CSH	Combat Support Hospital
Ctr	Center
Det	Detachment
DISCOM	Division Support Command
Dismtd	Dismounted
Dist	Distribution
Div	Division
DIVARTY	Division Artillery
DOD	Department of Defense
DS	Direct Support
DSG	Direct Support Group (USMC)
EAC	Echelons Above Corps
Eng	Engineer
EPW	Enemy Prisoner of War
Evac	Evacuation
FA	Field Artillery
Fin	Finance
FIST	Fire Integration Support Team
FMF	Fleet Marine Force
FOB	Forward Operating Base
FORSCOM	U.S. Army Forces Command
FR	French
FSSG	Force Service Support Group (USMC)
Fwd	Forward
GCE	Ground Combat Element (USMC)
G Day	"Ground Day" - the day the ground war began, 24 Feb 91 in the KTO (23 Feb 91 on the east coast)
GEN	General (full (four star) general) (U.S. Army)
Gen	General (full (four star) general) (USMC)
Gp	Group
GS	General Support

GSR	General Support-Reinforcing[3] [or] Ground Surveillance Radar
Hel	Helicopter
HHB	HQ & HQ Battery
HHC	HQ & HQ Company
HHT	HQ & HQ Troop
HMMWV	High Mobility Multipurpose Wheeled Vehicle[4]
HNH	Host Nation Hospital
Hosp	Hospital
HQ	Headquarters
H&S	HQ & Service
ID(M)	Mechanized Infantry Div
IFV	Infantry Fighting Vehicle
Inf	Infantry
Info	Information
INTSCOM	Intelligence & Security Command
IRR	Individual Ready Reserve
ITV	Improved TOW Vehicle
JFC	Joint Forces Command
JTF	Joint Task Force
KKMC	King Khalid Military City
KTF	Kuwait Task Force[5]
KTO	Kuwaiti Theater of Operations
LAAD	Low Altitude Air Defense (USMC)
LAAM	Light Antiaircraft Missile (USMC)
LAI	Light Armored Infantry (USMC)
LAV	Light Armored Vehicle (USMC)
LCAC	Landing Craft, Air Cushion (U.S. Navy)
LHA	Amphibious Assault Ship (General Purpose) (U.S. Navy)
LKA	Amphibious Cargo Ship (U.S. Navy)
LPD	Amphibious Transport Dock (U.S. Navy)
LPH	Amphibious Assault Ship (Helicopter) (U.S. Navy)
LRS	Long Range Surveillance[6]
LSD	Dock Landing Ship (U.S. Navy)
LST	Tank Landing Ship (U.S. Navy)
Lt	Light
LTG	Lieutenant (three star) General (U.S. Army)

---

[3] General Support-Reinforcing is a field artillery mission in which the FA unit provides general support artillery fires for the force it is supporting and, as a second priority, reinforces the fires of another specified FA unit.

[4] This vehicle replaced the jeep.

[5] Many sources refer to this unit as the "Kuwaiti TF."

[6] Similar to the LRRPs (Long Range Reconnaissance Patrol) of the Vietnam era.

Order of Battle

LtGen	Lieutenant (three star) General (USMC)
LZ	Landing Zone
(M)	Mechanized
MAC	Maneuver Area Command
MACG	Marine Air Control Group
MAG	Marine Aircraft Group
MajGen	Major (two star) General (USMC)
MARCENT	Marine Element, CENTCOM
MASH	Mobile Army Surgical Hospital
MAW	Marine Aircraft Wing
MBT	Main Battle Tank
MC	Movement Control
MEU	Marine Expeditionary Unit
MEB	Marine Expeditionary Brigade
MEF	Marine Expeditionary Force
Med	Medical
MG	Major (two star) General (U.S. Army)
MI	Military Intelligence
MICLIC	Mine Clearing Line Charge
MLRS	Multiple Launch Rocket System
MMC	Material Management Center
MP	Military Police
MPS	Maritime Prepositioning Ships (U.S. Navy)
MSC	Military Sealift Command (U.S. Navy)
Mtn	Mountain
Mtzd	Motorized
NAVCENT	Navy Element, CENTCOM
NTC	National Training Center
o/a	On or about
ODS	Operation Desert Storm
OP	Observation Post
OPCON	Operational Control[7]
OpFor	Opposing Forces[8]
Opns	Operations
Ord	Ordnance

---

[7] A type of command relationship. When Unit X is OPCON to Unit Y, Unit Y has the authority to direct the actions of Unit X, but is not responsible for providing logistical or administrative support to Unit X. OPCON relationships are typically short in duration, measured by days or even hours, and are typically limited from the outset to a set period of time or until a certain event occurs. See also TACON.

[8] The OpFor are the units at the specialized training centers, such as the National Training Center at Fort Irwin, that replicate enemy units for force-on-force maneuver training.

ORF	Operational Readiness Float[9]
Para	Parachute
PERSCOM	Personnel Command
Pers	Personnel
PhibGru	Amphibious Group (U.S. Navy)
PhibRon	Amphibious Squadron (U.S. Navy)
Plt	Platoon
POW	Prisoner of War
Prov	Provisional
QM	Quartermaster
RA	Royal Artillery (UK)
RAC	Royal Armoured Corps (UK)
RAF	Royal Air Force (UK)
Recon	Reconnaissance
Regt	Regiment
Rein	Reinforced (USMC)
Reinf	Reinforcing[10]
RLT	Regimental Landing Team (USMC)
RN	Royal Navy (UK)
Rngr	Ranger
RS	Royal Saudi
RSLF	Royal Saudi Land Forces
RTR	Royal Tank Regt (UK)
SAM	Surface to Air Missile
SANG	Saudi Arabian National Guard
SAS	Special Air Service (UK)
SCT	Squad/Crew/Team
Sec	Section
SF	Special Forces[11]
SFOD	Special Forces Operational Det
Sig	Signal
SOAR	Special Operations Aviation Regiment
SOC	Special Operations Capable (USMC)
SOCCENT	Special Operations Command, CENTCOM
SOCEUR	Special Operations Command, Europe

---

[9] The ORF consisted of vehicles and other equipment that were present in the theater of operations to replace equipment that was out of action due to combat or mechanical problems.

[10] Reinforcing is a field artillery mission in which the FA unit reinforces the fires of another specified FA unit. This increases the weight of fire support available to the maneuver unit supported by these FA units and facilitates command and control of these fires.

[11] Special Forces are the Army's "Green Berets."

SOCOM	Special Operations Command
SOF	Special Operations Forces[12]
SOSC(TA)	Special Operations Support Command(Theater Army)
Spec	Special
Spt	Support
Spt'd	Supported
Sqdn	Squadron
SRI	Surveillance, Recon & Intelligence (USMC)
SRISG	SRI Support Group (USMC)
Sta	Station
SUPCOM	Support Command
Svc	Service
Sys	System
TA	Theater Army [or, for artillery units] Target Acquisition
TAA	Tactical Assembly Area
TAACOM	Theater Army Area Command
TACON	Tactical Control[13]
TARP	Target Acquisition & Reconnaissance Platoon
TDA	Table of Distributions & Allowances[14]
TF	Task Force
Tng	Training
TOE	Table of Organization & Equipment[15]
TOW	Tube Launched, Optically Tracked, Wire Guided Command Link Antitank Missile
Trans	Transportation
TTU	Transportation Terminal Unit
UAE	United Arab Emirates
UK	United Kingdom
USAR	U.S. Army Reserve
USAREUR	U.S. Army Europe
USARS	U.S. Army Regimental System
USMC	U.S. Marine Corps

---

[12] Special Operations Forces include elements from all of the armed services. Army SOF includes Special Forces, Rangers, special operations aviation, psychological operations, and civil affairs.

[13] A type of command relationship. When Unit X is TACON to Unit Y, Unit Y has the authority to direct the actions of Unit X, but is not responsible for providing logistical or administrative support to Unit X. TACON relationships are typically short in duration, measured by days or even hours, and are typically limited from the outset to a set period of time or until a certain event occurs. See also OPCON. The main difference between OPCON and TACON is that under OPCON, the senior unit has the authority to reorganize the OPCON'd unit, whereas the senior unit lacks this authority with regard to a TACON unit.

[14] A nontactical unit, as opposed to TOE units, which are tactical (field) units. TDA units include installation support units, such as the military police who patrol the base and man its gates, and training units.

[15] A tactical (field) unit, as opposed to a TDA (nontactical) unit.

USMCR	U.S. Marine Corps Reserve
USN	U.S. Navy
VAdm	Vice Admiral (U.S. Navy)
V/A/S	Vulcan/Avenger/Stinger
V/C/S	Vulcan/Chaparral/Stinger
V/S	Vulcan/Stinger
Vulc	Vulcan
Wpns	Weapons
WSRO	Weapon System Replacement Operations. See Chart 12.
(105 T)	105mm towed howitzers
(155 T)	155mm towed howitzers
(155 SP)	155mm self-propelled howitzers
(203 SP)	203mm self-propelled howitzers
(-)	A unit that is significantly understrength, e.g., a battalion that is short one of its companies.
(+)	A unit that is significantly overstrength, e.g., a division that has an extra brigade.

Military Installations

Selected U.S. Army Installations

Installation	State
Belvoir	VA
Benning	GA
Bliss	TX
Bragg	NC
Campbell	KY
Carson	CO
Devens	MA
Dix	NJ
Drum	NY
Eustis	VA
Gillem	GA
Gordon	GA
Hood	TX
Sam Houston	TX
Huachuca	AZ

Order of Battle

Installation	State
Irwin	CA
Jackson	SC
Knox	KY
Lee	VA
Lewis	WA
McClellan	AL
McPherson	GA
Monmouth	NJ
Ord	CA
Polk	LA
Redstone Arsenal	AL
Riley	KS
Rucker	AL
Shelby	MS
Sill	OK
Stewart	GA
Story	VA
Leonard Wood	MO

Selected U.S. Marine Corps Installations

Installation	State
Kaneohe Bay	HI
Lejeune	NC
Pendleton	CA
Twentynine Palms	CA
Yuma	AZ

Selected U.S. Navy Installations

Installation	State
Little Creek	VA

Maps

These maps were prepared by the author, primarily using the maps that appear in several official histories of Operation Desert Storm. Unfortunately, these official maps contradict each other in several major ways. I have attempted to resolve these discrepancies using other sources, but cannot swear to the absolute accuracy of the maps. They should, however, provide a basic understanding of the course of the ground war and the scheme of maneuver of Coalition units.

Legend

Armored Division

Mechanized Division

Air Assault Division

Air Assault Infantry Brigade

Airborne Division

French Light Armored Division

Armored Cavalry Regiment

Marine Infantry Regiment/Task Force (Map 4)

Marine Mechanized Task Force (Map 4)

Marine Division

Order of Battle

Map 1 – Coalition Ground Forces Prior To The Ground War

This map depicts the approximate locations of the Coalition's major command and major ground combat maneuver units just prior to the beginning of the ground war, as of approximately 0400 hours, 24 Feb 91. This map was based primarily upon BG Robert H. Scales, Jr., et al., *Certain Victory: The United States Army in the Gulf War*. Washington, DC: Office of the Chief of Staff, U.S. Army, 1993. See Figure 5-1.

Map 2 - ARCENT Units As Of 1800 Hours, 26 Feb 91

This map depicts the approximate locations of ARCENT's major maneuver units about mid-way through the ground war, as of 1800 hours on 26 Feb 91. This map is based primarily upon BG Robert H. Scales, Jr., et al., *Certain Victory: The United States Army in the Gulf War*. Washington, DC: Office of the Chief of Staff, U.S. Army, 1993. See Figures 5-1 and 5-4.

At this time, in the VII Corps, the 1st and 3rd Armored Divisions, and 2nd Armored Cavalry Regiment, were on line charging due east at the Republican Guard. The 1st (UK) Armoured Division had passed through the breach created by the 1st Infantry Division(Mech) and was attacking due east toward Kuwait City. The 1st Infantry Division(Mech) had completed its breach of the Iraqi front lines and was moving north to join the remainder of the VII Corps. The 1st Cavalry Division(-) had been released from its role as the theater reserve and was moving north to join the remainder of the VII Corps.

In the XVIII Airborne Corps, the 24th Infantry Division(Mech) and 3rd Armored Cavalry Regiment were attacking northeast toward Tallil and Jalibah Airbases. The 3rd Brigade, the 101st Airborne Division(Air Aslt) had seized control of Area of Operations (AO) Eagle and severed Highway 8, while the remainder of the division was at Forward Operating Base (FOB) Cobra. In the West, the 6th (French) Light Armored Division had completed its attack and was screening the Coalition's western flank. The 82nd Airborne Division was moving north in the XVIII Airborne Corps rear area.

Map 3 – Coalition Ground Forces At The End Of Desert Storm

This map depicts the approximate locatons of ARCENT's major maneuver units at the end of Operation Desert Storm, as of approximately 0800 hours, 28 Feb 91. This map was based primarily upon BG Robert H. Scales, Jr., et al., *Certain Victory: The United States Army in the Gulf War*. Washington, DC: Office of the Chief of Staff, U.S. Army, 1993. See Figures 5-1 and 5-6.

Map 4 – I Marine Expeditionary Force

This map depicts the approximate locations of the major maneuver units of I Marine Expeditionary Force during the ground war. This map shows the approximate locations of those units before the ground war (as of approximately 0400 hours, 24 Feb 91), their general scheme of maneuver, and the approximate locations of these units at the end of Operation Desert Storm, as of approximately 0800 hours, 28 Feb 91. Not depicted on this map, to prevent information overload, are (1) the 5th Marines (Rein), 5th MEB, which began landing off map in Saudi territory at Al Mish'ab and Al Jubayl in the afternoon of 24 Feb 91, and ended the war in the vicinity of Al Jaber Airfield; and (2) the 24th Marines(-), which performed rear area security for 1 MEF. This map was based primarily upon the maps in Col Charles J. Quilter II, _U.S. Marines In The Persian Gulf, 1990-1991: With the I Marine Expeditionary Force In Desert Shield And Desert Storm_. Washington, DC: History and Museums Div, HQ, U.S. Marine Corps, 1993. See pages 81 and 105.

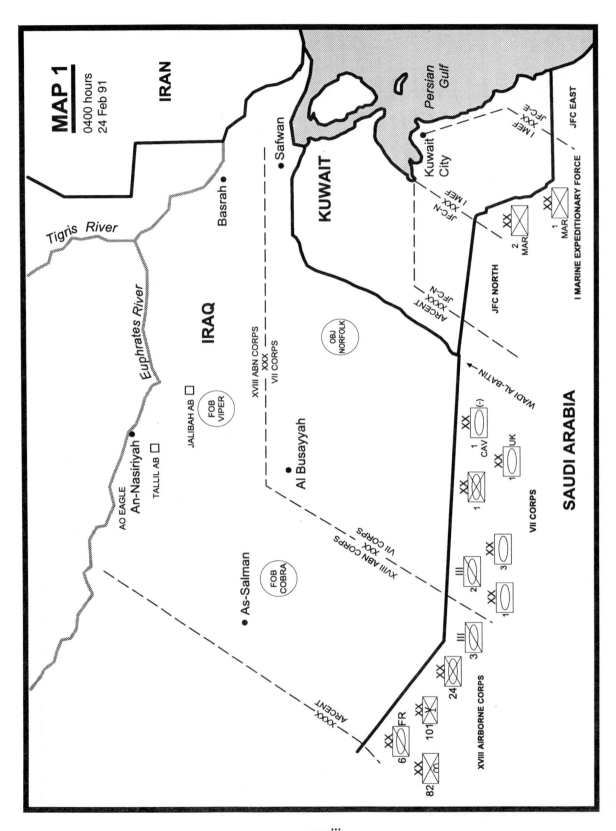

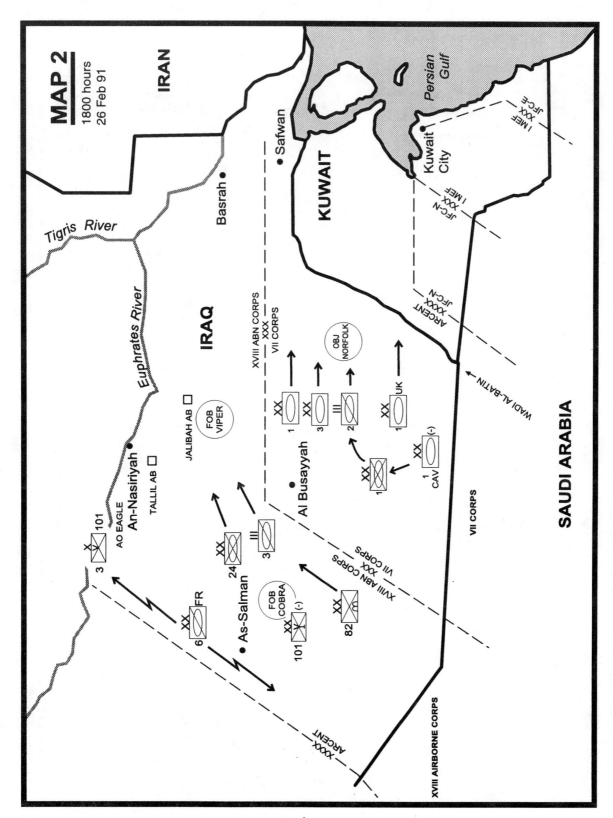

MAP 2
1800 hours
26 Feb 91

IRAN

Persian Gulf

Safwan •

KUWAIT

Kuwait City

JFCE
XXX
I MEF

I MEF
XXX
JFC-N

ARCENT
XXX
JFC-N

Basrah •

Tigris River

Euphrates River

IRAQ

XVIII ABN CORPS
XXX
VII CORPS

OBJ
NORFOLK

UK

CAV (-)
1

1

2 III

3 XX

1 XX

JALIBAH AB

FOB
VIPER

Al Busayyah •

TALLIL AB

AO EAGLE
An-Nasiriyah •

3 X 101

24 XX

III
3

XVIII ABN CORPS
XXX
VII CORPS

WADI AL-BATIN

SAUDI ARABIA

VII CORPS

FR
6 XX

As-Salman •

FOB
COBRA

101 XX (-)

82 XX

XXXX
ARCENT

XVIII AIRBORNE CORPS

xxix

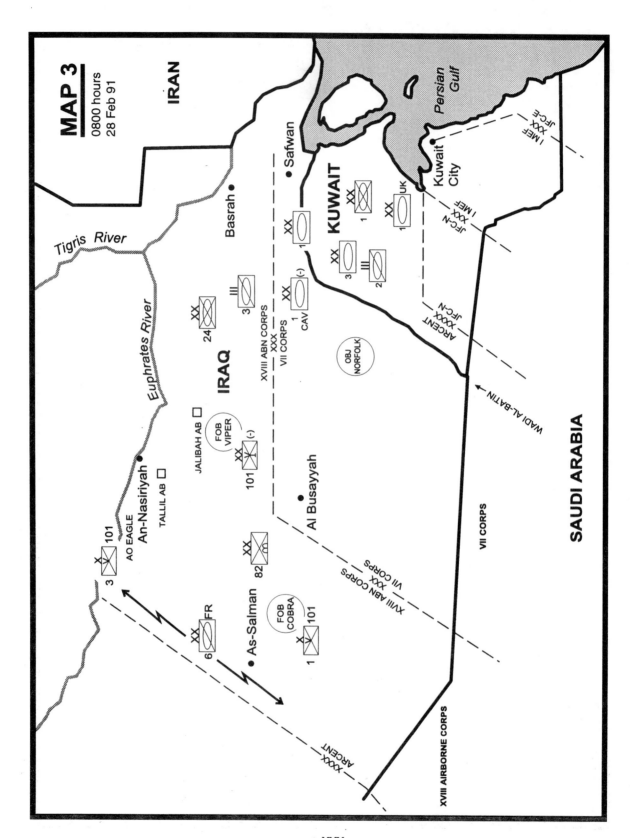

MAP 3
0800 hours
28 Feb 91

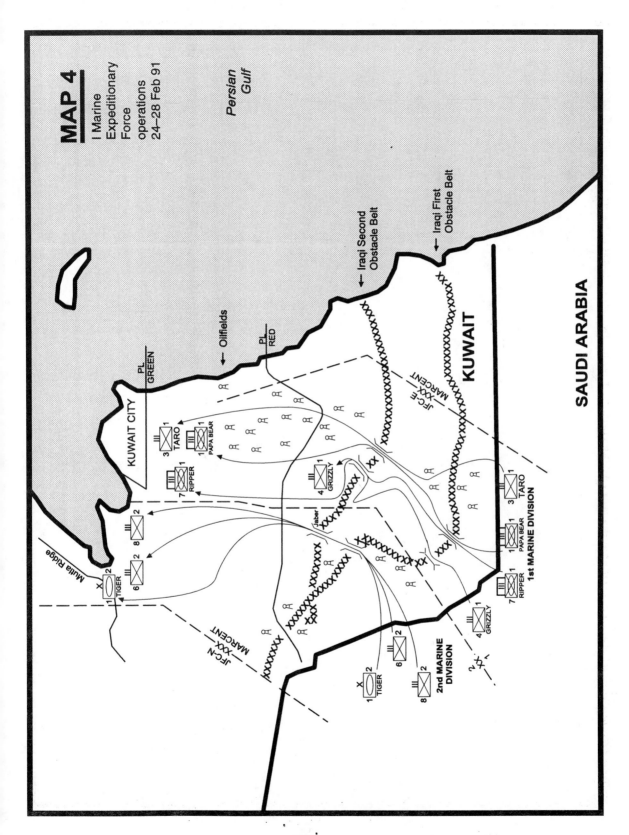

MAP 4

I Marine
Expeditionary
Force
operations
24–28 Feb 91

Persian Gulf

Iraqi Second Obstacle Belt

Iraqi First Obstacle Belt

Oilfields

PL GREEN

PL RED

KUWAIT CITY

Mutla Ridge

KUWAIT

SAUDI ARABIA

JFC-E MARCENT

JFC-N MARCENT

Jaber

1st MARINE DIVISION

2nd MARINE DIVISION

TARO

PAPA BEAR

RIPPER

GRIZZLY

TIGER

TIGER

xxxi

Operation Desert Storm

*In war, then, let our great object be victory,
not lengthy campaigns.*

Sun Tzu, *The Art of War*

The Ground War

At 1430 hours on February 24, 1991, the VII Corps — the most powerful armored corps in history — initiated its attack and headed north into the featureless wastes of the Iraqi desert. The VII Corps consisted of four heavy divisions,[1] an armored cavalry regiment, a combat aviation brigade, and a corps artillery with four field artillery brigades, for a total of more than 1,300 tanks, more than 1,100 infantry/cavalry fighting vehicles, more than 600 self-propelled artillery pieces, and approximately 175-plus attack helicopters.[2] As CENTCOM's main effort, the success of Operation Desert Storm was largely dependent on whether the VII Corps would accomplish its mission.

The VII Corps was, of course, not alone. Less than 12 hours previously, the Marines and Arab-Islamic coalition forces to the east of VII Corps initiated the ground war by attacking into the main body of the Iraqi defenses in Kuwait. Most of the defending Iraqi units succumbed to the onslaught after offering limited resistance.

---

[1] The 1st Cav Div(-) joined the VII Corps on 26 Feb 91, expanding the VII Corps to five heavy divisions. See Chart 2, Footnote 1.

[2] When the 1st Cav Div(-) was added to VII Corps, these numbers grew to: more than 1,500 main battle tanks, more than 1,300 IFVs/CFVs, more than 650 self-propelled artillery pieces, and more than 200 attack helicopters.

1

Order of Battle

Those that did not were quickly outmaneuvered and outfought by the Marines. Marine commanders were soon faced with long lines of surrendering Iraqi soldiers streaming south as the Marines advanced inexorably toward Kuwait City.

Shortly after the Marines' attack, the XVIII Airborne Corps kicked-off its offensive. The XVIII Airborne Corps was to the west of the VII Corps, and formed the coalition's left flank. In the western portion of the XVIII's zone, the French 6th Light Armored Division, reinforced by the 2nd Brigade, 82nd Airborne Division, attacked to secure the coalition's western flank. Several hours later, to the right of the French (and in the center of the XVIII Airborne Corps zone) the 101st Airborne Division(Air Aslt) began what was to become the largest air assault in history. By the evening of February 25, the 101st had severed Highway 8 near the Iraqi city of As-Samawah, sealing that important escape route from the Kuwaiti Theater of Operations. And at 1500 hours on February 24, the 24th Infantry Division(Mech), its right flank secured by the 3rd Armored Cavalry Regiment, raced into the desert in the eastern portion of the XVIII Airborne Corps zone.

All of these efforts, while critically important to the success of Operation Desert Storm, were of secondary importance. In addition to ejecting the Iraqis from Kuwait, Desert Storm was intended to inflict heavy casualties upon Saddam Hussein's Republican Guard. If the war ended with Iraq forced from Kuwait, but the Republican Guard intact and still a major offensive force that could threaten the stability of the region, American war aims would be only partially fulfilled. Thus, to a substantial degree, the overall success of the operation depended upon the outcome of the VII Corps' attack on the Republican Guard.

The war ended just 89 hours after the VII Corps began its attack. Maneuvering unerringly through the desert, day and night, with the assistance of advanced thermal sights and the Global Positioning System, the VII Corps had crushed the cream of the Iraqi Army, the "elite" Republican Guard Forces Command.

In the eastern (or right-hand) portion of the VII Corps zone, the breach of the Iraqi front line was conducted by the 1st Infantry Division(Mech), with three field artillery brigades and the division artillery of the British 1st Armoured Division in support. In a period of 30 minutes, 11,000 artillery rounds struck Iraqi positions in the breach area.[3]

---

[3] This barrage was so effective that virtually no Iraqi artillery fire hit the breach zone during the 1st Infantry Div(Mech)'s breach. The Iraqi 48th Inf Div, which defended the breach area, had 100 artillery pieces before the air war began. It lost 17 artillery pieces during the five and a half-week air campaign that preceded G-Day. It lost every remaining artillery piece — all 83 tubes — during the 30 minute artillery prep that preceded the breach.

In order to minimize casualties and exploit its mobility, the 1st Infantry Division(Mech) conducted an unusual mounted breach in which its infantry remained mounted in their M2 "Bradley" Fighting Vehicles instead of attacking on foot. Iraqi soldiers who refused to surrender were buried alive in their trenches by M9 Armored Combat Earthmovers and M1 and M1A1 "Abrams" Main Battle Tanks with dozer blades, while the Bradleys forced the Iraqis to keep their heads down by firing their 25mm chain guns down the length of the Iraqi trenches. Once the breach had been completed, the British 1st Armoured Division passed through the 1st Infantry Division(Mech) and, shortly beyond the breach, pivoted to the right to attack local Iraqi reserves that could threaten the VII Corps' lines of communications.

The 2nd Armored Cavalry Regiment, leading the American 1st and 3rd Armored Divisions, attacked to the left of the 1st Infantry Division(Mech) in the western (or left-hand) part of the VII Corps zone. This area was beyond the Iraqi front lines, and thus these units did not have to conduct a breach. On the other hand, because they were further to the west, these units had significantly further to go before they could close with and destroy the Republican Guard.

The VII Corps attack disproved that old maxim, "No plan survives contact with the enemy." The Iraqis were unable to wrest the initiative from the attacker, leaving VII Corps free to execute its plan at will. The 2nd Armored Cavalry Regiment, operating as the Corps' covering force, encountered Republican Guard units early on February 26, 1991, and shortly after 1600 hours, began to attack the main body of the Tawakalna Division in the vicinity of the 73 Easting, a map grid line used by allied forces. The regiment overran and destroyed the Iraqi forces arrayed in front of it and, late in the evening of February 26, handed the battle off to the 1st Infantry Division(Mech). The 1st Infantry Division had raced north to catch up with the remainder of the VII Corps after completing its breach of the Iraqi defenses. At this point the VII Corps had three heavy divisions, the 1st Armored, 3rd Armored, and 1st Infantry,[4] arrayed on line from north to south, driving inexorably toward the east — right at the heart of the Republican Guard.

By shortly after midnight on February 26, 1991, these three powerful divisions had slammed into the Republican Guard's Medina and Tawakalna Divisions and were proceeding to destroy them, and the 10th and 12th Armored Divisions of the Iraqi regular army, in detail. Iraqi T-72 tanks, which were only able to engage allied armor out to 1,800 meters or so, vainly attempted to stop the American onslaught. American M1A1 Main Battle Tanks routinely killed Iraqi armor — even the vaunted T-72 — at ranges well in excess of 3,000 meters, even when the firing tanks and/or targets were

---

[4] Although designated a (mechanized) infantry division, the 1st Inf Div(Mech) was organized and equipped as an armored division, with six tank battalions and three mechanized infantry battalions. See Chart 4, page 4-10.

on the move.[5] M2 and M3 series Bradley Fighting Vehicles added to the carnage using their long-range TOW wire-guided antitank missiles and 25mm automatic cannon. American hits frequently detonated the Iraqi vehicle's ammunition and fuel, causing a "catastrophic kill" in which the hapless victim exploded in a fireball that reduced a supposedly first-rate combat vehicle to a burning, turretless wreck in a matter of seconds.

Throughout the fight, field artillery, Army attack helicopters, and Air Force fixed-wing aircraft hammered the Iraqis. Army AH-64 "Apache" attack helicopters — long vilified by the media and the GAO for supposedly being unreliable and ineffective[6] — executed repeated deep strikes into the Iraqi rear, day and night, to destroy vehicles that were attempting to escape from the theater of operations. Veteran field artillery cannon systems — the M109 self-propelled 155mm howitzer and the M110 self-propelled 203mm howitzer — along with two new rocket/missile systems, the M270 Multiple Launch Rocket System and the Army Tactical Missile System, pounded Iraqi forces, suppressed and destroyed Iraqi artillery during counter-battery missions, and took out high priority targets such as headquarters, air defense units, and logistics centers.

On the third day of the war the 1st Cavalry Division(-), which had initially been held back as the theater reserve,[7] was released to the VII Corps and charged north to join the fight on the morning of February 26, 1991. The VII Corps continued to smash Iraqi forces right up to the cease-fire, aided by the XVIII Airborne Corps' 24th Infantry Division(Mech) and 3rd Armored Cavalry Regiment, which had wheeled around to the east to attack toward Basrah. After consulting with his commanders, President Bush declared a cease-fire effective at 0800 hours on February 28, 1991.[8]

The cease fire generally held. The one notable exception occurred on March 2, 1991, when Iraqi units attempting to escape to Basrah foolishly engaged the 24th Mech's 1st Brigade. The brigade returned fire, maneuvered to the flanks, and

---

[5] The M1A1 represents a quantum leap in capability from the previous generation of American tanks. According to official Army statistics, the M60A1 Main Battle Tank that the author commanded in the early 1980s had only a 50 percent chance of scoring a hit (whether this would result in a kill was uncertain) on a Soviet tank at 1,500 meters — if the firing tank was stationary and the target tank was fully exposed in the open and stationary — improbably favorable conditions that were highly unlikely to occur in combat.

[6] Because of its reliability and lethality, the Apache was selected to fire the opening shots of Desert Storm. At 0237 hours on January 17, 1991, eight AH-64s from the 1st Bn(AH), 101st Avn, 101st Airborne Div(AAslt), destroyed a key Iraqi early warning installation. This attack was completely successful and opened a large hole in the Iraqi air defense system which allowed coalition aircraft to penetrate undetected deep into Iraqi airspace. See Chart 4, Footnote 58.

[7] At the beginning of the ground war the 1st Cavalry Div(-) had performed a feinting attack at the Wadi al Batin to conceal the location of the coalition's main effort.

[8] This was midnight, February 27, 1991, Eastern Standard Time. Although the 1st Cavalry Div(-) arrived in time to join the attack on the left flank of the VII Corps, concerns over friendly fire led the VII Corps commander to hold the 1st Cav in reserve.

destroyed over 185 armored vehicles, 400 wheeled vehicles, 34 artillery pieces, nine multiple rocket launchers, and seven FROG missile systems, primarily from the Republican Guard's Hammurabi Armored Division, in just a few short hours. Total American casualties in this engagement were one soldier wounded, one Bradley Fighting Vehicle damaged by enemy action, and one Abrams Main Battle Tank inadvertently destroyed when an exploding T-72 set the Abrams on fire.

Air Defense Artillery

The coalition's air defense artillery had a schizophrenic experience in Desert Storm. Most of the air defenders were unable to perform their primary mission because the Iraqi air force never even attempted to attack allied ground forces. The Army's Patriot missile units, however, had a completely different experience, as they were kept busy blasting Iraq's Scud missiles out of the skies over Saudi Arabia and Israel. Although Iraq's Scud missiles posed no military threat to the coalition so long as they carried only high explosive warheads, the Scuds could have fractured the coalition if Israel had entered the war to avenge Scud missile attacks. Accordingly, the Army's Patriot units made a special contribution to our Desert Storm victory.[9]

Special Operations Forces

Desert Storm was unusual in that, although the battlefield was dominated by heavy forces, special operations forces also played an extremely important role. Army Special Forces performed two important missions: (1) training and coordination for coalition armies that did not normally operate with U.S. forces; and (2) deep reconnaissance into Iraq. The deep reconnaissance mission included a particularly-important sub-mission: finding Iraq's mobile Scud missiles. This mission was performed by the Joint Special Operations Task Force(Forward) (JSOTF-F), which was based in Ar'ar in western Saudi Arabia. In conjunction with British special operations forces (primarily the Special Air Service), the JSOTF-F hunted mobile Scud missile launchers in western Iraq. This operation began on February 7, 1991, well before the start of the ground war. The JSOTF-F included elements of "Delta Force," the Army's special counter-terrorist commando unit, and a reinforced company of Army Rangers.[10]

---

[9] Post-war analysis has called into question the Patriot's high intercept rate. These critiques ignore the fact that the war-time perception that the Patriot was invincible — whether accurate or not — kept Israel out of the war and the coalition intact. Thus, in a very real sense, the Patriot's success rate was 100 percent.

[10] The Rangers conducted at least one "direct action" mission, in which a reinforced ranger platoon raided an Iraqi communications facility. Surprisingly, relatively few Rangers deployed for Operation Desert Storm. See Chart 6.

Logistics

No discussion of the Gulf War would be complete without an acknowledgment of the critically important contribution made by the Army's support units. Throughout the war, the coalition's logisticians, under the direction of the Army's 22nd Support Command, ensured that the necessary ammunition, fuel, food, water, repair parts, and other key supplies arrived in the right place and at the right time. All of this was accomplished under a hectic schedule, in an austere theater that lacked most of the infrastructure that had generally been considered necessary for the conduct of a modern military campaign.

Medical Care

Above the divisional level, medical care is provided by a hierarchy of hospitals ranging from small (60 bed) mobile army surgical hospitals (MASH) to extremely large (1,000 bed) general hospitals. The Army deployed 44 hospitals to SWA with a total capacity of 13,580 beds. The light casualties sustained by the allies meant that most of this capacity was not needed, although it was put to good use treating large numbers of EPWs, many of whom were in dire need of medical care after receiving none from their own chain of command for weeks or months. The 44 Army hospitals in SWA were assigned as follows:[11]

	Total	VII Corps	XVIII Abn Corps	3rd MEDCOM
MASH	8	5	3	
CSH	9	5	4	
Evacuation	22	5	5	12
Field	3			3
Station	1			1
General	1			1
TOTAL:	44	15	12	17

---

[11] These figures include the 115th MASH, which was broken up and did not serve as a cohesive unit. These figures also count the 345th CSH as a combat support hospital, notwithstanding that it was converted to a MASH. See Chart 2, Footnotes 14 & 15.

When the size (number of beds) of the various hospitals is taken into account, it becomes clear that the Army's medical force structure was solidly weighted toward the EAC level. Equally interesting is the fact that the VII Corps, which was larger than the XVIII Airborne Corps and expected to do most of the heavy fighting, received only a slight weighting of medical assets:[12]

Number of Beds

	Total	VII Corps	XVIII Abn Corps	3rd MEDCOM
MASH	480	300	180	
CSH	1,800	1,000	800	
Evacuation	8,800	2,000	2,000	4,800
Field	1,200			1,200
Station	300			300
General	1,000			1,000
TOTAL:	13,580	3,300	2,980	7,300
By Percentage	100%	24%	22%	54%

The WSRO/SCT Program[13]

One of the unique things about Desert Storm was how the United States Army and at least one of our allies, Great Britain,[14] planned to respond to battlefield casualties. Instead of replacing personnel and equipment losses in combat units with individual soldiers and pieces of equipment, as has generally been done in the past, the Army deployed intact platoons (complete with personnel, equipment, and platoon leadership), as the means for replacing front line losses. The Army calls this approach "Weapon System Replacement Operations."

---

[12] The weighting of hospital beds toward the VII Corps was most pronounced closest to the front lines. Thus, while both corps had the same number of evacuation hospitals, the VII Corps had 25 percent more combat support hospitals and 67 percent more MASHs. These figures include the 115th MASH, which was broken up and did not serve as a cohesive unit. These figures also count the 345th CSH as a combat support hospital, notwithstanding that it converted to a MASH. See Chart 2, Footnotes 14 & 15.

[13] "SCT" stands for "Squad/Crew/Team" and "WSRO" stands for "Weapon System Replacement Operations." WSRO units were deployed as organized platoons, while SCT units were deployed as organized squads, crews, or teams. See Chart 12.

[14] See Chart 27, Footnote 29.

Some of these platoons were assigned to divisions, while others were held at corps or army level. The VII Corps formed all or most of its WSRO units into a provisional battalion called Task Force Jayhawk, which assisted the corps with rear area security. In the XVIII Airborne Corps, however, it appears that most WSRO units were assigned below corps level. Three tank and two mechanized infantry platoons were formed into a provisional company and attached to the 24th Infantry Division(Mech),[15] while a scout platoon from the 11th Armored Cavalry Regiment served with the 3rd Armored Cavalry Regiment.

The U.S. Army deployed sufficient tank, infantry, and field artillery crews and equipment, pursuant to the WSRO program, to replace the "trigger pullers" in:

- 2 Tank battalions equipped with the M1A1 Abrams
- 2 Mechanized infantry battalions equipped with the M2 Bradley
- 1 Light infantry battalion
- 4 Scout platoons equipped with the M3 Bradley
- 1 155mm self-propelled field artillery battalion
- 1 203mm self-propelled field artillery battery
- 1+ 105mm towed field artillery battery
- 1 155mm towed field artillery battery
- 1 MLRS field artillery battery

Aviation units were handled differently. An Active Army aviation unit, the 5th Bn(AH), 229th Aviation, deployed to the KTO from Fort Hood, was assigned to the ARCENT Aviation Brigade, and administered the WSRO/SCT program for all ARCENT aviation units.[16]

Unfortunately, none of the WSRO units have received campaign participation credit for Desert Storm, and the Army has done nothing to memorialize or publicize their participation. As a result, little information is readily available concerning which units served in this capacity. These units were contributed primarily by the units stationed in Germany that did not deploy for Desert Storm.[17] Because of the short duration of the ground war, and the low casualty levels sustained by Army units, the WSRO/SCT system was barely tested. Very few WSRO/SCT units were used to replace front line losses.

---

[15] By the beginning of the ground war, however, the 24th Mech had reassigned some or all of the vehicles belonging to its WSRO units to its organic units. The Bradleys of at least one of the mechanized infantry platoons were used to replace M113 APCs in brigade headquarters, while at least some of the tanks were used to replace tanks that were down for maintenance problems. One tank platoon reportedly provided security for the division's Assault CP. See Chart 12.

[16] In addition to administering the WSRO/SCT program for aviation units, several sources indicate that the 5th Bn(AH), 229th Avn served as Third Army's reserve attack helicopter battalion. See Chart 4, Footnote 77.

[17] USAREUR sent 9,000 personnel to the KTO as individual augmentees and replacement crew members.

The Reserve Components

Desert Storm was both the reserve components' biggest success story, and a significant failure. Huge numbers of reserve component support units were mobilized and deployed, and they performed admirably. Quite literally, Desert Storm would have been impossible without the reserves. For example, 58 percent of the Army transportation units deployed in Southwest Asia came from the reserve components.

With regard to combat units, however, the story is decidedly mixed. The Army declined to mobilize any of its reserve component maneuver units until very late, in November and December of 1990, and this effectively guaranteed that none of these units would see combat. Unsurprisingly, the three maneuver brigades that were mobilized were found to be less than 100 percent combat ready, and were then subjected to a massive training effort to get them into top condition. The lead brigade, Georgia's 48th Infantry Brigade(Mech), trained at the National Training Center and — ironically — was certified as fully combat ready on February 28, 1991, the day the war ended.

The Army also mobilized two National Guard field artillery brigades, and both of these units were deployed. One brigade, the 196th, arrived too late to see combat, but the remaining units, HQ & HQ Battery, 142nd Field Artillery Brigade, and four field artillery battalions, saw combat and acquitted themselves well.

The Marine Corps approach to the reserves was completely different. A large percentage of the Marine Corps Reserve was mobilized, and many combat units deployed to the Gulf and saw combat. The Marines deployed to the Gulf the following reserve combat units:

- One of their three infantry regiment headquarters
- Approximately half of their nine infantry battalions
- Almost all of their two tank battalions
- All or almost all of their only LAV battalion
- Six of approximately 16 field artillery firing batteries
- Their only assault amphibian battalion
- Both of their force reconnaissance companies
- Part of their only reconnaissance battalion
- Some of their air defense artillery units

The remaining USMCR combat units that were mobilized were deployed to Okinawa, sent to Norway on an exercise, or used to create a small strategic reserve in CONUS.

Moreover, while some Marine Corps Reserve combat units that deployed did not serve in the front lines — such as the 24th Marines(-), which performed rear area security for I MEF — other reserve units were right in the thick of the fighting. Company B, 4th Tank Battalion, a Marine Corps Reserve unit from Yakima, Washington, distinguished itself when, shortly before dawn on February 25, 1991, it was attacked by an Iraqi armored force that outnumbered the Marines almost three-to-one. The Marines annihilated the Iraqi force — without sustaining a single friendly casualty — in just seven minutes. Amazingly, this unit had just transitioned from the 30-year old M60A1 Main Battle Tank to the state-of-the-art M1A1 only two months previously, when it completed a truncated M1A1 training course after being mobilized in December 1990.

Conclusion

Desert Storm was the most successful use of military force in the Twentieth Century. In addition, Desert Storm was one of the very few occasions in our nation's history when our armed forces were prepared to fight at the beginning of the conflict; this time, Task Force Smith stayed home.[18]

By any measure, Desert Storm was an extraordinary event. We accomplished our war goals quickly, with amazingly few friendly casualties and without having to contend with a long-term friendly POW/MIA problem. Moreover, we so completely dominated the battlefield that at no time during the 42-day war was the enemy able to wrest the initiative from us, or even interfere significantly with the execution of our campaign plan. And, when Iraqi soldiers decided that they had suffered enough and wanted to surrender, American soldiers promptly transitioned from warriors to humanitarians.[19]

Since Desert Storm, a debate has raged with regard to the contributions made by the different armed services. Some factions in the Air Force have argued that airpower won the Gulf War virtually single-handedly, and that the ground war was largely unnecessary. While airpower made a critically important contribution to the war effort, these arguments ignore the fact that Iraq showed no inclination to leave Kuwait during the air war. Moreover, post-war analysis has raised questions with regard to the

---

[18] "Task Force Smith" was the first U.S. Army unit to deploy to Korea in response to North Korea's invasion of South Korea in 1950. Poorly equipped and trained, the task force was destroyed in action during its first battle, and has come to symbolize poor readiness and the consequences of a "hollow army."

[19] Significantly, there has not been even a single allegation of improper treatment of EPWs by U.S. personnel. The International Red Cross, which inspected Allied prisoner of war facilities, reported that the care provided by the Allies to captured Iraqis was the best that has ever been provided to captured soldiers.

high BDA claimed by the Air Force during the war. In retrospect, it appears clear that Saddam had no intention of retreating from Kuwait voluntarily, and the kind of unambiguous victory we achieved in Desert Storm would have been impossible without the decisive commitment of overwhelming ground forces.

There has also been a substantial amount of controversy with regard to whether the coalition terminated the war prematurely. In retrospect, it is clear that the entire Iraqi Army in the KTO had not been rendered combat ineffective, notwithstanding General Schwarzkopf's statements to the contrary at the famous "Mother of All Briefings" near the end of the war. Some Iraqi units were able to retreat into Iraq without suffering catastrophic losses. Nonetheless, there can be no doubt that the Iraqi Army was thoroughly and completely routed. Without exception, those Iraqi units that stood and fought were destroyed without inflicting even nominal losses on the allied forces that attacked them. The Iraqi units that did escape the KTO only did so because they deserted their fellow soldiers and ran from the Allied juggernaut to save their own skins. This was most assuredly not a retreat in good order that would have allowed the Iraqi Army to maintain some measure of dignity with regard to its performance in the Gulf. Furthermore, the units that did escape from the KTO suffered significant losses from Army attack helicopters and artillery, and from Air Force fixed-wing aircraft.[20]

In retrospect, a case can be made that the war should have been continued for another 12 to 24 hours. That would have allowed the allies to inflict that much more of a decisive defeat upon the Iraqi Army. However, this slight increase in the degree of our victory would have been paid for with the blood of allied soldiers — primarily American soldiers. Moreover, as the campaign continued, and bone-tired U.S. Army units that were operating at the end of an increasingly longer logistical lifeline came into contact with new Iraqi Army units — some of which almost certainly would have been relatively fresh and unblooded — the likelihood of significant or substantial friendly casualties would have increased materially.

---

[20] For an analysis that takes a contrary position, arguing that the VII Corps attacked too slowly and allowed much of the Republican Guard to escape the KTO, see "Pushing Them Out the Back Door," *U.S. Naval Institute Proceedings*, 37-42 (June 1993), by Air Force Colonel James G. Burton. Compelling counterarguments are contained in: LTC Steve E. Dietrich, "From Valhalla With Pride," *U.S. Naval Institute Proceedings*, 59-60 (Aug. 1993); COL Richard M. Swain, "Compounding the Error," *U.S. Naval Institute Proceedings*, 61-62 (Aug. 1993); LTG Ronald H. Griffith, "Mission Accomplished — In Full," *U.S. Naval Institute Proceedings*, 63-65 (Aug. 1993); and COL Richard M. Swain, "Reflections on the Revisionist Critique," *Army*, 24-31 (Aug. 1996). See also LTG John H. Cushman, "Desert Storm's End Game," *U.S. Naval Institute Proceedings*, 76-80 (Oct. 1993).

Order of Battle

Thus, any argument that the war was halted prematurely must answer one fundamental question: How many U.S. lives would it have been worth to achieve a slightly more decisive victory in the Gulf? In my opinion, the answer is clear: Such a victory would not be worth the life of even one allied soldier.

America is a safer nation today because of the unprecedented victory we achieved in Operation Desert Storm. Potential future enemies will think long and hard before they risk a course of action that could lead to the destruction of their armed forces, national infrastructure, and way of life. If you have the privilege of meeting Desert Storm veterans, shake their hand and thank them for all they accomplished. They deserve your gratitude and respect.

Chart 1

Allied Coalition, Operation Desert Storm

Under the principle of "unity of command," all the military units participating in a campaign usually operate under one chain of command and ultimately report to one commander. This principle was compromised during Desert Storm for political reasons, however, as it would have been awkward for Saudi and other Arab-Islamic forces to report to an American commander in a campaign pitting them against another Arab nation. Accordingly, there were two separate, theoretically co-equal chains of command within the allied coalition, with General H. Norman Schwarzkopf in command of the American and European forces, and Saudi Lieutenant General Prince Khalid bin Sultan in command of the Arab-Islamic forces. In reality, Schwarzkopf led the entire coalition.

Order of Battle

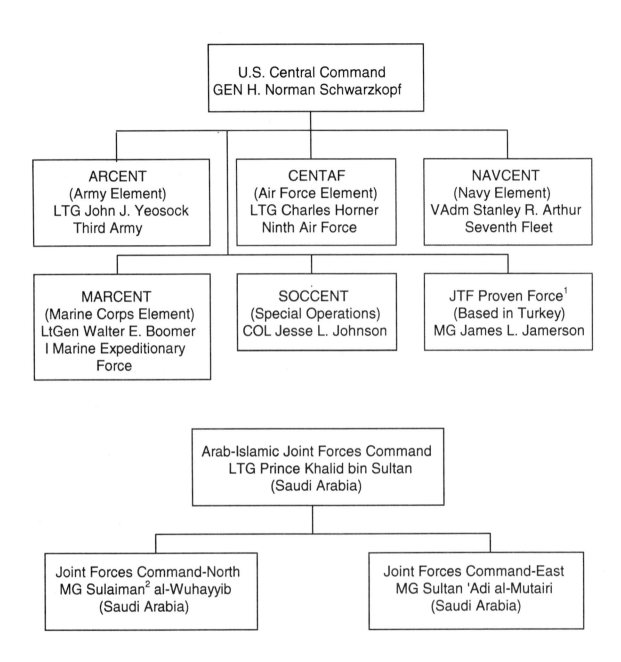

---

[1] Was under "operational control" of the U.S. European Command, but CENTCOM exercised "tactical control" over JTF Proven Force.

[2] Some sources spell this name "Suleman."

1 - 2

Chart 2

Major U.S. Army Formations By Unit Type

This chart lists all of the major U.S. Army units that participated in Operation Desert Storm, by unit type.

Unit	Assignment, Desert Storm	Assignment & Location Prior to Desert Storm
Third Army	CENTCOM	FORSCOM, McPherson
VII Corps	Third Army	USAREUR, Germany
XVIII Abn Corps	Third Army	FORSCOM, Bragg
1st Armd Div(-)	VII Corps	VII Corps, Germany
3rd Armd Div	VII Corps	V Corps, Germany
1st Cav Div(-)	VII Corps[1]	III Corps, Hood
1st Inf Div(M)(-)	VII Corps	III Corps, Riley
24th Inf Div(M)(-)	XVIII Abn Corps	XVIII Abn Corps, Stewart
82nd Abn Div	XVIII Abn Corps	XVIII Abn Corps, Bragg
101st Abn Div(AAslt)	XVIII Abn Corps	XVIII Abn Corps, Campbell

---

[1] The 1st Cav Div(-) was attached to the VII Corps from 13 Jan 91 to 23 Feb 91, when it became CENTCOM's theater reserve. The 1st Cav Div(-) was then released to VII Corps at approximately 0930 hours on 26 Feb 91 and served with VII Corps through the end of the war.

Order of Battle

Unit	Assignment, Desert Storm	Assignment & Location Prior to Desert Storm
1st Bde, 2nd Armd Div	2nd Mar Div	2nd Armd Div, Hood
3rd Bde, 2nd Armd Div	1st Inf Div(M)	2nd Armd Div, Germany
3rd Bde, 3rd Inf Div(M)	1st Armd Div	3rd Inf Div(M), Germany
197th Inf Bde(M)	24th Inf Div(M)	XVIII Abn Corps, Benning
2nd Armd Cav Regt	VII Corps	VII Corps, Germany
3rd Armd Cav Regt	XVIII Abn Corps[2]	III Corps, Bliss
ARCENT Avn Bde[3]	Third Army	KTO(?)[4]
11th Avn Bde	VII Corps	VII Corps, Germany
12th Avn Bde	XVIII Abn Corps	V Corps, Germany
18th Avn Bde(Abn)	XVIII Abn Corps	XVIII Abn Corps, Bragg
29th Avn Gp(ATC)	Third Army	MD ARNG
VII Corps Arty	VII Corps	VII Corps, Germany
XVIII Abn Corps Arty	XVIII Abn Corps	XVIII Abn Corps, Bragg
18th FA Bde(Abn)	XVIII Abn Corps Artillery	XVIII Abn Corps Arty, Bragg
42nd FA Bde	VII Corps Arty	V Corps Arty, Germany
75th FA Bde	VII Corps Arty	III Corps Arty, Sill
142nd FA Bde	VII Corps Arty	AR ARNG
196th FA Bde[5]	XVIII Abn Corps Artillery	TN ARNG
210th FA Bde	VII Corps Arty	VII Corps Arty, Germany
212th FA Bde	XVIII Abn Corps Artillery	III Corps Arty, Sill
11th ADA Bde	Third Army	XVIII Abn Corps, Bliss

---

[2] The 3rd ACR was OPCON to the 24th Inf Div(M) at various times during the ground war. One such period began at noon on 26 Feb 91. The final such period began at 0600 hours on 27 Feb 91 and lasted until the end of the war.

[3] This unit was sometimes called the 2nd Avn Bde because HQ, ARCENT Avn Bde was formed from HQ, Avn Bde, 2nd Armd Div. This apparently occurred in January 1991. The Army has credited HQ, Avn Bde, 2nd Armd Div with participating in Operation Desert Storm.

[4] See Footnote 3.

[5] The 196th arrived too late to see combat. See Chart 4, Footnote 105.

Unit	Assignment, Desert Storm	Assignment & Location Prior to Desert Storm
3rd SF Gp(Abn)(-)	SOCCENT	1st SOCOM,[6] Bragg
5th SF Gp(Abn)	SOCCENT	1st SOCOM, Campbell
10th SF Gp(Abn)(-)	JTF Proven Force	1st SOCOM,[7] Devens
416th Eng Cmd	Third Army	IL USAR
7th Eng Bde	VII Corps	VII Corps, Germany
20th Eng Bde(Abn)	XVIII Abn Corps	XVIII Abn Corps, Bragg
411th Eng Bde	416th Eng Cmd	NY USAR
36th Eng Gp	20th Eng Bde	FORSCOM(?), Benning
109th Eng Gp	7th Eng Bde	SD ARNG
176th Eng Gp	7th Eng Bde	VA ARNG
265th Eng Gp	20th Eng Bde	GA ARNG
926th Eng Gp	7th Eng Bde	AL USAR
937th Eng Gp	20th Eng Bde	III Corps(?), Riley
14th MP Bde	VII Corps	VII Corps, Germany
16th MP Bde(Abn)	XVIII Abn Corps	XVIII Abn Corps, Bragg
89th MP Bde	Third Army	III Corps, Hood
800th MP Bde(EPW)	22nd SUPCOM	NY USAR
301st MP POW Cp	800th MP Bde	MI USAR
400th MP POW Cp	800th MP Bde	FL USAR
401st MP POW Cp	800th MP Bde	TN USAR
402nd MP POW Cp	800th MP Bde	PA USAR
403rd MP POW Cp	800th MP Bde	NE USAR
3rd MP Gp(CID)(Prov)[8]	Third Army	CIC, Gillem
6th Theater Sig Cmd(Army)	Third Army	[9]
11th Sig Bde	6th Sig Cmd	Info Sys Cmd, Huachuca
35th Sig Bde(Abn)	XVIII Abn Corps	XVIII Abn Corps, Bragg
93rd Sig Bde	VII Corps	VII Corps, Germany

---

[6] On 27 Nov 90, Army special operations forces were reorganized and the special forces groups were reassigned from the 1st SOCOM to the newly-activated U.S. Army Special Forces Cmd. The 3rd and 10th SF Gps(Abn) deployed for ODS after this reassignment.

[7] See Footnote 6.

[8] This unit was previously designated the 3rd Region, CID. It was formally redesignated the 3rd MP Gp(CID) on 16 Sep 92. It is unclear when it adopted the designation 3rd MP Gp(CID)(Prov), but it used this designation during Desert Storm.

[9] The 6th Sig Cmd was activated at Fort Huachuca, AZ, on 4 Dec 90, and departed for SWA on 25 Dec 90. It was fully operational in the KTO by 11 Jan 91.

Order of Battle

Unit	Assignment, Desert Storm	Assignment & Location Prior to Desert Storm
3rd Med Cmd	Third Army	KTO[10]
44th Med Bde	1st COSCOM	1st COSCOM, Bragg
332nd Med Bde	2nd COSCOM	TN USAR
1st Med Gp	44th Med Bde	13th COSCOM, Hood
30th Med Gp[11]	332nd Med Bde	2nd COSCOM, Germany
62nd Med Gp	44th Med Bde	I Corps, Lewis
127th Med Gp	332nd Med Bde	AL ARNG
173rd Med Gp	3rd Med Cmd	MA USAR
202nd Med Gp[12]	3rd Med Cmd	FL ARNG
244th Med Gp	3rd Med Cmd	NY ARNG
341st Med Gp	332nd Med Bde	TX USAR
803rd Med Gp	3rd Med Cmd	MA USAR
TF EVAC(Prov)[13]	332nd Med Bde	KTO(?)
2nd MASH	1st Med Gp	(?), Benning
5th MASH	1st Med Gp	44th Med Bde(?), Bragg
10th MASH	1st Med Gp	43rd Spt Gp, Carson
115th MASH[14]	332nd Med Bde	DC ARNG
159th MASH	341st Med Gp	LA ARNG
475th MASH	341st Med Gp	KY ARNG
807th MASH	341st Med Gp	KY USAR
912th MASH	341st Med Gp	TN USAR

---

[10] The 3rd Med Cmd was activated as the ARCENT Med Gp(Prov) on 5 Dec 90 and became the ARCENT Med Cmd(Prov) on 26 Dec 90. It became the 3rd Med Cmd on 15 Mar 91. Some of the personnel needed to operate HQ, 3rd Med Cmd were provided by HQ, 202nd Med Gp.

[11] HQ, 30th Med Gp was the senior medical headquarters in VII Corps before ODS. This headquarters was absorbed into HQ, 332nd Med Bde for Desert Storm, however. Because the 30th did not serve as a separate unit during ODS, it is not listed on Chart 3. HQ, 30th Med Gp did receive campaign participation credit for ODS, however.

[12] See Footnote 10.

[13] This unit was created to control VII Corps' evacuation hospitals. See Chart 3, Footnote 22.

[14] The 115th MASH was dissolved in SWA because of concerns over its readiness, and its personnel were assigned to other units within the 332nd Med Bde. It appears the majority of the 115th MASH's personnel went to the 31st CSH. As a result of these developments, the 345th CSH was converted into a MASH. Because the 115th MASH did not serve as a separate unit during ODS, it is not listed on Chart 3. The 115th did receive campaign participation credit for ODS, however.

Unit	Assignment, Desert Storm	Assignment & Location Prior to Desert Storm
28th CSH	1st Med Gp	44th Med Bde(?), Bragg
31st CSH	127th Med Gp	30th Med Gp(?), Germany
41st CSH	1st Med Gp	(?), Sam Houston
46th CSH	1st Med Gp	(?), Devens
47th CSH	1st Med Gp	62nd Med Gp, Lewis
128th CSH	127th Med Gp	30th Med Gp(?), Germany
345th CSH[15]	341st Med Gp	FL USAR
377th CSH	127th Med Gp	TN USAR
403rd CSH	127th Med Gp	AZ USAR
8th Evac Hosp	173rd Med Gp	(?), Ord
12th Evac Hosp	TF EVAC(Prov)	3rd COSCOM(?), Germany
13th Evac Hosp	TF EVAC(Prov)	WI ARNG
15th Evac Hosp	62nd Med Gp	Devil Troop Bde,[16] Polk
44th Evac Hosp	62nd Med Gp	OK/TX USAR
85th Evac Hosp	173rd Med Gp	(?), Lee
86th Evac Hosp	62nd Med Gp	101st Spt Gp, Campbell
93rd Evac Hosp	62nd Med Gp	(?), Leonard Wood
109th Evac Hosp	62nd Med Gp	AL ARNG
114th Evac Hosp	803rd Med Gp	TX USAR
129th Evac Hosp [HNH]	202nd Med Gp	CA USAR
144th Evac Hosp	244th Med Gp	UT ARNG
148th Evac Hosp	TF EVAC(Prov)	AR ARNG
201st Evac Hosp	173rd Med Gp	PR ARNG
207th Evac Hosp [HNH]	173rd Med Gp	MI ARNG
217th Evac Hosp [HNH]	244th Med Gp	TX ARNG
251st Evac Hosp [HNH]	803rd Med Gp	SC ARNG
311th Evac Hosp [HNH]	202nd Med Gp	ND USAR
312th Evac Hosp	TF EVAC(Prov)	NC USAR
350th Evac Hosp	803rd Med Gp	OH USAR
365th Evac Hosp [HNH]	202nd Med Gp	NY USAR
410th Evac Hosp	TF EVAC(Prov)	KS USAR
47th Field Hosp	173rd Med Gp	214th FA Bde(?), Sill
300th Field Hosp	173rd Med Gp	PA USAR
382nd Field Hosp [HNH]	244th Med Gp	GA USAR

---

[15] The 345th was reconfigured as a MASH in late January 1991. It is unclear if this unit was redesignated as a MASH, however. See Footnote 14.

[16] The Devil Trp Bde was a TDA unit that commanded the nondivisional units at Fort Polk.

Order of Battle

Unit	Assignment, Desert Storm	Assignment & Location Prior to Desert Storm
316th Sta Hosp [HNH]	244th Med Gp	PA USAR
50th Gen Hosp [HNH]	244th Med Gp	WA USAR
321st MMC	22nd SUPCOM	LA/AR USAR
22nd SUPCOM	Third Army	KTO[17]
1st COSCOM	XVIII Abn Corps	XVIII Abn Corps, Bragg
2nd COSCOM	VII Corps	VII Corps, Germany
7th Spt Gp(Corps)	2nd COSCOM	2nd COSCOM, Germany
16th Spt Gp(Corps)	2nd COSCOM	3rd COSCOM, Germany
30th Spt Gp(Corps)	2nd COSCOM	NC ARNG
43rd Spt Gp(Corps)	2nd COSCOM[18]	13th COSCOM(?), Carson
46th Spt Gp(Corps)	1st COSCOM	1st COSCOM, Bragg
101st Spt Gp(Corps)[19]	1st COSCOM	1st COSCOM, Campbell
159th Spt Gp(Corps)	2nd COSCOM	MT USAR
171st Spt Gp(Corps)	1st COSCOM	NC USAR
507th Spt Gp(Corps)[20]	1st COSCOM	1st COSCOM, Bragg
226th Spt Gp(Area)	22nd SUPCOM	AL ARNG
301st Spt Gp(Area)	22nd SUPCOM	NY USAR
593rd Spt Gp(Area)	22nd SUPCOM	I Corps, Lewis
Area Spt Gp Dhahran(Prov)	22nd SUPCOM	KTO

---

[17] The 22nd SUPCOM was formally activated as the ARCENT SUPCOM(Prov) on 19 Aug 90, but had been in operation since 10 Aug 90. One source indicates it was redesignated the 22nd SUPCOM(Prov) on 27 Aug 90. All sources agree, however, that this unit was redesignated the 22nd SUPCOM on 16 Dec 90. According to one source the 22nd SUPCOM was activated at Ft. McPherson on 16 Dec 90 and the command's flag was transferred to Saudi Arabia on 17 Dec 90.

[18] The 43rd Spt Gp supported the 1st Cav Div(-). The 43rd joined the 2nd COSCOM when the 1st Cav Div(-) was assigned to the VII Corps. See Footnote 1.

[19] The Eagle Spt Bde, a TDA unit, became the 101st Corps Spt Gp(Prov) on 25 May 89. On 1 Oct 90, this unit became the 101st Spt Gp(Corps), a TOE unit.

[20] Although officially designated a corps support group, the 507th focused on transportation matters, was commanded by a transportation corps officer, and was sometimes unofficially referred to as the 507th Trans Gp. Some sources indicate the 507th Spt Gp was redesignated the 324th Spt Gp on 15 Jan 91. It is clear, however, that this unit was referred to as the 507th Spt Gp throughout ODS. Moreover, this unit remained active at Fort Bragg as the 507th Spt Gp(Corps) through at least early 1999.

Unit	Assignment, Desert Storm	Assignment & Location Prior to Desert Storm
318th Trans Agency(MC)	22nd SUPCOM	NY USAR
7th Trans Gp(Terminal)	22nd SUPCOM	FORSCOM, Eustis/Story
32nd Trans Gp(Composite)	22nd SUPCOM	FL USAR
111th Ord Gp(Ammunition)	22nd SUPCOM	AL ARNG
475th QM Gp(Petroleum)	22nd SUPCOM	PA USAR
207th MI Bde	VII Corps	VII Corps, Germany
513th MI Bde	Third Army	INTSCOM, Monmouth
525th MI Bde(Abn)	XVIII Abn Corps	XVIII Abn Corps, Bragg
4th PSYOP Gp(Abn)	Third Army	1st SOCOM,[21] Bragg
5th SOSC(TA)(Abn)	22nd SUPCOM[22]	KTO[23]
7th SOSC(TA)(Abn)	JTF Proven Force	SOCEUR, Germany
1st EOD Gp(Prov)	22nd SUPCOM	[24]
TF Freedom[25]	Third Army	KTO[26]
Combined CA TF	TF Freedom	KTO[27]
Kuwait TF[28]	CCATF	[29]
Spt Cmd TF[30]	TF Freedom	KTO (?)

---

[21] On 27 Nov 90, the 4th PSYOP Gp was reassigned from the 1st SOCOM to the newly-activated U.S. Army Civil Affairs and Psychological Operations Cmd. HQ, 4th PSYOP Gp deployed to the KTO after this reassignment, in January 1991.

[22] The 5th SOSC was apparently assigned directly to Third Army as of 15 Feb 91, but was later reassigned to the 22nd SUPCOM. It is unclear when this reassignment occurred, however.

[23] The 5th SOSC was activated on 16 Sep 90, but no personnel were assigned until October 1990. The 5th SOSC was authorized a full colonel as commander, but was commanded by a lieutenant colonel during Desert Storm.

[24] The 1st EOD Gp was activated at Fort Gillem on 29 Nov 90 specifically for Desert Storm, and then deployed to the KTO. HQ, 1st EOD Gp was formed from the 547th EOD Control Team.

[25] Task Force Freedom, the Combined CA TF, and the Kuwait TF were provisional civil affairs units that were formed specifically for ODS. Task Force Freedom focused on Kuwait's short-term recovery.

[26] Task Force Freedom was activated on 13 Feb 91 and was disestablished on 30 Apr 91.

[27] The CCATF was activated on 14 Feb 91 and apparently concluded operations on 30 Apr 91.

[28] Some sources refer to this unit as the "Kuwaiti TF."

[29] The Kuwait TF was activated in the Washington, DC, area on 1 Dec 90, primarily from personnel of the 352nd CA Cmd [MD USAR], and deployed to the KTO in late January 1991. The KTF focused on Kuwait's long term recovery. Most of the KTF had returned to CONUS by 10 May 91.

[30] This was a provisional logistics unit commanded by the Deputy CG of the 22nd SUPCOM.

Order of Battle

Unit	Assignment, Desert Storm	Assignment & Location Prior to Desert Storm
352nd CA Cmd	CCATF	MD USAR
354th CA Bde	VII Corps	MD USAR
360th CA Bde	XVIII Abn Corps	SC USAR
304th CA Gp	22nd SUPCOM	PA USAR
10th PERSCOM	Third Army	KTO[31]
3rd Pers Gp	22nd SUPCOM[32]	III Corps, Hood
7th Pers Gp	VII Corps	VII Corps, Germany
18th Pers Gp(Abn)	XVIII Abn Corps	XVIII Abn Corps, Bragg
7th Corps Fin Gp	VII Corps	VII Corps, Germany
18th Corps Fin Gp(Abn)	XVIII Abn Corps	XVIII Abn Corps, Bragg
Dragon Bde[33]	XVIII Abn Corps	XVIII Abn Corps, Bragg
3rd Bde(-),[34] 1st Inf Div(M)	VII Corps	VII Corps, Germany
1st BCD[35]	CENTAF	XVIII Abn Corps, Bragg
ARCENT Contracting Cmd[36]	22nd SUPCOM	KTO(?)[37]
U.S. Army Spt Gp[38]	22nd SUPCOM(?)	KTO(?)

[31] The 10th PERSCOM was activated as the 3rd PERSCOM(Prov) on 29 Aug 90, and became the 10th PERSCOM on 16 Dec 90.

[32] The 3rd Pers Gp was initially assigned to the 10th PERSCOM, but was reassigned to the 22nd SUPCOM by the beginning of the ground war.

[33] The Dragon Bde was a provisional unit that consisted of various XVIII Abn Corps units not assigned to any other higher headquarters. It included a number of NBC defense units. The Dragon Bde performed a number of roles for the XVIII Abn Corps, including force protection, managing the corps rear area, and operating the corps alternate CP.

[34] Did not serve as a combat arms unit. Assisted VII Corps with its arrival in the KTO. See Chart 4, page 4-28.

[35] This unit was responsible for coordinating operational and intelligence matters between ARCENT and CENTAF. This included providing updates to CENTAF with regard to the Army's situation on the ground, submitting tactical air support requests and providing Army input into the Air Tasking Order (the Air Force document that governed each day's air missions), and coordinating adjustments of the Fire Support Coordination Line (FSCL). Beyond the FSCL, any unit could engage the enemy without first coordinating with Army maneuver units to determine their precise location.

[36] The ARCENT Contracting Cmd was a provisional unit created for Desert Storm that was responsible for all procurement actions, with the exception of real property, construction, and host nation support.

[37] The ARCENT Contracting Cmd was active in the KTO at the very beginning of Desert Shield, on 6 Aug 90. The command was probably created in the KTO.

[38] A provisional unit created by the Army Material Command to provide theater-level repair parts supply and maintenance support in the KTO. At peak strength had over 1,300 personnel, many of whom were civilians. The group was operating in Saudi Arabia by 5 Nov 90, but was apparently not officially activated until 17 Nov 90.

Notes:

➢ "KTO" in the "Assignment & Location Prior to Desert Storm" column indicates that the unit was activated in the Kuwaiti Theater of Operations during Operations Desert Shield/Storm.

➢ In the "Assignment & Location Prior to Desert Storm" column, reserve component units are indicated by state and component, e.g., the 142nd FA Bde was an Army National Guard unit from Arkansas.

➢ Hospitals that have "[HNH]" after their designation operated out of Host Nation Hospitals. These U.S. Army units shared a hospital operated by a host nation, rather than having their own medical facilities in buildings or tents. All were located in Saudi Arabia, with the exceptions of the 129th Evac Hosp (UAE); 311th Evac Hosp (UAE); and 365th Evac Hosp (Oman).

Chart 3

Major Formations, ARCENT

Third Army was the senior Army headquarters in the Gulf and served as ARCENT, the Army component command of the U.S. Central Command. This chart depicts all of the major units (American and allied) that served under ARCENT/Third Army, and the command relationships of these units.

THIRD ARMY

11th ADA Bde
ARCENT Avn Bde[1]
29th Avn Gp(ATC) [MD ARNG]
22nd SUPCOM
   318th Trans Agency(MC) [NY USAR]
   321st Material Management Ctr [LA/AR USAR]
   226th Spt Gp(Area) [AL ARNG]
   301st Spt Gp(Area) [NY USAR]
   593rd Spt Gp(Area)
   Area Support Gp Dhahran(Prov)
   7th Trans Gp(Terminal)[2]
   32nd Trans Gp(Composite)[3] [FL USAR]
   111th Ord Gp(Ammunition) [AL ARNG]
   475th QM Gp(Petroleum) [PA USAR]
   5th SOSC(TA)(Abn)[4]

---

[1] See Chart 2, Footnote 3.

[2] Operated ports of Dammam and Jubayl, and moved supplies inland to initial Log Bases in northeast Saudi Arabia.

[3] Moved supplies north from initial Log Bases to subsequent Log Bases, where responsibility passed to the COSCOMs.

[4] See Chart 2, Footnote 23.

THIRD ARMY (continued)

22nd SUPCOM (continued)
    800th MP Bde(EPW)[5] [NY USAR]
        301st MP POW Cp [MI USAR] (Spt'd XVIII Abn Corps)
        400th MP POW Cp [FL USAR] (Spt'd MARCENT & ARCENT)
        401st MP POW Cp [TN USAR] (Spt'd MARCENT)
        402nd MP POW Cp [PA USAR] (Spt'd VII Corps)
        403rd MP POW Cp [NE USAR] (Spt'd MARCENT)
    1st EOD Gp(Prov)
    304th CA Gp [PA USAR]
    3rd Pers Gp
    ARCENT Contracting Cmd
    U.S. Army Spt Gp(?)[6]
416th Eng Cmd [IL USAR]
    411th Eng Bde [NY USAR]
6th Theater Sig Cmd(Army)
    11th Sig Bde
3rd Med Cmd
    173rd Med Gp [MA USAR]
        8th Evac Hosp
        85th Evac Hosp
        201st Evac Hosp [PR ARNG]
        207th Evac Hosp [MI ARNG] [HNH]
        47th Field Hosp
        300th Field Hosp[7] [PA USAR]
    202nd Med Gp [FL ARNG]
        129th Evac Hosp [CA USAR] [HNH]
        311th Evac Hosp [ND USAR] [HNH]
        365th Evac Hosp [NY USAR] [HNH]
    244th Med Gp [NY ARNG]
        144th Evac Hosp [UT ARNG]
        217th Evac Hosp [TX ARNG] [HNH]
        382nd Field Hosp [GA USAR] [HNH]
        316th Sta Hosp [PA USAR] [HNH]
        50th Gen Hosp [WA USAR] [HNH]

---

[5] Four of the 800th MP Bde's POW Camps were organized into two task forces, designated the Bronx Area and the Brooklyn Area. The Bronx Area was in the east and supported MARCENT. The Bronx Area included the 401st and 403rd MP POW Cps, with the commander of the 401st as the overall commander. The Brooklyn Area was in the west and supported the VII and XVIII Abn Corps. The Brooklyn Area included the 301st and 402nd MP POW Cps, with the commander of the 402nd as the overall commander.

[6] The U.S. Army Spt Gp was an EAC unit that was probably assigned to the 22nd SUPCOM.

[7] Primarily responsible for providing medical care to EPWs.

THIRD ARMY (continued)

    3rd Med Cmd (continued)
        803rd Med Gp [MA USAR]
            114th Evac Hosp [TX USAR]
            251st Evac Hosp [SC ARNG] [HNH]
            350th Evac Hosp [OH USAR]
    89th MP Bde
    3rd MP Gp(CID)(Prov)
    513th MI Bde
    4th PSYOP Gp(Abn)[8]
    TF Freedom[9]
        Combined CA TF
            352nd CA Cmd [MD USAR]
            Kuwait TF[10]
        Spt Cmd TF[11]
    10th PERSCOM

---

[8] Although assigned to the Third Army, the 4th PSYOP Gp(Abn) was OPCON to CENTCOM and received its orders directly from HQ, CENTCOM.

[9] Task Force Freedom was responsible for the reconstruction of Kuwait.

[10] See Chart 2, Footnotes 28 & 29.

[11] See Chart 2, Footnote 30.

XVIII Airborne Corps

24th Inf Div(Mech)
    197th Inf Bde(Mech)
82nd Abn Div
101st Abn Div(Air Aslt)
6th (FR) Lt Armd Div[12]
    2nd Bde, 82nd Abn Div[13]
3rd Armd Cav Regt[14]
12th Avn Bde (Spt'd 6 (FR) Lt AD; 101 Abn Div(AAslt))
18th Avn Bde(Abn)
XVIII Abn Corps Arty
    18th FA Bde(Abn) (Spt'd 6 (FR) Lt AD[15]; 24 ID(M))
    196th FA Bde[16] [TN/KY ARNG]
    212th FA Bde (Spt'd 24 ID(M))
20th Eng Bde(Abn)
    36th Eng Gp (Spt'd 24 ID(M))
    265th Eng Gp [GA ARNG] (Spt'd 24 ID(M); XVIII Abn Corps)
    937th Eng Gp (Spt'd 6 (FR) Lt AD; XVIII Abn Corps)
1st COSCOM
    46th Spt Gp(Corps) (Spt'd 82 Abn Div)
    101st Spt Gp(Corps) (Spt'd 101 Abn Div(AAslt))
    171st Spt Gp(Corps) [NC USAR] (Spt'd 24 ID(M))
    507th Spt Gp(Corps)

---

[12] French Army units were under the command of the French government, but were under the tactical control of the XVIII Airborne Corps. French and other european sources indicate that this unit was actually designated "The Daguet Division" (apparently because France code named its participation in Desert Storm "Operation Daguet") and that the 6th (FR) Lt Armd Div merely provided some of the units for this provisional unit. I refer to this unit as the 6th (FR) Lt Armd Div because U.S. sources consistently use this designation.

[13] The 2nd Bde, 82nd Abn Div was OPCON to the 6th (FR) Lt Armd Div during the initial stages of the ground war, but returned to 82nd Abn Div control at approximately 1300 hours on 26 Feb 91, and became the 82nd's reserve at that time.

[14] See Chart 2, Footnote 2.

[15] Also supported the 2nd Bde, 82nd Abn Div, during this period.

[16] The 196th arrived too late to see combat. See Chart 4, Footnote 105.

XVIII Airborne Corps (continued)

    1st COSCOM (continued)
        44th Med Bde[17]
            1st Med Gp
                2nd MASH
                5th MASH
                10th MASH
                28th CSH
                41st CSH
                46th CSH
                47th CSH
            62nd Med Gp
                15th Evac Hosp
                44th Evac Hosp [OK/TX USAR]
                86th Evac Hosp
                93rd Evac Hosp
                109th Evac Hosp [AL ARNG]
    16th MP Bde(Abn)
    35th Sig Bde(Abn)
    525th MI Bde(Abn)
    360th CA Bde [SC USAR]
    18th Pers Gp(Abn)
    18th Corps Fin Gp(Abn)
    Dragon Bde[18]

---

[17] The 44th Med Bde adopted the same non-doctrinal approach used by the 332nd Med Bde, with its forward medical assets (MASHs and CSHs) controlled by the 1st Med Gp and its rear medical assets (evacuation hospitals) controlled by the 62nd Med Gp. See Footnote 22.

[18] See Chart 2, Footnote 33.

VII Corps

1st Armd Div
    3rd Bde, 3rd Inf Div(Mech)
3rd Armd Div
1st Inf Div(Mech)
    3rd Bde, 2nd Armd Div
1st Cav Div(-)[19]
1st (UK) Armd Div[20]
2nd Armd Cav Regt
11th Avn Bde
VII Corps Arty
    42nd FA Bde (Spt'd 1 ID(M); 3 AD)
    75th FA Bde (Spt'd 1 ID(M); 1 AD)
    142nd FA Bde [AR/OK ARNG] (Spt'd 1 ID(M); 1 (UK) AD)
    210th FA Bde (Spt'd 2 ACR; 1 ID(M))
7th Eng Bde
    109th Eng Gp [SD ARNG] (Spt'd VII Corps)
    176th Eng Gp [VA ARNG] (Spt'd 1 ID(M); VII Corps)
    926th Eng Gp [AL USAR] (Spt'd 3 AD)
2nd COSCOM
    7th Spt Gp(Corps) (Forward support)
    16th Spt Gp(Corps) (Rear area support)
    30th Spt Gp(Corps) [NC ARNG] (Rear area support)
    43rd Spt Gp(Corps)[21] (Spt'd 1 Cav Div(-))
    159th Spt Gp(Corps) [MT USAR] (Forward support)

---

[19] See Chart 2, Footnote 1.

[20] British Army units were under the command of the British government, but were under the tactical control of the VII Corps.

[21] See Chart 2, Footnote 18.

VII Corps (continued)

2nd COSCOM (continued)
    332nd Med Bde[22] [TN USAR]
        127th Med Gp [AL ARNG]
            31st CSH
            128th CSH
            377th CSH [TN USAR]
            403rd CSH [AZ USAR]
        341st Med Gp [TX USAR]
            159th MASH [LA ARNG]
            475th MASH [KY ARNG]
            807th MASH [KY USAR]
            912th MASH [TN USAR]
            345th CSH[23] [FL USAR]
        TF EVAC(Prov)[24]
            12th Evac Hosp
            13th Evac Hosp [WI ARNG]
            148th Evac Hosp [AR ARNG]
            312th Evac Hosp [NC USAR]
            410th Evac Hosp [KS USAR]
14th MP Bde
93rd Sig Bde
207th MI Bde
354th CA Bde [MD USAR]
7th Pers Gp
7th Corps Fin Gp
3rd Bde(-),[25] 1st Inf Div(M)

---

[22] See Chart 2, Footnotes 11 & 14. According to doctrine, each medical group within a corps medical brigade was supposed to be "vertically integrated," including MASHs, CSHs, and evacuation hospitals, and would be responsible for all aspects of medical care within its portion of the corps zone. The 332nd Med Bde adopted a non-doctrinal approach, organizing its medical groups horizontally so that each covered the entire corps zone and provided one level of medical care within its horizontal band. The 332nd adopted this approach because of the distances VII Corps expected to travel, and the fact the battlefield was expected to be deeper than it was wide. Only the MASHs were expected to move into Iraq. See also Appendix D, page D-20.

[23] See Chart 2, Footnote 15.

[24] See Chart 2, Footnote 13.

[25] See Chart 2, Footnote 34.

Notes:

➢ When a listed unit supported several other units at different times, the supported units are separated by a semicolon and listed in chronological order. Thus, the 937th Eng Gp initially supported the 6th (FR) Lt Armd Div, and then later supported the XVIII Abn Corps.

➢ Hospitals that have "[HNH]" after their designation operated out of Host Nation Hospitals. These U.S. Army units shared a hospital operated by a host nation, rather than having their own medical facilities in buildings or tents. All were located in Saudi Arabia, with the exceptions of the 129th Evac Hosp (UAE); 311th Evac Hosp (UAE); and 365th Evac Hosp (Oman).

➢ ARCENT should have had a Transportation Command as the senior transportation unit for the theater, but no Transportation Command was established in SWA. The functions that should have been performed by a Transportation Command were performed by staff officers at the 22nd SUPCOM Headquarters, under the direction of COL David A. Whaley, the 22nd SUPCOM's Assistant Chief of Staff for Transportation. Several sources report that a Transportation Command was active in the Gulf, but this is incorrect.

➢ ARCENT should have had a Finance Command as the senior finance unit for the theater, but no Finance Command was established in SWA. The functions that should have been performed by a Finance Command were performed by staff officers at Third Army Headquarters under the direction of COL Richard B. Granger, the ARCENT Deputy Chief of Staff for Resource Management (comptroller), and by the 18th Corps Fin Gp(Abn). Several sources report that a Finance Command was active in the Gulf, but this is incorrect.

Chart 4

U.S. Army Combat Arms Units
Assigned To ARCENT,
By Division/Brigade

This chart lists all U.S. Army combat arms units that were assigned to ARCENT. This chart does not cover U.S. Army units assigned to MARCENT (see Chart 5); U.S. Army units assigned to SOCCENT (see Chart 6); U.S. Army units assigned to Joint Task Force Proven Force (see Chart 7); or U.S. Army units assigned to Task Force Patriot Defender (see Chart 8). Major non-combat arms units are listed only if they had combat arms units assigned to them. Thus, for example, the 207th MI Bde is listed here because it had an infantry company assigned, but the 513th MI Bde is not listed because no combat arms units were assigned to the 513th.

This chart also provides a short combat narrative for the major maneuver units that fought in Desert Storm.

VII CORPS

TF Jayhawk[1]
TF 8-43 ADA[2]
    8-43 ADA(Patriot)[3] [Fr. 69 ADA Bde, 32 AADCOM]
    Btrys A & C, 6-52 ADA(Hawk) [Fr. 69 ADA Bde, 32 AADCOM]

---

[1] This was a provisional battalion that VII Corps formed to control its WSRO units. See Chart 12, page 12-4, "Notes."

[2] Was under the operational control of VII Corps, although the 11th ADA Bde exercised tactical control over the task force.

[3] Consisted of HHB and Btrys A-D.

XVIII AIRBORNE CORPS

(1) Abn Inf Bn[4] [Fr. 82 Abn Div]
2-502 Inf(Air Aslt)[5] [Fr. 2 Bde, 101 Abn Div(AAslt)]
(1) Stinger Sec, 2-52 ADA(Hawk) [Fr. 11 ADA Bde]
TF 2-1 ADA[6]
    2-1 ADA(Hawk)[7] [Fr. 11 ADA Bde]
    Btrys A, B & E, 3-43 ADA(Patriot) [Fr. 11 ADA Bde]
    Fire Dist Sec, 1-43 ADA(Patriot) [Fr. 11 ADA Bde]
    (4) Inf Plts [Fr. 10 Mtn Div(Lt Inf)]

1st ARMORED DIVISION[8]

The 1st Armored Division served as the left-hand portion of the VII Corps fist that attacked the Republican Guard. The division initiated its attack at 1434 hours on 24 Feb 91, moving northeast behind elements of the 2nd Armored Cavalry Regiment. The division advanced north in a wedge formation, with the 3rd Brigade, 3rd Infantry Division(Mech) in the lead in the center, with the other two brigades echeloned behind the lead brigade, the 2nd Brigade to the left (next to the XVIII Airborne Corps zone) and the 3rd Brigade to the right (next to the 3rd Armored Division).

By the evening of 25 Feb 91, the 1st Armored Division had changed to a two up, one back formation, with 2nd Brigade on the left, 3rd Brigade, 3rd Infantry Division(Mech) on the right, and 3rd Brigade in reserve. The 1st Armored Division attacked Al Busayyah the night of 25-26 Feb 91, and then curved around to the right on 26 Feb 91 so that it was headed east. At the same time, the division transitioned to a new formation, with three brigades on line, the 2nd Brigade on the left (next to the XVIII Airborne Corps zone), 3rd Brigade, 3rd Infantry Division(Mech) in the center, and 3rd Brigade on the right (next to the 3rd Armored Division). The 1st Armored Division maintained this formation for the rest of the war.

---

[4] OPCON to the Dragon Bde for rear area protection. The designation of this battalion is unknown, however it came from either the 1st or 3rd Bdes of the 82nd Abn Div.

[5] Initially detached from the 101st Abn Div(AAslt) to the XVIII Abn Corps as the "corps tactical force for rear battle." Apparently OPCON to the Dragon Bde during this period. Reassigned to the 2nd Bde, 101st Abn Div(AAslt) at 1850 hours, 26 Feb 91. However, the 2-502 Inf was reassigned to the 1st Bde, 101st Abn Div(AAslt) on 27 Feb 91, before it was able to link up with the 2nd Bde.

[6] Also known as TF Scorpion. The attached infantry platoons provided local security; their designations are unknown. They were probably deployed to SWA under the WSRO/SCT program. See text, pages 7 and 8, and Chart 12.

[7] Consisted of HHB and Btrys A-C.

[8] Was supported by the 75th FA Bde. See Footnote 88.

The 1st Armored Division attacked the Republican Guard in the afternoon of 26 Feb 91 and continued to attack right up to the cease fire at 0800 hours on 28 Feb 91. The division saw heavy combat throughout this period, culminating in the "Battle of Medina Ridge" the afternoon of 27 Feb 91, when the division destroyed a large portion of the RGFC Medina Division. This was arguably the largest and most violent battle of the Gulf War. It was inarguably a huge, lopsided victory for the 1st Armored Division.

Organization of the 1st Armored Division

<u>3rd Bde, 3rd Inf Div(Mech)</u>[9] "Phantom Brigade" [Served as the 1st Armd Div's 1st Bde]

    4-66 Armor [M1A1 or M1A1(Mod)][10]
    1-7 Inf(M)
    4-7 Inf(M)(-)
       Co A, 1-35 Armor [Fr. 2 Bde, 1 AD]
    2-41 FA(155 SP) [3 x 8]
    Btry A, 6-3 ADA(Vulc/Chap/Stinger)

<u>2nd Brigade</u> "Iron Brigade"

    1-35 Armor(-) [M1A1 or M1A1(Mod)]
       Co D, 4-7 Inf(M) [Fr. 3 Bde, 3 ID(M)]
    2-70 Armor [M1A1 or M1A1(Mod)]
    4-70 Armor [M1A1 or M1A1(Mod)]
    6-6 Inf(M) [Fr. 3 Bde, 1 AD]
    2-1 FA(155 SP) [3 x 8]
    Btry B, 6-3 ADA(Vulc/Chap/Stinger)

<u>3rd Brigade</u> "Bulldog Brigade"

    3-35 Armor [M1A1 or M1A1(Mod)]
    1-37 Armor [M1A1HA] [Fr. 1 Bde, 1 AD]
    7-6 Inf(M)
    3-1 FA(155 SP) [3 x 8]
    Btry C, 6-3 ADA(Vulc/Chap/Stinger)

---

[9] Replaced the 1st Armd Div's 1st Bde. Left behind in Germany were: HQ, 1st Bde; 2-37 Armor; 1-6 Inf(M); and 6-1 FA(155 SP). Also left behind was the 2nd Bde's 2-6 Inf(M). The infantry units left behind were still equipped with the M113 series APC or were in the process of transitioning to the M2 Bradley IFV.

[10] Of the five 1st Armd Div tank battalions marked "[M1A1 or M1A1(Mod)]," three had the M1A1 and two had the M1A1(Mod).

Aviation Brigade[11]

    1-1 Cav
    2-1 Avn(AH)[12] [AH-64]
    3-1 Avn(AH) [AH-64]

DIVARTY

    4-27 FA(MLRS)(-) [2 x 9] [Fr. 72 FA Bde]
      Btry A(MLRS), 94th FA [1 x 9]
    Btry B(TA), 25th FA

Division Troops

    6-3 ADA(Vulc/Chap/Stinger)(-)
    LRS Det, 501st MI Bn(CEWI)

Regimental Engineer

DISCOM

3rd ARMORED DIVISION[13]

The 3rd Armored Division served as the center portion of the VII Corps fist that attacked the Republican Guard. The division initiated its attack at 1445 hours on 24 Feb 91, moving northeast behind elements of the 2nd Armored Cavalry Regiment. The 3rd Armored Division advanced north in a column of brigades, with 2nd Brigade in the lead, followed by 1st Brigade and then 3rd Brigade.

The 3rd Armored Division curved around to the right on 26 Feb 91 so that it was headed east and, in the late morning, deployed for combat with two brigades on line

---

[11] Typically referred to as the "4th Bde."

[12] Was OPCON to the 2nd ACR at the beginning of the ground war. Rejoined the 1st Armd Div mid-day on 27 Feb 91.

[13] Was supported by the 42nd FA Bde (see Footnote 87) and the 926th Eng Gp. See Footnote 14. The 2-6 Cav(AH), 11th Avn Bde, became OPCON to the Avn Bde, 3rd Armd Div at 1000 hours, 27 Feb 91, and remained with the division for the rest of the war. Certain 3rd Armd Div units were left behind in Germany and replaced by units from the 8th Inf Div(M) because they had begun inactivating as part of the post-Cold War drawdown of the Army and were no longer combat ready. Left behind in Germany were: 2-32 Armor and 3-5 ADA. However, 1st Plt, Co B, 2-32 Armor deployed to the KTO in mid-February 1991, probably as a WSRO unit.

and one in reserve. By noon this maneuver had been completed and 2nd Brigade was on the left (with the 1st Armored Division to its left), 1st Brigade was on the right (with the 2nd Armored Cavalry Regiment to its right in what would become the 1st Infantry Division(Mech) zone), and 3rd Brigade was in reserve. The division maintained a two up, one back formation for the remainder of the war.

The 3rd Armored Division began encountering substantial elements of the Republican Guard in the afternoon of 26 Feb 91. On 27 Feb 91, the 3rd Brigade passed through the 2nd Brigade and the 2nd Brigade became the division reserve. This hand-off was complete by around noon on 27 Feb 91. By 2130 hours on 27 Feb 91, the 3rd Armored Division had reached Phase Line (PL) Kiwi, its limit of advance, after inflicting heavy casualties on the defending Republican Guard and Iraqi regular army armored units. The division held at PL Kiwi because the 1st Infantry Division(Mech) to the south was angling to the left and attacking in front of the 3rd Armored Division.

Organization of the 3rd Armored Division

1st Brigade "Ready First Combat Team" or "RFCT"

    4-32 Armor [M1A1]
    4-34 Armor [M1A1] [Fr. 1 Bde, 8 ID(M)]
    3-5 Cav(M)
    5-5 Cav(M)[14]
    2-3 FA(155 SP) [3 x 8]
    Btry A, 5-3 ADA(Vulc/Chap/Stinger) [Fr. 8 ID(M)]
    1st Plt, Btry D, 5-3 ADA(Vulc/Chap/Stinger) [Fr. 8 ID(M)]

2nd Brigade (No Brigade Nickname)

    3-8 Cav(A) [M1A1HA]
    4-8 Cav(A) [M1A1HA]
    4-18 Inf(M)
    4-82 FA(155 SP) [3 x 8]
    Btry B, 5-3 ADA(Vulc/Chap/Stinger) [Fr. 8 ID(M)]

---

[14] The 5-5 Cav(M) began the ground war with the 1st Bde, but left that unit and apparently operated directly under divisional control some time after the 3rd Armd Div initiated its attack. The 5-5 Cav(M) was re-attached to the 1st Bde in the late afternoon of 26 Feb 91, and was then attached to the 3rd Bde around midnight on 26 Feb 91. The 5-5 Cav(M) organized a provisional "Security Plt" equipped with M113 series APCs to provide rear area security to the battalion trains. The Security Plt was formed from Co E [M901A1], which was inactivated before the battalion deployed to SWA.

3rd ARMORED DIVISION (continued)

3rd Brigade[15] "Thundering Third Brigade"

    2-67 Armor [M1A1]
    4-67 Armor [M1A1HA]
    5-18 Inf(M)
    2-82 FA(155 SP) [3 x 8]
    Btry D, 5-3 ADA(Vulc/Chap/Stinger) [Fr. 8 ID(M)]

Aviation Brigade[16]

    4-7 Cav
       Stinger Plt(Prov), 5-3 ADA(Vulc/Chap/Stinger) [Fr. 8 ID(M)]
    2-227 Avn(AH)[17] [AH-64]
       Co A, 5-229 Avn(AH)[18] [AH-64] [Fr. Apache Tng Bde]

DIVARTY

    Btry A(MLRS), 40th FA [1 x 9]
    Btry F(TA), 333rd FA

Division Troops

    5-3 ADA(Vulc/Chap/Stinger)(-) [Fr. 8 ID(M)]
       Stinger Teams, 3-5 ADA
    LRS Det, 533rd MI Bn(CEWI)

Regimental Engineer

DISCOM

---

[15] See Footnote 14.

[16] Typically referred to as the "4th Cbt Avn Bde." See Footnote 13.

[17] Six OH-58Ds from the 7-227 Avn were attached to the 2-227 Avn throughout the ground war.

[18] See Footnote 77.

1st CAVALRY DIVISION(-)[19]

The 1st Cavalry Division(-) served as the theater reserve until approximately 0930 hours on 26 Feb 91, when it was assigned to the VII Corps. Prior to that, on 24 Feb 91 the 2nd Brigade and Aviation Brigade committed a feinting attack up the Wadi al Batin as part of the Coalition deception plan.

The 1st Cavalry Division(-) began moving north to join the VII Corps at 1100 hours on 26 Feb 91 and, by 1100 hours on 27 Feb 91, had arrived behind the 1st Armored Division in the left-hand portion of the VII Corps zone. At this point, the 1st Cavalry Division(-) was deployed with its two brigades on line, with 1st Brigade on the left and 2nd Brigade on the right. Plans to get the 1st Cavalry Division(-) into the fight by passing it through the 1st Armored Division, or by sliding the 1st Armored Division to the right and passing the 1st Cavalry Division(-) around the 1st Armored Division's left flank, were frustrated by the cease fire on 28 Feb 91. As a result, the war ended without the 1st Cavalry Division(-) having seen a substantial amount of combat.

Organization of the 1st Cavalry Division(-)

1st Brigade "Ironhorse Brigade"

    2-8 Cav(A) [M1A1(Mod)]
    3-32 Armor [M1A1(Mod)]
    2-5 Cav(M)
    1-82 FA(155 SP) [3 x 8]
    Btry A, 4-5 ADA(Vulc/Avenger/Stinger)

---

[19] Was supported by the 43rd Spt Gp(Corps) and, from 27 Feb 91 to the end of the war, by the 1-158 FA(MLRS)(-). See Footnote 90.

1st CAVALRY DIVISION(-) (continued)

2nd Brigade[20] "Blackjack Brigade"

    1-8 Cav(A) [M1A1(Mod)]
    1-32 Armor [M1A1(Mod)]
    1-5 Cav(M)
    3-82 FA(155 SP) [3 x 8]
    Btry C, 4-5 ADA(Vulc/Avenger/Stinger)

Aviation Brigade

    1-3 Avn(AH) [AH-64] [Fr. 2 AD(-)]
    1-227 Avn(AH) [AH-64]

DIVARTY

    Btry A(MLRS), 21st FA [1 x 9]
    Btry A(TA), 333rd FA

Division Troops

    1-7 Cav(-)[21]
        Trps A & B, 2-1 Cav [Fr. 2 AD(-)]
    4-5 ADA(Vulc/Avenger/Stinger)(-)[22]
    LRS Det, 312th MI Bn(CEWI)

DISCOM

---

[20] Beginning 7 Feb 91, the 2nd Bde executed a series of feints and artillery raids to the east of the VII Corps zone. These actions were intended to deceive the Iraqis into concluding that the main Allied effort would occur in the vicinity of the Wadi al Batin. The 1st Cav Div(-) dubbed these actions "The Battle of the Ruqi Pocket" because they occurred in the vicinity of the Saudi town of Ruqi. On 20 Feb 91, the 2nd Bde executed a brigade-sized attack across the border into Iraq near Ruqi. This attack was called "Operation Knight Strike."

[21] The 1-7 Cav was short one ground troop. Thus, with two ground troops attached from the 2nd Armd Div, the 1-7 Cav was over-strength by one troop.

[22] The 4-5 ADA formed Btry D(Avenger)(+), a provisional unit, in SWA. Battery D consisted of six Avenger platoons; three were formed from personnel of the 2nd Armd Div's 2-5 ADA.

1st INFANTRY DIVISION(MECH)[23]

The 1st Infantry Division(Mech) served as the right-hand portion of the VII Corps fist that attacked the Republican Guard. The division began breaching the Iraqi front lines at 1500 hours on 24 Feb 91 with 1st Brigade on the left and 2nd Brigade on the right, with 3rd Brigade, 2nd Armored Division in reserve.[24] At 0600 on 25 Feb 91 the 1st Infantry Division(Mech) continued the attack by passing the 3rd Brigade, 2nd Armored Division through the 2nd Brigade. The division completed the breach by 1100 and began passing the 1st (UK) Armoured Division though the breachhead at noon. Passage of the 1st (UK) Armoured Division was completed by 0200 on 26 Feb 91.

Starting at 0430 hours on 26 Feb 91, the 1st Infantry Division(Mech) raced northward in a column of brigades, with 1st Brigade in the lead, followed by 3rd Brigade, 2nd Armored Division, and finally 2nd Brigade, to join the other units of the VII Corps. The division caught up with the forward elements of the VII Corps later that day and executed a forward passage of lines through the 2nd Armored Cavalry Regiment from approximately 2200 hours on 26 Feb 91 to approximately 0210 hours on 27 Feb 91.

At that time, the 1st Infantry Division(Mech) became the right-hand element of the VII Corps juggernaut. The division attacked with two brigades on line, the 1st Brigade on the left (with the 3rd Armored Division to its left), and the 3rd Brigade, 2nd Armored Division on the right (with the 1st (UK) Armoured Division zone to its right), with 2nd Brigade in reserve. The 1st Infantry Division(Mech) was almost immediately thrust into what became known as the "Battle of [Objective] Norfolk," arguably the most chaotic and difficult engagement the Coalition fought during Desert Storm, a battle that was fought all night from late on 26 Feb 91 until 0400 hours on 27 Feb 91.

At 0600 on 27 Feb 91, the 1st Infantry Division(Mech) passed the 2nd Brigade through the 1st Brigade and continued the attack to the east with 2nd Brigade on the left, 3rd Brigade, 2nd Armored Division on the right, and 1st Brigade in reserve. At this point the division was in an exploitation and was able to move faster than the 1st and 3rd Armored Divisions, which were still encountering heavy Iraqi resistance.

---

[23] During the 1st Inf Div(M)'s breach of the Iraqi front lines on 24 Feb 91, the division was supported by the 42nd, 75th, and 142nd FA Bdes and by the division artillery of the 1st (UK) Armd Div. See Footnotes 87-90 & 93 and Chart 27, Footnote 17. The 1st Inf Div(M) was also initially supported by the 176th Eng Gp (until 26 Feb 91) and was later supported by the 210th FA Bde. See Footnote 96.

[24] The 1st Inf Div(M) began slowly advancing toward the Iraqi defenses at 0538 hours and then initiated an intense 30-minute artillery prep at 1430 hours, culminating with the attack through the breach at 1500 hours.

Order of Battle

The 1st Infantry Division(Mech) began angling to the left so that it was attacking northeast, moving diagonally across the front of the 3rd Armored Division. At 1900 hours on 27 Feb 91, however, VII Corps directed the 1st Infantry Division(Mech) to stop attacking northeast and to proceed due east. The division advanced until the cease fire at 0800 hours on 28 Feb 91. By this time the 1st Infantry Division(Mech) had cut the Basrah-Kuwait City highway, ending the war just to the north of the 1st (UK) Armoured Division, which was also astride this road.

Organization of the 1st Infantry Division(Mech)

1st Brigade "Devil Brigade"

> 1-34 Armor [M1A1(Mod)]
> 2-34 Armor [M1A1(Mod)]
> 5-16 Inf(M)
> 1-5 FA(155 SP) [3 x 8]
> Btry A(-), 2-3 ADA(Vulc/Stinger)

2nd Brigade "Dagger Brigade"

> 3-37 Armor [M1]
> 4-37 Armor [M1]
> 2-16 Inf(M)
> 4-5 FA(155 SP) [3 x 8]
> Btry B(-), 2-3 ADA(Vulc/Stinger)

3rd Bde, 2nd Armd Div "Blackheart Brigade" [Served as the 1st Inf Div(Mech)'s 3rd Bde]

> 2-66 Armor [M1A1HA]
> 3-66 Armor [M1A1HA]
> 1-41 Inf(M)
> 4-3 FA(155 SP)[25] [3 x 8]
> Btry C(-), 2-3 ADA(Vulc/Stinger)
>   4th Plt(Stinger), Btry C, 2-5 ADA

---

[25] This battalion was under the control of the 42nd FA Bde during the 1st Inf Div(M)'s breach of the Iraqi front lines on 24 Feb 91.

Aviation Brigade[26]

    1-4 Cav[27]
        (1) Stinger Tm, 4th Plt, Btry A, 2-3 ADA(Vulc/Stinger)
        LRS Det, Co D, 101st MI Bn(CEWI)
    1-1 Avn(AH) [AH-64]

DIVARTY

    Btry B(MLRS), 6th FA [1 x 9]
    Btry D(TA)(-),[28] 25th FA
        (1) Radar Sec, Btry C(TA), 26th FA[29] [Fr. 2 AD(Fwd)]

Division Troops

    2-3 ADA(Vulc/Stinger)(-)

Regimental Engineer

DISCOM

---

[26] Typically referred to as the "4th Bde."

[27] Troop A, a ground troop stationed in Germany with the 1st Inf Div(M)(Fwd), was inactivated on 17 Jul 90. The 1-4 Cav activated a new Troop A on 19 Nov 90 to bring the squadron back up to full strength. It is unclear why Trp D(Air), 2-1 Cav, 3rd Bde, 2nd Armd Div did not deploy with that brigade. The 1-4 Cav secured the site at Safwan, Iraq, that was used for the cease fire talks between GEN Schwarzkopf and senior Iraqi leaders on 3 Mar 91.

[28] Battery D at Fort Riley was short one AN/TPQ-36 Radar, which was stationed in Germany with the 1st Inf Div(M)(Fwd). This radar did not deploy for Operation Desert Storm.

[29] One AN/TPQ-36 Radar from Btry C(TA), 26th FA (the 2nd Armd Div's TA battery) was serving with the 2nd Armd Div(Fwd) in Germany prior to Desert Storm. It appears this radar deployed to SWA with the 3rd Bde, 2nd Armd Div and served with Btry D(TA)(-), 25th FA, standing in for the one "missing" radar section from Btry D. See Footnote 28.

24th INFANTRY DIVISION(MECH)[30]

The 24th Infantry Division(Mech) attacked in the right-hand portion of the XVIII Airborne Corps zone, with the 101st Airborne Division(Air Aslt) on its left and the 3rd Armored Cavalry Regiment on its right. The 24th Infantry Division(Mech) crossed the line of departure at 1500 hours on 24 Feb 91 with three brigades on line, the 197th Infantry Brigade(Mech) on the left, the 1st Brigade in the center, and the 2nd Brigade on the right. Later in the day, however, the division transitioned to a two up, one back formation, with the 1st Brigade following the 2nd Brigade in its zone. Thus, the 24th Infantry Division(Mech) was concentrated in the eastern portion of its zone, a trend that was to continue and to influence the remainder of the division's war.

Beginning in the early morning hours of 25 Feb 91, the 197th Infantry Brigade(Mech) attacked northward in the left hand portion of the division zone, while the 1st and 2nd Brigades each attacked their own objectives in the right hand portion of the division zone. For the 197th Infantry Brigade(Mech), these efforts culminated on 27 Feb 91, when the brigade seized Tallil Air Base. The 1st and 2nd Brigades attacked north until 27 Feb 91, when they wheeled to the east and attacked Jalibah Air Base. During these attacks, the 1st Brigade was generally on the left and in the lead, while the 2nd Brigade was on the right; the division main effort alternated between these two brigades. The 3rd Armored Cavalry Regiment joined the division's attack from 0600 hours on 27 Feb 91.

During the final phase of the war, the 24th Infantry Division(Mech) attacked east toward the Republican Guard forces outside of Basrah. Commencing at 1300 hours on 27 Feb 91, the division attacked with its 1st Brigade on the left, 2nd Brigade in the center, and the 3rd Armored Cavalry Regiment (OPCON to the division) on the right, next to the VII Corps zone. The 197th Infantry Brigade(Mech) was the division reserve and advanced behind the 2nd Brigade. The division halted its advance at 0500 on 28 Feb 91, but pounded the enemy with heavy artillery fire right up to the 0800 cease fire. At this time, the 24th Infantry Division(Mech) was 50 kilometers west of Basrah. Finally, the 1st Brigade fought the only major post-cease fire battle on 2 Mar 91 when it engaged Republican Guard units that attacked the brigade as they attempted to escape the KTO. See text at pages 4 and 5.

---

[30] Was supported by the 212th FA Bde, 36th Eng Gp, and 171st Spt Gp(Corps) throughout the ground war. Was initially also supported by the 265th Eng Gp, until approximately 26 Feb 91. Was later supported by the 18th FA Bde(Abn)(-) starting at 0400 hours on 28 Feb 91. See Footnote 99. See also Footnote 105. The 3rd ACR was OPCON to the 24th Inf Div(M) for portions of the ground war. See Chart 2, Footnote 2. The 5-6 Cav(AH), 12th Avn Bde, was attached to the 24th Inf Div(M) in the evening of 27 Feb 91.

Organization of the 24th Infantry Division(Mech)

<u>Division Headquarters</u>

    Division Assault CP
       2nd Plt, Btry A, 1-5 ADA(Vulc/Stinger)

    Division Tactical CP
       3rd Plt, Btry B, 1-5 ADA(Vulc/Stinger)

    Division Main CP
       3rd Plt, Btry C, 1-5 ADA(Vulc/Stinger)

<u>1st Brigade</u>[31] "Liberty Brigade"

    4-64 Armor [M1A1(Mod)] [Fr. 2 Bde,[32] 24 ID(M)]
    2-7 Inf(M)
    3-7 Inf(M)
    1-41 FA(155 SP) [3 x 8]
    Btry A(-), 1-5 ADA(Vulc/Stinger)

<u>2nd Brigade</u>[33] "Vanguard Brigade"

    1-64 Armor [M1A1(Mod)]
    3-69 Armor(-)[34] [M1A1(Mod)] [Fr. 1 Bde,[35] 24 ID(M)]
    3-15 Inf(M)
    3-41 FA(155 SP) [3 x 8]
    Btry B(-), 1-5 ADA(Vulc/Stinger)

---

[31] See Footnotes 34, 37 & 40. On 2 Mar 91 the 1st Bde, reinforced by the 1-24 Avn(AH) and one air cavalry troop from the 2-4 Cav, fought the only large battle that occurred after the Desert Storm cease fire. See text at pages 4 and 5.

[32] When Operation Desert Shield began the 4-64 Armor was only at 50 percent strength, as its line companies were rotating to the 2nd Inf Div in Korea under the COHORT program. The 4-64 Armor was brought to full strength with tankers from the Armor Center at Fort Knox. Because the 2nd Bde was the first unit of the 24th Inf Div(M) to deploy, the 4-64 Armor was traded to the 1st Bde for the 3-69 Armor to allow the 4-64 to do additional training before deployment.

[33] The first M1 series Main Battle Tanks arrived in Saudi Arabia in late August 1990. These tanks belonged to the 2nd Bde's 1-64 Armor and 3-69 Armor. See Footnote 40.

[34] Was temporarily assigned to the 1st Bde, 24th Inf Div(M) during Operation Desert Shield.

[35] See Footnote 32.

24th INFANTRY DIVISION(MECH) (continued)

197th Inf Bde(Mech) "Sledgehammer Brigade" [Served as the 24th Inf Div(Mech)'s 3rd Bde]

    2-69 Armor [M1A1(Mod)]
    1-18 Inf(M) [M113 APC]
    2-18 Inf(M) [M113 APC]
    Trp D, 4th Cav[36]
    4-41 FA(155 SP)[37] [3 x 8]
    Btry C(-), 1-5 ADA(Vulc/Stinger)
        3rd Squad, 4th Plt, Btry A, 1-5 ADA(Vulc/Stinger)

Aviation Brigade

    TF Air Cav
        Trp C(Air), 2-4 Cav
        Trp D(Air), 2-4 Cav
        Trp E(AVUM), 2-4 Cav
    1-24 Avn(AH)[38] [AH-64]
    4th Plt(Stinger), HQ Btry, 1-5 ADA(Vulc/Stinger)

DIVARTY[39]

    Btry G(TA)(-), 333rd FA
    4th Plt(Stinger)(-), HQ Co, 197th Inf Bde(M)

Division Troops

    TF 2-4 Cav[40]
        HHT, 2-4 Cav
        Trp A, 2-4 Cav
        Trp D, 4th Cav[41] [Fr. 197 Inf Bde(M)]
        Co D, 3-69 Armor

---

[36] Was assigned to the 197th Inf Bde(M) at the beginning of the ground war. Was reassigned to TF 2-4 Cav at 1000 hours on 25 Feb 91; linked up with TF 2-4 Cav shortly before 1400 hours.

[37] May have been detached from the 197th Inf Bde(M) to support the 1st Bde, 24th Inf Div(M) at the end of the war.

[38] See Footnote 31.

[39] See Footnote 42.

[40] Was OPCON to the 2nd Bde until approximately 0630 hours, 25 Feb 91, when it became OPCON to the 1st Bde. At 0230 hours, 26 Feb 91, came under division control. Became OPCON to DISCOM at 1200 hours on 28 Feb 91.

[41] See Footnote 36.

Division Troops (continued)

TF 2-4 Cav (continued)
Btry A(MLRS), 13th FA[42] [1 x 9]
(1) AN/TPQ-37 Radar, Btry G(TA), 333rd FA
1st Squad,[43] 4th Plt(Stinger), HQ Co, 197th Inf Bde(M)
1st & 2nd Squads, 4th Plt, Btry B, 1-5 ADA(Vulc/Stinger)
1-5 ADA(Vulc/Stinger)(-)
LRS Det, 124th MI Bn(CEWI)

DISCOM

2nd Squad, 4th Plt, Btry A, 1-5 ADA(Vulc/Stinger)
2nd & 3rd Squads, 4th Plt, Btry C, 1-5 ADA(Vulc/Stinger)

82nd AIRBORNE DIVISION[44]

The 82nd Airborne Division(-) served a relatively minor role during the ground war. It was tasked with clearing MSR Texas, a main supply route into Iraq, and generally clearing areas seized by other XVIII Airborne Corps units. The 2nd Brigade served in a more significant role, as it was OPCON to the 6th (FR) Light Armored Division and fought in the left-hand portion of the XVIII Airborne Corps zone. The 2nd Brigade initiated its attack at 0400 hours on 24 Feb 91 and was released by the French on 26 Feb 91 at about 1300 hours. At that point the 2nd Brigade became the 82nd Airborne Division's reserve.

Organization of the 82nd Airborne Division

1st Brigade "Devil Brigade"

1-504 Inf(Abn)
2-504 Inf(Abn)
3-504 Inf(Abn)
Co C, 3-73 Armor(Abn) [M551A1(TTS)]
3-319 FA(Abn)(105 T) [3 x 6]
Btry A(-), 3-4 ADA(Abn)(Vulc/Stinger)

---

[42] Left TF 2-4 Cav and served with DIVARTY for most of 26-27 Feb 91.

[43] This may be the 1st Section rather than the 1st Squad.

[44] Was supported by the 46th Spt Gp(Corps). One airborne infantry battalion was OPCON to the Dragon Bde. See Footnote 4.

Order of Battle

2nd Brigade[45] "Falcon Brigade"

    1-325 Inf(Abn)
    2-325 Inf(Abn)
    4-325 Inf(Abn)
    Co B, 3-73 Armor(Abn)[46] [M551A1(TTS)]
    2-319 FA(Abn)(105 T) [3 x 6]
    Btry B(-), 3-4 ADA(Abn)(Vulc/Stinger)

3rd Brigade[47] "Panther Brigade"

    1-505 Inf(Abn)
    2-505 Inf(Abn)
    3-505 Inf(Abn)
    Co A, 3-73 Armor(Abn)[48] [M551A1(TTS)]
    1-319 FA(Abn)(105 T) [3 x 6]
    Btry C(-), 3-4 ADA(Abn)(Vulc/Stinger)

Aviation Brigade[49]

    1-82 Avn(AH) [AH-64]
    Stinger Sec, Team D(Prov), 3-4 ADA(Abn)(Vulc/Stinger)

DIVARTY

    1-39 FA(Abn)(155 T)[50] [3 x 8]

---

[45] Was OPCON to the 6th (FR) Lt Armd Div during the initial stages of the ground war. See Chart 3, Footnote 13. During this period, was supported by the 18th FA Bde(Abn). See Footnote 99; see also Footnote 105. The 2nd Bde, 82nd Abn Div was the first major U.S. Army combat arms unit to deploy to Saudi Arabia during Desert Shield. Its lead elements began departing Fort Bragg on 8 Aug 90 and arrived in Saudi Arabia the following day. The entire brigade had arrived in Saudi Arabia by 14 Aug 90.

[46] Company B was assigned to the 2nd Bde only during the first phase of the ground war, when the 2nd Bde was attached to the 6th (FR) Lt Armd Div. Thereafter, Co B served under TF 3-73 Armor.

[47] Deployed to Riyadh o/a 8-10 Jan 91 to perform an anti-terrorist security mission. Returned to the 82nd's location and control during the period 3-6 Feb 91. One infantry company was left in Riyadh as a quick reaction force. This was initially Co C, 1-505 Inf(Abn), which was later replaced by Co A, 1-505 Inf(Abn).

[48] During the first phase of the ground war, when the 2nd Bde was attached to the 6th (FR) Lt Armd Div, this company served under TF 3-73 Armor. Company A joined the 3rd Bde for clearing operations at Tallil Air Base near the end of the war.

[49] Sometimes referred to as the "82nd Avn Bde." See Footnote 52.

[50] Initially assigned to the 18th FA Bde(Abn). Attached to the 82nd Abn Div at approximately noon, 26 Feb 91.

Division Troops

    TF 3-73 Armor
      3-73 Armor(Abn)(-)[51] [M551A1(TTS)]
      (1) Inf Co from 1st Bde (?)
      Stinger Sec, Team D(Prov), 3-4 ADA(Abn)(Vulc/Stinger)
    1-17 Cav(Air)[52]
      LRS Det, 313th MI Bn(CEWI)
    3-4 ADA(Abn)(Vulc/Stinger)(-)[53]

DISCOM

    Stinger Sec, Team D(Prov), 3-4 ADA(Abn)(Vulc/Stinger)

TF Provider

    Stinger Sec, Team D(Prov), 3-4 ADA(Abn)(Vulc/Stinger)

101st AIRBORNE DIVISION(AIR ASLT)[54]

    The 101st Airborne Division(Air Aslt)'s experience in Desert Storm was unique, as this division conducted three separate brigade-level operations. The first occurred on the morning of 24 Feb 91, when the 1st Brigade(+) air assaulted 95 miles north from Tactical Assembly Area (TAA) Campbell to Forward Operating Base (FOB) Cobra. FOB Cobra was then used as a base to support subsequent operations.

    The second operation occurred on 25-26 Feb 91 when the 3rd Brigade air assaulted 150 miles north from TAA Campbell to Area of Operations (AO) Eagle to cut Highway 8, the major highway connecting Baghdad and Basrah. The first 500 troops arrived at Highway 8 at 1508 hours on 25 Feb 91 and, by 2200 hours, the 3rd Brigade had substantial forces in place on Highway 8.

---

[51] The Sheridans of the 3-73 Armor were the first U.S. tanks to deploy to Saudi Arabia, arriving by air in mid August 1990. Throughout the ground war, TF 3-73 Armor had HHC & Co D, 3-73 Armor. At the beginning of the ground war, TF 3-73 Armor also had Co A, 3-73 Armor, which it later traded for Co B, 3-73 Armor. See Footnotes 46 & 48.

[52] The 1-17 Cav(Air) began the ground war under division control and joined the Avn Bde during the last phase of the war.

[53] The 3-4 ADA formed a provisional fourth firing battery, Team D, in SWA by reorganizing the battalion's assets. See Appendix D at page D-19.

[54] Was supported by the 101st Spt Gp(Corps) and, beginning at approximately noon on 26 Feb 91, by the 12th Avn Bde.

Order of Battle

The 101st Airborne Division(Air Aslt)'s final operation occurred the morning of 27 Feb 91. The 2nd Brigade, which had moved administratively from TAA Campbell to FOB Cobra on 24-25 Feb 91, air assaulted 93 miles to the east, to Objective Tim. This was not a combat assault, however, as Tim was already in allied hands. Objective Tim was converted into FOB Viper within four hours and was then used to support attack helicopter operations north of Basrah. The division's organization was basically the same for the first two operations, but underwent substantial changes for the final operation:

Organization of the 101st Airborne Division(Air Aslt)
For The First Two Operations (24-26 Feb 91)

1st Brigade[55] "Always First Brigade"

> 1-327 Inf(Air Aslt)
> 2-327 Inf(Air Aslt)
> 3-327 Inf(Air Aslt)
> 1-502 Inf(Air Aslt) [Fr. 2 Bde, 101 Abn Div(AAslt)]
> Team, Pathfinder Det
> 2-320 FA(Air Aslt)(105 T) [3 x 6]
> > Btry C, 5-8 FA(155 T) [1 x 8] [Fr. 18 FA Bde(Abn)]
> > 2nd FA Det(TA)
> Btry A(-), 2-44 ADA(Vulc/Stinger)

2nd Brigade[56] "Strike Brigade"

> 3-502 Inf(Air Aslt)
> 1-320 FA(Air Aslt)(105 T) [3 x 6]
> Btry B(-), 2-44 ADA(Vulc/Stinger)

3rd Brigade "Rakkasans"

> 1-187 Inf(Air Aslt)
> 2-187 Inf(Air Aslt)
> 3-187 Inf(Air Aslt)
> 3-320 FA(Air Aslt)(105 T) [3 x 6]
> Btry C(-), 2-44 ADA(Vulc/Stinger)

---

[55] The 1st Bde's air assault into FOB Cobra was supported by the 2-17 Cav(Air), 1-101 Avn(AH), and 3-101 Avn(AH).

[56] See Footnote 5.

Aviation Brigade[57]

    2-17 Cav(Air)
    1-101 Avn(AH)[58] [AH-64]
       Target Acquisition Plt, Trp A, 1-9 Cav(Air)[59] [OH-58D] [Fr. 9 ID(Mtzd)]
    3-101 Avn(AH) [AH-1]
    2-229 Avn(AH) [AH-64] [Fr. 18 Avn Bde(Abn)]
    Pathfinder Det(-)[60]

DIVARTY

    5-8 FA(155 T)(-)[61] [2 x 8] [Fr. 18 FA Bde(Abn)]
    2nd FA Det(TA)

Division Troops

    LRS Det,[62] 311th MI Bn(CEWI)
    Team, Pathfinder Det
    2-44 ADA(Vulc/Stinger)(-)[63]

DISCOM

    Team, Pathfinder Det

---

[57] Sometimes referred to as the "101st Avn Bde."

[58] The opening shots of Desert Storm were fired at approximately 0237 hours on 17 Jan 91, when TF Normandy, consisting of elements of the 1-101 Avn(AH), destroyed a radar facility in western Iraq. This allowed hundreds of coalition fixed-wing aircraft to enter Iraqi airspace undetected. Task Force Normandy consisted of nine AH-64 Apache Attack Helicopters and one UH-60 Black Hawk, organized into a "Red Team" and a "White Team" (each with four Apaches), and a reserve (the Black Hawk and the ninth Apache). The eight Apaches in the Red and White Teams engaged the target; the ninth Apache and the Black Hawk remained inside Saudi airspace.

[59] Other than the fact that it flew the OH-58D "Kiowa" helicopter, very little is known about this unit. Some sources refer to it as the "TARP," or "Target Acquisition and Reconnaissance Plt." Some sources claim it was part of Trp E, 1-9 Cav, rather than Trp A. Other sources suggest it was assigned directly to the 1-9 Cav and was not part of either Trp A or Trp E.

[60] One source reports that the Pathfinder Det served under the 2-17 Cav(Air).

[61] Initially assigned to the 18th FA Bde(Abn). Attached to the 101st Abn Div(AAslt) at approximately noon, 26 Feb 91.

[62] Some sources report that the 101st's LRS detachment was the size of a company and that it served under the 2-17 Cav(Air).

[63] Included in this element were the 3rd plts of Btrys A-C.

Order of Battle

Organization of the 101st Airborne Division(Air Aslt)
For The Final Operation (27 Feb 91)

1st Brigade "Always First Brigade"

    1-327 Inf(Air Aslt)
    2-327 Inf(Air Aslt)
    2-502 Inf(Air Aslt)[64] [Fr. 2 Bde, 101 Abn Div(AAslt)]
    Team, Pathfinder Det
    2-320 FA(Air Aslt)(105 T) [3 x 6]
    Btry A(-), 2-44 ADA(Vulc/Stinger)

2nd Brigade[65] "Strike Brigade"

    3-327 Inf(Air Aslt) [Fr. 1 Bde, 101 Abn Div(AAslt)]
    1-502 Inf(Air Aslt)
    3-502 Inf(Air Aslt)
    1-320 FA(Air Aslt)(105 T) [3 x 6]
        Btry C, 5-8 FA(155 T) [1 x 8] [Fr. 18 FA Bde(Abn)]
    Btry B(-), 2-44 ADA(Vulc/Stinger)

3rd Brigade "Rakkasans"

    1-187 Inf(Air Aslt)
    2-187 Inf(Air Aslt)
    3-187 Inf(Air Aslt)
    3-320 FA(Air Aslt)(105 T) [3 x 6]
    Btry C(-), 2-44 ADA(Vulc/Stinger)

Aviation Brigade[66]

    2-17 Cav(Air)
    1-101 Avn(AH) [AH-64]
        Target Acquisition Plt, Trp A, 1-9 Cav(Air)[67] [OH-58D] [Fr. 9 ID(Mtzd)]
    3-101 Avn(AH) [AH-1]
    2-229 Avn(AH) [AH-64] [Fr. 18 Avn Bde(Abn)]
    Pathfinder Det(-)

---

[64] See Footnote 5.

[65] See Footnote 5.

[66] Sometimes referred to as the "101st Avn Bde."

[67] See Footnote 59.

DIVARTY

5-8 FA(155 T)(-)[68] [2 x 8] [Fr. 18 FA Bde(Abn)]
2nd FA Det(TA)

Division Troops

LRS Det,[69] 311th MI Bn(CEWI)
Team, Pathfinder Det
2-44 ADA(Vulc/Stinger)(-)

DISCOM

Team, Pathfinder Det

2nd ARMORED CAVALRY REGIMENT[70]

The 2nd Armored Cavalry Regiment advanced northeast at 1430 hours on 24 Feb 91 as the VII Corps covering force. The regiment initially operated in the left-hand portion of the VII Corps zone, in front of the 1st and 3rd Armored Divisions. On 25 Feb 91, the 2nd Armored Cavalry Regiment began to slide to the right within the VII Corps zone, so that by 26 Feb 91 the regiment was no longer in front of the 1st and 3rd Armored Divisions, and now was on-line with those divisions and driving east toward the Republican Guard in what would later become the 1st Infantry Division(Mech) zone.

The 2nd Armored Cavalry Regiment encountered elements of the Republican Guard early on 26 Feb 91. The regiment defeated major elements of the RGFC Tawakalna Division that afternoon, at the Battle of 73 Easting. Commencing at approximately 2200 hours on 26 Feb 91, the 2nd Armored Cavalry Regiment began passing the 1st Infantry Division(Mech) through its zone. This process was completed by approximately 0210 hours on 27 Feb 91, at which point the 2nd Armored Cavalry Regiment went into corps reserve, continuing to advance behind the 1st Infantry Division(Mech) until the cease fire went into effect.

---

[68] See Footnote 61.

[69] See Footnote 62.

[70] Was supported by the 210th FA Bde until approximately 0210 hours on 27 Feb 91. See Footnote 96.

Organization of the 2nd Armored Cavalry Regiment

1/2 ACR [M2A2 & M1A1HA]
2/2 ACR [M2A2 & M1A1HA]
3/2 ACR [M2A2 & M1A1HA]
4/2 ACR(Avn)
2-1 Avn(AH)[71] [AH-64] [Fr. 1 AD]
Stinger Plt, Regt HQ Trp
ORF Plt[72]

3rd ARMORED CAVALRY REGIMENT[73]

The 3rd Armored Cavalry Regiment crossed the line of departure at 1500 hours on 24 Feb 91 and began advancing north as the right flank guard of the XVIII Airborne Corps, with the VII Corps to its right and the 24th Infantry Division (Mech) to its left. The regiment was placed under the temporary operational control of the 24th Infantry Division(Mech) at noon on 26 Feb 91 and attacked to the east, seizing an airfield at Umm Hajul, Iraq.[74]

The 3rd Armored Cavalry Regiment again came under the operational control of the 24th Infantry Division(Mech) at 0600 hours on 27 Feb 91 and began attacking toward the east. The regiment would remain under the 24th's control for the remainder of the war. By 1300 on 27 Feb 91, the 3rd Armored Cavalry Regiment was on line with the 24th Infantry Division(Mech)(-) and attacking east into the Republican Guard, with the 2nd Brigade, 24th Infantry Division(Mech) on the regiment's left and the VII Corps zone on its right. Although it performed several important missions during Desert Storm, the 3rd Armored Cavalry Regiment encountered relatively few Iraqi units and did not see much combat.

---

[71] Was OPCON to the 2nd ACR at the beginning of the ground war. Rejoined the 1st Armd Div mid-day on 27 Feb 91.

[72] This was a tank platoon that was apparently formed from war reserve equipment stocks and 2nd ACR personnel o/a 16 Feb 91. It was attached to the 2nd ACR's Spt Sqdn. It was apparently not a WSRO unit. It saw combat briefly on 26 Feb 91 when it helped repulse an Iraqi attack on the 2nd ACR's Spt Sqdn.

[73] See Chart 2, Footnote 2. The first M1A1 series Main Battle Tanks to arrive in the KTO belonged to the 3rd ACR and arrived in September 1990. On 22 Jan 91, the 3rd ACR became the first Third Army unit to take Iraqi soldiers as prisoners.

[74] Unfortunately, intelligence reports were erroneous and this airfield was not defended by Iraqi troops. During this attack, friendly fire from 3/3 ACR killed a soldier from the VII Corps. This became one of the most acrimonious and controversial friendly fire accidents of the war.

Organization of the 3rd Armored Cavalry Regiment

1/3 ACR [M3A2 & M1A1HA]
2/3 ACR [M3A2 & M1A1HA]
3/3 ACR [M3A2 & M1A1HA]
4/3 ACR(Avn)
3-18 FA(155 SP) [3 x 6(?)] [Fr. 212 FA Bde]
   Det,[75] Btry C(TA), 25th FA [Fr. 214 FA Bde]
Avenger Plt(Avenger/Stinger), Regt HQ Trp
Btry B, 5-62 ADA(Vulc/Stinger) [Fr. 11 ADA Bde]
Btry B, 6-52 ADA(Hawk) [Fr. 69 ADA Bde, 32 AADCOM]

ARCENT AVIATION BRIGADE[76]

5-229 Avn(AH)(-)[77] [AH-64] [Fr. Apache Tng Bde][78]
(4) Stinger Teams, 3-5 ADA [Fr. 3 AD]

11th AVIATION BRIGADE[79]

2-6 Cav(AH)[80] [AH-64]
4-229 Avn(AH) [AH-64] [Fr. 12 Avn Bde]
Co D(?) (Scout), 4-159 Avn [OH-58D]

---

[75] Consisted of one AN/TPQ-36 Radar and one AN/TPQ-37 Radar.

[76] See Chart 2, Footnote 3.

[77] The status of this unit is unclear. The 5-229 Avn was activated at Fort Hood on 16 Sep 90 and deployed to the KTO in January or February of 1991. Although it is not listed in the Army's General Order that supposedly covers all the units that served in the Gulf War, this battalion clearly did participate. It participated in the WSRO/SCT program by training the aviation crews that deployed as part of that program. At the same time, it appears that the 5-229 Avn existed in-theater as a fully-equipped attack helicopter unit. Two sources describe the 5-229 Avn as ARCENT's reserve attack helicopter battalion. Company A, however, was attached to the 2-227 Avn(AH), 3rd Armd Div, throughout the ground war.

[78] The Apache Tng Bde (now called the Combat Avn Tng Bde) was stationed at Fort Hood and was responsible for training new Apache attack helicopter battalions, which then moved to their new duty stations.

[79] Left behind in Germany was the 6-6 Cav(AH), which had only recently transitioned to the AH-64 Apache.

[80] Was OPCON to the Avn Bde, 3rd Armd Div from 1000 hours, 27 Feb 91, until the end of the war.

12th AVIATION BRIGADE

(Spt'd 6 (FR) Lt AD; 101 Abn Div(AAslt))[81]

5-6 Cav(AH)[82] [AH-64]
3-227 Avn(AH) [AH-64] [Fr. 3 AD]
Co D(Scout), 5-158 Avn [OH-58D]
4th Plt(Stinger),[83] Btry D, 3-5 ADA [Fr. 3 AD]

18th AVIATION BRIGADE(ABN)

4-17 Cav(Air)(-)[84] [Armed OH-58D][85]

VII CORPS ARTILLERY

42nd FA Bde[86] (Spt'd 1 ID(M); 3 AD)[87]

3-20 FA(155 SP) [3 x 8] [Fr. 41 FA Bde]
1-27 FA(MLRS) [3 x 9] [Fr. 41 FA Bde]
2-29 FA(155 SP) [3 x 8] [Fr. 8 ID(M)]

---

[81] The 12th Avn Bde ceased supporting the French and began supporting the 101st Abn Div(AAslt) around noon on 26 Feb 91. When the 12th Avn Bde deployed during the early days of Desert Shield, it left its 4-229 Avn(AH) behind, for reasons that are unclear. The 4-229 Avn later deployed with the 11th Avn Bde.

[82] Was attached to the 24th Inf Div(M) in the evening of 27 Feb 91.

[83] Some sources indicate this was a platoon(-).

[84] This squadron was formed in the Gulf on 15 Jan 91 from TF 118, which had patrolled the Persian Gulf and helped protect Kuwaiti tankers during the late 1980s, pursuant to "Operation Prime Chance." Task Force 118 operated Army Armed OH-58D Helicopters off of Navy ships. The 4-17 Cav(Air) consisted of HHT, Trps A & B, and a maintenance troop. The squadron continued to fly in support of the Navy during Desert Storm, operating off a number of Navy warships, primarily FFG 7 *Perry*-class guided missile frigates. Included among these were the USS *Jarrett* (FFG 33), the USS *Curts* (FFG 38), the USS *Nicholas* (FFG 47), and the USS *O'Brien* (DD 975), a DD 963 *Spruance*-class destroyer. Troop A left the squadron and began supporting the 3rd SF Gp(Abn) the second week of February 1991. .

[85] These aircraft were produced in the late 1980s under a then-secret program called "Prime Chance." They were armed with a variety of weapons, including Hellfire and Stinger missiles, Hydra 70 unguided rockets, and a .50 cal machine gun. They were used by TF 118; see Footnote 84. Since the Gulf War, the Army has fielded an improved version of the Prime Chance aircraft which is called the OH-58D(I) "Kiowa Warrior." The "(I)" stands for "Improved."

[86] All of the FA battalions normally assigned to the 42nd were left behind when the brigade deployed. Remaining in Germany were: 5-3 FA(203 SP), 4-7 FA(203 SP), 2-20 FA(203 SP), 2-32 FA(MLRS), and 3-32 FA(Lance).

[87] Fired in support of the 1st Inf Div(M)'s breach of the Iraqi front lines on 24 Feb 91. See Footnotes 25 & 89. The 42nd was released by the 1st Inf Div(M) at 1300 hours on 25 Feb 91 and had linked-up with the 3rd Armd Div by nightfall on 25 Feb 91.

VII CORPS ARTILLERY (continued)

75th FA Bde (Spt'd 1 ID(M); 1 AD)[88]

    1-17 FA(155 SP) [3 x 6]
    5-18 FA(203 SP)[89] [3 x 8]
    1-158 FA(MLRS)(-)[90] [2 x 9] [OK ARNG] [Fr. 45 FA Bde]
    Btry A,[91] 6-27 FA(MLRS/ATACMS) [1 x 9]
    Btry C(TA)(-),[92] 26th FA [Fr. 2 AD(-)]

142nd FA Bde [AR/OK ARNG] (Spt'd 1 ID(M); 1 (UK) AD)[93]

    1-142 FA(203 SP) [3 x 4] [AR ARNG]
    2-142 FA(203 SP) [3 x 4] [AR ARNG]
    Btry A, 1-158 FA(MLRS)[94] [1 x 9] [OK ARNG] [Fr. 45 FA Bde]

---

[88] Fired in support of the 1st Inf Div(M)'s breach of the Iraqi front lines on 24 Feb 91. The 75th was released by the 1st Inf Div(M) at 1300 hours on 25 Feb 91. Sources disagree concerning when the brigade linked-up with the 1st Armd Div. One source indicates this occurred by noon on 26 Feb 91, while according to another source, this did not occur until 1600 hours on 26 Feb 91.

[89] This battalion was under the control of the 42nd FA Bde during the 1st Inf Div(M)'s breach of the Iraqi front lines on 24 Feb 91.

[90] The entire battalion fired in support of the 1st Inf Div(M)'s breach of the Iraqi front lines on 24 Feb 91 as an element of the 75th FA Bde. Battery A then left the battalion early on 25 Feb 91 to join the 142nd FA Bde. The 1-158 FA(-) left the 75th FA Bde apparently shortly before noon on 26 Feb 91 and moved to join the 210th FA Bde. The link-up with the 210th was apparently not completed, however, and at approximately 0630 hours on 27 Feb 91 the 1-158 FA(-) began moving to link up with the 1st Cav Div(-). The 1-158 FA(-) completed this link-up several hours later and ended the war attached to the 1st Cav Div(-).

[91] The first use of ATACMS in combat, and the first round fired in combat by the VII Corps since World War II, occurred o/a 18 Jan 91 when Btry A engaged an SA-2 ADA missile site. This was also the first shot fired in Desert Storm by a U.S. Army field artillery unit.

[92] Consisted of two AN/TPQ-36 Radars and two AN/TPQ-37 Radars. One AN/TPQ-36 Radar from Btry C was stationed in Germany with the 2nd Armd Div(Fwd) prior to Desert Storm. See Footnote 29.

[93] Fired in support of the 1st Inf Div(M)'s breach of the Iraqi front lines on 24 Feb 91. The 142nd was released by the 1st Inf Div(M) at approximately 0200 hours on 26 Feb 91 and thereafter supported the 1st (UK) Armd Div.

[94] See Footnote 90.

VII CORPS ARTILLERY (continued)

210th FA Bde[95] (Spt'd 2 ACR; 1 ID(M))[96]

    3-17 FA(155 SP)[97] [3 x 8]
    Btry C, 4-27 FA(MLRS) [1 x 9] [Fr. 72 FA Bde]
    6-41 FA(155 SP)[98] [3 x 8] [Fr. 3 ID(M)]
    Btry E(TA), 333rd FA [Fr. 9 ID(Mtzd)]

XVIII AIRBORNE CORPS ARTILLERY

5-62 ADA(Vulc/Stinger)(-) [Fr. 11 ADA Bde]

18th FA Bde(Abn) (Spt'd 6 (FR) Lt AD & 2 Bde, 82 Abn Div; 24 ID(M))[99]

    3-8 FA(155 T) [3 x 8]
    5-8 FA(155 T)(-)[100] [2 x 8]
    6-27 FA(MLRS/ATACMS)(-)[101] [2 x 9] [Fr. 75 FA Bde]
    1-39 FA(Abn)(155 T)[102] [3 x 8]
    1-201 FA(155 SP) [3 x 6] [WV ARNG][103] [Fr. 138 FA Bde]
    Btry A, 5-62 ADA(Vulc/Stinger)[104] [Fr. 11 ADA Bde]
    1st FA Det(TA) [Fr. XVIII Abn Corps Arty]

---

[95] See Footnote 90. Several of the FA battalions normally assigned to the 210th were left behind when the brigade deployed. Remaining in Germany were: 3-5 FA(203 SP), 2-12 FA(Lance), and 5-17 FA(203 SP).

[96] Was released by the 2nd ACR to support the 1st Inf Div(M) at approximately 0210 hours on 27 Feb 91, when the 2nd ACR became VII Corps reserve.

[97] Was DS to the 3/2 ACR while the 210th FA Bde supported the 2nd ACR.

[98] Was DS to the 2/2 ACR while the 210th FA Bde supported the 2nd ACR.

[99] Initially supported the 6th (FR) Lt Armd Div and the 2nd Bde, 82nd Abn Div in the western portion of the XVIII Abn Corps zone. Completed this mission at approximately noon on 26 Feb 91, when the 18th FA Bde(Abn)(-) (see Footnotes 100 & 102) began moving to join the 24th Inf Div(M) in the eastern portion of the corps zone. The 18th FA Bde(Abn)(-) began supporting the 24th at 0400 hours on 28 Feb 91.

[100] Was initially assigned to the 18th FA Bde(Abn). Was later attached to the 101st Abn Div(AAslt) at approximately noon on 26 Feb 91.

[101] Technically, this battalion was assigned directly to XVIII Abn Corps Arty during the initial stage of the ground war and was not attached to the 18th FA Bde(Abn) until approximately noon on 26 Feb 91. However, the 6-27 FA(-) was controlled by the 18th FA Bde(Abn) throughout the ground war.

[102] Was initially assigned to the 18th FA Bde(Abn). Was later attached to the 82nd Abn Div at approximately noon on 26 Feb 91.

[103] Was supposed to serve with the 196th FA Bde, but when the 196th had not arrived in-theater by the beginning of the ground war, the 1-201 FA was assigned to the 18th FA Bde(Abn). The 1-201 FA was later reassigned to the 196th FA Bde after the cease fire, effective 1 Mar 91.

[104] This battery also reportedly supported the 6th (FR) Lt Armd Div.

XVIII AIRBORNE CORPS ARTILLERY (continued)

196th FA Bde[105] [TN/KY ARNG]

    1-181 FA(203 SP) [3 x 4] [TN ARNG]
    1-623 FA(203 SP) [3 x 4] [KY ARNG] [Fr. 138 FA Bde]

212th FA Bde (Spt'd 24 ID(M))

    2-17 FA(155 SP)[106] [3 x 6]
    2-18 FA(203 SP) [3 x 8]
    3-27 FA(MLRS) [3 x 9] [Fr. XVIII Abn Corps Arty]
    Btry C(TA)(-),[107] 25th FA [Fr. 214 FA Bde]
    Btry C, 5-62 ADA(Vulc/Stinger) [Fr. 11 ADA Bde]

11th AIR DEFENSE ARTILLERY BRIGADE[108]

    Btry D, 1-7 ADA(Patriot)[109] [Fr. 94 ADA Bde, 32 AADCOM]
    2-7 ADA(Patriot)[110]
    2-43 ADA(Patriot)[111] [Fr. 10 ADA Bde, 32 AADCOM]
    3-43 ADA(Patriot)(-)[112]
    2-52 ADA(Hawk)[113]

---

[105] The 196th FA Bde was supposed to support the 6th (FR) Lt Armd Div and the 2nd Bde, 82nd Abn Div in the western portion of the XVIII Abn Corps zone. The 196th, however, arrived in the theater late and the battle in the western part of the corps zone was over before it arrived. The 196th was, therefore, reassigned to support the 24th Inf Div(M) in the eastern portion of the corps zone. The 196th was en route to join the 24th when the cease fire was declared. Thus, the 196th FA Bde never got into the fight. See Footnote 103. The 196th deployed without one of its organic units, the 1-115 FA(155 T) [TN ARNG].

[106] Was temporarily assigned to the 75th FA Bde during Operation Desert Shield.

[107] Consisted of two AN/TPQ-36 Radars and one AN/TPQ-37 Radar.

[108] One of the ADA battalions normally assigned to the 11th was left behind when the brigade deployed. Remaining at Fort Stewart was the 1-2 ADA(Chap).

[109] Located at Tabuk, Saudi Arabia. Part of HHB, 1-7 ADA, was attached to Btry D.

[110] Consisted of HHB and Btrys A-F, located as follows: HHB and Btrys A & B, Dhahran; Btry C, Bahrain; Btry D, Dammam; Btry E, King Fahd International Airport; and Btry F, Jubayl. On 18 Jan 91, Btry A, 2-7 ADA became the first air defense artillery unit in history to engage a hostile ballistic missile. Battery B, 2-7 ADA was the first Patriot unit to deploy to SWA. It arrived in Saudi Arabia on 13 Aug 90 with the Army's only three Patriot PAC-2 missiles, the version that was able to engage theater ballistic missiles. Battery B also brought two Avengers from the 6th ADA Bde's 2nd Bn, 6th ADA, a training unit at Fort Bliss.

[111] Consisted of HHB and Btrys A-D. The entire battalion was located at King Khalid Military City. Battery E(Prov) was formed in the Gulf with three Patriot launchers and was active until 26 Jan 91, when it was disbanded.

[112] Consisted of HHB and Btrys C, D & F. The 3-43 ADA(-) was located at Riyadh.

207th MILITARY INTELLIGENCE BRIGADE

Co F(LRS), 51st Inf[114]

525th MILITARY INTELLIGENCE BRIGADE

Co D(LRS), 522nd MI Bn(CEWI)[115] [Fr. 2 AD(-)]

Several combat arms units deployed to Saudi Arabia reconfigured to provide logistical support:

3-2 ADA(Chap)[116] [Fr. 35 ADA Bde(-)]

3rd Bde(-), 1st Inf Div(Mech)

The 1st Inf Div(Mech)(Fwd) was in the process of being inactivated in the fall of 1990. Elements of this unit deployed to Saudi Arabia (without equipment) to support VII Corps' arrival in the KTO. This mission was performed by the 1st Inf Div(Mech)(Fwd) Port Support Activity (PSA), a brigade-level unit that consisted of two identical 725-man battalion task forces that included tankers, infantrymen, artillerymen, engineers, medics, mechanics, and communications specialists from all units of the 1st Inf Div(Mech)(Fwd). Headquarters, 3rd Bde, 1st Inf Div(Mech) was the headquarters that supervised this effort. This mission, known as "Operation Desert Duty," was completed on 17-18 Feb 91, and the brigade began departing the KTO on 19 Feb 91. Assigned to the 1st Inf Div(Mech)(Fwd) PSA were:

3-34 Armor[117]
4-16 Inf(M)[118]
1st Inf Div(Mech)(Fwd) Scout Plt[119]

---

[113] Consisted of HHB and Btrys A-C. At the beginning of the air war, the entire battalion defended King Khalid Military City. At the beginning of the ground war, Btry B moved to Log Base Echo, and Btry C moved to the Hafir Al Batin. Prior to Desert Shield, the 2-52 ADA had been stationed at Fort Bragg and attached to the Dragon Bde, although it was assigned to the 11th ADA Bde.

[114] During the war Co F was assigned to the 511th MI Bn.

[115] During the war Co D was assigned to the 519th MI Bn(AE).

[116] This battalion, which left its ADA weapons in CONUS, was augmented by the 73rd Eng Co and IRR fillers, and converted to a truck battalion. It served in the 7th Trans Gp. Battery A formed a provisional unit that provided security to the Port of Dammam. It consisted of one M1A1 Abrams tank and seven Bradley Fighting Vehicles.

[117] Known as Port Assistance Task Force North. Operated an intermediate staging area at Jubayl.

[118] Known as Port Assistance Task Force South. Provided security and facilities support at Dammam.

Notes:

➢ "[M1A1(Mod)]" refers to M1A1 Main Battle Tanks that were modified in-theater to M1A1HA standard. See Chart 13, page 13-2.

➢ All U.S. Army mechanized infantry units used the M2 "Bradley" series Infantry Fighting Vehicle, unless noted otherwise. See Chart 13, pages 13-5 and 13-6, for information on which versions of the Bradley were used by the various units.

➢ The entries for field artillery firing units show the number of batteries and the number of howitzers or MLRS launchers authorized per battery in brackets, e.g., the 2nd Bn(155 SP), 1st FA, 1st Armored Division, had three firing batteries each authorized eight howitzers [3 x 8]. Some units, however, acquired extra weapons, typically from the operational readiness float stocks that were intended to replace vehicles and weapons that were not operationally ready, or "down," for various reasons. For example, at least three MLRS batteries acquired one extra launcher and operated ten launchers during Desert Storm. These were Btry A, 21st FA, 1st Cav Div(-); Btry A, 40th FA, 3rd Armd Div; and Btry A, 92nd FA, which was attached to the 2nd Marine Div.

➢ When a listed unit supported several other units at different times, the supported units are separated by a semicolon and listed in chronological order. Thus, the 75th FA Bde initially supported the 1st Inf Div(M) and then later supported the 1st Armd Div. When a listed unit supported several other units simultaneously, the supported units are separated by an ampersand (&). Thus, the 18th FA Bde(Abn) simultaneously supported the 6th (FR) Lt Armd Div and the 2nd Bde, 82nd Abn Div, during the early stages of the ground war.

➢ Only two combat arms battalions had elements that served in both U.S. Army corps. The 6th Bn(MLRS/ ATACMS)(-), 27th FA served with the XVIII Abn Corps' 18th FA Bde(Abn), while Btry A was assigned to the 75th FA Bde in VII Corps. Batteries A & C, 6th Bn(Hawk), 52nd ADA served with the VII Corps in TF 8-43 ADA, while Btry B was assigned to the XVIII Abn Corps' 3rd Armd Cav Regt.

➢ Which was the most powerful brigade in the Gulf? This honor goes to the 2nd Bde, 1st Armd Div, which had four maneuver battalions (three tank and one mechanized infantry) for the entire ground war. Most heavy maneuver brigades had only three maneuver battalions. The only other brigades that had four maneuver battalions — the 1st and 3rd Bdes, 3rd Armd Div — had four such battalions for only a portion of the ground war. See Footnote 14.

➢ Most U.S. Army maneuver brigades have official or semi-official nicknames that are used in addition, or occasionally in lieu of, their formal designation. These nicknames are indicated in quotation marks after the brigade's formal designation. Only the 2nd Bde, 3rd Armd Div did not use a nickname during Desert Storm.

---

[119] Was the security force for the U.S. Army staging camp outside Jubayl. The platoon consisted of 26 soldiers. The vehicle(s) used by the platoon are unknown.

Chart 4A

Task Organization of U.S. Army
Heavy Maneuver Battalions

This chart shows the task organization of U.S. Army tank and mechanized infantry battalions. In heavy brigades, tank and mechanized infantry battalions typically swap one or two companies so that each battalion is a combined arms unit, which is then known as a "battalion task force." There are no set rules concerning how this is done; the specifics of each situation control how many companies are swapped, which companies are swapped, and with whom they are swapped.[1] Some battalions do not participate in this process, however, and are then known as "pure" battalions.[2] All of this is up to the brigade commander.

In some battalion task forces, the tank and mechanized infantry companies remain as pure companies, but in other cases, tank and mechanized infantry companies swap platoons to form combined arms "company teams." This chart presents the task organization of all U.S. Army heavy maneuver battalions. I present this information here, as opposed to including it on Charts 4 (U.S. Army units assigned to ARCENT) and 5 (U.S. Army units assigned to MARCENT) to avoid "information overload" on those charts. Where known, I also indicate whether companies fought as pure companies or as company teams.

---

[1] Some unusual examples saw combat in Desert Storm. For example, TF 3-69 Armor, 2nd Bde, 24th Inf Div(M), had three tank companies and one antiarmor company equipped with the M901A1 ITV.

[2] Battalion task forces were referred to as, for example, "TF 2-34 Armor," while pure battalions used their standard designation, for example, "1-34 Armor." See entries for 1st Bde, 1st Inf Div(M).

1st ARMORED DIVISION

3rd Bde, 3rd Inf Div(Mech) "Phantom Brigade" [Served as the 1st Armd Div's 1st Bde]

  TF 4-66 Armor
    Co B, 4-66 Armor [Team]
    Co C, 4-66 Armor
    Co D, 4-66 Armor
    Co A, 1-7 Inf(M)
  TF 1-7 Inf(M)
    Co B, 1-7 Inf(M)
    Co C, 1-7 Inf(M)
    Co D, 1-7 Inf(M)
    Co A, 4-66 Armor [Team]
  TF 4-7 Inf(M)
    Co A, 4-7 Inf(M)
    Co B, 4-7 Inf(M)
    Co C, 4-7 Inf(M)
    Co A, 1-35 Armor [Fr. 2 Bde, 1 AD]

2nd Brigade "Iron Brigade"

  TF 1-35 Armor
    Co B, 1-35 Armor
    Co C, 1-35 Armor
    Co D, 1-35 Armor
    Co D, 4-7 Inf(M) [Fr. 3 Bde, 3 ID(M)]
  TF 2-70 Armor
    Co A, 2-70 Armor
    Co B, 2-70 Armor
    Co D, 2-70 Armor
    Co B, 6-6 Inf(M)
  TF 4-70 Armor
    Co A, 4-70 Armor [Team]
    Co C, 4-70 Armor
    Co D, 4-70 Armor
    Co D, 6-6 Inf(M)

2nd Brigade (continued)

    TF 6-6 Inf(M)
        Co A, 6-6 Inf(M) [Team]
        Co C, 6-6 Inf(M) [Team]
        Co C, 2-70 Armor
        Co B, 4-70 Armor [Team]

3rd Brigade "Bulldog Brigade"

    TF 3-35 Armor
        Co A, 3-35 Armor
        Co B, 3-35 Armor
        Co C, 3-35 Armor
        Co B, 7-6 Inf(M)
    TF 1-37 Armor
        Co B, 1-37 Armor [Pure]
        Co C, 1-37 Armor [Pure]
        Co D, 1-37 Armor [Pure]
        Co C, 7-6 Inf(M) [Pure]
    TF 7-6 Inf(M)
        Co A, 7-6 Inf(M)
        Co D, 7-6 Inf(M)
        Co D, 3-35 Armor
        Co A, 1-37 Armor

3rd ARMORED DIVISION

1st Brigade "Ready First Combat Team" or "RFCT"

    TF 4-32 Armor
        Co A, 4-32 Armor [Pure]
        Co B, 4-32 Armor [Team]
        Co C, 4-32 Armor [Pure]
        Co D, 5-5 Cav(M) [Team]
    TF 4-34 Armor
        Co A, 4-34 Armor
        Co B, 4-34 Armor
        Co D, 4-34 Armor
        Co D, 3-5 Cav(M)

3rd ARMORED DIVISION (continued)

<u>1st Brigade</u> (continued)

    TF 3-5 Cav(M)
        Co A, 3-5 Cav(M) [Team]
        Co B, 3-5 Cav(M) [Pure ?]
        Co C, 3-5 Cav(M) [Team]
        Co C, 4-34 Armor [Team]
    TF 5-5 Cav(M)[3]
        Co A, 5-5 Cav(M) [Pure]
        Co B, 5-5 Cav(M) [Team]
        Co C, 5-5 Cav(M) [Pure]
        Co D, 4-32 Armor [Team]

<u>2nd Brigade</u> (No Brigade Nickname)

    3-8 Cav(A) [Pure]
        Co A, 3-8 Cav(A)
        Co B, 3-8 Cav(A)
        Co C, 3-8 Cav(A)
        Co D, 3-8 Cav(A)
    TF 4-8 Cav(A)
        Co B, 4-8 Cav(A)
        Co C, 4-8 Cav(A)
        Co D, 4-8 Cav(A)
        Co D, 4-18 Inf(M)
    TF 4-18 Inf(M)[4]
        Co A, 4-18 Inf(M) [Pure]
        Co B, 4-18 Inf(M) [Team]
        Co C, 4-18 Inf(M) [Pure]
        Co A, 4-8 Cav(A) [Team]

---

[3] During the ground war, the 5-5 Cav(M) was assigned to, in order: 1st Bde; HQ, 3rd Armd Div; 1st Bde; and 3rd Bde. See Chart 4, Footnote 14.

[4] At 0300 hours on 27 Feb 91, Co D, 3-8 Cav(A) was transferred from 3-8 Cav(A) to TF 4-18 Inf(M).

3rd Brigade "Thundering Third Brigade"

TF 2-67 Armor
    Co A, 2-67 Armor
    Co C, 2-67 Armor
    Co D, 2-67 Armor
    Co D, 5-18 Inf(M)
TF 4-67 Armor
    Co B, 4-67 Armor [Team]
    Co C, 4-67 Armor [Pure]
    Co D, 4-67 Armor [Pure]
    Co A, 5-18 Inf(M) [Team]
TF 5-18 Inf(M)
    Co B, 5-18 Inf(M)
    Co C, 5-18 Inf(M)
    Co B, 2-67 Armor
    Co A, 4-67 Armor

1st CAVALRY DIVISION(-)

1st Brigade "Ironhorse Brigade"

2-8 Cav(A) [Pure ?]
    Co A, 2-8 Cav(A) (?)
    Co B, 2-8 Cav(A) (?)
    Co C, 2-8 Cav(A) (?)
    Co D, 2-8 Cav(A) (?)
TF 3-32 Armor
    Co A, 3-32 Armor
    Co C, 3-32 Armor
    Co D, 3-32 Armor
    Co B, 2-5 Cav(M)
TF 2-5 Cav(M)
    Co A, 2-5 Cav(M)
    Co C, 2-5 Cav(M)
    Co D, 2-5 Cav(M)
    Co E(Antiarmor), 2-5 Cav(M)
    Co B, 3-32 Armor (?)

1st CAVALRY DIVISION(-) (continued)

2nd Brigade[5] "Blackjack Brigade"

    1-8 Cav(A) [Permanently Task Organized][6]
        Co A, 1-8 Cav(A) [Mech Inf]
        Co B, 1-8 Cav(A) [Tank]
        Co C, 1-8 Cav(A) [Tank]
        Co D, 1-8 Cav(A) [Tank]
    1-32 Armor [Permanently Task Organized][7]
        Co A, 1-32 Armor [Tank]
        Co B, 1-32 Armor [Tank]
        Co C, 1-32 Armor [Mech Inf]
        Co D, 1-32 Armor [Tank]
    1-5 Cav(M) [Permanently Task Organized][8]
        Co A, 1-5 Cav(M) [Mech Inf]
        Co B, 1-5 Cav(M) [Tank]
        Co C, 1-5 Cav(M) [Mech Inf]
        Co D, 1-5 Cav(M) [Tank]
        Co E(Antiarmor), 1-5 Cav(M) [Antiarmor]

1st INFANTRY DIVISION(MECH)

1st Brigade "Devil Brigade"

    1-34 Armor [Pure]
        Co A, 1-34 Armor
        Co B, 1-34 Armor
        Co C, 1-34 Armor
        Co D, 1-34 Armor

---

[5] Before Desert Storm began, the 2nd Bde adopted an unusual approach by permanently task organizing its three maneuver battalions as combined arms battalion task forces.

[6] This battalion permanently task organized its companies and had three tank companies and one mechanized infantry company. See Footnote 5.

[7] This battalion permanently task organized its companies and had three tank companies and one mechanized infantry company. See Footnote 5.

[8] This battalion permanently task organized its companies and had two tank companies, two mechanized infantry companies, and one antiarmor company. See Footnote 5.

1st Brigade (continued)

TF 2-34 Armor
Co B, 2-34 Armor [Team]
Co C, 2-34 Armor [Team]
Co A, 5-16 Inf(M) [Team]
Co D, 5-16 Inf(M) [Team]
TF 5-16 Inf(M)
Co B, 5-16 Inf(M)
Co C, 5-16 Inf(M)
Co E(Antiarmor), 5-16 Inf(M)
Co A, 2-34 Armor
Co D, 2-34 Armor

2nd Brigade "Dagger Brigade"

TF 3-37 Armor
Co B, 3-37 Armor
Co C, 3-37 Armor
Co A, 2-16 Inf(M)
Co D, 2-16 Inf(M)
4-37 Armor[9] [Pure]
Co A, 4-37 Armor
Co B, 4-37 Armor
Co C, 4-37 Armor
Co D, 4-37 Armor
TF 2-16 Inf(M)
Co B, 2-16 Inf(M) [Team]
Co C, 2-16 Inf(M)
Co E(Antiarmor), 2-16 Inf(M)
Co A, 3-37 Armor
Co D, 3-37 Armor [Team]

---

[9] It is unclear if this battalion fought with three or four tank companies under its command and, if it only had three companies, which companies it had and where the fourth tank company was.

Order of Battle

<u>3rd Bde, 2nd Armd Div</u> "Blackheart Brigade" [Served as the 1st Inf Div(Mech)'s 3rd Bde]

    2-66 Armor [Pure]
        Co A, 2-66 Armor
        Co B, 2-66 Armor
        Co C, 2-66 Armor
        Co D, 2-66 Armor
    TF 3-66 Armor
        Co C, 3-66 Armor
        Co D, 3-66 Armor
        Co A, 1-41 Inf(M)
        Co D, 1-41 Inf(M)
    TF 1-41 Inf(M)
        Co B, 1-41 Inf(M)
        Co C, 1-41 Inf(M)
        Co A, 3-66 Armor
        Co B, 3-66 Armor

24th INFANTRY DIVISION(MECH)

<u>1st Brigade</u> "Liberty Brigade"

    TF 4-64 Armor
        Co A, 4-64 Armor [Team]
        Co C, 4-64 Armor [Team]
        Co A, 2-7 Inf(M) [Team]
        Co C, 3-7 Inf(M) [Team]
    TF 2-7 Inf(M)
        Co B, 2-7 Inf(M)
        Co C, 2-7 Inf(M)
        Co D, 2-7 Inf(M)
        Co E(Antiarmor), 2-7 Inf(M)
        Co B, 4-64 Armor
    TF 3-7 Inf(M)
        Co A, 3-7 Inf(M)
        Co B, 3-7 Inf(M)
        Co D, 3-7 Inf(M)
        Co E(Antiarmor), 3-7 Inf(M)
        Co D, 4-64 Armor

2nd Brigade "Vanguard Brigade"

    TF 1-64 Armor
        Co C, 1-64 Armor (?)
        Co D, 1-64 Armor (?)
        Co A, 3-15 Inf(M) [Team ?]
        Co B, 3-15 Inf(M) (?)
    TF 3-69 Armor(-)[10]
        Co A, 3-69 Armor
        Co B, 3-69 Armor
        Co C, 3-69 Armor
        Co E(Antiarmor), 3-15 Inf(M)
    TF 3-15 Inf(M)
        Co C, 3-15 Inf(M) (?)
        Co D, 3-15 Inf(M) (?)
        Co A, 1-64 Armor
        Co B, 1-64 Armor

197th Inf Bde(Mech) "Sledgehammer Brigade" [Served as the 24th Inf Div(Mech)'s 3rd Bde]

    TF 2-69 Armor
        Co _, 2-69 Armor
        Co _, 2-69 Armor
        Co A, 1-18 Inf(M)
        Co _, 2-18 Inf(M)
    TF 1-18 Inf(M)
        Co B, 1-18 Inf(M)
        Co C, 1-18 Inf(M)
        Co D, 1-18 Inf(M)
        Co E(Antiarmor), 1-18 Inf(M)
        Co B, 2-69 Armor
    TF 2-18 Inf(M)
        Co __, 2-18 Inf(M)
        Co __, 2-18 Inf(M)
        Co __, 2-18 Inf(M)
        Co E(Antiarmor), 2-18 Inf(M)
        Co __, 2-69 Armor

---

[10] Company D was attached to the 2-4 Cav.

1st BRIGADE, 2nd ARMORED DIVISION "Tiger Brigade"

TF 1-67 Armor
    Co A, 1-67 Armor
    Co B, 1-67 Armor
    Co D, 1-67 Armor
    Co D, 3-41 Inf(M) [11]
TF 3-67 Armor
    Co A, 3-67 Armor [Team]
    Co B, 3-67 Armor
    Co D, 3-67 Armor
    Co C, 3-41 Inf(M) [Team]
TF 3-41 Inf(M)
    Co A, 3-41 Inf(M) [Team]
    Co B, 3-41 Inf(M)
    Co E(Antiarmor), 3-41 Inf(M)
    Co C, 1-67 Armor
    Co C, 3-67 Armor

Notes:

➢ Battalions that fought as combined arms battalion task forces by cross attaching companies with another battalion are listed as "TF _____." Battalions that did not cross attach companies with another battalion are listed with their battalion designation, followed by "[Pure]". Where known, companies that formed combined arms company teams by cross attaching platoons with another company have "[Team]" after their designation, whereas companies that did not cross attach platoons have "[Pure]" after their designation.

➢ In each case, whether a battalion fought as a combined arms task force or as a pure battalion, the battalion's headquarters & headquarters company served with its parent battalion.

➢ In addition to the task organization shown here, each maneuver battalion received a plethora of other attachments, such as ADA and engineers. I have not attempted to depict these attachments, as the detail would swamp this chart, I do not have reliable information for all units, and some of these attachments changed during the ground war.

➢ Most U.S. Army maneuver brigades have official or semi-official nicknames that are used in addition, or occasionally in lieu of, their formal designation. These nicknames are indicated in quotation marks after the brigade's formal designation. Only the 2nd Bde, 3rd Armd Div did not use a nickname during Desert Storm.

---

[11] To avoid confustion between Co D, 1-67 Armor and Co D, 3-41 Inf(M), Co D, 3-41 Inf(M) was referred to as "Team F."

Chart 5

U.S. Army Combat Arms Units
That Served With MARCENT,
By Division/Brigade

This chart lists all U.S. Army combat arms units that served under the Marine Corps as elements of MARCENT. For a narrative of the 1st Brigade, 2nd Armored Division's operations in Desert Storm, see Chart 19, pages 19-8 and 19-9.

I Marine Expeditionary Force

2nd Marine Division

1st Brigade, 2nd Armored Division "Tiger Brigade"

> 1-67 Armor [M1A1(Mod)]
> 3-67 Armor [M1A1(Mod)]
> 3-41 Inf(M)
> Elements, 2nd LAI Bn(Rein)[1] [USMC]
> 1-3 FA(155 SP)[2] [3 x 8]
> Btry B(Vulc/Stinger), 4-5 ADA [Fr. 1 Cav Div(-)]

---

[1] See Chart 19, Footnotes 77 & 78.
[2] Was GS to the 2nd Mar Div until 1600 hours, 24 Feb 91. From the morning of 25 Feb 91, was reinforced by the 5/10 Marines (Arty). See Chart 19, Footnote 90.

Order of Battle

10th Marines (Artillery) [USMC]

Btry A(MLRS), 92nd FA [1 x 9] [Fr. 2 AD(-)]
4th Radar Sec, Btry A(TA), 26th FA [Fr. 4 ID(M)(-)]

Notes:

➢ All units are U.S. Army unless indicated otherwise, e.g., "[USMC]"

➢ "[M1A1(Mod)]" refers to M1A1 Main Battle Tanks that were modified in-theater to M1A1HA standard. See Chart 13, page 13-2.

➢ All U.S. Army mechanized infantry units used the M2 "Bradley" series Infantry Fighting Vehicle, unless noted otherwise.

➢ The entries for field artillery firing units show the number of batteries and the number of howitzers or MLRS launchers authorized per battery in brackets, e.g., the 1st Bn(155 SP), 3rd FA, 1st Brigade, 2nd Armored Division had three firing batteries each authorized eight howitzers [3 x 8]. Some units, however, acquired extra weapons, typically from the operational readiness float stocks that were intended to replace vehicles and weapons that were not operationally ready, or "down," for various reasons. For example, Btry A(MLRS), 92nd FA, which was attached to the 10th Marines (Artillery), acquired one extra launcher and operated ten launchers during Desert Storm.

➢ Most U.S. Army units have official or semi-official nicknames that are used in addition, or occasionally in lieu of, their official designation. For some reason, during Desert Shield/Storm the 1st Bde, 2nd Armd Div was known almost exclusively by its nickname, the "Tiger Brigade."

➢ The Tiger Bde was OPCON to the 2nd Marine Div. During Desert Shield, the Tiger Bde had been attached to the 1st Cav Div(-). See Chart 27, page 27-7 ("Notes").

Chart 6

U.S. Army Special Operations Units, Central Command

The Special Operations Command, Central Command (SOCCENT) was the joint (multi-service) command within the U.S. Central Command that was responsible for special operations forces. This chart depicts the Army units that were assigned to SOCCENT. This chart also shows the Army units assigned to the Joint Special Operations Task Force(Forward), which reported directly to HQ, CENTCOM.

SOCCENT

3rd SF Gp(Abn)[1] [Fr. 1 SOCOM][2]
   1/3 SF Gp(Abn)
      Co A, 3/10 SF Gp(Abn) [Fr. 10 SF Gp(Abn)]
   Trp A, 4-17 Cav(Air)[3] [Armed OH-58D][4]
   1st SF Bn (Kuwait)

---

[1] According to official Army sources, elements of the 3rd SF Gp(Abn) were the first U.S. personnel to re-enter the U.S. Embassy in Kuwait City. These claims are disputed, however, by the 5th SF Gp(Abn) and the Marines. See Chart 19, Footnote 4.

[2] See Chart 2, Footnote 6.

[3] See Chart 4, Footnote 84.

[4] See Chart 4, Footnote 85.

Order of Battle

5th SF Gp(Abn)[5] [Fr. 1 SOCOM]
    1/5 SF Gp(Abn)
    2/5 SF Gp(Abn)
    3/5 SF Gp(Abn)
    TF 3/160 Spec Opns Avn Regt(Abn)
        3/160 Spec Opns Avn Regt(Abn) [Fr. 160 SOAR(Abn)]
        2/160 Spec Opns Avn Regt(Abn)(-) [Fr. 160 SOAR(Abn)]

Joint Special Operations Task Force(Forward)[6] "JSOTF-F"

Elements of 1st SF Operational Det-Delta(Abn)[7] [Fr. 1 SOCOM ?]
Co B(+), 1/75 Ranger Regt(Abn)[8] [Fr. 75 Rngr Regt(Abn)]
Elements of 160th Spec Opns Avn Regt(Abn)[9] [Fr. 160 SOAR(Abn)]

Notes:

➢ The Army reportedly deployed elements of several other SOF units, including the U.S. Special Operations Command (USSOCOM), Joint Special Operations Command (JSOC), and U.S. Army Special Operations Command (USASOC). It is unclear, however, whether these commands sent sub-elements that participated as discrete units, or whether they merely contributed personnel who served with the JSOTF-F.

➢ British (see Chart 27) and French (see Chart 28) special operations units, and the Army's 10th SF Gp(Abn)(-) (assigned to JTF Proven Force in Turkey, see Chart 7) were all under the tactical control of SOCCENT, although not assigned to SOCCENT.

➢ The Marine Corps does not possess special operations units per se. The two special operations-capable Marine expeditionary units that were afloat in the Gulf were assigned to NAVCENT, rather than SOCCENT. See Chart 18.

---

[5] See Footnote 1. During the Gulf War, the 5th SF Gp(Abn), with attachments, was known as "ARSOTF," for "Army Special Operations Task Force."

[6] This 877-man task force was engaged in hunting for mobile Scud missiles in Western Iraq commencing on 7 Feb 91. Some sources refer to this task force as the "CENTCOM JSOTF." British special operations units participated in the "Scud Hunt." See Chart 27, Footnote 30.

[7] This is the Army's "Delta Force," commandos normally assigned counter-terrorist duties. Delta Force reportedly deployed two of its three squadrons; these were apparently the 1st & 2nd Sqdns.

[8] Company B was reinforced by the 1st Plt, Co A, 1/75 Rngr Regt(Abn), and selected personnel from HHC, 1/75 Rngr Regt(Abn) and Regimental HHC. Some sources state that all or a portion of the Weapons Plt of Co A also deployed. The Rangers reportedly deployed on 12 Feb 91 and redeployed on 6 Apr 91, without suffering any casualties.

[9] This was apparently the 1st Bn(-), 160th Spec Opns Avn Regt(Abn).

Chart 7

Ground Combat Formations,
Joint Task Force Proven Force

Joint Task Force Proven Force operated out of Turkey. It consisted primarily of Air Force units based at Incirlik Air Base.

JTF Proven Force

<u>Army Forces, JTF Proven Force</u>

7th SOSC(TA)(Abn) [Fr. SOCEUR]
4-7 ADA(-)[1] (Patriot) [Fr. 108 ADA Bde, 32 AADCOM]
324th Netherlands Sqdn (Hawk)[2]
328th Netherlands Sqdn (Hawk)
502nd Netherlands Sqdn (Patriot)
503rd Netherlands Sqdn (Patriot)

---

[1] Consisted of HHB and Btrys A & B. This unit began deploying to Turkey on 14 Jan 91 and completed this deployment by 25 Jan 91.
[2] It is unclear how the Dutch units fit into the chain of command.

Order of Battle

<u>Joint Special Operations Task Force[3]</u>

    10th SF Gp(Abn)(-) [Fr. 1 SOCOM][4]
        1/10 SF Gp(Abn)
        2/10 SF Gp(Abn)

Notes:

➤ JTF Proven Force operated under the U.S. European Command, but was under the tactical control of CENTCOM.

➤ The U.S. Army deployed a total of 16 Patriot launchers to Turkey. The two Dutch squadrons added another ten Patriot launchers.

➤ Iraq did not fire any Scud Missiles at Turkey. As a result, none of the U.S. or Dutch Patriot units in Turkey fired a Patriot missile.

➤ Turkish units provided short range air defense for Incirlik Air Base, but it is unclear how these units fit into the chain of command.

---

[3] The headquarters of this task force was apparently formed using personnel from HQ, SOCEUR. BG Richard W. Potter, then-CG of SOCEUR, was the CG of the task force during ODS.

[4] See Chart 2, Footnote 6.

Chart 8

U.S. And Allied Air Defense Artillery Units
Stationed in Israel
During Operation Desert Storm

In response to Iraqi Scud missile attacks on Israel on 18 Jan 91, Israel agreed to allow allied Patriot units to deploy to Israel because Israel's Patriot units were not yet fully trained and ready. Israel's two firing units did not achieve operational status until 21 Jan 91 and, in the early morning hours of 22 Jan 91, engaged Scuds that had been fired at Israel. In the meantime, on 18 Jan 91, the 4th Bn(Patriot)(-), 43rd ADA had been ordered to deploy to Israel with two firing batteries. Deployment began approximately twelve hours later, at 0635 hours on 19 Jan 91, and was completed on 22 Jan 91. Two additional batteries, Batteries A & B, 1st Bn(Patriot), 7th ADA, deployed to Israel 25-26 Jan 91, within 24 hours of being alerted. The 327th Netherlands Sqdn deployed o/a 24 Feb 91, but did not engage any Scuds.

Task Force Patriot Defender[1]

4-43 ADA(Patriot)(-)[2] [Fr. 10 ADA Bde, 32 AADCOM]
Btrys A & B, 1-7 ADA(Patriot) [Fr. 94 ADA Bde, 32 AADCOM]

---

[1] The task force was commanded by the commander of the 10th ADA Bde, but it is unclear if HHB, 10th ADA Bde deployed to Israel. This unit has not received campaign participation credit from the Army, but this may have been driven by political considerations. It is likely that HHB, 10th ADA Bde provided the personnel used to staff the task force's headquarters.

[2] Consisted of HHB and Btrys A & B.

Order of Battle

Israeli Air Force

    IDF-1 (Patriot)[3]
    IDF-2 (Patriot)
    327th Netherlands Sqdn (Patriot)

Notes:

➤ The exact command relationship between these seven Patriot units is unclear. One source reports that all were under the tactical control of Task Force Patriot Defender, while another source reports that all Patriot units in Israel were under the operational control of the Israeli Defense Forces.

➤ The areas of responsibility for U.S. joint commands are assigned on a geographic basis and Israel is assigned to the U.S. European Command, rather than Central Command. As a result, Task Force Patriot Defender reported to HQ, U.S. European Command in Stuttgart, Germany, rather than HQ, Central Command.

➤ The two Israeli Patriot units defended Tel Aviv. The Dutch Patriot squadron defended Jerusalem. Two of the U.S. batteries defended Tel Aviv and the other two defended Haifa. It appears that the units that defended Tel Aviv were Btry B, 1st Bn, 7th ADA and Btry B, 4th Bn, 43rd ADA, while Btry A, 1st Bn, 7th ADA and Btry A, 4th Bn, 43rd ADA defended Haifa.

➤ The U.S. Army deployed a total of 32 Patriot launchers to Israel. The two Israeli units and the Dutch squadron together contributed another 16 launchers.

---

[3] These are Israeli Defense Force Patriot batteries.

Chart 9

U.S. Army Combat Arms Units
That Participated In Operation Desert Storm,
By Parent Regiment

This chart lists all U.S. Army combat arms units that deployed to the KTO, Turkey, or Israel, and shows the major command to which they were assigned.

Cavalry Units

1st Cavalry

1st Sqdn	1st Armd Div
Trps A & B, 2nd Sqdn	1st Cav Div(-)

2nd Armored Cavalry

1st Sqdn	2nd Armd Cav Regt
2nd Sqdn	2nd Armd Cav Regt
3rd Sqdn	2nd Armd Cav Regt
4th Sqdn(Avn)	2nd Armd Cav Regt

3rd Armored Cavalry

1st Sqdn	3rd Armd Cav Regt
2nd Sqdn	3rd Armd Cav Regt
3rd Sqdn	3rd Armd Cav Regt
4th Sqdn(Avn)	3rd Armd Cav Regt

Cavalry Units (continued)

4th Cavalry

1st Sqdn	1st Inf Div(Mech)
2nd Sqdn(-)	24th Inf Div(Mech)
Trp D	197th Inf Bde(Mech); 24th Inf Div(Mech)

7th Cavalry

1st Sqdn(-)	1st Cav Div(-)
4th Sqdn	3rd Armd Div

9th Cavalry

Target Acquisition Plt, Trp A, 1st Sqdn(Air)[1]	101st Abn Div(Air Aslt)

17th Cavalry

1st Sqdn(Air)	82nd Abn Div
2nd Sqdn(Air)	101st Abn Div(Air Aslt)
4th Sqdn(Air)(-)	18th Avn Bde(Abn)
Trp A, 4th Sqdn(Air)	3rd SF Gp(Abn)

Other Cavalry Units

1st Inf Div(Mech)(Fwd), Scout Plt[2]	3rd Bde(-), 1st Inf Div(Mech)

Armor Units

8th Cavalry[3] (Armor)

1st Bn	1st Cav Div(-)
2nd Bn	1st Cav Div(-)
3rd Bn	3rd Armd Div
4th Bn	3rd Armd Div

---

[1] See Chart 4, Footnote 59.

[2] Evidently a provisional unit. Was the security force for the U.S. Army staging camp outside Jubayl. See Chart 4, page 4-28 and Footnote 119.

[3] The 8th Cavalry is listed here, rather than with the cavalry units, because its units were armor (tank) units, not true cavalry units that performed reconnaissance and security missions.

Armor Units (continued)

32nd Armor

1st Bn	1st Cav Div(-)
3rd Bn	1st Cav Div(-)
4th Bn	3rd Armd Div

34th Armor

1st Bn	1st Inf Div(Mech)
2nd Bn	1st Inf Div(Mech)
3rd Bn[4]	3rd Bde, 1st Inf Div(Mech)
4th Bn	3rd Armd Div

35th Armor

1st Bn	1st Armd Div
3rd Bn	1st Armd Div

37th Armor

1st Bn	1st Armd Div
3rd Bn	1st Inf Div(Mech)
4th Bn	1st Inf Div(Mech)

64th Armor

1st Bn	24th Inf Div(Mech)
4th Bn	24th Inf Div(Mech)

66th Armor

2nd Bn	3rd Bde, 2nd Armd Div
3rd Bn	3rd Bde, 2nd Armd Div
4th Bn	3rd Bde, 3rd Inf Div(Mech)

67th Armor

1st Bn	1st Bde, 2nd Armd Div
2nd Bn	3rd Armd Div
3rd Bn	1st Bde, 2nd Armd Div
4th Bn	3rd Armd Div

---

[4] Did not serve as an armor unit. See Chart 4, page 4-28 and Footnote 117.

Armor Units (continued)

69th Armor

2nd Bn	197th Inf Bde(Mech)
3rd Bn	24th Inf Div(Mech)

70th Armor

2nd Bn	1st Armd Div
4th Bn	1st Armd Div

73rd Armor

3rd Bn(Abn)	82nd Abn Div

Other Armor Units

ORF Plt[5]	2nd Armd Cav Regt

Infantry Units

5th Cavalry[6]

1st Bn(M)	1st Cav Div(-)
2nd Bn(M)	1st Cav Div(-)
3rd Bn(M)	3rd Armd Div
5th Bn(M)	3rd Armd Div

6th Infantry

6th Bn(M)	1st Armd Div
7th Bn(M)	1st Armd Div

---

[5] A provisional unit. See Chart 4, Footnote 72.

[6] The 5th Cavalry is listed here, rather than with the cavalry units, because its units were mechanized infantry units, not true cavalry units that performed reconnaissance and security missions.

Infantry Units (continued)

7th Infantry

1st Bn(M)	3rd Bde, 3rd Inf Div(Mech)
2nd Bn(M)	24th Inf Div(Mech)
3rd Bn(M)	24th Inf Div(Mech)
4th Bn(M)	3rd Bde, 3rd Inf Div(Mech)

15th Infantry

3rd Bn(M)	24th Inf Div(Mech)

16th Infantry

2nd Bn(M)	1st Inf Div(Mech)
4th Bn(M)[7]	3rd Bde, 1st Inf Div(Mech)
5th Bn(M)	1st Inf Div(Mech)

18th Infantry

1st Bn(M)	197th Inf Bde(Mech)
2nd Bn(M)	197th Inf Bde(Mech)
4th Bn(M)	3rd Armd Div
5th Bn(M)	3rd Armd Div

41st Infantry

1st Bn(M)	3rd Bde, 2nd Armd Div
3rd Bn(M)	1st Bde, 2nd Armd Div

75th Ranger Regiment(Abn)

Elements, HHC	Joint Spec Opns TF(Fwd)
Elements, HHC, 1st Bn	Joint Spec Opns TF(Fwd)
1st Plt, Co A,[8] 1st Bn	Joint Spec Opns TF(Fwd)
Co B, 1st Bn	Joint Spec Opns TF(Fwd)

---

[7] Did not serve as an infantry unit. See Chart 4, page 4-28 & Footnote 118.

[8] Some sources state that all or a portion of the Weapons Plt of Co A also deployed.

Infantry Units (continued)

187th Infantry

1st Bn(Air Aslt)	101st Abn Div(Air Aslt)
2nd Bn(Air Aslt)	101st Abn Div(Air Aslt)
3rd Bn(Air Aslt)	101st Abn Div(Air Aslt)

325th Infantry

1st Bn(Abn)	82nd Abn Div
2nd Bn(Abn)	82nd Abn Div
4th Bn(Abn)	82nd Abn Div

327th Infantry

1st Bn(Air Aslt)	101st Abn Div(Air Aslt)
2nd Bn(Air Aslt)	101st Abn Div(Air Aslt)
3rd Bn(Air Aslt)	101st Abn Div(Air Aslt)

502nd Infantry

1st Bn(Air Aslt)	101st Abn Div(Air Aslt)
2nd Bn(Air Aslt)	XVIII Abn Corps; 101st Abn Div (Air Aslt)
3rd Bn(Air Aslt)	101st Abn Div(Air Aslt)

504th Infantry

1st Bn(Abn)	82nd Abn Div
2nd Bn(Abn)	82nd Abn Div
3rd Bn(Abn)	82nd Abn Div

505th Infantry

1st Bn(Abn)	82nd Abn Div
2nd Bn(Abn)	82nd Abn Div
3rd Bn(Abn)	82nd Abn Div

Infantry Units (continued)

Long Range Surveillance Units

Co F(LRS), 51st Inf	207th MI Bde
LRS Det, Co D, 101st MI Bn	1st Inf Div(Mech)
LRS Det, 124th MI Bn	24th Inf Div(Mech)
LRS Det, 311th MI Bn	101st Abn Div(Air Aslt)
LRS Det, 312th MI Bn	1st Cav Div(-)
LRS Det, 313th MI Bn	82nd Abn Div
LRS Det, 501st MI Bn	1st Armd Div
Co D(LRS), 522nd MI Bn	525th MI Bde
LRS Det, 533rd MI Bn	3rd Armd Div

Other Infantry Units

Pathfinder Det	101st Abn Div(Air Aslt)

Special Forces Units

3rd Special Forces Gp(Abn)

1st Bn	3rd SF Gp(Abn)

5th Special Forces Gp(Abn)

1st Bn	5th SF Gp(Abn)
2nd Bn	5th SF Gp(Abn)
3rd Bn	5th SF Gp(Abn)

10th Special Forces Group(Abn)

1st Bn	10th SF Gp(Abn)(-)
2nd Bn	10th SF Gp(Abn)(-)
Co A, 3rd Bn	3rd SF Gp(Abn)

Other Special Operations Units

Elements, 1st SFOD-Delta(Abn)[9]	Joint Spec Opns TF(Fwd)

---

[9] See Chart 6, Footnote 7.

Aviation Units[10]

1st Aviation

1st Bn(AH)	1st Inf Div(Mech)
2nd Bn(AH)	2nd Armd Cav Regt; 1st Armd Div
3rd Bn(AH)	1st Armd Div

3rd Aviation

1st Bn(AH)	1st Cav Div(-)

6th Cavalry[11]

2nd Sqdn(AH)	11th Avn Bde; 3rd Armd Div
5th Sqdn(AH)	12th Avn Bde; 24th Inf Div(Mech)

24th Aviation

1st Bn(AH)	24th Inf Div(Mech)

82nd Aviation

1st Bn(AH)	82nd Abn Div

101st Aviation

1st Bn(AH)	101st Abn Div(Air Aslt)
3rd Bn(AH)	101st Abn Div(Air Aslt)

158th Aviation

Co D(Scout), 5th Bn	12th Avn Bde

159th Aviation

Co D(?) (Scout), 4th Bn	11th Avn Bde

---

[10] This chart lists only attack helicopter, scout, and special operations aviation units.

[11] The 6th Cavalry is listed here, rather than with the cavalry units, because its units were attack helicopter units, not true cavalry units that performed reconnaissance and security missions.

Aviation Units (continued)

160th Special Operations Aviation Regt(Abn)

1st Bn(-) (?)[12]	Joint Spec Opns TF(Fwd)
2nd Bn(-)	5th SF Gp(Abn)
3rd Bn	5th SF Gp(Abn)

227th Aviation

1st Bn(AH)	1st Cav Div(-)
2nd Bn(AH)	3rd Armd Div
3rd Bn(AH)	12th Avn Bde

229th Aviation

2nd Bn(AH)	101st Abn Div(Air Aslt)
4th Bn(AH)	11th Avn Bde
5th Bn(AH)(-)	ARCENT Avn Bde
Co A, 5th Bn(AH)	3rd Armd Div

Field Artillery Units

1st Field Artillery

2nd Bn(155 SP)	1st Armd Div
3rd Bn(155 SP)	1st Armd Div

3rd Field Artillery

1st Bn(155 SP)	1st Bde, 2nd Armd Div
2nd Bn(155 SP)	3rd Armd Div
4th Bn(155 SP)	42nd FA Bde; 3rd Bde, 2nd Armd Div

5th Field Artillery

1st Bn(155 SP)	1st Inf Div(Mech)
4th Bn(155 SP)	1st Inf Div(Mech)

---

[12] See Chart 6, Footnote 9.

Field Artillery Units (continued)

6th Field Artillery

    Btry B(MLRS)   1st Inf Div(Mech)

8th Field Artillery

    3rd Bn(155 T)   18th FA Bde(Abn)
    5th Bn(155 T)(-)   18th FA Bde(Abn);101st Abn Div(Air Aslt)
    Btry C, 5th Bn(155 T)   101st Abn Div(Air Aslt)

13th Field Artillery

    Btry A(MLRS)   24th Inf Div(Mech)

17th Field Artillery

    1st Bn(155 SP)   75th FA Bde
    2nd Bn(155 SP)   212th FA Bde
    3rd Bn(155 SP)   210th FA Bde

18th Field Artillery

    2nd Bn(203 SP)   212th FA Bde
    3rd Bn(155 SP)   3rd Armd Cav Regt
    5th Bn(203 SP)   42nd FA Bde; 75th FA Bde

20th Field Artillery

    3rd Bn(155 SP)   42nd FA Bde

21st Field Artillery

    Btry A(MLRS)   1st Cav Div(-)

25th Field Artillery

    Btry B(TA)   1st Armd Div
    Btry C(TA)(-)   212th FA Bde
    Det, Btry C(TA)   3rd Armd Cav Regt
    Btry D(TA)(-)   1st Inf Div(Mech)

Field Artillery Units (continued)

26th Field Artillery

4th Radar Sec, Btry A(TA)	2nd Mar Div
Btry C(TA)(-)	75th FA Bde
(1) Radar Sec, Btry C(TA)	1st Inf Div(Mech)

27th Field Artillery

1st Bn(MLRS)	42nd FA Bde
3rd Bn(MLRS)	212th FA Bde
4th Bn(MLRS)(-)	1st Armd Div
Btry C, 4th Bn(MLRS)	210th FA Bde
6th Bn(MLRS/ATACMS)(-)	18th FA Bde(Abn)[13]
Btry A, 6th Bn(MLRS/ATACMS)	75th FA Bde

29th Field Artillery

2nd Bn(155 SP)	42nd FA Bde

39th Field Artillery

1st Bn(Abn)(155 T)	18th FA Bde(Abn); 82nd Abn Div

40th Field Artillery

Btry A(MLRS)	3rd Armd Div

41st Field Artillery

1st Bn(155 SP)	24th Inf Div(Mech)
2nd Bn(155 SP)	3rd Bde, 3rd Inf Div(Mech)
3rd Bn(155 SP)	24th Inf Div(Mech)
4th Bn(155 SP)	197th Inf Bde(M); 24th Inf Div(M)(?)[14]
6th Bn(155 SP)	210th FA Bde

---

[13] See Chart 4, Footnote 101.

[14] See Chart 4, Footnote 37.

Field Artillery Units (continued)

82nd Field Artillery

1st Bn(155 SP)	1st Cav Div(-)
2nd Bn(155 SP)	3rd Armd Div
3rd Bn(155 SP)	1st Cav Div(-)
4th Bn(155 SP)	3rd Armd Div

92nd Field Artillery

Btry A(MLRS)	2nd Mar Div

94th Field Artillery

Btry A(MLRS)	1st Armd Div

142nd Field Artillery [AR ARNG]

1st Bn(203 SP)	142nd FA Bde
2nd Bn(203 SP)	142nd FA Bde

158th Field Artillery [OK ARNG]

1st Bn(MLRS)(-)	75th FA Bde; 1st Cav Div(-)[15]
Btry A, 1st Bn(MLRS)	75th FA Bde; 142nd FA Bde

181st Field Artillery [TN ARNG]

1st Bn(203 SP)	196th FA Bde

201st Field Artillery [WV ARNG]

1st Bn(155 SP)	18th FA Bde(Abn)

---

[15] See Chart 4, Footnote 90.

Field Artillery Units (continued)

319th Field Artillery

1st Bn(Abn)(105 T)	82nd Abn Div
2nd Bn(Abn)(105 T)	82nd Abn Div
3rd Bn(Abn)(105 T)	82nd Abn Div

320th Field Artillery

1st Bn(Air Aslt)(105 T)	101st Abn Div(Air Aslt)
2nd Bn(Air Aslt)(105 T)	101st Abn Div(Air Aslt)
3rd Bn(Air Aslt)(105 T)	101st Abn Div(Air Aslt)

333rd Field Artillery

Btry A(TA)	1st Cav Div(-)
Btry E(TA)	210th FA Bde
Btry F(TA)	3rd Armd Div
Btry G(TA)	24th Inf Div(Mech)

623rd Field Artillery [KY ARNG]

1st Bn(203 SP)	196th FA Bde

Other Field Artillery Units

How Btry(155 SP), 1st Sqdn	2nd Armd Cav Regt
How Btry(155 SP), 2nd Sqdn	2nd Armd Cav Regt
How Btry(155 SP), 3rd Sqdn	2nd Armd Cav Regt
How Btry(155 SP), 1st Sqdn	3rd Armd Cav Regt
How Btry(155 SP), 2nd Sqdn	3rd Armd Cav Regt
How Btry(155 SP), 3rd Sqdn	3rd Armd Cav Regt
1st FA Det(TA)	18th FA Bde(Abn)
2nd FA Det(TA)	101st Abn Div(Air Aslt)

Air Defense Artillery Units

1st Air Defense Artillery

    2nd Bn(Hawk)   XVIII Abn Corps

2nd Air Defense Artillery

    3rd Bn(Chap)[16]   7th Trans Gp(Terminal)

3rd Air Defense Artillery

    2nd Bn(Vulc/Stinger)   1st Inf Div(Mech)[17]
    5th Bn(Vulc/Chap/Stinger)   3rd Armd Div
    6th Bn(Vulc/Chap/Stinger)   1st Armd Div[18]

4th Air Defense Artillery

    3rd Bn(Abn)(Vulc/Stinger)   82nd Abn Div

5th Air Defense Artillery

    1st Bn(Vulc/Stinger)   24th Inf Div(Mech)[19]
    4th Plt(Stinger), Btry C, 2nd Bn   3rd Bde, 2nd Armd Div
    4th Plt(Stinger),[20] Btry D, 3rd Bn   12th Avn Bde
    Stinger Teams, 3rd Bn   3rd Armd Div
    (4) Stinger Teams, 3rd Bn   ARCENT Avn Bde
    4th Bn(V/A/S)(-)   1st Cav Div(-)
    Btry B(V/S), 4th Bn(V/A/S)   1st Bde, 2nd Armd Div

---

[16] Did not serve as an ADA unit. See Chart 4, Footnote 116.

[17] Elements of the 2-3 ADA were also assigned to the 3rd Bde, 2nd Armd Div, which served as part of the 1st Inf Div(M) during Desert Storm.

[18] Elements of the 6-3 ADA were also assigned to the 3rd Bde, 3rd Inf Div(M), which served as part of the 1st Armd Div during Desert Storm.

[19] Elements of the 1-5 ADA were also assigned to the 197th Inf Bde(M), which served as part of the 24th Inf Div(M) during Desert Storm.

[20] Some sources indicate this was a platoon(minus).

Air Defense Artillery Units (continued)

7th Air Defense Artillery

Btrys A & B, 1st Bn(Patriot)	TF Patriot Defender
Btry D,[21] 1st Bn(Patriot)	11th ADA Bde
2nd Bn(Patriot)	11th ADA Bde
4th Bn(Patriot)(-)	JTF Proven Force

43rd Air Defense Artillery

Fire Dist Sec,1st Bn(Patriot)	XVIII Abn Corps
2nd Bn(Patriot)	11th ADA Bde
3rd Bn(Patriot)(-)	11th ADA Bde
Btrys A, B & E, 3rd Bn(Patriot)	XVIII Abn Corps
4th Bn(Patriot)(-)	TF Patriot Defender
8th Bn(Patriot)	VII Corps

44th Air Defense Artillery

2nd Bn(AAslt)(Vulc/Stinger)	101st Abn Div(Air Aslt)

52nd Air Defense Artillery

2nd Bn(Hawk)	11th ADA Bde
(1) Stinger Sec, 2nd Bn	XVIII Abn Corps
Btrys A & C, 6th Bn(Hawk)	VII Corps
Btry B, 6th Bn(Hawk)	3rd Armd Cav Regt

62nd Air Defense Artillery

5th Bn(Vulc/Stinger)(-)	XVIII Abn Corps Arty
Btry B, 5th Bn(V/S)	3rd Armd Cav Regt

---

[21] Included a portion of HHB, 1-7 ADA.

Air Defense Artillery Units (continued)

Other Air Defense Artillery Units

4th Plt(Stinger),
    HQ Co, 197th Inf Bde   24th Inf Div(Mech)
Stinger Plt, HQ Trp,
    2nd Armd Cav Regt   2nd Armd Cav Regt
Avenger Plt(A/S), HQ Trp,
    3rd Armd Cav Regt   3rd Armd Cav Regt

Notes:

➢ When a listed unit was assigned to two different major commands at different times, the commands are separated by a semi-colon and listed in chronological order.

➢ This chart demonstrates that, among the combat arms, the 41st Field Artillery was the U.S. Army regiment that was best represented in the Gulf, with five battalions present for duty during Operation Desert Storm. Ten combat arms regiments tied for second place, each with four battalions present:

> 2nd Armored Cavalry
> 3rd Armored Cavalry
> 8th Cavalry(Armor)
> 34th Armor
> 67th Armor
> 5th Cavalry(Mech Inf)
> 7th Infantry
> 18th Infantry
> 27th Field Artillery
> 82nd Field Artillery

➢ Units that participated as WSRO/SCT units are not listed on this chart, and are instead listed on Chart 12. The 5th Bn(AH), 229th Avn is listed on this chart because, although it supported the WSRO/SCT program, it was not a WSRO/SCT unit. See Chart 4, Footnote 77.

Chart 10

Selected Army National Guard and Army Reserve Units That Were Mobilized For Operation Desert Storm

This chart lists selected Army National Guard and Army Reserve units that were mobilized for Operation Desert Storm. This chart also addresses several collateral issues, including reserve component units that were almost mobilized and those that should have been mobilized (because of established command relationships with Active Army units that were in the Gulf), but were not.

Combat Arms Units That Deployed To the Gulf

Unit & State	Gaining Command	Mobilization Site
142nd FA Bde [AR/OK ARNG] 1-142 FA(203 SP) [AR ARNG] 2-142 FA(203 SP) [AR ARNG] * Btry A, 1-158 FA(MLRS)[2] [OK ARNG]	VII Corps Arty	Sill[1]

---

[1] The 142nd was federalized on 21 Nov 90, arrived at Fort Sill o/a 24 Nov 90, and arrived in the KTO in mid-January 1991. The brigade's main body left Saudi Arabia on 10 May 91 and returned to Fort Sill. The 142nd was released from active duty on 3 Jul 91.

[2] See Chart 4, Footnote 90.

Combat Arms Units That Deployed To the Gulf (continued)

Unit & State	Gaining Command	Mobilization Site

196th FA Bde [TN/KY ARNG]
    1-181 FA(203 SP) [TN ARNG]
  * 1-623 FA(203 SP) [KY ARNG]
	XVIII Abn Corps Arty	Campbell[3]

1-158 FA(MLRS)(-) [OK ARNG]	VII Corps Arty[4]	Sill[5]
1-201 FA(155 SP) [WV ARNG]	18th FA Bde(Abn)[6]	Campbell[7]

Combat Arms Units That Deployed To Europe

Unit & State	Gaining Command	Mobilization Site
3-87 Inf[8] [CO USAR]	18th MP Bde	Carson[9]

---

[3] The 196th was federalized on 9 Dec 90, arrived at Fort Campbell 10-12 Dec 90, and arrived in the KTO 2-11 Feb 91. The brigade returned to Fort Campbell 6-17 May 91 and was released from active duty on 27 May 91.

[4] See Chart 4, Footnote 90.

[5] The 1-158 FA was federalized on 21 Nov 90, arrived at Fort Sill o/a 24 Nov 90, and arrived in the KTO on 1 Feb 91. The battalion returned to Fort Sill 11-15 May 91, and most personnel had been released from active duty by 9 Jun 91.

[6] See Chart 4, Footnote 103.

[7] The 1-201 FA was federalized on 9 Dec 90, arrived at Fort Campbell on 12 Dec 90, and arrived in the KTO on 2 Feb 91. The 1-201 FA apparently arrived back at Fort Campbell sometime between 6 and 17 May 91, and had apparently left Fort Campbell for its home stations by 24 May 91.

[8] Performed an anti-terrorist security mission for V Corps.

[9] The 3-87 Inf was mobilized on 17 Jan 91 and arrived at Fort Carson on 19 Jan 91. The battalion moved to Germany on 5 Feb 91. The 3-87 returned to Fort Carson on 1 May 91, and began terminal leave pending release from active duty on 15 May 91.

Combat Arms Units That Were Mobilized But Not Deployed

Unit & State	Training Sites	Round-Out During ODS
48th Inf Bde(M)(+) [GA/SC ARNG]	Stewart/Irwin[10]	None[11]
1-108 Armor [GA ARNG]	" "	
* 1-263 Armor [SC ARNG]	" "	
1-121 Inf(M) [GA ARNG]	" "	
2-121 Inf(M) [GA ARNG]	" "	
Trp E, 348th Cav [GA ARNG]	" "	
1-230 FA(155 SP) [GA ARNG]	" "	
155th Armd Bde(+) [MS/TX ARNG]	Shelby/Hood/Irwin[12]	4 ID(M)(-)[13]
1-198 Armor [MS ARNG]	" " "	
2-198 Armor [MS ARNG]	" " "	
* 3-141 Inf(M) [TX ARNG]	Hood/Irwin	
1-155 Inf(M) [MS ARNG]	Shelby/Hood/Irwin	
Trp A, 98th Cav [MS ARNG]	Shelby/Hood[14]	
2-114 FA(155 SP) [MS ARNG]	Shelby/Hood/Irwin	

---

[10] The 48th was federalized on 30 Nov 90, arrived at Fort Stewart o/a 3 Dec 90, and moved to Fort Irwin in late December 1990/early January 1991. The brigade completed its NTC training and was certified combat ready on 28 Feb 91, the day the Gulf War ended. The units of the 48th were released from active duty between 27 Mar 91 and 10 Apr 91.

[11] Prior to ODS, the 48th Inf Bde(M) and the 1-263 Armor had been Round-Out to the 24th Inf Div(M).

[12] With the exception of the 3-141 Inf(M), which was federalized on 7 Dec 90 and arrived at Fort Hood on 10 Dec 90, the 155th was federalized on 7 Dec 90, arrived at Camp Shelby on 10 Dec 90, and moved to Fort Hood in late December 1990. The brigade moved to Fort Irwin in early March 1991, after the war was over, and completed NTC training on 22 Mar 91. The units of the 155th were released from active duty between 7 Apr 91 and 14 May 91.

[13] Prior to ODS, the 155th Armd Bde and the 3-141 Inf(M) had been Round-Out to the 1st Cav Div(-).

[14] It appears that Trp A, 98th Cav did not accompany the 155th Armd Bde to the NTC.

Combat Arms Units That Were Mobilized But Not Deployed (continued)

Unit & State	Training Sites	Round-Out During ODS
256th Inf Bde(M)(+) [LA/AL ARNG]	Polk/Hood[15]	5 ID(M)(-)
* 2-152 Armor [AL ARNG]	" "[16]	
1-156 Armor [LA ARNG]	" "	
2-156 Inf(M) [LA ARNG]	" "	
3-156 Inf(M) [LA ARNG]	" "	
Trp E, 256th Cav [LA ARNG]	Polk/Hood	
1-141 FA(155 SP) [LA ARNG]	" "	
20th SF Gp(Abn) [AL/FL/MS/MD ARNG][17]	Bragg[18]	None
1st Bn [AL/MD ARNG]	"	
2nd Bn [MS/MD ARNG]	"	
3rd Bn [FL ARNG]	"	
1-130 Avn(AH) [AH-64] [NC ARNG]	Hood[19]	None

Combat Arms Units That Were Almost Mobilized

The Army seriously considered mobilizing the following units, but ultimately decided against their mobilization:

> 1-151 Avn(AH) [AH-64] [SC ARNG]
> 1-168 Avn(AH) [AH-1] [WA ARNG]
> 1-140 FA(155 T) [UT ARNG]

---

[15] The 256th was federalized on 30 Nov 90, arrived at Fort Polk in early December, and later moved to Fort Hood, apparently in late 1990. Training at the NTC, which had been scheduled for 2-13 Apr 91, was cancelled when the war ended. The units of the 256th were released from active duty between 9 Apr 91 and 10 May 91.

[16] It is unclear if the 2-152 Armor mobilized at Camp Shelby with the rest of the 256th Inf Bde(M) and later moved to Fort Hood, or whether it mobilized at Fort Hood.

[17] Also mobilized with the 20th was the 165th Weather Flight, a Kentucky Air National Guard unit.

[18] The 20th was federalized on 20 Feb 91 and arrived at Fort Bragg on 23 Feb 91. The group was certified as combat ready, apparently in early April 1991, departed Fort Bragg on 17 May 91, and was released from active duty on 23 May 91.

[19] The 1-130 Avn(AH) was federalized on 12 Feb 91 and arrived at Fort Hood on 18 Feb 91. After completing its training, the battalion departed Fort Hood on 7 Apr 91 and was released from active duty on 19 Apr 91.

USAR Combat Arms Training Units That Were Mobilized[20]

Unit	Mobilization Station	Branch
HQ, 1st Bde, 70th Div(Tng)[21] [MI USAR]	Benning	Infantry
3rd Bde, 70th Div(Tng)[22] [IN USAR]	Benning	Infantry
* 2-333 Regt[23] [MI USAR]	"	"
1-423 Regt [IN USAR]	"	"
2-423 Regt [IN USAR]	"	"
3-423 Regt [IN USAR]	"	"
Tng Spt Bde, 70th Div(Tng)[24] [MI USAR]	"	"
2nd Bde, 78th Div(Tng)[25] [NJ USAR]	Dix	Infantry
3-309 Regt [NJ USAR]	"	"
1-310 Regt [NJ USAR]	"	"
3-310 Regt [NJ USAR]	"	"
Det 1, Tng Spt Bde, 78th Div(Tng)[26] [NJ USAR]	"	"
3rd Bde(-), 84th Div(Tng)[27] [WI USAR]	Sill	Armor
2-334 Regt [WI USAR]	"	"
3-334 Regt [WI USAR]	"	"

---

[20] Training units provide training to individuals when they enter the Army, including basic training and branch-specific advanced individual training (AIT). All reserve component training units are in the Army Reserve. Listed here are those training units that were intended to provide AIT to combat arms soldiers.

[21] HQ, 1st Bde was mobilized on 25 Jan 91 to command Active Army training units at Fort Benning, and was released from active duty on 26 Mar 91.

[22] Was mobilized on 22 Jan 91 and released from active duty on 26 Mar 91.

[23] Normally assigned to the 2nd Bde, 70th Div(Tng).

[24] Was mobilized on 22 Jan 91 and released from active duty on 26 Mar 91. Some sources refer to this unit as "Training Gp, 70th Div(Tng)."

[25] These units were mobilized o/a 25 Jan 91 and released from active duty o/a 31 Mar 91.

[26] This unit was mobilized o/a 25 Jan 91 and released from active duty on 31 Mar 91.

[27] All 84th Div(Tng) units were mobilized on 22 Jan 91, arrived at Fort Sill on 25 Jan 91, and were released from active duty o/a 22 Mar 91.

USAR Combat Arms Training Units That Were Mobilized[28] (continued)

Unit	Mobilization Station	Branch
1st Bde, 100th Div(Tng)[29] [KY USAR]	Knox	Armor
*1-302 Cav [KY USAR]	"	"
2-397 Regt [KY USAR]	"	"
*Cos A & B, 1-398 Regt [KY USAR]	"	"
2-399 Regt [KY USAR]	"	"
Tng Gp, 100th Div(Tng) [KY USAR]	"	"
FA Tng Gp, 402nd FA Tng Bde[30] [OK USAR]	Sill	FA
3-318 Regt[31] [VA USAR] (80th Div(Tng))	Eustis	Infantry[32]
1-335 Regt[33] [IL USAR] (85th Div(Tng))	Bliss	Armor
1-485 Regt[34] [NC USAR] (108th Div(Tng))	Jackson	Infantry
2-485 Regt[35] [NC USAR] (108th Div(Tng))	Jackson	Infantry

Other Selected Units That Were Mobilized

➤ The 21st Theater Army Area Command(Continental U.S. Augmentation) [IN USAR] was created to supplement the 21st TAACOM, the senior logistics unit in Europe, during a general war in Europe. Instead, these reservists deployed to the KTO and were assigned to the 22nd SUPCOM. Because these personnel served with the 22nd SUPCOM, the 21st TAACOM Augmentation is not listed as a separate unit on any of the other charts.

---

[28] Training units provide training to individuals when they enter the Army, including basic training and branch-specific advanced individual training (AIT). All reserve component training units are in the Army Reserve. Listed here are those training units that were intended to provide AIT to combat arms soldiers.

[29] All 100th Div(Tng) units were mobilized on 22 Jan 91 and released from active duty 17-26 Mar 91. The 1-302 Cav was normally assigned to the 3rd Bde, and Cos A & B, 1-398 Regt were normally assigned to the 2nd Bde.

[30] Mobilized on 22 Jan 91 and released from active duty on 19 Mar 91. The Army also considered mobilizing the 402nd's 4th Bn, 89th Regt [TX USAR], but did not mobilize this battalion.

[31] Mobilized on 25 Jan 91 and released from active duty on 20 Mar 91.

[32] Although apparently an infantry training unit, the 3-318 Regt provided non-infantry branch training to aviation and transportation IRR soldiers.

[33] Mobilized on 25 Jan 91, arrived at Fort Bliss on 28 Jan 91, and was released from active duty on 21 Mar 91.

[34] Mobilized on 22 Jan 91 and released from active duty on 31 Mar 91.

[35] Mobilized on 22 Jan 91 and released from active duty on 31 Mar 91.

➤ A portion of the 353rd Civil Affairs Command [NY USAR] deployed to Europe to coordinate host nation support for U.S. forces in Southwest Asia.

➤ About 30 percent of the 75th Maneuver Area Command [TX USAR] was mobilized to assist with the NTC training of the 48th Infantry Brigade(Mech)(+).

➤ The Army Reserve includes 24 TDA hospital units that are designed to augment existing Army hospitals in CONUS. All of these units were mobilized for Desert Storm, but in some instances not all of the personnel were mobilized with the unit. These units are commanded by full colonels or general officers, and were assigned to the Health Services Command:

Unit & State	Location During Desert Storm
1125th US Army Hosp [ME USAR]	Devens
1207th US Army Hosp [AL/GA USAR]	Benning
1208th US Army Hosp [NY USAR]	Monmouth
2289th US Army Hosp [DE USAR]	Dix
2290th US Army Hosp [MD USAR]	Walter Reed AMC[36]
2291st US Army Hosp [OH USAR]	Lee
3270th US Army Hosp [SC USAR]	Jackson
3271st US Army Hosp [SC/GA USAR]	Stewart
3273rd US Army Hosp [SC USAR]	Campbell
3274th US Army Hosp [NC USAR]	Bragg
3297th US Army Hosp [GA/NC/FL USAR]	Gordon
3343rd US Army Hosp [AL USAR]	Redstone
3344th US Army Hosp [FL USAR	Rucker
3345th US Army Hosp [AL USAR]	McClellan
4005th US Army Hosp [TX USAR]	Hood
4010th US Army Hosp [LA USAR]	Polk
5010th US Army Hosp [KY USAR]	Knox
5501st US Army Hosp [MN USAR	Sam Houston
5502nd US Army Hosp [CO USAR]	Fitzsimmons AMC[37]
5503rd US Army Hosp [MO USAR	Leonard Wood
6250th US Army Hosp [WA USAR]	Lewis
6251st US Army Hosp [AZ USAR]	Bliss
6252nd US Army Hosp [CA USAR]	Ord
6253rd US Army Hosp [CA USAR]	Carson

[36] Walter Reed Army Medical Center is in Washington, DC.

[37] Fitzsimmons Army Medical Center is in Aurora, CO.

➢ One of the specialized missions assigned to the Army Reserve is the support of unit deployments. The Army Reserve performs this mission using a variety of units, including deployment control units and transportation terminal units. These units are quite small, but are each commanded by a full colonel. DCUs assist deploying units at their home installations, while TTUs operate sea ports through which the units deploy. Listed here are the units that were called to active duty; other units contributed volunteers, or helped deploy Army units during their regularly-scheduled annual training:

Unit & State	Assisted Units In
1190th DCU [LA USAR]	Eastern part of CONUS Europe
1394th DCU [CA USAR]	Forts Hood, Riley & Carson USMC units at Camp Pendleton

Unit & State	Ports Operated[38]
1176th TTU [MD USAR]	Wilmington, NC Charleston, SC Bayonne, NJ Jacksonville, FL Savannah, GA
1181st TTU [MS USAR]	Jacksonville, FL Antwerp, Belgium Jacksonville, FL
1185th TTU [PA USAR]	Savannah, GA Wilmington, NC Newport News, VA Bayonne, NJ Sunny Point, NC Rotterdam, The Netherlands Bayonne, NJ

---

[38] The ports are listed in chronological order. Some units served at the same port at several different times, hence those ports are listed more than once.

Unit & State	Ports Operated[39]
1186th TTU [FL USAR]	Rotterdam, The Netherlands
1191st TTU [LA USAR]	Houston, TX New Orleans, LA Houston, TX
1192nd TTU [LA USAR]	Beaumont, TX

➤ Three strategic military intelligence detachments, each commanded by a full colonel, were mobilized for Operation Desert Storm. These units served at Fort Belvoir, VA, and were assigned to the Defense Intelligence Agency:

> 446th MI Det(Strat) [PA USAR]
> 480th MI Det(Strat) [IN USAR]
> 484th MI Det(Strat) [MA USAR]

➤ Other reserve component units were mobilized and deployed to Europe:[40]

> 300th MASH [TN ARNG]
> 45th Sta Hosp [WA USAR]
> 56th Sta Hosp [VA USAR]
> 44th Gen Hosp [WI USAR]
> 94th Gen Hosp [TX USAR]
> 328th Gen Hosp [UT USAR]

Major Commands That Should Have Been Mobilized, But Were Not

The following units had a long-term relationship with Third Army under the Capstone program and were supposed to mobilize and go to war with the Third Army. Despite years of training to perform this mission, these units were not called, and their place was taken by Active Army units:

---

[39] The ports are listed in chronological order. Some units served at the same port at several different times, hence those ports are listed more than once.

[40] One source states that the 300th Spt Gp(Area) [VA USAR] was mobilized and sent to Rotterdam, however it appears that this is incorrect.

Unit & State[41]	Mission Performed By
377th TAACOM[42] [LA USAR]	22nd SUPCOM
143rd Trans Cmd[43] [FL USAR	22nd SUPCOM[44]
220th MP Bde [MD USAR]	89th MP Bde
335th Sig Cmd[45] [GA USAR]	6th Theater Sig Cmd(Army)
164th ADA Bde [FL ARNG]	11th ADA Bde
336th Fin Cmd [LA USAR]	Third Army HQ and
	18th Corps Fin Gp(Abn)[46]

Finally, the 332nd Medical Brigade [TN USAR], which had a Capstone assignment to ARCENT as an EAC unit, was not mobilized to perform this mission, which was instead performed by the 3rd Medical Command.[47] Instead, the 332nd served as the VII Corps' medical brigade — a mission for which the 213th Medical Brigade [MS ARNG] had a Capstone assignment. The 213th was not mobilized, however. The 213th Medical Brigade was apparently one of several reserve component units that had a Capstone assignment with the VII Corps that was not mobilized for Desert Storm.

Notes:

* = Not normally assigned to the unit with which it mobilized.

➤ "Round-Out" was a long-standing program under which reserve component units were used to "flesh-out" Active Army divisions that lacked one of the three maneuver brigades they were supposed to have.

➤ All of the units that mobilized with the 48th Inf Bde(M), 155th Armd Bde, and 256th Inf Bde(M) were equipped with the M1 "Abrams" and the M2/M3 series "Bradley" Fighting Vehicle. The 256th Inf Bde(M) had just received its Bradleys in March 1990, however, and was still undergoing New Equipment Training at the time it was mobilized.

---

[41] State listed is location of unit's headquarters; some subordinate units were probably located in other states. Some other Third Army Capstone units that were smaller than commands or brigades were also not mobilized. Not surprisingly, the Army is not publicizing this aspect of Desert Storm, so information on these units is hard to come by.

[42] The 377th received an alert order on 23 Aug 90, but was taken off alert status on 27 Sep 90.

[43] The 143rd received an alert order, but it is unclear when this occurred and when the order was cancelled.

[44] See Chart 3, page 3-8, "Notes."

[45] The 335th never received an alert order. The decision to not mobilize this unit was made very early, o/a 11-12 Aug 90.

[46] See Chart 3, page 3-8, "Notes."

[47] The commander of the 3rd Med Cmd was an active duty full colonel, while the 332nd Med Bde was commanded by an Army Reserve brigadier general. As a result, the brigadier general commanding the 332nd was subordinate to the lower-ranking colonel who commanded the 3rd Med Cmd.

Chart 11

Major U.S. Army Combat Arms Units Stationed Outside the KTO At the Beginning Of Operation Desert Storm

In order to place the Gulf War in perspective it is necessary to consider the Army units that were active outside the Gulf during the war. This chart lists all of the major Army combat arms units that were active outside the KTO at the beginning of Operation Desert Storm, including the reserve component units that had been mobilized and were on active duty.

Unit	Location
HQ, I Corps[1]	Lewis
HQ, III Corps	Hood
HQ, V Corps	Germany
2nd Inf Div[2]	Korea
3rd Inf Div(Mech)(-)	Germany
4th Inf Div(Mech)(-)	Carson
5th Inf Div(Mech)(-)	Polk
6th Inf Div(Lt)(-)	Alaska
7th Inf Div(Lt)	Ord
8th Inf Div(Mech)	Germany

[1] Served as the Army's contingency corps while the XVIII Abn Corps was in SWA.

[2] The 2nd Inf Div used a hybrid organization that included tank, mechanized infantry, and air assault infantry units, along with both towed and self-propelled field artillery. The 2nd Inf Div was also on the small side, having only seven maneuver battalions (compared to 11 for an armored or mechanized division), but had extra field artillery (4.3 battalions, as opposed to 3.3 in an armored or mechanized division). Thus, the 2nd Inf Div had about 80 percent of the combat power of a standard heavy division. Nonetheless, I treat it here and in the other charts as a full-strength division, not a division(-).

Order of Battle

Unit	Location
10th Mtn Div(Lt Inf)(-)	Drum
25th Inf Div(Lt)	Hawaii
1st Bde, 1st Armd Div	Germany
11th Armd Cav Regt	Germany
6th Cav Bde(Air Cbt)[3]	Hood
155th Armd Bde(+) [MS/TX ARNG]	Hood[4]
177th Armd Bde(-)[5]	Irwin
48th Inf Bde(Mech)(+) [GA/SC ARNG]	Irwin
256th Inf Bde(Mech)(+) [LA/AL ARNG	Hood[6]
193rd Inf Bde(-)	Panama Canal Zone
199th Inf Bde(Mtzd)[7]	Lewis
Berlin Bde	Berlin
56th FA Cmd(-)[8]	Germany
17th FA Bde	Germany
41st FA Bde	Germany
72nd FA Bde	Germany
214th FA Bde	Sill
HQ, 32nd AADCOM	Germany
10th ADA Bde(-)	Germany
31st ADA Bde(-)	Hood
35th ADA Bde(-)	Lewis
69th ADA Bde(-)	Germany
94th ADA Bde(-)	Germany
108th ADA Bde	Germany

---

[3] One of the mysteries of the Gulf War is why the Army did not deploy the 6th Cav Bde, its preeminent attack helicopter unit. The 6th was apparently alerted for movement, but the Army cancelled the orders when it became apparent that this unit had substantial equipment readiness problems, supposedly due to a severe wind storm that had devastated Fort Hood in 1989.

[4] See Chart 10, Footnote 12.

[5] The 177th served as the OpFor at the NTC. Because this brigade would have been heavily involved in the training of Army units that were tasked to deploy, the 177th could not be counted as a deployment asset.

[6] See Chart 10, Footnote 15.

[7] See Footnote 10.

[8] The 56th was equipped with the Pershing II Missile, a nuclear-only weapons system. Accordingly, there was no possibility the 56th would deploy to the Gulf. Moreover, pursuant to the Intermediate-Range Nuclear Forces (INF) Treaty, the 56th terminated Pershing Missile operations in September 1990 and thereafter focused its efforts upon inactivation. The last Pershing launcher left Germany on 17 Apr 91 and the 56th FA Cmd was inactivated on 31 May 91.

Unit	Location
75th Ranger Regt(Abn)	Benning, Stewart & Lewis
1st SF Gp(Abn)	Lewis, Okinawa & Korea
7th SF Gp(Abn)	Bragg & Panama
20th SF Gp(Abn) [AL/FL/MS/MD ARNG][9]	Bragg

Notes:

➤ By the time Desert Storm was initiated, the Army had inactivated the following units following its high-water mark during the height of the Cold War in the late 1980s:

> HQ and 2nd Bde, 2nd Armd Div
> HQ and 1st & 2nd Bdes, 9th Inf Div(Mtzd)[10]
> 2nd Bde, 4th Inf Div(M)
> 194th Armd Bde(-)[11]

In addition, some U.S. Army units in Germany were in the process of being inactivated and were, therefore, unavailable for combat operations in January 1991. Included among these was the 3rd Bde, 1st Inf Div(M). For this reason, and because part of this brigade deployed to the Gulf without its equipment to perform a support/logistics mission, see Chart 4, page 4-28, the 3rd Bde, 1st Inf Div(M) is not included on this chart.

➤ Other units deployed significant elements to the KTO as fillers or as WSRO units. For example, the 8th Inf Div(M) deployed the 4th Bn, 34th Armor and 5th Bn(Vulc/Chap/Stinger), 3rd ADA with the 3rd Armd Div, and the 2nd Bn(155 SP), 29th FA with the 42nd FA Bde. In addition, the 8th Inf Div(M) deployed at least 12 tank platoons — equivalent to a tank battalion — as WSRO units. See Chart 12.

---

[9] Did not arrive at Fort Bragg until 23 Feb 91. See Chart 10, Footnote 18.

[10] The 3rd Bde, 9th Inf Div(Mtzd) was reflagged as the 199th Inf Bde(Mtzd) on 16 Feb 91. HQ, 9th Inf Div(Mtzd) remained active, on paper, until 15 Dec 91, however this division effectively ceased to exist when the 3rd Bde was reflagged. Accordingly, HQ, 9th Inf Div(Mtzd) is not included in the totals reflected in this chart.

[11] When the 194th was inactivated one battalion task force was retained on active duty.

Chart 12

U.S. Army WSRO And SCT Units

Weapon System Replacement Operations (WSRO) and Squad/Crew/Team (SCT) units were intended to be used to replace battlefield losses. They consisted of pre-existing, trained units or crews, rather than individual replacements. See text, pages 7 and 8, for more details on this program. Most of these units came from USAREUR.

Part 1: WSRO/SCT Units By Type

WSRO Units	WSRO Units Contributed By	Gaining Command	Notes
29 Tank Platoons:			
12 Tank Plts	USAREUR[1]	VII Corps	[2]
3 Tank Plts	USAREUR[3]	24th ID(M)	[4]
14 Tank Plts	USAREUR[5]	ARCENT(?)	

---

[1] VII Corps organized its WSRO units into TF Jayhawk. See Page 12-4, "Notes." Of the 12 tank platoons in TF Jayhawk, six came from the 2-68 Armor, 8th Inf Div(M), four came from the 3-77 Armor, 8th Inf Div(M), and the unit that contributed the final two platoons is unknown. Apparently Cos A-C of the 2-68 Armor each contributed two platoons. One of the platoons from B Co was the 3rd Plt. The platoons from C Co were the 2nd & 3rd Plts.

[2] One of the platoons from the 3-77 Armor was attached to the 1st Armd Div and saw combat after it replaced a unit that had sustained casualties.

[3] Two of these platoons came from Co D, 2-68 Armor, 8th Inf Div(M). The unit that contributed the final platoon is unknown.

[4] One of the WSRO platoons was reportedly used to provide security to HQ, 24th Inf Div(M).

[5] It is unknown which specific unit contributed these platoons.

Part 1: WSRO/SCT Units By Type (continued)

WSRO Units	WSRO Units Contributed By	Gaining Command	Notes
4 Scout Platoons:			
1 Scout Plt[6]	11th ACR	3rd ACR	[7]
3 Scout Plts[8]	11th ACR	ARCENT	[9]
27 Mech Inf Platoons:			
9 Mech Inf Plts	USAREUR	VII Corps[10]	
2 Mech Inf Plts	USAREUR	24th ID(M)	
16 Mech Inf Plts	USAREUR	ARCENT(?)	

SCT Units	SCT Units Contributed By	Gaining Command	Notes
27 Lt Inf Squads	Various[11]	XVIII Abn Corps(?)	[12]
24 SP 155mm FA Crews	USAREUR[13]	?	
8 SP 203mm FA Crews	USAREUR	?	
9 MLRS Crews	?	?	
8 Towed 105mm FA Crews	?	XVIII Abn Corps(?)	
8 Towed 155mm FA Crews	9th ID(Mtzd)[14]	XVIII Abn Corps(?)	

---

[6] This was apparently the 1st Plt, Trp E, 2/11 ACR.

[7] Provided security for the 3rd ACR TOC, fuel trucks, and EPWs.

[8] These were apparently the 3rd Plt, Trp E, 2/11 ACR, and the 1st & 3rd Plts, Trp K, 3/11 ACR.

[9] Remained at King Khalid Military City during the war.

[10] VII Corps organized its WSRO units into TF Jayhawk. See Page 12-4, "Notes."

[11] These units were apparently contributed by the 10th Mtn Div(Lt Inf), 25th Inf Div(Lt), and 199th Inf Bde(Mtzd).

[12] Four of these platoons apparently provided local security to TF 2-1 ADA. See Chart 4, Footnote 6.

[13] Eight of these crews apparently came from the 4-29 FA(155 SP), 8th Inf Div(M).

[14] These crews came from the 1-11 FA(155 T) and/or the 3-11 FA(155 T).

Part 2: The Designations Of WSRO Units

WSRO Units	Owning Command	Gaining Command	Notes
Tank Platoons			
1st Plt, Co B, 2-32 Armor	3rd AD	?	[15]
(1) Plt, 2-64 Armor	3rd ID(M)	ARCENT(?)	
(2) Plts, Co A, 2-68 Armor	8th ID(M)	VII Corps	
(2) Plts, Co B, 2-68 Armor	8th ID(M)	VII Corps	[16]
(2) Plts, Co C, 2-68 Armor	8th ID(M)	VII Corps	[17]
(2) Plts, Co D, 2-68 Armor	8th ID(M)	24th ID(M)	
(4) Plts, 4-69 Armor	8th ID(M)	ARCENT(?)	[18]
(4) Plts, 3-77 Armor	8th ID(M)	VII Corps	
Scout Platoons			
(2) Plts, Trp E, 2/11 ACR	11th ACR		[19]
(2) Plts, Trp K, 3/11 ACR	11th ACR	ARCENT	[20]

Notes:

➢ WSRO units consisted of personnel and major end items such as vehicles. SCT units had only personnel and minor pieces of equipment (no major end items), either because this type of unit was not authorized major end items (e.g., light infantry) or because the end items had not been issued to the unit (e.g., field artillery).

➢ The WSRO and SCT units were the equivalent of:

  2 Tank Bns equipped with M1A1 series MBTs (116 M1A1s)
  2 Mechanized Infantry Bns equipped with M2 series IFVs (108 M2s)
  4 Scout Platoons equipped with M3 series CFVs (24 M3 CFVs)
  1 Light Infantry Bn
  1 SP 155mm FA Bn (24 M109A2/A3s)
  1 SP 203mm FA Btry (8 M110A2s)
  1 MLRS Btry (9 MLRSs)
  1+ Towed 105mm Btry (8 M102s)
  1 Towed 155mm Btry (8 M198s)

This is the equivalent of two brigades of combat troops.

---

[15] This platoon was probably a WSRO unit. It arrived in the KTO in mid-February 1991. See Chart 4, Footnote 13.

[16] One of these was the 3rd Plt.

[17] These were the 2nd & 3rd Plts.

[18] Each line company contributed one platoon. The platoon from Co D was 3rd Plt.

[19] The 1st Plt was assigned to 3rd ACR while the 3rd Plt was assigned to ARCENT.

[20] These were the 1st & 3rd Plts.

Order of Battle

➢ The smallest units for which the Army awards campaign participation credit are companies, and separate detachments and platoons (those not assigned to a company). Accordingly, platoons that were detached from their parent company to participate in Desert Storm as WSRO units are not eligible to receive campaign participation credit, and the Army is doing nothing to publicize or record the Gulf War service of these WSRO units. As a result, it has been extremely difficult to identify WSRO units that served in the Gulf.

➢ The VII Corps organized its WSRO units into a provisional battalion called Task Force Jayhawk, which assisted the corps with rear area security. Task Force Jayhawk was formed on 6 Feb 91 and was assigned to the 7th Pers Gp. The task force consisted of 48 M1A1 series tanks, 36 M2A2 IFVs, and their crews, enough to equip 12 tank platoons and nine mechanized infantry platoons (i.e., the fighting elements of four tank and three mechanized infantry ompanies). Platoons from this task force provided security for Log Base Echo and possibly the VII Corps main and rear CPs. In addition, one tank platoon was OPCON to the 207th MI Bde for two weeks to provide security to units that operated unmanned aerial vehicles (UAV) that were used to gather intelligence. During the ground war TF Jayhawk dispatched four M1A1s to the 1st Armd Div, two M2A2s to the 1st Cav Div(-), and one M2A2 to the 1st Inf Div(M) to replace combat losses. After the cease fire, the task force sent four M2A2s to the 3rd Armd Div and eight M2A2s to the 3rd Bde, 2nd Armd Div.

➢ The 2nd Bn, 68th Armor, 8th Inf Div(M) had more than half of its tank crews in the Gulf as WSRO units. This battalion and its subordinate units are not eligible for campaign participation credit for Desert Storm, however, because of the Army's policy of not awarding campaign participation credit to platoons

➢ The 2nd Bn(AH), 25th Avn, a 10th Mtn Div(Lt Inf) unit at Fort Drum, deployed most of its AH-1F Cobra Attack Helicopter and OH-58 Kiowa Observation Helicopter crews to the Gulf as individual crews pursuant to the SCT program. It is unclear how many crews deployed and the command(s) to which they were attached.

➢ USAREUR deployed ten OH-58 crews as SCT units.

➢ The 5th Bn(AH), 229th Avn supported the WSRO/SCT program by providing training to aviation crews that deployed to SWA as SCT assets. The 5th Bn(AH), 229th Avn, however, was not a WSRO/SCT unit. See Chart 4, Footnote 77.

Chart 13

Selected U.S. Army Equipment

Tanks

While the Army always fights as a combined arms team, in different situations different branches dominate the Army's operations. Desert Storm was dominated by the Army's armor units, and was the only conflict since World War II for which that has been true. Army armor units took three basic types of tanks into combat in Desert Storm: (1) the M1 "Abrams" Main Battle Tank, armed with a 105mm main gun; (2) the M1A1 Abrams, armed with a 120mm main gun; and (3) the M551 "Sheridan" Armored Reconnaissance/Airborne Assault Vehicle (in reality, a light tank), armed with a 152mm "Shillelagh" dual purpose gun and missile launcher.

M1 and M1A1 "Abrams" Main Battle Tanks

The M1 Abrams was developed in the 1970s as a replacement for the M60 series Main Battle Tank. The M60 had been introduced in the early 1960s and had culminated with the M60A3, which entered service in the late 1970s. The M1 Abrams was fielded in U.S. Army armor units in Germany in 1982. By the time Desert Shield began, the Abrams had been fielded in four versions: the M1, the IPM1, the M1A1, and the M1A1HA.

The basic M1, which was in production from 1980 through 1985, was equipped with a 105mm main gun. The IPM1, or "Improved Performance" version, was in production from 1984 through 1986. The IPM1 mounted the same 105mm main gun but had better armor protection and a host of other minor improvements. The M1A1, which was in production from 1985 through 1988, had a 120mm main gun. Finally, the most advanced version of the M1 was the M1A1HA, for "Heavy Armor."[1] This tank went into production in 1988 and had depleted uranium armor that was virtually impenetrable.

The Army conducted a massive in-theater upgrade of its tanks before the ground war commenced. Almost all of the units that had deployed from CONUS had been equipped with the 105mm-armed M1 or IPM1, rather than the 120mm-armed M1A1 or M1A1HA, as the Army had been fielding the new M1A1 primarily in its forward-deployed units in Germany.[2] All but two of these tank battalions were re-equipped with 120mm-armed M1A1 series tanks for Desert Storm.[3]

As part of this effort, the Army created a new version of the M1 by upgrading M1A1s in-theater to the M1A1HA standard. This upgrade involved five modifications to the basic M1A1, including adding armored plate to the outside of the turret and improving the optical systems. These upgraded tanks were apparently known as the "Modified M1A1."[4]

Twenty-nine of the Active Army's 49 then-active tank battalions fought in Operation Desert Storm.[5] All but three of the 29 tank battalions in SWA were equipped with 120mm-armed M1A1, Modified M1A1, or M1A1HA tanks. Two of the 29 tank battalions in SWA were equipped with the basic version of the M1 with a 105mm main gun. Thus, 90 percent of the Army's tank units in the Gulf had 120mm-armed M1A1 series tanks, and another seven percent had 105mm-armed M1s.

All six of the armored cavalry squadrons assigned to the 2nd and 3rd Armored Cavalry Regiments were equipped with the M1A1HA. Although not authorized by the TOE, two of the five heavy division cavalry squadrons in the Gulf had M1A1 series tanks.[6]

---

[1] There was also another version called the "M1A1 Common." This version was used exclusively by the Marine Corps. See Chart 24, page 24-2.

[2] The first M1 series Main Battle Tanks arrived in Saudi Arabia in late August 1990. These tanks belonged to the 2nd Bde, 24th Inf Div(M)'s 1-64 Armor and 3-69 Armor. The Army deployed ten M1-equipped tank battalions and four IPM1-equipped tank battalions from CONUS, as follows: 24th Inf Div(M)(-), three IPM1 battalions; 197th Inf Bde(M), one IPM1 battalion; 1st Cav Div(-), four M1 battalions; 1st Bde, 2nd Armd Div, two M1 battalions; and 1st Inf Div(M)(-), four M1 battalions. The only unit that deployed from CONUS with the M1A1 was the 3rd Armd Cav Regt, which arrived in September 1990. The 3rd Armd Cav Regt was the first unit to bring M1A1 series tanks to the KTO.

[3] Only the 1st Inf Div(M)'s 3-37 Armor and 4-37 Armor took 105mm-armed M1s into combat. No IPM1s served in Desert Storm.

[4] I abbreviate this as "M1A1(Mod)". It is not clear what the Army's official abbreviation is.

[5] The 49 tank battalion total does not include (1) an Active Army tank battalion at Fort Irwin that, as part of the OpFor at the NTC, was responsible for training other Army units, and (2) six National Guard tank battalions that had been federalized in late 1990.

[6] These were the 1-4 Cav, 1st Inf Div(M), and the 2-4 Cav, 24th Inf Div(M). See Appendix D, pages D-10 and D-11, for

No M60 series Main Battle Tanks fought with Army tank or cavalry units in Operation Desert Storm.[7] Several M60 derivatives served during Desert Storm, however, including the M728 Combat Engineer Vehicle, the M60 Armored Vehicle Launching Bridge (AVLB), and the Armored Vehicle Launched MICLIC (AVLM).[8]

U.S. Army M1 Series Tank Battalions In Combat During Desert Storm

Unit[9]	M1	M1A1	M1A1(Mod)	M1A1HA	Total
1st Armd Div		3	2	1	6
3rd Armd Div		3		3	6
1st Cav Div(-)			4		4
1st Inf Div(M)	2		2	2	6
24th Inf Div(M)			4		4
1st Bde, 2nd Armd Div			2		2
Total	2	6	14	6	28

Desert Storm was the Abrams' combat debut, as none served in Grenada or Panama. During Desert Storm, the Army's M1 and M1A1 series tanks achieved an operational readiness rate in excess of 90 percent.

The 105mm-armed M1 and IPM1 are no longer in service with the Active Army, having been replaced by M1A1 series tanks and an improved version, the M1A2, which began to enter service in 1995. The M1 and/or IPM1 continue to serve in the Army National Guard, however.[10]

M551 "Sheridan" Armored Reconnaissance/Airborne Assault Vehicle

The M551 was introduced in the mid-1960s as a dual-purpose light tank for cavalry units and airborne light tank for airborne forces. The M551 suffered from

---

details.

[7] However, nine M60A3s deployed to SWA during Desert Shield with Trp D, 4th Cav, 197th Inf Bde(M). These tanks were replaced by the M1A1(Mod) before the ground war began. The Army then probably provided the left over M60A3s to the Marine Corps. See Chart 24, page 24-2 and Footnote 4.

[8] The AVLM consisted of two MICLIC launchers mounted on an AVLB in lieu of the bridge. The MICLIC, or Mine Clearing Line Charge, was a mine clearing device. The AVLM was a field expedient created by the 1st Inf Div(M) during Desert Storm.

[9] These figures include the 3rd Bde, 3rd Inf Div(M) within the totals for the 1st Armd Div; the 3rd Bde, 2nd Armd Div within the totals for the 1st Inf Div(M); and the 197th Inf Bde(M) within the totals for the 24th Inf Div(M).

[10] The last unit in the U.S. military (Army and Marine Corps, active and reserve) to use M60 series tanks was the 1-635 Armor [KS ARNG], which traded its M60A3s for IPM1s in May 1997.

numerous shortcomings, however, and by 1990 was only in service with one tactical unit: the 3rd Bn(Abn), 73rd Armor, the 82nd Airborne Division's airborne light tank battalion. This battalion deployed to SWA with its parent division, via C-5 aircraft, during the early days of Desert Shield. These Sheridans were the first U.S. armored vehicles to arrive in Saudi Arabia and were probably the only armored vehicles to deploy by air.

The M551 saw limited combat in Vietnam. No Sheridans served in Grenada, but a company's worth saw combat in Panama. The Sheridans that served in Desert Storm were the M551A1(TTS), the most advanced version of the Sheridan. With the A1 version, the Army added a laser range finder. In late 1990, the Army further modified a battalion's worth of M551A1s by adding a thermal sight from the M60A3 MBT, and this version was designated the M551A1(TTS).[11] In November and December 1990, these M551A1(TTS) Sheridans replaced the M551A1s that the 3rd Bn(Abn), 73rd Armor had deployed to SWA in August.

The 3rd Bn(Abn), 73rd Armor saw relatively limited action in Desert Storm. For example, it is unclear if any of the Sheridan's long range Shillelagh heavy antitank missiles were fired in combat during Desert Storm.[12] Desert Storm was the Sheridan's final combat action, as the 82nd Airborne Division's airborne tank battalion was inactivated in July 1997.

Bradley Fighting Vehicle

The Army introduced the Bradley Fighting Vehicle in 1983 as a replacement for the M113 series Armored Personnel Carrier in mechanized infantry and cavalry units. The Bradley comes in two types, the M2 Infantry Fighting Vehicle (IFV) and M3 Cavalry Fighting Vehicle (CFV).[13] The M2 IFV served as the carrier for the infantry squad and as a command vehicle in mechanized infantry units. The M3 CFV served as a scout vehicle and command vehicle in heavy division cavalry squadrons and regimental armored cavalry squadrons, and as a scout vehicle in the scout platoons of most tank and mechanized infantry battalions.[14] Of the 19 mechanized infantry

---

[11] "TTS" stands for "Tank Thermal Sight." The M60A3 with a thermal sight is designated "M60A3(TTS)".

[12] The Army Missile Command's history of Desert Storm states no Shillelaghs were fired. According to the commander of the 3-73 Armor during Desert Storm, however, one Shillelagh was fired in combat.

[13] The principal difference is that the M2 IFV carries more dismounts, while the M3 CFV carries more ammunition. The M2 IFV carries nine soldiers (track commander/squad leader, gunner, driver, and six dismounts) while the M3 CFV carries five soldiers (track commander, gunner, driver, and two dismounts). In addition, on the earlier versions the M2 had six firing ports for individual weapons, whereas the M3 had none. On the M2A2, these firing ports were reduced from six to two.

[14] See Appendix D, pages D-5 and D-6, and Footnote 10.

battalions in the Gulf, all but two were equipped with the Bradley.[15] Thus, 90 percent of the Army's mechanized infantry in the Gulf was equipped with the Bradley. All six of the regimental armored cavalry squadrons and all five of the heavy division cavalry squadrons used Bradleys.[16]

Desert Storm was the Bradley's combat debut, as none served in Grenada or Panama. The Bradley achieved an operational readiness rate during the ground war in excess of 90 percent. By the time Desert Storm began, three versions of the Bradley had been fielded: the original version (known informally as the "A0"), the A1 version (first fielded in 1987), and the A2 version (first fielded in 1988). The M2 IFV and M3 CFV were both fielded in all three versions.

As with the Abrams, during Desert Shield the Army upgraded its Bradley force in-theater by issuing early-deploying CONUS-based units, which typically had early versions of the Bradley, with the more advanced later versions. As part of this upgrade effort, the 2nd Armored Cavalry Regiment was primarily issued M2A2 Infantry Fighting Vehicles instead of the M3 series Cavalry Fighting Vehicles it was authorized. Of the 2,200 BFVs in SWA during the ground war, almost half were A2s and another third were A1s. As a result of these force modernization efforts, the following units went to war equipped with the listed version(s) of the Bradley:[17]

1st Armored Division
    Primarily M2A2/M3A2
    Four mechanized infantry battalions and one cavalry squadron

3rd Armored Division
    Primarily M2A1/M3A1
    Four mechanized infantry battalions and one cavalry squadron

1st Cavalry Division(-)
    Primarily M2A2/M3A2
    Two mechanized infantry battalions and one cavalry squadron(+)

---

[15] These were the 197th Inf Bde(M)'s 1-18 Inf(M) and 2-18 Inf(M), which used the M113 series APC.

[16] However, one cavalry troop was equipped with M113 series APCs and M901 ITVs. This was Trp D, 4th Cav, which served with the 197th Inf Bde(M) and the 2-4 Cav(-) in the 24th Inf Div(M).

[17] These entries include the 3rd Bde, 3rd Inf Div(M) with the 1st Armd Div, and the 3rd Bde, 2nd Armd Div with the 1st Inf Div(M). The 197th Inf Bde(M) was part of the 24th Inf Div(M), but had M113 series APCs in lieu of Bradleys.

Order of Battle

1st Infantry Division(Mech)
Primarily M2A0[18]
Three mechanized infantry battalions and one cavalry squadron

24th Infantry Division(Mech)
Primarily M2A1/M3A1, with some M2A0
Three mechanized infantry battalions and one cavalry squadron(-)

1st Brigade, 2nd Armored Division
Primarily M2A2, with some M2A1 and M3A0
One mechanized infantry battalion

2nd Armored Cavalry Regiment
Primarily M2A2, with some M3A2
Three armored cavalry squadrons

3rd Armored Cavalry Regiment
Primarily M3A2, with some M2A2[19]
Three armored cavalry squadrons

The Bradley continues to serve in the same role in today's Army, primarily in a modernized version, the M2A2(ODS) and M3A2(ODS), which incorporated improvements based upon Operation Desert Storm. All Active Army mechanized infantry and cavalry units have now been equipped with the Bradley, although some National Guard units continue to use the M113 series APC.

Infantry

In addition to the Bradley, the Army's mechanized infantry units took three major weapon systems into combat in Operation Desert Storm: (1) the M113 series Armored Personnel Carrier, (2) the M901A1 Improved TOW Vehicle; and (3) the M106 series self-propelled 4.2" mortar.

---

[18] The 1st Inf Div(M) was the only division that took a large number of the original "M2A0" version of the Bradley into combat. At least one 1st Inf Div(M) unit, the 1-4 Cav, had M3A2s, however.

[19] The 3rd Armd Cav Regt had 108 M3A2 CFVs and 14 M2A2 IFVs, which made it overstrength by six Bradleys.

M113 Series Armored Personnel Carrier

The M113 series APC entered service in the early 1960s and saw extensive combat in Vietnam. The M113 did not serve in Grenada, but a mechanized infantry battalion equipped with M113s saw combat in Panama. In Desert Storm, the M113 served as the armored personnel carrier for two mechanized infantry battalions in the 197th Infantry Brigade(Mech) that had not upgraded to the Bradley before they deployed during Desert Shield,[20] and in a variety of support roles in all heavy units, such as maintenance section track, engineer squad carrier, and medic track. The most modern version of the M113 to see service in the Gulf was the M113A3, which the Army began fielding in 1986. The M113A2 version, which the Army began introducing in the early 1980s, also served in Desert Storm.

At the time of Desert Storm, many Active Army mechanized infantry units stationed outside SWA continued to use M113 series APCs because they had yet to be upgraded with Bradleys. Since then, all Active Army mechanized infantry units have received Bradleys as their squad carriers, although the M113 continues to serve in this role in the Army National Guard. The M113 continues to perform the many supporting roles that it did during Desert Storm, however, in both the Active Army and the reserve components.

M901 Improved TOW Vehicle

The M901 Improved TOW Vehicle (ITV) is an antitank version of the M113 APC which mounts a double-barrelled launcher for the TOW antitank missile on an articulated device carried on a rotating cupola. This allows the ITV to hide behind, for example, a ridge, with only its TOW launcher elevated above the ridge to engage the enemy. The ITV was first fielded in Europe in 1980 and did not see action in Grenada. A handful of ITVs served in Panama. The basic M901 was based upon the M113A2. An improved version that was able to fire the TOW 2 missile, the M901A1, entered production in 1984. Presumably all of the ITVs that served in the Gulf were M901A1s.

The ITV was an interim solution that was needed to supplement the antitank capability of mechanized infantry units equipped with the M113 series APC. The ITV served little purpose in a Bradley-equipped battalion, however, as every Bradley had its own double-barreled TOW launcher. Moreover, the ITV had reliability problems and a high center of gravity that limited its mobility.

---

[20] These were the 1-18 Inf(M) and 2-18 Inf(M). The M113 also served as a scout track in Trp D, 4th Cav, which served with the 197th Inf Bde(M) and the 2-4 Cav(-) in the 24th Inf Div(M). It is unclear why these units were not upgraded with Bradleys before Desert Storm began.

Order of Battle

The ITV played a relatively limited role in Desert Storm, as it was a defensive weapon that was out of place once the Army transitioned from the defensive mindset of the early days of Desert Shield to the offensive focus that we adopted for Desert Storm. Furthermore, the ITVs that were present had great difficulty keeping up with the more mobile Bradleys. Indeed, the VII Corps mechanized infantry units that deployed from Germany did not even bring their ITVs with them.[21] The ITV has now been phased out of the Active Army, but is probably still in service with Army National Guard units that have not yet received Bradleys to replace their M113 series APCs.

M106 Series Self-Propelled 4.2" Mortar

The M106 series self-propelled 4.2" (107mm) mortar (typically called a "mortar track") is an infantry-branch weapon system that served in the mortar platoon of tank and mechanized infantry battalions, and in the mortar section of armored cavalry troops assigned to armored cavalry regiments and cavalry troops assigned to heavy division cavalry squadrons. The M106 has been in service since at least 1965 and saw combat in Vietnam and apparently in Panama, but not in Grenada. It appears that all of the M106s that served in Desert Storm were the M106A2 model. Desert Storm was probably the M106's last combat, as it is being replaced by the M1064, a 120mm mortar on an M113 series vehicle. The M1064 entered service in 1995 and fielding to the Active Army was scheduled to be completed in 1998.

Field Artillery

Army field artillery units took a variety of old and new weapon systems to war in the Persian Gulf. For some of these weapons, Desert Storm turned out to be their last opportunity to fire in anger with the United States Army. For others, Desert Storm was their baptism by fire. Army field artillery units used the following six weapon systems in Desert Storm: (1) the M102 towed 105mm howitzer; (2) the M198 towed 155mm howitzer; (3) the M109 series self-propelled 155mm howitzer; (4) the M110 series self-propelled 203mm howitzer; (5) the M270 MLRS; and (6) the Army Tactical Missile System (ATACMS).

---

[21] Basically, only the following units brought ITVs to the Gulf: 24th Inf Div(M)(-), three mechanized infantry battalions; 197th Inf Bde(M), two mechanized infantry battalions and one cavalry troop; 1st Cav Div(-), two mechanized infantry battalions; 1st Bde, 2nd Armd Div, one mechanized infantry battalion; and 1st Inf Div(M)(-), two mechanized infantry battalions. One (or perhaps a few) battalion scout platoons that deployed from Europe were equipped with M113s and ITVs, although the one scout platoon that definitely brought ITVs to the Gulf (1-37 Armor, 1st Armd Div) exchanged them for HMMWVs before the ground war began.

M102 Towed 105mm Howitzer

The M102 towed 105mm howitzer was an old system that entered service in the mid-1960s and first saw combat in Vietnam. The M102 also served in Grenada and Panama, and was the only field artillery weapon system to serve with the Army in those two conflicts. In Desert Storm, the M102 provided direct support artillery fires in the 82nd Airborne Division and 101st Airborne Division(Air Aslt). Thus, the M102 served in six of the Army's 47 field artillery battalion equivalents,[22] and comprised 13 percent of the Army's field artillery force in the Gulf. The Army began fielding a replacement for the M102, the M119 towed 105mm howitzer, in 1989. No M119s made it to the Gulf, however. Since Desert Storm, the M119 has completely replaced the M102 in the Active Army, although the M102 continues to serve in the National Guard.

M198 Towed 155mm Howitzer

The M198 towed 155mm howitzer was a relatively new system, having been fielded in the late 1970s to replace the M114 towed 155mm howitzer. The M198 did not serve with the Army in Grenada or Panama, however, due to the fact that heavy artillery was not required in those conflicts. In Desert Storm, the M198 equipped three battalions in the 18th Field Artillery Brigade(Abn), a corps artillery unit, and comprised six percent of the Army's field artillery force in the Gulf.[23] The M198 continues to serve in the same role today.

M109 Series Self-Propelled 155mm Howitzer

The M109 series self-propelled 155mm howitzer was the workhorse of Army field artillery in Desert Storm. First fielded in the early 1960s, the M109 saw a significant amount of combat in Vietnam, but did not serve in Grenada or Panama.

In Desert Storm, the M109 served as the direct support field artillery weapon system in all Army heavy brigades and armored cavalry regiments, a total of 18 battalion equivalents. In addition, the M109 equipped seven of the Army's 20 corps artillery battalions and thus constituted just over one-third of the Army's corps artillery firing units. Overall, the M109 was the most common Army field artillery system in the

---

[22] This counts the six howitzer batteries assigned to the 2nd and 3rd Armd Cav Regts as two battalion equivalents, and the six divisional MLRS batteries as another two battalion equivalents. See Chart 33, Footnote 6. This only counts the Army's field artillery firing units, however; target acquisition units are not included in this total. The Marines used the M101A1 towed 105mm howitzer rather than the M102. See Chart 24, pages 24-6 and 24-7.

[23] The M198 was far away the most important Marine Corps field artillery system deployed to SWA, however. Almost 85 percent of Marine field artillery units were equipped with the M198. See Chart 24, page 24-7.

Gulf, equipping 25 battalion equivalents,[24] just over 50 percent of the Army's total field artillery force in the Gulf.

The Army's M109s fired over 43,000 rounds during Desert Storm. The M109s that served in the Gulf were the M109A2 and M109A3 versions. More modern versions of the M109, the M109A5 and M109A6 "Paladin," continue to serve in the same roles in the Active Army today.

M110 Series Self-Propelled 203mm Howitzer

The M110 series self-propelled 203mm (eight inch) howitzer was an old system that has seen substantial Army service. First fielded in the early 1960s, the M110 saw a significant amount of combat in Vietnam, but did not serve in Grenada or Panama.

In Desert Storm, the M110 served strictly as corps artillery.[25] The M110 equipped six battalions, which constituted 30 percent of corps artillery firing units and 13 percent of the Army's total field artillery force in the Gulf.[26] The M110s that served in the Gulf were the M110A2 version, which entered service in the early 1980s.

Desert Storm was the M110's last war, as it left Active Army service in 1996 and was phased out of the Army National Guard in 1997. The M110 has been replaced by the MLRS.

M270 Multiple Launch Rocket System (MLRS)

MLRS was a relatively new system that received its baptism of fire during Desert Storm. It was first fielded in 1983, and did not serve in Panama. In Desert Storm, MLRS served in the general support battery of heavy divisions and in corps

---

[24] This consisted of 15 battalions DS to heavy brigades; two battalion equivalents organic to the 2nd and 3rd Armd Cav Regts; one battalion attached to the 3rd Armd Cav Regt; and seven battalions of corps artillery. One of the corps artillery battalions was an Army National Guard unit. Thus, the National Guard contributed just over five percent of the U.S. Army M109 units that served in Desert Storm. The Marines also used the M109, but for them it was a relatively minor player, equipping only ten percent of Marine field artillery units. See Chart 24, page 24-7.

[25] Prior to a major reorganization of the Army in the mid-1980s, the M110 had also equipped a general support field artillery battalion in each heavy division, and one of the general support batteries in the old conventional infantry division. The M110 was replaced in the GS role in heavy divisions by an MLRS battery. The conventional infantry division was replaced by a light infantry division, and the GS role in that unit was assumed by the M198 towed 155mm howitzer.

[26] Four of these six battalions were Army National Guard units, however only two of the four Guard battalions actually engaged the enemy during Desert Storm. See Chart 4, Footnote 105. Thus, the National Guard contributed two-thirds of the M110 units that served with the Army in Desert Storm. Although used by the Marines, the M110 equipped only five percent of Marine field artillery units in SWA. See Chart 24, page 24-8.

artillery units. MLRS equipped the equivalent of seven battalions,[27] which constituted 15 percent of the Army's total field artillery force in the Gulf.

The Army's then-only reserve component MLRS unit, the 1st Bn, 158th FA [OK ARNG] served with great success in Desert Storm.[28] Indeed, the record of the most MLRS rockets fired by a single battery is held by Battery A, 1st Bn, 158th FA, 142nd Field Artillery Brigade, which fired 699 rockets during Desert Storm. Battery A, 21st FA, 1st Cavalry Division(-) is in second place with 550 rockets. Battery A, 21st FA was also the first unit to fire MLRS in combat, which occurred during an artillery raid on 13 Feb 91. MLRS continues to serve in the same roles in today's Army.

Army Tactical Missile System (ATACMS)

The Army Tactical Missile System was a brand new weapon system that had just completed its operational testing in June 1990. The ATACMS is fired from the same tracked launcher that fires the MLRS, but during the Gulf War most MLRS units lacked the ability to fire ATACMS. The Army had a single ATACMS-capable battalion in the Gulf, the 6th Bn, 27th FA.[29] The first use of ATACMS in combat occurred o/a 18 Jan 91, when Battery A, 6th Bn, 27th FA fired an ATACMS at an Iraqi SA-2 ADA missile site. This was also the first shot fired by U.S. Army field artillery in Desert Storm, and the first shot fired by the VII Corps in combat since 1945.[30] The Army shipped just over 100 ATACMS missiles to the Gulf, all that were in the inventory. The Army fired 32 of these missiles and all were apparently successful. ATACMS continues to serve in the same role in today's Army.

"Firefinder" Target Acquisition Radars

In addition to its firing units, Army field artillery deployed a number of target acquisition units to the Gulf. Target acquisition units use radar to detect and track incoming enemy mortar and artillery rounds so that friendly artillery can return fire and suppress or destroy the enemy's indirect fire assets. The Army's target acquisition units were equipped with the AN/TPQ-36 "Firefinder" Mortar Locating Radar and the AN/TPQ-37 "Firefinder" Artillery Locating Radar. Fielding of both these radars began in

---

[27] This consisted of six divisional batteries (the equivalent of two battalions), a battalion(-) attached to the 1st Armd Div, and four(+) battalions assigned to corps artillery. The Marines did not have the MLRS, however the Army's Btry A(MLRS), 92nd FA was attached to the 2nd Mar Div. See Chart 5, page 5-2 & Chart 19, page 19-14. Thus, about five percent of the Army's MLRS firing batteries supported the Marine Corps.

[28] Thus, the National Guard contributed almost 15 percent of the MLRS units that served in Desert Storm.

[29] Two of this battalion's three firing batteries were ATACMS-capable when they deployed to the Gulf, and the third battery may have added ATACMS capability while deployed in SWA. The Marines did not use ATACMS.

[30] The XVIII Airborne Corps did not fire its first ATACMS until 28 Feb 91, when Btry B, 6-27 FA successfully engaged 40 stationary vehicles.

the early 1980s and was completed in Active Army units by 1990. The AN/TPQ-36 did not deploy to Grenada, but was used in action by the Army in Panama. The AN/TPQ-37 apparently did not see combat before Desert Storm.

During Desert Storm the AN/TPQ-36 and Q-37 served in target acquisition batteries and detatchments that were assigned to divisions or to field artillery brigades that were part of corps artillery. Both systems continue to serve in the same role in today's Army.

M992 FAASV and M548 Tracked Cargo Carrier

The field artillery needs a means for transporting its ammunition. In light units, unarmored wheeled vehicles such as the two-and-a-half ton truck fulfill this role, but heavy units have specialized tracked vehicles for this purpose. The M548 Tracked Cargo Carrier, an unarmored vehicle based upon the M113, has performed this role since the mid-1960s. Beginning in 1985 the Army began to replace its M548s with a larger vehicle that was armored, the M992 Field Artillery Ammunition Support Vehicle (FAASV). The M992 is based upon the M109 self-propelled howitzer and consists of a fixed superstructure mounted on the M109's chassis in place of the turret. Both the M548 and the M992 served in the Gulf.

Lance and Pershing Missiles

Two veteran field artillery systems did not serve in the Gulf even though they were still in Army service in 1991. These were the Lance missile and the Pershing II missile.

Lance was fielded in 1972 and was never fired in combat. It was equipped with conventional and nuclear warheads and was a corps-level weapon. It was phased out of Army service in 1993 and replaced by ATACMS. The Army began deploying a Lance unit from Fort Sill to Saudi Arabia during Desert Shield, but terminated this deployment before the unit left CONUS. This decision was driven by political considerations and the fact that Lance was nuclear-capable.

The original Pershing I was fielded in the early 1960s and was replaced in 1985 by the Pershing II. Pershing was a nuclear-only theater-level missile that served primarily in Germany. In light of its nuclear-only payload, there was no place for the Pershing in SWA. The Pershing II was eliminated as a result of the Intermediate-Range Nuclear Forces (INF) Treaty, and was in the process of being phased out in 1990. No weapon system has taken Pershing's place.

Air Defense Artillery

Like the field artillery, air defense artillery brought a variety of old and new weapons to the Gulf. Army air defense artillery units used the following seven weapon systems in Desert Storm: (1) the M167 "Vulcan" towed 20mm gatling gun; (2) the M163A1 "Vulcan" self-propelled 20mm gatling gun; (3) the M730 "Chaparral" self-propelled missile system; (4) the "Stinger" manportable missile; (5) the "Avenger" air defense system; (6) the "Hawk" missile system; and (7) the "Patriot" missile system. Of these, only the Patriot was fired in combat against aerial targets.[31]

M167 "Vulcan" Towed 20mm Gatling Gun

The M167 towed 20mm gatling gun, also known as the Vulcan, is an old system that entered Army service in the late 1960s. It apparently did not serve in Vietnam. It did not deploy to Grenada but did serve in Panama, although it did not see combat in its primary role of providing air defense for friendly forces.

In Desert Storm, the M167 served in the divisional air defense artillery battalions of the 82nd Airborne Division and 101st Airborne Division(Air Aslt). In both battalions, the M167 served in mixed Vulcan/Stinger batteries. The M167A2 was the most modern version in service at the time of Desert Storm. Of the approximately 70 air defense artillery firing battery equivalents that deployed to Saudi Arabia, Israel, or Turkey during Desert Storm,[32] seven were equipped with the M167 towed Vulcan, for a total of ten percent of the Army's air defense artillery force in the Gulf. Since Desert Storm, the M167 has been phased out of the Army inventory and replaced by Avenger and Stinger.

M163 "Vulcan" Self-Propelled 20mm Gatling Gun

The M163 was the self-propelled version of the M167. It consisted of a 20mm gatling gun and radar mounted on an M113 series vehicle and, like the M167, was known as the Vulcan. The M163 was fielded during 1968 and was used in combat in Vietnam, providing fire support against ground targets, rather than in its primary role as an air defense system. The M163 did not see service during Grenada or Panama, however.

In Desert Storm, the M163 served in the divisional air defense artillery battalions of all five Army heavy divisions, and in the 5th Bn, 62nd ADA, a former

---

[31] The M163 self-propelled Vulcan, and possibly the M167 towed Vulcan, were fired against ground targets, however.

[32] This is an approximate number because ADA firing batteries had a varying number of platoons, and the headquarters batteries of ADA battalions included varying numbers of Stinger teams that need to be included within these totals.

Order of Battle

11th Air Defense Artillery Brigade unit that supported the 3rd Armored Cavalry Regiment and XVIII Airborne Corps Artillery. Each of these six battalions had three mixed M163 Vulcan/Stinger batteries. Of the approximately 70 air defense artillery firing battery equivalents that deployed to Saudi Arabia, Israel, or Turkey during Desert Storm, 18 were equipped with the M163 self-propelled Vulcan, for a total of 25 percent of the Army's air defense artillery force in the Gulf.

The M163A2 was the most modern version in service at the time of Desert Storm. Since Desert Storm, the M163 has been phased out of the Active Army and replaced by the Bradley Stinger Fighting Vehicle, which consists of a Stinger missile team carried in a Bradley Fighting Vehicle.[33] The M163 has also been phased out of the National Guard, where it has been replaced by Avenger and Stinger.

M730 "Chaparral" Missile Carrier

The M730 "Chaparral" self-propelled missile carrier was another veteran ADA weapon. It consisted of four modified "Sidewinder" air-to-air heat seeking missiles mounted on a traversing unit on the back of an unarmored, M548 Tracked Cargo Carrier. Chaparral was fielded in 1969, and had not seen combat when Desert Storm began. The M730A2 version, which brought the M730 up to the M113A3 standard, was being fielded as of October 1989.

Historically, Chaparral had served in the mixed Vulcan/Chaparral ADA battalions of heavy divisions, however by the time Desert Shield began the Army was phasing Chaparral out of that role and making it a corps level weapon, organized in pure Chaparral battalions. As a result, it appears that only two Chaparral batteries served in Desert Storm: Battery D, 6th Bn, 3rd ADA, 1st Armored Division, and Battery D, 5th Bn, 3rd ADA, 3rd Armored Division. No corps-level Chaparral battalions deployed to SWA in that role, although one such battalion, the 3rd Bn, 2nd ADA, deployed without its Chaparrals and served as a provisional truck battalion. See Chart 4, Footnote 116. Of the approximately 70 air defense artillery firing battery equivalents that deployed to Saudi Arabia, Israel, or Turkey during Desert Storm, only two were equipped with Chaparral, for less than three percent of the Army's air defense artillery force in the Gulf. Since Desert Storm, Chaparral has left Army service and been replaced by Avenger.

---

[33] The Army began to field a new system in 1997, "Bradley Linebacker" (also known as the Bradley Stinger Fighting Vehicle-Enhanced, or BSFV-E). This vehicle consists of two Stinger launchers mounted on a Bradley in lieu of its TOW launcher so that it can fire its Stingers without exposing the crew, and even while on the move.

"Stinger" Missile

Stinger was a manportable, shoulder-fired, heat-seeking air defense missile. Stinger entered service in 1981 as a replacement for the "Redeye" missile, which was similar to Stinger but much less capable, as it could only be fired at the tail of enemy aircraft as they exited the area after completing their attack on friendly forces. Stinger served in Grenada and Panama, but apparently did not see combat.

In Desert Storm, Stinger served in divisional air defense artillery battalions, with 15-20 Stinger teams in the battalion headquarters battery and one platoon in each of the three firing batteries, which otherwise were equipped with the Vulcan (M163 SP Vulcan in heavy divisions and M167 towed Vulcan in light divisions). Stinger also served in other ADA units, including the headquarters battery of Hawk and Patriot battalions and in separate ADA platoons assigned to, for example, the 2nd and 3rd Armored Cavalry Regiments. Of the approximately 70 air defense artillery firing battery equivalents that deployed to Saudi Arabia, Israel, or Turkey during Desert Storm, the equivalent of approximately 12 batteries were equipped with Stinger, for a total of 17 percent of the Army's air defense artillery force in the Gulf. Stinger continues to serve in the same role in today's Army.

"Avenger" Air Defense System

Avenger was a brand new system that the Army only began fielding in 1990. Avenger consisted of an HMMWV mounting a traversing pedestal with eight Stinger missiles and a single M2 .50 cal. machine gun. During Desert Storm, Avenger equipped the six platoons of Battery D, 4th Bn, 5th ADA, 1st Cavalry Division(-), and the Avenger Platoon of the 3rd Armored Cavalry Regiment. In addition, Battery B, 2nd Bn(Patriot), 7th ADA, 11th Air Defense Artillery Brigade deployed to SWA in August 1990 with two Avengers. See Chart 4, Footnote 110.

A total of 48 Avengers deployed to the Gulf, but no Avenger system engaged the enemy during Desert Storm. Of the approximately 70 air defense artillery firing battery equivalents that deployed to Saudi Arabia, Israel, or Turkey during Desert Storm, approximately two battery's worth were equipped with Avenger, for a total of three percent of the Army's air defense artillery force in the Gulf. Avenger now serves in divisional air defense artillery battalions and in corps-level air defense artillery battalions, typically on the basis of one per corps.

Order of Battle

"Hawk" Missile System[34]

Hawk is a medium range, low-to-medium altitude missile designed to engage enemy aircraft. It entered service in 1960 and served in Vietnam in limited numbers. Hawk did not serve in Grenada or Panama.

In Desert Storm, Hawk served at corps level in the air defense artillery battalion task forces assigned to the VII and XVIII Airborne Corps, and at the theater level in the 11th Air Defense Artillery Brigade. Of the approximately 70 air defense artillery firing battery equivalents that deployed to Saudi Arabia, Israel, or Turkey during Desert Storm, nine were equipped with Hawk, for a total of 13 percent of the Army's air defense artillery force in the Gulf. No Hawks were fired at enemy aircraft, however. Hawk was phased out of the Active Army in 1994 and left National Guard service in 1997.

"Patriot" Missile System

Patriot is a low-to-high altitude, long range missile designed to engage enemy aircraft. It was first fielded in Germany in 1985, replacing the Nike-Hercules missile. Patriot did not serve in Panama. In Desert Storm, Patriot served at corps level in the air defense artillery battalion task forces assigned to the VII and XVIII Airborne Corps, and at the theater level in the 11th Air Defense Artillery Brigade. Patriot was also deployed to Israel and Turkey.

As originally designed, Patriot did not possess the ability to engage ballistic missiles. This capability was added through software changes implemented with the PAC-2 (Patriot ATM Capability 2) missile. When Desert Shield began in August 1990, the Army had a grand total of three Patriot PAC-2 missiles. These still-experimental missiles were deployed to Saudi Arabia with the first Patriot unit to deploy, Battery B, 2nd Bn, 7th ADA, 11th Air Defense Artillery Brigade. Battery B arrived in Saudi Arabia on 13 Aug 90.

Battery A, 2nd Bn, 7th ADA made history at approximately 0445 hours on 18 Jan 91 when it successfully engaged a Scud theater ballistic missile. The Army fired 158 Patriot missiles during Desert Storm. Of the approximately 70 air defense artillery firing battery equivalents that deployed to Saudi Arabia, Israel, or Turkey during Desert Storm, 27 were equipped with Patriot, for a total of 39 percent of the Army's air defense artillery force in the Gulf. Patriot achieved an operational readiness rate in SWA of 95 percent. Patriot continues to serve in the same role in today's Army.

---

[34] According to some sources, the correct name is "HAWK," an acronym for "Homing All the Way Killer." Most sources state the name as "Hawk," however, and I have used that spelling in this order of battle. The Army fielded an improved version of Hawk known as "I-Hawk," in the early 1970s. However, prior to Desert Storm the Army retired all of its Basic Hawks and, once this had occurred, dropped the term "I-Hawk."

Aviation

Army aviation units took six main types of helicopters into action during Desert Storm: (1) the OH-58 "Kiowa" Observation Helicopter; (2) the AH-1 "Cobra" Attack Helicopter; (3) the AH-64 "Apache" Attack Helicopter; (4) the UH-1 "Huey" Utility Helicopter; (5) the UH-60 "Black Hawk" Utility Helicopter; and (6) the CH-47 "Chinook" Cargo Helicopter.

OH-58 "Kiowa" Observation Helicopter

The OH-58 "Kiowa" was fielded in 1969. It saw substantial combat in Vietnam, and served in Grenada and Panama. At least three versions of the Kiowa served in Desert Storm: the OH-58C, OH-58D, and the Armed OH-58D.[35] The OH-58C, an improved version of the original OH-58A, apparently entered service in the early 1980s. The OH-58D entered service in the mid-1980s. It was a substantial improvement over the OH-58C, and featured a mast-mounted sight through which the crew could observe the enemy and guide Hellfire missiles fired by Apache Attack Helicopters. This mast-mounted sight was on top of the rotor assembly and allowed the helicopter to hide behind buildings, ridgelines, or trees, with only the mast-mounted sight exposed. The OH-58C and OH-58D were completely unarmed. The Armed OH-58D was an armed version of the OH-58D that was fielded on a very limited basis in the late 1980s.

In Desert Storm, the OH-58 served primarily as a scout helicopter in air cavalry and attack helicopter units. OH-58s were assigned to (1) the seven cavalry squadrons assigned to the Army's divisions, (2) the two aviation squadrons assigned to the 2nd and 3rd Armored Cavalry Regiments, (3) the 16 attack helicopter battalions that served in the Gulf,[36] and (4) the scout helicopter companies that served in the 11th and 12th Aviation Brigades.[37] It appears that the majority of the OH-58s that served in Desert Storm were the OH-58C. OH-58Ds served primarily in attack helicopter battalions that were equipped with the AH-64 Apache, and in the two scout helicopter companies assigned to the 11th and 12th Aviation Brigades.[38] The Armed OH-58D served only with the 4th Sqdn(Air), 17th Cavalry, a specialized air cavalry unit.[39]

---

[35] It appears a limited number of OH-58As also served in Desert Storm.

[36] This total includes the 5-229 Avn(AH). See Chart 4, Footnote 77.

[37] These were Co D, 5-158 Avn, 12th Avn Bde, and a company of the 4-159 Avn (probably Co D), 11th Avn Bde.

[38] Some Apache battalions had OH-58Cs, however. The Army deployed 132 OH-58Ds to SWA, which was 80 percent of the OH-58D fleet. The OH-58D's operational readiness rate was in excess of 85 percent.

[39] See Chart 4, Footnotes 84 & 85 for more information on the 4-17 Cav and the Armed OH-58D.

Order of Battle

Since Desert Storm, the Armed OH-58D has been standardized as the OH-58D(I) "Kiowa Warrior."[40] Kiowa Warrior has now replaced the earlier versions of the Kiowa in Active Army air cavalry units. In addition, Kiowa Warrior is now serving as the attack helicopter in attack helicopter battalions assigned to light units, replacing the Cobra and Apache in that role.

AH-1 "Cobra" Attack Helicopter

The AH-1 "Cobra" was fielded in the late 1960s as the Army's first purpose-built attack helicopter. The Cobra saw extensive combat in the Vietnam War and served in Grenada and Panama.

In Desert Storm, the Cobra served primarily in air cavalry units, providing heavy firepower to back up the OH-58s in the seven cavalry squadrons assigned to the Army's divisions and in the two aviation squadrons assigned to the 2nd and 3rd Armored Cavalry Regiments. In addition, one of the Army's 16 attack helicopter battalions, the 3rd Bn(AH), 101st Aviation, 101st Airborne Division(Air Aslt), was equipped with the Cobra. All of the Cobras that served in Desert Storm were the AH-1F model, a modernized version that was apparently fielded in the late 1980s.

The last Cobras left Active Army service in March 1999. In air cavalry units, and attack helicopter units assigned to light infantry divisions or the 82nd Airborne Division, the AH-1 has been replaced by the OH-58D(I) Kiowa Warrior. In all other attack helicopter units the AH-1 has been replaced by the AH-64 Apache. The Cobra continues to serve in the National Guard, however.

AH-64 "Apache" Attack Helicopter

The AH-64 "Apache" was fielded in 1986 as a replacement for the Cobra, and saw limited combat in Panama. Apaches equipped 15 of the Army's 16 attack helicopter battalions in SWA.[41] Thus, almost 95 percent of the attack helicopter units in the Gulf had the Apache. No AH-64s served in air cavalry units.

The Army deployed 274 Apaches to SWA, which was 45 percent of the Apache fleet. All of the Apaches that served in Desert Storm were the initial model, the AH-64A. The Apache's operational readiness rate during the ground war was in excess of 90 percent.

---

[40] The "(I)" stands for "Improved."

[41] This includes the 5-229 Avn(AH). See Chart 4, Footnote 77. The exception was the 3-101 Avn(AH), which had the AH-1 Cobra.

The Apache continues to play the same role in today's Army, however it has been replaced in light units by the OH-58D(I) Kiowa Warrior, which is much smaller and easier to deploy on short notice. An improved version of the Apache, the AH-64D "Apache Longbow," began entering service with the Army in 1998.

UH-1 "Huey" Utility Helicopter

The UH-1 "Huey" was fielded in 1959 and saw extensive service in the Vietnam War as the Army's standard helicopter for airmobile operations, command and control, medevac, and resupply missions. The UH-1 also served in Grenada and Panama. Although partially replaced by the UH-60 "Black Hawk," large numbers of the UH-1H model served in Desert Storm. Although now largely replaced by the Black Hawk, the Huey continues to serve in the Active Army today.

UH-60 "Black Hawk" Utility Helicopter[42]

The UH-60 "Black Hawk" was fielded in 1979 as a replacement for the UH-1. The Black Hawk saw combat in Grenada and Panama. The original model was the UH-60A, which was supplemented from late 1989 by the UH-60L, with a more powerful engine and more durable main gear box. It appears that the majority of Black Hawks in the Gulf War were the earlier UH-60A version.

Large numbers of Black Hawks served in Desert Storm, in assault helicopter companies and battalions and in many other types of aviation units. The Army deployed 489 Black Hawks to SWA, which was 46 percent of the UH-60 fleet. The Black Hawk's operational readiness rate in SWA was in excess of 80 percent. The UH-60 continues to serve in the same roles in today's Army.

CH-47 "Chinook" Medium Lift Helicopter

The CH-47 "Chinook" was fielded in 1962 and saw extensive combat in Vietnam, where it served as the Huey's larger brother and participated in numerous airmobile assault and resupply missions. The CH-47 also served in Panama, but did not serve in Grenada. A modernized version, the CH-47D, was fielded in 1984 and served in Desert Storm in medium helicopter units assigned to the 11th, 12th, and 18th Aviation Brigades, and in the 8th Bn, 101st Aviation, the 101st Airborne Division(Air Aslt)'s medium helicopter battalion. The CH-47D continues to serve the same role in today's Army, with no replacement in sight.

---

[42] Although many reliable sources refer to the UH-60 as the "Blackhawk," it is clear that the correct name is two words, "Black Hawk."

Special Operations Aviation

    The Army's special operations aviation unit, the 160th Special Operations Aviation Regiment(Abn), used a number of specialized helicopters. The 160th SOAR concentrated on night flying in support of special operations forces such as the Rangers and Special Forces, and used specialized models of the UH-60 and CH-47 helicopters. The 160th SOAR also used an updated version of the venerable OH-6 "Cayuse" Light Observation Helicopter, which served during the initial stages of the Vietnam War and was replaced by the OH-58 Kiowa. Some of these OH-6s were armed and served as attack helicopters, designated the AH-6. Elements of the 160th SOAR served in the Gulf, however information with regard to the missions they performed and the aircraft they operated is very difficult to come by. See Chart 6.

Notes:

➢   All information with regard to the current status of weapon systems is "as of" mid-1998.

➢   "M1A1 series tank" refers to the M1A1, the Modified M1A1, and the M1A1HA.

➢   The statements with regard to the percentage of the Army's field artillery force in the Gulf that was provided by the various weapon systems are done on a unit basis, not on the basis of the number of weapons deployed. The number of weapons per battery varied (see Appendix D, page D-17) and, therefore, percentages based on weapon systems would yield the following slightly different results:

	Percentage	Number Of Weapons
M102 Towed 105mm Howitzer	10%	108
M198 Towed 155mm Howitzer	7%	72
M109 SP 155mm Howitzer	55%	576
M110 SP 203mm Howitzer	9%	96
M270 MLRS	18%	189
Total:	100%[43]	1,043

These numbers are based on the quantities of weapon systems authorized for each unit by the TOE. Some units obtained some additional systems, primarily from operational readiness float stocks. The small quantities involved would not materially alter the results.

➢   The statements with regard to the percentage of the Army's air defense artillery force in the Gulf that was provided by the various weapon systems are done on a unit basis, not on the basis of the number of weapons deployed. The number of weapons per battery varied (see Appendix D, pages D-18 and D-19) and, therefore, percentages based on weapon systems would yield different results.

---

[43] Percentages do not add up to exactly 100 percent due to rounding.

Chart 14

U.S. Army Campaign Participation Credit and Unit Awards For Operation Desert Storm

Campaign Participation Credit

The Army recognizes a unit's participation in combat by according it campaign participation credit (CPC). "An organization will be given campaign participation credit if it actually engaged the enemy in combat, was stationed in the combat zone, or performed duties either in the air or on the ground in any part of the combat zone during the time limitations of the campaign."[1]

Major wars, such as World War Two, are divided into numerous campaigns, each defined using geographic and chronological factors. Smaller conflicts, such as Grenada, constitute a single campaign. Desert Shield/Storm was divided into three campaigns:

Defense of Saudi Arabia (2 Aug 90 through 16 Jan 91)
Liberation and Defense of Kuwait (17 Jan through 11 Apr 91)
Southwest Asia Cease-Fire (12 Apr 91 through 30 Nov 95)

Department of the Army General Orders (DAGO) No. 7 (2 Apr 93), announced campaign participation credit for the majority of the units that fought in Operation Desert Storm. Other DAGOs have amended DAGO 7 and are listed in the bibliography to this order of battle. This process will undoubtedly continue for some time; at least once a year or so, the Army amends the CPC awarded for World War Two. Moreover,

---

[1] All of the quotations in this chart are from Army Regulation (AR) 672-5-1, <u>Military Awards</u> (1 Oct 90), which was in effect during Desert Storm. This regulation has been superseded by AR 600-8-22, <u>Military Awards</u> (25 Feb 95).

the DAGOs issued to date only address the units that have been awarded CPC for the Defense of Saudi Arabia and the Liberation and Defense of Kuwait. The units awarded CPC for the third "campaign" of Desert Storm — the Southwest Asia Cease-Fire — has yet to be addressed by a DAGO.[2]

Assault Landing Credit

Units that conduct amphibious, airborne, or helicopter-borne assaults are awarded a bronze "arrowhead device" in addition to campaign participation credit. In order to receive such credit, however, the unit must participate in the initial phases of an assault that was actively and meaningfully contested by the enemy. A mere insertion into enemy territory does not qualify. Nor does a raid type operation. "The forces committed should be spearheading a major assault into enemy controlled territory . . . such that the committed forces will ultimately control the area in which they have landed and will not rely on immediate link-up with other forces or extraction after a hit-and-run type of mission."

As a result, no Army unit was awarded assault landing credit for Desert Storm.[3] No Army units participated in an amphibious or airborne assault, and the closest the Army came to a helicopter-borne assault was when the 3rd Brigade, 101st Airborne Division(Air Aslt) seized AO Eagle. While this bold move played an important role in cutting off the KTO, the landing was not significantly contested by the Iraqis. As a result, no units of the 101st Airborne Division(Air Aslt) have been awarded assault landing credit for Desert Storm.

The Army Unit Award System

The Army recognizes superior unit performance through unit awards.[4] Army units were eligible for four such awards during Operation Desert Storm (listed in order of precedence, from highest to lowest):

---

[2] These campaigns were established by the Department of Defense and apply to all of the Armed Services. In light of the fact that essentially no combat occurred during this time period it is difficult to understand why this third period of time qualifies as a campaign for CPC purposes.

[3] By contrast, some units that participated in Operations Urgent Fury (Grenada) and Just Cause (Panama) received assault landing credit.

[4] The Army also has a series of awards for individuals, some of which are limited to valor in combat (e.g., the Congressional Medal of Honor), while others can be awarded under other circumstances. Army units are also eligible for awards from the other Armed Services and from certain foreign nations. For example, Army units that served with I MEF received Navy unit awards for Desert Storm. No foreign nations issued unit awards to U.S. Army units for Desert Storm, however.

1. Presidential Unit Citation (Army)
2. Valorous Unit Award
3. Meritorious Unit Commendation (Army)
4. Army Superior Unit Award

In order to receive the Presidential Unit Citation (PUC) or the Valorous Unit Award (VUA), the unit must display "extraordinary heroism in action against an armed enemy of the United States . . . The unit must display such gallantry, determination, and esprit de corps in accomplishing its mission under extremely difficult and hazardous conditions as to set it apart and above other units participating in the same campaign." The PUC requires the level of heroism that would justify award of the Distinguished Service Cross (DSC) to an individual.[5] The VUA requires the level of heroism that would justify award of the Silver Star to an individual.[6] Only rarely will the PUC or VUA be awarded to a unit larger than a battalion.

The Meritorious Unit Commendation (MUC) is awarded "for exceptionally meritorious conduct in performance of outstanding services for at least 6 continuous months during the period of military operations against an armed enemy." Although "[s]ervice in [a] combat zone is not required," the unit's activities "must be directly related to the combat effort." The MUC requires the level of achievement that would justify award of the Legion of Merit to an individual.[7] Only combat service support type units — not senior headquarters, combat, or combat support units — are eligible for the MUC, and only rarely will the MUC be awarded to a unit larger than a battalion.

Finally, the Army Superior Unit Award (ASUA) is awarded for "outstanding meritorious performance of a unit during peacetime of a difficult and challenging mission under extraordinary circumstances."

Army Unit Awards For Desert Storm

Surprisingly, as of 31 Dec 98, the Army has still not completed the unit award process for Desert Storm, and it is unclear when this process will be completed. The Presidential Unit Citation has not been awarded to any unit for Desert Storm, and it appears that a conscious decision was made, early in the awards process, that no PUCs would be awarded. A recommendation that the entire XVIII Airborne Corps

---

[5] The DSC is the second-highest individual award for heroism. The Congressional Medal of Honor is the highest individual award for heroism.

[6] The Silver Star is the third-highest individual award for heroism.

[7] The Legion of Merit is the Army's second-highest individual award for meritorious service that does not involve heroism in combat.

receive the PUC — which would have been a gross violation of Army regulations — was rejected.[8] Many units received the Valorous Unit Award, however, and in many commands virtually every unit that engaged the enemy received the VUA.

For example, in the VII Corps, virtually every maneuver battalion in the 1st and 3rd Armored Divisions, 1st Infantry Division(Mech), and 2nd Armored Cavalry Regiment received the VUA. While the VII Corps saw tough combat against the Republican Guard, it seems unlikely that every maneuver battalion met the criteria for a VUA, which requires "extraordinary heroism . . . such gallantry, determination, and esprit de corps in accomplishing its mission under extremely difficult and hazardous conditions as to set it apart and above other units participating in the same campaign." This is particularly true in light of the fact that in some VII Corps divisions, some units were in reserve for a significant amount of the war and saw much less combat than other units.[9] In addition, six of the ten VII Corps maneuver brigade headquarters that saw substantial combat against the Republican Guard received the VUA[10] in contravention of the spirit, if not the letter, of AR 672-5-1's guidance that "[o]nly on rare occasions will a unit larger than a battalion qualify for award of [the VUA]." It appears that the Army's philosophy was to award a VUA to virtually every maneuver unit that saw a reasonable amount of combat, rather than limit the VUA to only those select units that did something extraordinary.

Moreover, in many instances the combat arms units that did not receive a VUA received the MUC, in violation of AR 672-5-1's statement that the MUC is limited to combat service support units. For example, the 82nd Airborne Division saw little combat during the ground war and, appropriately, no unit of the 82nd received a VUA. However, 12 of the 17 combat arms battalions assigned or attached to the 82nd received an MUC.

In many instances where equivalent units received different treatment in the awards process, this difference appears to derive from unit policies with regard to awards rather than genuine differences in unit performance. For example, both the 3rd Armored Division and the 1st Infantry Division(Mech) saw a substantial amount of combat and made a major contribution to the campaign by successfully attacking

---

[8] In World War II, however, on two occasions entire Army divisions were awarded the Distinguished Unit Citation (DUC). The DUC was renamed the PUC on 3 Nov 66.

[9] For example, the 3rd Bde, 3rd Armd Div was in reserve for much of the war and was not committed to front line combat until late in the morning of 27 Feb 91. The 3rd Armd Div reached its limit of advance and ceased meaningful offensive combat by 2130 hours that evening. Thus, the 3rd Brigade saw less than 12 hours of real combat during Desert Storm. Nonetheless, the brigade HHC, all three of its maneuver battalions, and its DS field artillery battalion all received the VUA.

[10] The 1st Armd Div, 3rd Armd Div, and 1st Inf Div(M) each had three maneuver brigades, and the tenth maneuver brigade equivalent was the 2nd Armd Cav Regt.

elements of Iraq's Republican Guard. However, in the 3rd Armored Division all three of the maneuver brigade headquarters & headquarters companies received the VUA, whereas in the 1st Infantry Division(Mech) none of the three maneuver brigade headquarters & headquarters companies has received a VUA.

Other anomalies exist. For example, VII Corps Artillery consisted of four field artillery brigades and all four saw substantial combat against the Republican Guard. The entire 210th Field Artillery Brigade (including the brigade headquarters & headquarters battery) has received the VUA, however only one other VII Corps Artillery unit, the 2nd Bn(155 SP), 29th FA, 42nd Field Artillery Brigade, has received a VUA. The other seven-plus battalions and three brigade headquarters & headquarters batteries have received no award whatsoever.

Contrast this treatment to the 11th Air Defense Artillery Brigade, the most decorated unit of the war. That unit consisted of four air defense artillery battalions under the brigade's control, and two-plus battalions that were detached from the brigade: the 2nd Bn(Hawk), 1st ADA, which reported directly to the XVIII Airborne Corps, and the 5th Bn(Vulc/Stinger), 62nd ADA, which supported XVIII Airborne Corps Artillery and the 3rd Armored Cavalry Regiment. All six of these battalions received the VUA, notwithstanding that none of them faced the kind of danger that confronted every front-line maneuver unit.

Indeed, three of these battalions never fired a round in anger during Desert Storm. The 2nd Bn, 1st ADA and 2nd Bn, 52nd ADA were Hawk missile units, and the 5th Bn, 62nd ADA was equipped with the Vulcan and Stinger systems. Only the 11th Air Defense Artillery Brigade's three Patriot battalions actually had the opportunity to perform their mission of engaging an enemy aerial threat, because Iraq never attempted to use its aircraft to attack U.S. units. Nonetheless, every unit that was associated with the 11th Air Defense Artillery Brigade received the VUA.

Thus, high-level air defense artillery units — those at corps and theater level — enjoyed a much better "VUA rate" then did the Army's maneuver and field artillery units, even though those high-level air defense artillery units were far from the front lines, not subject to a significant amount of danger, and probably enjoyed a number of creature comforts denied to the maneuver units, such as hot food, latrines, and showers. Interestingly, the only ADA unit above division level that did not receive a VUA was Task Force 8-43 ADA, a composite Patriot/Hawk reinforced battalion that had been assigned to the 32nd Army Air Defense Command in Germany prior to Desert Storm. Thus, the only air defense artillery unit above division level that did not receive a VUA was also the only such unit that had no connection to the 11th Air Defense Artillery Brigade. Coincidence? Not likely.

Many non-combat arms units that served in SWA received the MUC and a handful received the VUA. Finally, some units received the ASUA for Desert Storm. It appears that all such awards went to units outside the KTO.

The Navy Unit Commendation

One final award was received by a handful of Army units: the Navy Unit Commendation (NUC), which ranks just below the MUC. The Navy awarded this commendation to the Tiger Brigade (1st Brigade, 2nd Armored Division), which served with I Marine Expeditionary Force. The Marine Corps is a separate military service within the Department of the Navy, hence it is the Navy — not the Marine Corps — that administers unit awards for the Marine Corps. See Chart 25 for more information on the NUC and the unit awards received by Marine Corps units.

Notes:

➤ Campaign participation credit is announced in general orders issued by the senior Army headquarters in the theater of operations. These awards are then confirmed by general orders issued by the Department of the Army (DAGO). DAGOs are numbered and dated, and the numbering scheme begins with "1" each new calendar year.

➤ Campaign participation credit is only awarded to companies, separate detachments and platoons (those not normally assigned to a company), and larger units. If a company does not serve in the theater of operations but sends one of its platoons, that platoon is not eligible for campaign participation credit. As a result of this policy, none of the WSRO units that served in SWA will receive campaign participation credit for Desert Storm. See Chart 12.

➤ Assault landing credit is awarded by Headquarters, Department of the Army and is announced in DAGOs. Authority to award assault landing credit may be delegated to the senior Army commander in the theater.

➤ Army unit awards are typically announced in permanent orders issued by unit headquarters that are authorized to approve the awards. These awards are then confirmed in DAGOs.

➤ The Army is considering issuing a Department of the Army Pamphlet that lists all of the units that participated in Desert Storm and the campaign participation credit and unit awards each unit received. The Army is also considering placing this document on the internet. The Army has already placed some limited information on campaign participation credit and unit awards for Desert Storm on the internet at:

> http://www.perscom.army.mil/tagd/awards/gulf.htm
> http://www.perscom.army.mil/tagd/awards/other.htm

➢ This order of battle does not identify each unit that has received an award because the list is simply too long, it is currently incomplete, and it will almost certainly need to be amended once it has been completed as errors are detected. The DAGOs issued to date that address unit awards are listed in the bibliography to this order of battle under "U.S. Army General/Permanent Orders."

➢ There is also a Joint Meritorious Unit Award (JMUA) which can be awarded to joint activities of the DOD "for meritorious achievement or service, superior to that which is normally expected, under one of the following conditions: (1) During action in combat with an armed enemy of the United States, (2) For a declared national emergency situation, (3) Under extraordinary circumstances that involved the national interest." Thus, joint headquarters to which Army personnel are assigned are eligible for the JMUA, but Army units are not. The JMUA for Desert Storm was awarded to:

Headquarters, U.S. Central Command
Headquarters, SOCCENT
Headquarters, JTF Proven Force
Joint Special Operations Task Force, JTF Proven Force
U.S. Special Operations Command

Chart 15

U.S. Army Post-Desert Storm Developments

With the end of the Gulf War on 28 Feb 91, the Army began the monumental task of standing down the huge war machine that had deployed to Southwest Asia. The Army had to move units, equipment, and supplies out of the Gulf, while ensuring the security of Saudi Arabia, Kuwait, and our other allies. Finally, notwithstanding our decisive victory, Saddam Hussein has continued to threaten our allies in the region, requiring periodic deployments of significant ground combat troops to Kuwait. This chart addresses the Army's drawdown in the KTO after the Gulf War, as well as the subsequent deployments in response to Saddam's continuing saber-rattling.

The Immediate Aftermath Of Desert Storm

➢ The last U.S. Army maneuver unit to leave the KTO after Operation Desert Storm was the 1st Brigade, 3rd Armored Division, which departed the theater in June 1991. As Task Force Positive Force, this brigade was responsible for the defense of Kuwait as the remaining U.S. Army units withdrew. The 1st Brigade was reorganized for this mission, and did not contain the same units that fought with the brigade during the war. Task Force Positive Force included the 2nd Bn, 67th Armor [Fr. 3rd Bde, 3rd AD]; 4th Bn, 67th Armor [Fr. 3rd Bde, 3rd AD]; 3rd Bn(Mech Inf), 5th Cav; and 2nd Bn(155 SP), 3rd FA.

➢ In early June 1991, Task Force Victory I deployed from Germany to Kuwait pursuant to Operation Positive Force. Task Force Victory I consisted of the

Order of Battle

11th Armored Cavalry Regiment(-).[1] This unit assumed the mission of defending Kuwait from the 1st Brigade, 3rd Armored Division o/a 13 Jun 91, and subsequently left the KTO in early September 1991.

➤ Operation Positive Force continued when Task Force Victory II began deploying from Germany to Kuwait in late August 1991. Task Force Victory II assumed the mission of defending Kuwait from Task Force Victory I o/a 7 Sep 91. Task Force Victory II consisted of two tank companies, two mechanized infantry companies, and supporting units.[2] This unit left the KTO in early/mid December 1991. At that point there was no longer any U.S. heavy maneuver unit in Kuwait.

➤ On 1 Jul 91, HQ, 22nd Support Command became the senior headquarters in Southwest Asia when HQ, CENTCOM(Main) left the theater. The 22nd SUPCOM was responsible for the retrograde of U.S. military equipment and supplies from the theater to the United States. The 22nd SUPCOM was inactivated in Southwest Asia on 31 Dec 91, and replaced by ARCENT Forward, which completed this mission and ceased operations in June 1992.

Army Prepositioned Stocks

➤ The United States wanted to establish substantial stocks of heavy equipment in SWA after Desert Storm to facilitate a quick re-deployment in the event of an emergency. The United States wanted to pre-position two-thirds of an armored division's equipment in Saudi Arabia with the remaining third in Kuwait, but the Saudis refused permission to place any Army equipment stocks in their country. Some prepositioned stocks were established in Kuwait, however. These stocks have been described in the popular press as sufficient to equip a heavy brigade, however they initially only added up to half a brigade's worth of equipment, as they were only sufficient to equip three tank companies, three mechanized infantry companies, and a few field artillery batteries. After the October 1994 crisis, the Army increased these stocks to a full heavy brigade's worth, including two tank battalions and one mechanized infantry battalion. The unit that maintains these prepositioned stocks was initially known as "Combat Equipment Group, Southwest Asia," but has been redesignated as "U.S. Army, Kuwait." The Army recently established prepositioned stocks for a second heavy brigade in Qatar and plans to

---

[1] The 11th Armd Cav Regt left behind Trps B, F & K, and almost all of the 4th Sqdn(Avn).

[2] The tank companies came from the 3-77 Armor and the mechanized infantry companies came from the 4-8 Inf(M). The 5-77 Armor and 5-3 ADA also contributed to the task force. All of these units were normally assigned to the 8th Inf Div(M). The 3rd Inf Div(M) also contributed to the task force.

have stocks for a division base in Qatar by the end of FY 2000. Finally, the Army plans to place a third brigade's worth of equipment in the region at a location to be determined.

➢ The Army also has a reinforced brigade's worth of equipment on "roll-on roll-off" (RO-RO) ships that are prepositioned at Guam in the Pacific Ocean and at Diego Garcia in the Indian Ocean. This set of equipment is currently called Army Prepositioned Stocks-3 (APS-3),[3] and consists of enough equipment for four maneuver battalions (two tank and two mechanized infantry), a direct support field artillery battalion with self-propelled 155mm howitzers, an MLRS battery, an air defense artillery battery, an engineer battalion, a reinforced forward support battalion, a military police company, a signal company, a chemical company, a military intelligence company, and a brigade headquarters & headquarters company. The brigade is supported by an additional three RO-RO ships that carry equipment for supporting units, including a transportation group and a corps support group, along with 15 days of supplies.

Post-Desert Storm Training Exercises

➢ In December 1991, the 1st Bn, 75th Ranger Regiment(Abn), and the Regimental HQ & HQ Co, deployed to Kuwait to participate in Exercise Iris Gold.

➢ Since 1991, various exercises have been conducted by U.S. Army units in Kuwait.

➢ For several years the Army has maintained at least a company from the 5th Special Forces Group(Abn) in Kuwait on a rotating basis. This unit assists the Kuwaiti Army with training.

➢ For many years the Army has rotated a heavy battalion task force to Kuwait on an intermittent basis, pursuant to Exercise Intrinsic Action. These deployments typically lasted 45 days. Beginning in the Fall of 1996, however, the Army decided to increase these rotations so that a heavy battalion task force would be present in Kuwait at all times. These units rotate in and out of Kuwait every three or four months.

---

[3] Formerly known as Army War Reserve-3 (AWR-3).

Post-Desert Storm Redeployments To the KTO

➢ In late September 1991, the 94th Air Defense Artillery Brigade(-) deployed from Germany to Saudi Arabia, pursuant to Operation Determined Resolve. The 94th consisted of two Patriot battalions, the 1st Bn, 7th ADA and 5th Bn, 7th ADA, each with three firing batteries. It is unclear when this unit left Saudi Arabia. Since then, the Army has maintained a Patriot presence in the Gulf by rotating battalions there from Germany and CONUS. In early 1998, the Army activated a new headquarters to control its Patriot units in SWA. This unit, designated the 32nd Army Air and Missile Defense Command, is the descendant of the 32nd Army Air Defense Command, which defended German airspace during the Cold War.

➢ In January 1993, the 1st Cavalry Division deployed a reinforced battalion task force based on the 1st Bn, 9th Cavalry[4] to Kuwait in response to Iraqi violations of the terms of the Gulf War cease fire.

➢ In October 1994, substantial elements of the 24th Infantry Division(Mech) deployed to Kuwait as part of Operation Vigilant Warrior in response to ominous Iraqi troop movements near the border. Although details are sketchy, it appears that the 24th initially deployed its 1st Brigade and then its 3rd Brigade, and at least elements of these units remained in Kuwait until December 1994. The 1st Brigade deployed its personnel by air to link up with equipment prepositioned in Kuwait, while the 3rd Brigade deployed its personnel by air to link up with equipment that had been prepositioned on ships in the Indian and Pacific Oceans. Had it been needed, the 2nd Brigade would have deployed its equipment from Fort Stewart via ship. The Army also deployed at least two Patriot batteries from the 108th Air Defense Artillery Brigade at Fort Polk, and at least a portion of the 24th Support Group(Corps) from Fort Stewart. The initial plan, which was not executed because Iraq pulled back from the border, envisioned deployment of the entire 24th Infantry Division(Mech) and apparently one other heavy division. This presumably would have been the 1st Cavalry Division. At the height of the deployment, total U.S. ground forces in Kuwait (Army and Marine Corps) apparently exceeded 10,000 personnel; original plans had been to send 36,000 ground troops.

➢ In August 1995, the 2nd Brigade, 1st Cavalry Division deployed to Kuwait, pursuant to Operation Vigilant Sentinel, when Iraq threatened its neighbors after several high-ranking Iraqi officials defected.

---

[4] Despite its designation, the 1-9 Cav was a mechanized infantry battalion.

➢ In September 1996, elements of the 1st Cavalry Division deployed to Kuwait during a period of increased tension between the United States and Iraq. The division's TF 1-9 Cavalry, a mechanized infantry battalion task force, was already in Kuwait on a routine exercise. Joining this unit were some 3,000 troops of the 1st Cavalry Division's 3rd Brigade. The Army also deployed to Kuwait the 5th Bn, 52nd ADA, a Patriot battalion from the 11th Air Defense Artillery Brigade at Fort Bliss.

➢ In February 1998, elements of the 3rd Infantry Division(Mech) deployed to Kuwait pursuant to Operation Desert Thunder. The division's TF 1-30 Infantry(M), a mechanized infantry battalion task force, was already in Kuwait on a routine exercise. Joining this unit were most of the division's 1st Brigade, along with other units, including the division's Apache attack helicopter battalion and MLRS battery.[5] This deployment was in response to increased tensions in the region as a result of Iraq's refusal to comply with a United Nations Security Council weapons inspection agreement. The ground troops were ordered to Kuwait as a deterrent in case air strikes were ordered against Iraq. Iraq backed down, the air strikes were never ordered, and the ground forces returned to the United States.

➢ In mid-November 1998, the Army began to deploy forces to the Persian Gulf in response to another round of Iraqi intransigence with regard to United Nations weapons inspectors. This deployment involved the 2nd Brigade, 3rd Infantry Division(Mech) at Fort Stewart, a light infantry battalion(-) from the 10th Mountain Division(Lt Inf) at Fort Drum, and several Patriot air defense artillery batteries from Fort Bliss. The United States was within one hour of launching an attack upon Iraq when Saddam appeared to back down. As a result, the deployment of Army units was put on hold and, with the exception of unit advance parties, no soldiers deployed to SWA.

➢ In mid-December 1998 it became clear that Iraq's stated willingness to cooperate with United Nations weapon inspectors had been disingenuous. As a result, the United States and the United Kingdom launched Operation Desert Fox, an extensive aerial attack upon targets in Iraq. As part of this operation, elements of the 2nd Brigade, 3rd Infantry Division(Mech) deployed by air from Fort Stewart to Kuwait to link up with prepositioned equipment.[6] This deployment involved a brigade, minus one maneuver battalion but possibly reinforced by other elements such as an MLRS battery and/or attack helicopter battalion. These units linked up with TF 4-64 Armor, an armor battalion task force that was already in Kuwait on a regular training rotation. In addition, about 500 soldiers from the 4th Bn, 31st Infantry, from the 10th Mountain Division(Lt Inf) at Fort Drum deployed to

---

[5] These were the 1-3 Avn(AH) and A-13 FA(MLRS).
[6] One of the units that deployed was the 3-15 Inf(M).

protect Patriot air defense artillery units in the region. It is unclear if any additional Patriot units deployed as part of this operation. No ground combat occurred during this operation. The Army has announced that the forces deployed to SWA may remain in the region for a significant amount of time.

The Current Status of U.S. Army Units That Served In Desert Storm

➤ After Desert Storm, the U.S. military continued the downsizing process that had begun in the late 1980s with the end of the Cold War. As a result, many of the units that served in the Gulf War were inactivated, "reflagged," relocated, or reorganized. Summarized here are some of the more significant developments.

➤ In the U.S. Army, most of the changes occurred in Active Army EAC units and the units of the VII Corps. All of the Army's reserve component units that served in SWA have been released from active duty and returned to their status as reserve units.

Echelons Above Corps Units

➤ All of the theater-level commands that were activated specifically for Desert Storm, such as the 22nd Support Command, have been inactivated. The 11th Air Defense Artillery Brigade returned to Fort Bliss and remains active as the Army's EAC air defense artillery brigade, however.

VII Corps Units

➤ The VII Corps and almost all of its supporting units (such as its corps support command and engineer brigade) were inactivated in 1992. Many of the VII Corps' combat units were also effected.

➤ The 1st Armored Division that fought in Desert Storm was inactivated in Germany in 1992, and the 8th Infantry Division(Mech) in Germany was reflagged as the 1st Armored Division and reassigned to the V Corps. The 3rd Brigade, 3rd Infantry Division(Mech), which served as the 1st Armored Division's 1st Brigade during Desert Storm, returned to Germany and its parent division. The 3rd Armored Division was inactivated in Germany in 1992.

➤ The 1st Infantry Division(Mech)(-) returned to Fort Riley, but the division headquarters was inactivated there in February 1996. At the same time, the 3rd Infantry Division(Mech)(-) in Germany was reflagged as the 1st Infantry Division(Mech)(-). As part of these reflaggings, the 1st Armored Division and 1st Infantry Division(Mech) each ended up with a division(-) in Germany and one brigade at Fort Riley.

➤ The 1st Cavalry Division(-) returned to its previous assignment at Fort Hood as a unit of the III Corps. The 1st Brigade, 2nd Armored Division also returned to Fort Hood and was reflagged as the 1st Cavalry Division's 3rd Brigade in May 1991, thereby bringing the 1st Cav to full strength. The 3rd Brigade, 2nd Armored Division, which served with the 1st Infantry Division(Mech) during Desert Storm, was inactivated in Germany in 1992.

➤ In 1992, the 2nd Armored Cavalry Regiment was inactivated in Germany and the 199th Infantry Brigade(Mtzd) at Fort Lewis was reflagged as the 2nd Armored Cavalry Regiment(Light). This unit then moved to Fort Polk in spring 1993. A "light" armored cavalry regiment is, in reality, a motorized infantry brigade that possesses no armored vehicles.

➤ The 11th Aviation Brigade returned to Germany, was redesignated as the 11th Aviation Regiment and reassigned to the V Corps, and was reorganized as an Apache-pure attack helicopter unit. Of the four field artillery brigades assigned to VII Corps Artillery, the 42nd moved from Germany to Fort Polk in September 1992 and was inactivated there in June 1995; the 75th returned to Fort Sill and its previous assignment with III Corps Artillery; the 142nd returned to its previous status as an Arkansas Army National Guard unit; and the 210th moved from Germany to Fort Lewis in January 1992 and was inactivated there in 1996.

XVIII Airborne Corps Units

➤ The XVIII Airborne Corps, most of its supporting units, the 82nd Airborne Division, and the 101st Airborne Division(Air Aslt), all returned to their pre-Desert Storm postings and assignments and continue to serve in those roles today. The 24th Infantry Division(Mech)(-) and 197th Infantry Brigade(Mech) returned to, respectively, Forts Stewart and Benning. The 197th was reflagged as the 24th Infantry Division(Mech)'s 3rd Brigade in June 1991, thereby bringing the division to full strength. Finally, in April 1996 the 24th Infantry Division(Mech) was reflagged as the 3rd Infantry Division(Mech).

➢ The 3rd Armored Cavalry Regiment returned to its pre-war assignment with the III Corps at Fort Bliss. In 1995-96, however, the 3rd ACR moved to Fort Carson. The 12th Aviation Brigade returned to Germany and its pre-Desert Storm assignment with the V Corps, while the 18th Aviation Brigade stayed with the XVIII Airborne Corps at Fort Bragg. The 12th was later reorganized, however, losing all of its Apache attack helicopter units because this role was assigned to the 11th Aviation Regiment. Of the three field artillery brigades that comprised XVIII Airborne Corps Artillery, the 18th returned to Fort Bragg; the 196th returned to its previous status as a Tennessee National Guard unit; and the 212th returned to Fort Sill and its assignment with III Corps Artillery.

Army Special Operations Forces

➢ The 3rd, 5th, and 10th Special Forces Groups(Abn) returned to their pre-Desert Storm postings at, respectively, Forts Bragg, Campbell, and Devens. The 3rd Special Forces Group, which had been substantially understrength during ODS, was expanded to a full group in 1992. The 10th Special Forces Group(-) moved from Fort Devens to Fort Carson in 1994-95.

➢ The 5th and 7th Special Operations Support Commands(TA)(Abn) were inactivated in the mid 1990s. The other Army special operations units that participated in Desert Storm — the 75th Ranger Regiment(Abn), 160th Special Operations Aviation Regiment(Abn), 1st Special Forces Operational Detachment-Delta(Abn), and 4th Psychological Operations Group(Abn) — remain active today.

Notes:

➢ "Reflagged" is an unofficial, but widely used, term that refers to what happens when a U.S. Army unit acquires a new designation but the Army does not recognize a historic connection between the two units. For example, in 1995 the 2nd Armd Div was active at Fort Hood and the 4th Inf Div(M) was active at Fort Carson. The Army decided it no longer needed a division flag at Fort Carson, but it wanted to maintain the 4th Inf Div(M) on active duty. The Army could have inactivated the 2nd Armd Div at Hood, sent the personnel and equipment of that division on to other assignments, and moved the 4th Inf Div(M) from Carson to Hood. The Army concluded, however, that it was more economical to inactivate the units at Carson and "reflag" the 2nd Armd Div at Hood as the 4th Inf Div(M). This was accomplished by having the soldiers at Hood remove their 2nd Armd Div shoulder patches and sew on 4th Inf Div(M) patches — thereby magically losing the history of the 2nd Armd Div and acquiring the history of the 4th Inf Div(M). The Army insists there is no historical relationship between the 2nd Armd Div and 4th Inf Div(M), and that the 2nd Armd Div was inactivated while the 4th Inf Div(M) was transferred from Carson to Hood. This fiction ignores the fact that it is a unit's personnel that provide continuity and a connection to the past — not the dry words recorded in orders that most soldiers never even see.

Chart 16

Major U.S. Marine Corps Units
That Participated In Operation Desert Storm,
By Unit Type

This chart lists all of the major U.S. Marine Corps units that participated in Operation Desert Storm, including units that were stationed in the Mediterranean, by unit type.

Unit	Assignment, Desert Storm	Assignment & Location Prior to Desert Storm
I MEF	CENTCOM	FMF Pacific, Pendleton
1st Mar Div(Rein)	I MEF	I MEF, Pendleton
2nd Mar Div(Rein)	I MEF	II MEF, Lejeune
4th MEB	NAVCENT	II MEF, Little Creek
5th MEB	NAVCENT; I MEF[1]	I MEF, Pendleton
24th Marines(-)	I MEF	KS/IL/WI/IA/MO/IN/TN USMCR
11th MEU(SOC)[2]	5th MEB	I MEF, Pendleton
13th MEU(SOC)	NAVCENT	I MEF, Pendleton

[1] The 5th MEB was initially afloat in the Gulf, assigned to NAVCENT. The 5th MEB began landing in Saudi territory on 24 Feb 91 and was, at that time, reassigned from NAVCENT to MARCENT as I MEF reserve.

[2] The 11th MEU(SOC) was "embedded" within the 5th MEB, which meant it normally operated under 5th MEB but could be broken out as an independent Marine expeditionary unit when necessary.

Order of Battle

Unit	Assignment, Desert Storm	Assignment & Location Prior to Desert Storm
24th MEU(SOC)[3]	Sixth Fleet	II MEF, Lejeune
26th MEU(SOC)[4]	Sixth Fleet	II MEF, Lejeune
1st SRI Gp	I MEF	I MEF, Pendleton
3rd CAG	I MEF	CA USMCR
4th CAG	I MEF	DC USMCR
1st FSSG	I MEF	I MEF, Pendleton
General Spt Gp 1	1st FSSG	KTO[5]
General Spt Gp 2	1st FSSG	KTO[6]
Direct Spt Cmd	I MEF	KTO[7]
Direct Spt Gp 1	Direct Spt Cmd	KTO[8]
Direct Spt Gp 2	Direct Spt Cmd	KTO[9]
Combat Replacement Regt	I MEF	KTO[10]

Notes:

➢ "KTO" in the "Assignment & Location Prior to Desert Storm" column indicates that the unit was activated in the Kuwaiti Theater of Operations during Operations Desert Shield/Storm.

➢ "USMCR" in the "Assignment & Location Prior to Desert Storm" column indicates that the unit was a Marine Corps Reserve unit located in the state(s) indicated.

---

[3] During Desert Storm the 24th and 26th MEU(SOC) were forward-deployed in the Mediterranean as the Landing Force, Sixth Fleet. See Chart 20.

[4] See Footnote 3.

[5] HQ, General Spt Gp 1 was formed in the KTO on 12 Sep 90 from HQ, BSSG-1, which had been assigned to the 1st MEB at Kaneohe Bay prior to Desert Storm.

[6] This unit was organized on 1 Dec 90.

[7] This unit was organized on 22 Dec 90 from HQ, 2nd FSSG (which had been stationed at Camp Lejeune and assigned to II MEF), and logistics units from the 1st & 2nd FSSGs and BSSG-1 (which had been stationed at Kaneohe Bay and assigned to the 1st MEB).

[8] This unit was organized on 12 Dec 90. The commanding officer of BSSG-7 (which had been stationed at Twentynine Palms and assigned to the 7th MEB) became the commander of DSG-1.

[9] This unit was organized on 20 Dec 90, primarily from 2nd FSSG units (which had been stationed at Camp Lejeune and assigned to II MEF). HQ, DSG-2 was formed from HQ, BSSG-6, which had been stationed at Camp Lejeune and assigned to the 6th MEB, a II MEF unit.

[10] Formed on 8 Feb 91 (one source says 22 Jan 91). The regiment was dissolved on 21 Mar 91.

Chart 17

Major Ground Formations,[1] MARCENT

I Marine Expeditionary Force was the senior Marine headquarters in the Gulf and served as MARCENT, the Marine Corps component command of the U.S. Central Command. This chart depicts all of the major units that served under MARCENT/I MEF.

I Marine Expeditionary Force

1st Mar Div(Rein)
2nd Mar Div(Rein) [Fr. II MEF]
    1st Bde, 2nd Armd Div ("Tiger Bde") [U.S. Army] [Fr. 2 AD(-)]
5th MEB[2]
24th Marines(-)[3] [KS/IL/WI/IA/MO/IN/TN USMCR]
1st SRI Gp
3rd CAG(Rein)[4] [CA/DC USMCR]

---

[1] I MEF also included substantial aviation elements, which were under the command of the 3rd Marine Aircraft Wing.

[2] The 5th MEB was initially afloat in the Gulf, assigned to NAVCENT. The 5th MEB began landing in Saudi territory on 24 Feb 91 and was, at that time, reassigned from NAVCENT to MARCENT as I MEF reserve.

[3] The 24th Marines(-) were tasked with rear area security and served as I MEF's Rear Area Operations Center. The 24th Marines(-) were OPCON to I MEF(Rear).

[4] The 3rd CAG [CA USMCR] was reinforced by the 4th CAG [DC USMCR] and the consolidated unit was called the 3rd CAG(Rein). It appears that the 4th CAG primarily supported the 2nd Mar Div(Rein).

I Marine Expeditionary Force (continued)

        3rd Naval Construc Regt[5]
        1st FSSG[6]
            General Support Group 1
            General Support Group 2
        Direct Support Cmd[7]
            Direct Support Group 1 (Spt'd 1 Mar Div(Rein))
            Direct Support Group 2 (Spt'd 2 Mar Div(Rein))
        Combat Replacement Regt[8]

Notes:

➢   The first Marine Corps units to deploy to the Gulf were the 7th MEB, from Twentynine Palms, and the subordinate units of the 1st MEB, from Kaneohe Bay. On 3 Sep 90, I MEF stood up in the KTO by "compositing" these units. On 6 Sep 90, the 1st Mar Div stood up in-theater; at that time, HQ, 1st Mar Div replaced HQ, 7th Marines as the senior headquarters for I MEF's Ground Combat Element. Accordingly, the 1st and 7th MEBs are not listed in any of the charts. Note also that the 1st MEB's Command Group did not deploy; its subordinate units were relieved from assignment to the 1st MEB when they deployed to the Gulf, and HQ, 1st MEB remained on Hawaii.

---

[5] This was a construction, or so-called "Sea Bee," unit. The designation 3rd Naval Construc Regt was adopted on 11 Dec 90, the previous designation of this unit's headquarters element had been Commander, Construc Bns, Pacific, Forward Deployed (COMCBPAC FOXTROT DELTA). This was a provisional headquarters created during Desert Shield from the staffs of COMCBPAC; Commander, Construc Bns, Atlantic (COMCBLANT); and the 31st Naval Construc Regt, which was a training unit at the Naval Construc Bn Ctr, Port Hueneme, CA

[6] The 1st FSSG functioned as a general support command, moving supplies from the ports and rear logistics bases to the Direct Spt Cmd, which then delivered the supplies to the forward-deployed units of I MEF. The CG of the 1st FSSG was the senior Marine logistician in I MEF and was responsible for the overall logistics effort.

[7] See Footnote 6.

[8] Created to control individual Marines who were deployed as replacements for combat losses. Was supposed to consist of 20 companies, but initially only ten were formed and apparently only one additional company was activated later, on 10 Feb 91. During the ground war the regiment apparently had between 1,700 and 1,800 personnel.

Chart 18

Major Ground Formations, NAVCENT

The Seventh Fleet was the senior Navy headquarters in the Gulf and served as NAVCENT, the Navy component command of the U.S. Central Command. Marine Corps units afloat in the Gulf were assigned to NAVCENT rather than MARCENT. This chart depicts all of the major units that served under NAVCENT. The Marine forces afloat in the Gulf during Desert Storm had almost 18,000 Marines and "constituted the largest Marine combat landing force since the Cuban Missile Crisis of 1962."[1]

| Seventh Fleet |

Amphibious Task Force[2]

Landing Force[3]

4th MEB [Fr. II MEF]
5th MEB[4] [Fr. I MEF]
13th MEU(SOC) [Fr. I MEF]

---

[1] LtCol Ronald J. Brown, USMCR, Retired, *U.S. Marines in the Persian Gulf, 1990-1991: With Marine Forces Afloat In Desert Shield And Desert Storm*, page 192. Washington, DC: History and Museums Division, Headquarters, U.S. Marine Corps, 1998.

[2] The Amphibious Task Force (ATF) was also known as Task Force 156. The ATF was a naval unit commanded by an admiral.

[3] The Landing Force (LF) was also known as Task Force 158. The LF was a Marine Corps unit commanded by a Marine major general.

[4] The 5th MEB began landing in Saudi territory on 24 Feb 91 and was, at that time, reassigned from NAVCENT to MARCENT as I MEF reserve. "Embedded" within the 5th MEB was the 11th MEU(SOC), which had a reinforced infantry battalion as its GCE. See Chart 19, Footnote 105.

Order of Battle

Notes:

➤ Many sources state that Marine units afloat in the Gulf were assigned to II MEF. This is incorrect. HQ, II MEF did not deploy to the Gulf. The Marines afloat in the Gulf were under the command of MajGen Harry Jenkins, who was dual-hatted as Commander, Landing Force and Commanding General, 4th MEB. The Marine Corps considered activating a new MEF headquarters, VI MEF (Forward), to command all Marine forces afloat in the Gulf, but ultimately did not activate this headquarters.

➤ The 4th MEB and 13th MEU(SOC) were "associated," which meant that the 13th MEU(SOC) remained a separate unit capable of independent action (rather than being composited into 4th MEB), but the 13th MEU(SOC) took its orders from the 4th MEB when operating in close proximity to that unit.

➤ These units were embarked upon the following Navy units:

　　4th MEB　　　　　Amphibious Group 2 (PhibGru 2)
　　5th MEB　　　　　Amphibious Group 3 (PhibGru 3)
　　13th MEU(SOC)　　Amphibious Squadron 5 (PhibRon 5)

These amphibious units totalled 41 ships, 31 Navy amphibious ships and 10 support ships operated by the Military Sealift Command (MSC). PhibGru 2, PhibGru 3, and Phibron 5 together comprised the Amphibious Task Force.

➤ Amphibious Group 2, which carried the 4th MEB, consisted of Amphibious Squadrons 6 and 8, with a total of 21 ships (13 Navy amphibious ships and eight support ships operated by MSC):

Navy Amphibious Ships

　　USS _Nassau_ (LHA 4)　[Flagship of ATF, LF & PhibGru 2]
　　USS _Iwo Jima_ (LPH 2)
　　USS _Guam_ (LPH 9)
　　USS _Portland_ (LSD 37)
　　USS _Pensacola_ (LSD 38)
　　USS _Gunston Hall_ (LSD 44)
　　USS _Raleigh_ (LPD 1)
　　USS _Trenton_ (LPD 14)
　　USS _Shreveport_ (LPD 12)
　　USS _Manitowoc_ (LST 1180)
　　USS _Saginaw_ (LST 1188)
　　USS _Spartanburg_ County (LST 1192)
　　USS _LaMoure County_ (LST 1194)

Military Sealift Command Support Ships

USNS *Wright* (T-AVB 3) [Aviation support ship]
MV *Cape Domingo* (T-AKR 5053) [Vehicle cargo ship]
MV *Strong Texan* (T-AKR[5] 9670) [Vehicle cargo ship]
MV *Bassro Polar*
MV *Pheasant*
MV *Aurora T*
MV *PFC William B. Baugh, Jr.*[6] (T-AK 3001) [MPS ship]
MV *1stLt Alex Bonnyman, Jr.* (T-AK 3003) [MPS ship]

➢   Amphibious Group 3, which carried the 5th MEB, had a total of 15 ships (13 Navy amphibious ships and two support ships operated by MSC):

Navy Amphibious Ships

USS *Tarawa* (LHA 1) [Flagship of PhibGru 3]
USS *Tripoli* (LPH 10)[7]
*USS *New Orleans* (LPH 11)[8]
USS *Anchorage* (LSD 36)
USS *Mount Vernon* (LSD 39)
*USS *Germantown* (LSD 42)
USS *Vancouver* (LPD 2)
*USS *Denver* (LPD 9)
USS *Juneau* (LPD 10)
*USS *Peoria* (LST 1183)
USS *Frederick* (LST 1184)
USS *Barbour County* (LST 1195)
*USS *Mobile* (LKA 115)

Military Sealift Command Support Ships

USNS *Flickertail State* (T-ACS 5) [Crane ship]
MV *Cape Girardeau* (T-AK 2039) [Cargo ship]

Those ships marked by an asterisk were assigned to PhibRon 1, which carried the 11th MEU(SOC), which was embedded within the 5th MEB. See Chart 19, Footnote 105.

---

[5] May have been T-AK 9670.

[6] The *Baugh* and *Bonnyman* were combination container and roll-on/roll-off (RO/RO) vehicle cargo ships previously assigned to Maritime Prepositioning Ship Squadron 2.

[7] The *Tripoli* left PhibGru 3 and was dedicated to clearing naval mines serving as a platform for Navy mine clearing helicopters. The *Tripoli* began reconfiguring its embarked assets in preparation for this mission on 21 Jan 91 and began mine clearing operations on 16 Feb 91. On 18 Feb 91, the *Tripoli* set off an Iraqi naval mine which caused heavy damage. As a result of this development, the USS *New Orleans* (LPH 11) left the ATF and replaced the *Tripoli* in support of mine clearing operations on 4 Mar 91, after the war was over.

[8] See Footnote 7.

Order of Battle

➢ Amphibious Squadron 5, which carried the 13th MEU(SOC), consisted of five Navy amphibious ships:

> USS _Okinawa_ (LPH 3) [Flagship of PhibRon 5]
> USS _Fort McHenry_ (LSD 43)
> USS _Ogden_ (LPD 5)
> USS _Cayuga_ (LST 1186)
> USS _Durham_ (LKA 114)

During Desert Storm, PhibRon 5 was also known as Amphibious Ready Group A or "ARG Alpha."

➢ The Seventh Fleet was the Navy command responsible for the Pacific area. A MEU was typically forward-deployed in the Pacific and assigned to the Seventh Fleet. This MEU was then known as Landing Force Seventh Fleet (LF7F). During Desert Storm, the 13th MEU(SOC) was LF7F.

➢ According to Marine Corps and Navy doctrine, all of the equipment and supplies needed to execute an amphibious assault are to be loaded on Navy amphibious ships, which are designed to be able to land these items efficiently on hostile beaches. The assault follow-on echelon (AFOE), which consists of the personnel, equipment, and supplies needed to sustain an amphibious assault, is carried on ships owned or leased by MSC. These ships are manned by civilian crews (which may include retired sailors) and are typically not optimally configured to support amphibious landings.

➢ Ships for which no alpha-numeric designators are given were leased from commercial sources, rather than owned by the Government, and thus did not have alpha-numeric designators.

Chart 18A

U.S. Navy Amphibious Ships
On Which Marine Units Were Embarked
During Operation Desert Storm

This chart lists the ships that supported Marine forces afloat in the Gulf or the Mediterranean during Desert Storm. The ships are listed by type, and within each type, by hull number.

Navy Amphibious Ships

Ship	Assignment
USS *Tarawa* (LHA 1)	PhibGru 3 (Flagship)
USS *Nassau* (LHA 4)	PhibGru 2 (Flagship)[1]
USS *Iwo Jima* (LPH 2)	PhibGru 2
USS *Okinawa* (LPH 3	PhibRon 5
USS *Guadalcanal* (LPH 7)	PhibRon 8 (Flagship)
USS *Guam* (LPH 9)	PhibGru 2
USS *Tripoli* (LPH 10)[2]	PhibGru 3
* USS *New Orleans* (LPH 11)[3]	PhibGru 3
USS *Inchon* (LPH 12)	PhibRon 2

---

[1] The *Nassau* was also flagship of the LF and ATF.
[2] See Chart 18, Footnote 7.
[3] See Chart 18, Footnote 8.

Order of Battle

Ship	Unit
USS *Anchorage* (LSD 36)	PhibGru 3
USS *Portland* (LSD 37)	PhibGru 2
USS *Pensacola* (LSD 38)	PhibGru 2
USS *Mount Vernon* (LSD 39)	PhibGru 3
USS *Whidbey Island* (LSD 41)	PhibRon 2
*USS *Germantown* (LSD 42	PhibGru 3
USS *Fort McHenry* (LSD 43)	PhibRon 5
USS *Gunston Hall* (LSD 44)	PhibGru 2
USS *Raleigh* (LPD 1)	PhibGru 2
USS *Vancouver* (LPD 2)	PhibGru 3
USS *Austin* (LPD 4)	PhibRon 8
USS *Ogden* (LPD 5)	PhibRon 5
* USS *Denver* (LPD 9)	PhibGru 3
USS *Juneau* (LPD 10)	PhibGru 3
USS *Shreveport* (LPD 12)	PhibGru 2
USS *Nashville* (LPD 13)	PhibRon 2
USS *Trenton* (LPD 14)	PhibGru 2
USS *Newport* (LST 1179)	PhibRon 2
USS *Manitowoc* (LST 1180)	PhibGru 2
* USS *Peoria* (LST 1183)	PhibGru 3
USS *Frederick* (LST 1184)	PhibGru 3
USS *Cayuga* (LST 1186)	PhibRon 5
USS *Saginaw* (LST 1188)	PhibGru 2
USS *Spartanburg County* (LST 1192)	PhibGru 2
USS *LaMoure County* (LST 1194)	PhibGru 2
USS *Fairfax County* (LST 1193)	PhibRon 2
USS *Barbour County* (LST 1195)	PhibGru 3
USS *Barnstable County* (LST 1197)[4]	PhibRon 2
USS *Charleston* (LKA 113)	PhibRon 8
USS *Durham* (LKA 114)	PhibRon 5
* USS *Mobile* (LKA 115)	PhibGru 3

---

[4] The sources disagree as to whether the *Barnstable County* was assigned to PhibRon 2.

Military Sealift Command Support Ships

Ship	Assignment
USNS *Wright* (T-AVB 3)	PhibGru 2
USNS *Flickertail State* (T-ACS 5)	PhibGru 3
MV *Cape Domingo* (T-AKR 5053)	PhibGru 2
MV *Cape Girardeau* (T-AK 2039)	PhibGru 3
MV *PFC William B. Baugh, Jr.* (T-AK 3001)	PhibGru 2
MV *1stLt Alex Bonnyman, Jr.* (T-AK 3003)	PhibGru 2
MV *Strong Texan* (T-AKR 9670) [5]	PhibGru 2
MV *Bassro Polar*	PhibGru 2
MV *Pheasant*	PhibGru 2
MV *Aurora T*	PhibGru 2

Notes:

➢ Those ships marked by an asterisk were assigned to PhibRon 1, which carried the 11th MEU(SOC), which was embedded within the 5th MEB. See Chart 19, Footnote 105.

➢ The Navy amphibious units listed here are addressed on the following charts:

Navy Unit	Chart	Embarked USMC Unit
PhibGru 2	Chart 18	4th MEB
PhibGru 3	Chart 18	5th MEB
PhibRon 2	Chart 20	26th MEU(SOC)
PhibRon 5	Chart 18	13th MEU(SOC)
PhibRon 8	Chart 20	24th MEU(SOC)

➢ Navy amphibious ship abbreviations are as follows:

LHA Amphibious Assault Ship (General Purpose)
LPH Amphibious Assault Ship (Helicopter)
LSD Dock Landing Ship
LPD Amphibious Transport Dock
LST Tank Landing Ship
LKA Amphibious Cargo Ship

---

[5] The sources disagree as to whether the *Barnstable County* was assigned to PhibRon 2.

Order of Battle

> Distribution Of Ships, By Ship Type and Unit

Ship	Total	PhibGru 2 (4th MEB)	PhibGru 3 (5th MEB)	PhibRon 2 (26th MEU)	PhibRon 5 (13th MEU)	PhibRon 8 (24th MEU)
LHA	2	1	1			
LPH	7	2	2	1	1	1
LSD	8	3	3	1	1	
LPD	9	3	3	1	1	1
LST	11[6]	4	3	3[7]	1	
LKA	3		1		1	1
MSC	10	8	2			
TOTAL	50[8]	21	15	6[9]	5	3

[6] May have only been ten. See Footnote 4.
[7] May have only been two. See Footnote 4.
[8] May have only been 49. See Footnote 4.
[9] May have only been five. See Footnote 4.

18A - 4

Chart 19

U.S. Marine Corps Ground Combat Units
That Deployed To the Gulf During Desert Storm,
By Division/Brigade

This chart lists all U.S. Marine Corps ground combat units that deployed to the Gulf, whether they were assigned to MARCENT or NAVCENT. It does not list units that were afloat in the Mediterranean, however (see Chart 20). This chart also provides a short combat narrative for the major units that fought in Desert Storm.

I MARINE EXPEDITIONARY FORCE

Det 2,[1] HQ Btry, 14th Marines (Artillery) [TX USMCR]

1st SRI Gp

Force Reconnaissance Gp(Composite)[2]
   1st Force Recon Co(-)[3]
   2nd Force Recon Co(-)[4] [Fr. 2 SRI Gp]
   3rd Force Recon Co(-) [AL USMCR]
   4th Force Recon Co(-) [HI USMCR]

---

[1] Supplemented the I MEF Fire Spt Coordination Cell.

[2] Formed in the KTO on 27 Dec 90. One source reports this unit was designated the "1st Force Recon Bn(Prov)."

[3] Consisted of Co HQ, the 5th-7th Plts, and probably other elements of the 1st Force Recon Co.

[4] According to the Marines, the 2nd Force Recon Co's 1st Plt was the first unit to enter the U.S. Embassy in Kuwait during the final hours of Desert Storm. The Army's 5th SF Gp(Abn) also claims credit for this, however, and it appears that — officially — the 3rd SF Gp(Abn) has been credited with this accomplishment.

I MARINE EXPEDITIONARY FORCE (continued)

24th Marines(-)[5] [KS/IL/WI/IA/MO/IN/TN USMCR]

    2/24 Marines[6] [IL/WI/IA USMCR]
    3/24 Marines [MO/IL/IN/TN USMCR]

1st Marine Division (Rein)

The 1st Marine Division(Rein) attacked north in the right-hand portion of the I MEF zone, with the 2nd Marine Division(Rein) to its left and the Joint Forces Command-East to its right. The 1st Marine Division organized most of its maneuver units into four task forces,[7] each commanded by an infantry regiment headquarters. Two were primarily dismounted infantry that used infiltration tactics to penetrate the Iraqi front lines. The other two had most of the division's armored vehicles and used a mechanized approach, mounting their infantry in assault amphibious vehicles. The two dismounted task forces began infiltrating Kuwait several days before the ground war began.

The 1st Marine Division initiated its attack at 0400 hours on 24 Feb 91. The division attacked toward the northeast with four task forces on line, from left to right, TF Grizzly, TF Ripper, TF Papa Bear, and TF Taro. The dismounted task forces were on the outside and secured the division's flanks. By the evening of 24 Feb 91, the 1st Marine Division had completely penetrated the Iraqi forward defenses with TF Ripper and TF Papa Bear, while TF Grizzly and TF Taro were still between the Iraqi first and second obstacle belts. Once through the second belt, TF Ripper turned to the left and attacked toward the northwest.

On 25 Feb 91, the 1st Marine Division fought off a determined Iraqi armored counterattack. By that evening, the 1st Marine Division had its two mechanized task forces, Ripper and Papa Bear, north of the second obstacle belt and on line, prepared to attack north. Task Force Grizzly was behind these two task forces, having successfully attacked Al Jaber Airfield that afternoon, while TF Taro was still between the first and second obstacle belts.

---

[5] See Chart 17, Footnote 3.
[6] A provisional rifle company was formed by H&S Co.
[7] The 1st Mar Div used named task forces in lieu of the standard numbered regimental designations to enhance cohesion among the many diverse units assigned to each task force.

Commencing at 0630 hours on 26 Feb 91, the 1st Marine Division attacked north, with TF Ripper on the left and TF Papa Bear on the right, to seize Kuwait International Airport. By 0800 hours on 27 Feb 91, TF Taro had joined this effort (while TF Grizzly remained at Al Jaber Airfield), and by 0900 hours the division had ceased offensive operations after seizing the airport.

Organization of the 1st Marine Division(Rein)

Division Forward CP[8]

    Co C, 1/1 Marines
    Co B,[9] 3rd LAI Bn [Fr. 3 Mar Div(-)]

Division Main CP

    1st Recon Bn(-)[10]
        Co A(-) [Dismtd ?],[11] 3rd Recon Bn [Fr. 3 Mar Div(-)]

Task Force Papa Bear[12] (1st Marines) "Armor Mech Force"

    1/1 Marines(-)[13]
        4th Plt,[14] AT Co [TOW], 1st Tank Bn
        Co B, 3rd Aslt Amphib Bn
    3/9 Marines(-)
        Co B, 1st Tank Bn [M60A1]
        1st Plt(-), AT Co [TOW], 1st Tank Bn
        Co C, 3rd Aslt Amphib Bn

---

[8] The Division Forward CP was also defended by TOW antitank units for most of the ground war. See Footnote 29.

[9] At 2300 hours on 24 Feb 91, Co B sent one platoon to provide security to the 1st Mar Div Forward CP. By 0700 hours on 25 Feb 91 this had been expanded to Co B(-) and, by 1330 hours on 25 Feb 91, to all of Co B. See Footnotes 33 & 35.

[10] Consisted of H&S Co and Cos A(-) & C(-). The 1st Plt of Co C was motorized; it is unclear if the remainder of Co C(-) was.

[11] Company A's 2nd Plt conducted a screen of the division's east flank until 26 Feb 91. While most of Co A(-) was apparently dismounted, the 1st Plt was motorized.

[12] Adopted the name "TF Papa Bear" o/a 1 Jan 91. Was the 1st Mar Div's reserve. See Footnote 44.

[13] Consisted of H&S Co, Cos A, B & D, and Wpns Co.

[14] See Footnote 117.

Task Force Papa Bear (continued)

    1st Tank Bn(-)[15] [M60A1]
        Co I, 3/9 Marines
            1st Sec, AT Plt [TOW], HQ Co, 3rd Marines [Fr. 1 MEB]
        AT Plt [TOW],[16] HQ Co, 1st Marines (?)
        1st Plt, Btry B, 3rd LAAD Bn [Stinger] [Fr. MACG 38]

Task Force Taro[17] (3rd Marines) "Infiltration Force"

    1/3 Marines(-)[18] [Fr. 1 MEB]
    2/3 Marines [Fr. 3 Mar Div(-)]
        1st Sec, 3rd Plt, AT Co [TOW], 1st Tank Bn [Fr. 3 Mar Div(-)]
        (1) Team, Sec C, 3rd Plt, Btry B, 3rd LAAD Bn [Stinger] [Fr. MACG 38]
    3/3 Marines [Fr. 1 MEB]
        Armor Det,[19] H&S Co, 1st Tank Bn
        (1) Sec, AT Plt [TOW], HQ Co, 3rd Marines [Fr. 1 MEB]
        3rd Sec, 3rd Plt, AT Co [TOW], 1st Tank Bn [Fr. 3 Mar Div(-)]
    AT Plt(-) [TOW], HQ Co, 3rd Marines (?) [Fr. 1 MEB]
    2nd Sec, 3rd Plt, AT Co [TOW], 1st Tank Bn [Fr. 3 Mar Div(-)]
    Co C,[20] 1st LAI Bn
    3rd Plt [Mtzd], Co D, 1st Recon Bn
    3rd Plt [Dismtd],[21] Co A, 3rd Recon Bn [Fr. 1 MEB]
    2nd Plt,[22] Co C, 3rd Recon Bn [Fr. 3 Mar Div(-)]
    Sec C(-), 3rd Plt, Btry B, 3rd LAAD Bn [Stinger] [Fr. MACG 38]

---

[15] Consisted of H&S Co, Cos C & D, and AT Co(-) [TOW]. This battalion had 58 M60A1 MBTs and five M60A3 MBTs. The AT Co(-) consisted of Co HQ, the 2nd Plt, and one section from the 1st Plt. Company D deployed to Saudi Arabia from an assignment with the 3rd Mar Div(-) on Okinawa. The 1st Tank Bn became 1st Mar Div reserve on 26 Feb 91.

[16] Some or all of this platoon's sections were probably attached to the other units of TF Papa Bear.

[17] See Footnotes 32, 40, 41 & 44. Had adopted the name "TF Taro" by 30 Nov 90. The 3rd Marines were assigned to the 1st MEB at Kaneohe Bay before Desert Shield began.

[18] Consisted of H&S Co(-), Co B, and Wpns Co(-). Apparently assisted TF Taro with rear area security. The battalion's "Bravo" Cmd Gp & Mor Plt, and Co B, departed TF Taro on 24 Feb 91, served briefly with TF Ripper commencing at 1500 hours, 24 Feb 91, and then became OPCON to TF Warden on 25 Feb 91. These elements left TF Warden at noon on 26 Feb 91 and rejoined TF Taro at 0300 hours on 27 Feb 91. See Footnote 32.

[19] Consisted of two M60A1 MBTs and two Amphibious Assault Vehicles.

[20] Company C returned to TF Shepherd at 1400 hours on 24 Feb 91. See Footnotes 33 & 34.

[21] The 3rd Plt had 2 teams in the town of Khafji during the Battle of Khafji, 29-31 Jan 91. See Chart 29, page 29-5.

[22] May have been the 1st Plt, rather than the 2nd Plt. One source states Co C(-) served in SWA, but I believe this is incorrect.

Task Force Grizzly[23] (4th Marines) "Infiltration Force"

    2/7 Marines
        (1) Sec, AT Plt [TOW], HQ Co, 4th Marines [Fr. 3 Mar Div(-)]
        (1) Tm, 3rd LAAD Bn [Fr. MACG 38]
    3/7 Marines [Fr. 3 Mar Div(-)]
    AT Plt(-) [TOW],[24] HQ Co, 4th Marines (?) [Fr. 3 Mar Div(-)]
    2nd Plt [Dismtd ?], Co A, 1st Recon Bn
    Co D(-), 1st Recon Bn
    (1) LAAD unit [Fr. _____?]

Task Force Ripper[25] (7th Marines) "Armor Mech Force"

    1/5 Marines[26]
        Co A, 1st Tank Bn [M60A1]
        3rd Plt, AT Co [TOW], 3rd Tank Bn
        Co A,[27] 3rd Aslt Amphib Bn [Fr. 3 Mar Div(-) & 1 MEB]
    1/7 Marines(-)[28]
        Co A, 3rd Tank Bn [M60A1]
        AT Plt(-) [TOW],[29] HQ Co, 7th Marines
        Co D(-), 3rd Aslt Amphib Bn

---

[23] See Footnotes 40 & 44. Adopted the name "TF Grizzly" on 15 Feb 91. The 4th Marines were assigned to the 3rd Mar Div(-) on Okinawa before Desert Shield began.

[24] Apparently consisted of six sections, three more than usual. Some or all of this platoon's sections were probably attached to the other units of TF Grizzly.

[25] Was the 1st Mar Div's main effort. See Footnotes 18 & 44. Adopted the name "TF Ripper" on 14 Sep 90.

[26] See Footnote 31.

[27] Before Desert Storm, there were two independent units bearing the Co A designation: Co A(-), with three platoons, on Okinawa with the 3rd Mar Div(-); and Det, Co A, with two platoons, in Hawaii with the 1st MEB. These units were apparently consolidated in SWA as follows: Co A (2nd-5th Plts) supported the 1/5 Marines, while 1st Plt, Co A, served with the 13th MEU(SOC). Because Co A had four platoons under its command, I have not listed it here as a company(-).

[28] Consisted of H&S Co, Cos B & C, and Wpns Co.

[29] The AT Plt began the war under the 1/7 Marines. In the morning of 25 Feb 91, the AT Plt was detached to defend the 1st Mar Div Forward CP. In the morning of 26 Feb 91, the AT Plt(-) returned to the 1/7 Marines leaving one section with HQ, 1st Mar Div for the remainder of the war.

Task Force Ripper (continued)

    3rd Tank Bn(-)[30] [M60A1]
        Co A, 1/7 Marines
        1st Plt, Co D, 3rd Aslt Amphib Bn
    Co D,[31] 3rd LAI Bn [Fr. 3 Mar Div(-)]
    2nd Plt(Mtzd), Co C, 1st Recon Bn
    2nd Plt, Co C, 2nd Aslt Amphib Bn [Fr. 3 Mar Div(-)]

Task Force X-Ray[32] "Airmobile Anti Armor Force"

Task Force Shepherd[33] "Exploitation Force"

    1st LAI Bn(-)[34]
    Det,[35] 3rd LAI Bn [Fr. 3 Mar Div(-)]
    Sec A, 2nd Plt, Btry B, 3rd LAAD Bn [Stinger] [Fr. MACG 38]

---

[30] Consisted of H&S Co, Cos B & C, and AT Co(-) [TOW], 3rd Tank Bn; and Co D, 1st Armd Aslt Bn. Company D was a tank company equipped with the M60A1 MBT that deployed to Saudi Arabia from an assignment with the 3rd Mar Div(-) on Okinawa. See Appendix E, pages E-13 and E-14, for more information on the 1st Armd Aslt Bn. The 3rd Tank Bn was the first USMC tank unit to arrive in SWA, arriving o/a 17 Aug 90. By the time the ground war began, the battalion had 58 M60A1s and five or six M60A3s. The AT Co(-) consisted of Co HQ and the 2nd Plt. The 1st Plt, AT Co was initially TF Ripper reserve but rejoined the 3rd Tank Bn in the evening of 24 Feb 91. During the early stages of Desert Shield the 3rd Tank Bn organized a fourth AT platoon, but this platoon left the battalion before the war began and it is unclear where it served. It may have been disbanded to beef-up one or more regimental AT platoons. See Footnotes 24, 48 & 74.

[31] Company D left TF Ripper and rejoined TF Shepherd by 1330 hours on 25 Feb 91. Company D was then re-attached to TF Ripper at 0600 hours, 26 Feb 91. From around 1800 hours, 26 Feb 91, until apparently a little after 0900 hours on 27 Feb 91, Co D was attached to the 1/5 Marines. See Footnotes 33 & 35.

[32] The 1st Mar Div initially planned to use TF Taro as a three-battalion heliborne regiment. By mid-February, however, this had been scaled back to a single battalion, the 1/3 Marines [Fr. 1 MEB], which was then detached from TF Taro and redesignated TF X-Ray. Just before the ground war, limited helicopter assets forced a further reduction of this effort, to a combined antiarmor team (CAAT) of 125 marines from the 1/3 Marines equipped with TOW-armed jeeps. Task Force X-Ray's first mission was scrubbed in the early evening of 24 Feb 91 because of poor visibility and concerns that the landing zone was not secure from enemy fire. Task Force X-Ray successfully landed at BP X-Ray at 1100 hours on 25 Feb 91 and was joined by Co A, 1/3 Marines, on 26 Feb 91. Task Force X-Ray(-) and Co A(-) departed BP X-Ray and linked up with TF Taro on 27 Feb 91. The remainder of TF X-Ray and Co A remained at BP X-Ray until the end of the war. See Footnotes 40 & 41.

[33] Elements of the 1st and 3rd LAI Bns were deployed in August and September 1990 and were merged into a full strength LAI battalion that was initially known simply as "LAI Bn" without any numerical designation. Soon after, this unit adopted the designation "TF Shepherd," named after Gen Lemuel C. Shepherd, Jr., former Commandant of the Marine Corps, who passed away on 6 Aug 90, just before Operation Desert Shield began. See Footnotes 9, 20 & 31.

[34] Consisted of H&S Co and Cos A & C, 1st LAI Bn. See Footnote 20. Company A was attached to TF Troy 21-23 Feb 91. See Footnote 45.

[35] Consisted of Det, H&S Co, and Cos B & D, 3rd LAI Bn. See Footnotes 9 & 31.

Task Force King (11th Marines) (Artillery)

    1/11 Marines [155 T, 3 x 8] [DS TF Papa Bear][36]
        HQ Btry, 1/11 Marines
        Btry A, 1/11 Marines
        Btry I, 3/11 Marines
        Btry H, 3/14 Marines [VA USMCR]
    3/11 Marines [155 T, 3 x 8] [DS TF Ripper]
        HQ Btry, 3/11 Marines
        Btry G, 3/11 Marines
        Btry H, 3/11 Marines [Fr. 3 Mar Div(-)]
        Btry E,[37] 2/12 Marines
    5/11 Marines [155 T/155 SP/203 SP, 4 x 6][38] [GS][39]
        HQ Btry, 5/11 Marines
        Btry Q [155 T], 5/11 Marines
        Btry R [155 T], 5/11 Marines
        Btry S [155 SP], 5/11 Marines
        Btry T [203 SP], 5/11 Marines
    1/12 Marines [155 T, 3 x 8] [DS TF Taro][40] [Fr. 1 MEB]
        HQ Btry, 1/12 Marines [Fr. 1 MEB]
        Btry A, 1/12 Marines [Fr. 1 MEB]
        Btry C, 1/12 Marines [Fr. 1 MEB]
        Btry F, 2/12 Marines [Fr. 1 MEB]
        Co C,[41] 1/3 Marines [Fr. 1 MEB]
    3/12 Marines [155 T, 3 x 8] [DS TF Grizzly][42] [Fr. 3 Mar Div(-)]
        HQ Btry, 3/12 Marines [Fr. 3 Mar Div(-)]
        Btry B, 1/10 Marines [Fr. 3 Mar Div(-)]
        Btry F, 2/10 Marines [Fr. 3 Mar Div(-)]
        Btry I, 3/14 Marines [PA USMCR]

---

[36] Served as GS to the 1st Mar Div from 1500 hours on 25 Feb 91 to 1641 hours on 26 Feb 91.

[37] Was assigned to TF Troy as a dedicated battery from 15 Feb 91 until the morning of 23 Feb 91. See Footnote 45.

[38] In June 1990, the 5/11 Marines had just completed a transition from a self-propelled GS battalion to a towed GS battalion consisting of HQ Btry and Btrys Q-S. During Desert Shield this unit was converted to a composite self-propelled/towed battalion and Btry T was activated.

[39] Served as GSR to the 3/11 Marines from 0355 hours on 24 Feb 91 to 1500 hours on 25 Feb 91.

[40] The 1/12 Marines(-) reinforced the 1/11 Marines from 1100 hours on 24 Feb 91 to 1500 hours on 25 Feb 91, when it became DS to TF Taro and TF X-Ray, with Btry A dedicated to TF Grizzly. One AN/TPQ-36 "Firefinder" Radar was attached to the 1/12 Marines.

[41] Provided security to the 1/12 Marines until 2000 hours on 27 Feb 91, when Co C(-) departed and moved to join Task Forces Taro & X-Ray. The 3rd Plt remained with the 1/12 Marines until the end of the war.

[42] The 3/12 Marines reinforced the 3/11 Marines from the evening of 25 Feb 91 (one source says 1500 hours) until apparently the end of the war.

Task Force Warden[43] "EPW Force"

    1/25 Marines[44] [MA/NY/NH/CT/ME USMCR]
      Wpns Plt, Co D, 2/25 Marines [NJ USMCR]

Task Force Troy[45] "Ambiguity Force"

H&S Co,[46] 3rd Aslt Amphib Bn

2nd Marine Division(Rein)

The 2nd Marine Division(Rein) attacked north in the left-hand portion of the I MEF zone, with the 1st Marine Division(Rein) to its right and the Joint Forces Command-North to its left. The 2nd Marine Division was the I MEF main effort and included a disproportionate amount of the Marines' combat power. The 2nd Marine Division was organized into three regimental-level units: 6th Marines, 8th Marines, and the U.S. Army's 1st Brigade, 2nd Armored Division (the "Tiger Brigade").

The 2nd Marine Division initiated its artillery preparation at 0430 hours on 24 Feb 91 and then began crossing the line of departure at 0530 hours. The 6th Marines(Rein) conducted the breach of the Iraqi front line defenses for the division. The 2nd Marine Division passed through the breach in column, first the 6th Marines, then the Tiger Bde, and finally the 8th Marines. The 8th Marines did not cross the breach until the morning of 25 Feb 91.

The 2nd Marine Division attacked north with its three task forces on line, with the Tiger Brigade on the left (with Joint Forces Command-North to its left), the 6th Marines in the center, and the 8th Marines on the right (with the 1st Marine Division to its right), commencing at approximately 1330 hours on 25 Feb 91. By the evening of 26 Feb 91, the 2nd Marine Division had reached its final position just west of Kuwait City, still with its three task forces on line. The 2nd Marine Division held in this position

---

[43] Task Force Warden was responsible for processing EPWs captured by the 1st Mar Div. See Footnote 18.

[44] Companies A & B both supported TFs Taro & Grizzly, while Co C supported TF Ripper. Company A also apparently supported TF Papa Bear. See Footnote 45.

[45] Task Force Troy was a provisional unit that performed deception operations. Its mission was to conceal from the Iraqis the fact that I MEF had redeployed its forces to new locations after commencement of the air war. Task Force Troy apparently consisted of small detachments from various units. See Footnotes 34, 37 & 62. A reinforced platoon-sized element from Co B, 1/25 Marines was assigned to TF Troy until 26 Feb 91, when it returned to the 1/25 Marines.

[46] This unit's assignment and role are unclear. All of its subordinate units were attached to 1st Mar Div task forces. Also active was Det G, 3rd Aslt Amphib Bn, which was apparently a provisional unit formed in SWA. It was attached to the 1st Cbt Eng Bn.

and passed Egyptian forces of Joint Forces Command-North through to Kuwait City from the west during the morning of 27 Feb 91.

Organization of the 2nd Marine Division(Rein)

<u>HQ Battalion</u>

Co A, Marine Barracks, Washington, DC[47] [Fr. HQ, USMC]
AT Co(-) [TOW], 4th Tank Bn [OK USMCR]
Btry B(-), 2nd LAAD Bn [Stinger] [Fr. MACG 28]

<u>6th Marines</u>[48]

2/2 Marines[49]
    Co A, 8th Tank Bn [M60A1] [KY USMCR]
    2nd Plt(-),[50] AT Co [TOW], 8th Tank Bn [FL USMCR]
    (1) Sec, 3rd Plt, AT Co [TOW], 8th Tank Bn (?) [FL USMCR]
    Co B,[51] 2nd Aslt Amphib Bn
1/6 Marines [Fr. 3 Mar Div(-)]
    Co C,[52] 8th Tank Bn [M60A1] [FL USMCR]
    2nd Sec, AT Plt [TOW], HQ Co, 6th Marines
    1st Plt(-),[53] AT Co [TOW], 8th Tank Bn [FL USMCR]
    Co B,[54] 1st Armd Aslt Bn
3/6 Marines[55]
    3rd Sec, AT Plt [TOW], HQ Co, 6th Marines
    1st Sec, 3rd Plt, AT Co [TOW], 8th Tank Bn (?) [FL USMCR]

---

[47] Served as a rifle company providing security to HQ, 2nd Mar Div. See Footnote 56.

[48] On 24 Feb 91 the 6th Marines conducted the breach of the Iraqi front lines for the 2nd Mar Div. See Footnotes 59, 61 & 68. The 2/2 Marines and 1/6 Marines were mechanized (mounted in AAV7s), while the 3/6 Marines was motorized (mounted in trucks). During Desert Storm the 6th Marines' AT Plt had 36 TOWs, 12 more than usual.

[49] See Footnote 56.

[50] May have been the 1st Plt, rather than the 2nd Plt(-).

[51] May have been a company(-).

[52] Company C was transferred to the 3/6 Marines the evening of 27 Feb 91.

[53] See Footnote 50.

[54] An assault amphibian unit. May have been a company(-). See Appendix E, pages E-13 and E-14, for additional information on the 1st Armd Aslt Bn.

[55] See Footnote 52.

6th Marines (continued)

    8th Tank Bn(-)[56] [M60A1] [NY/SC/FL USMCR]
        Det, 2nd Aslt Amphib Bn
    AT Plt(-) [TOW],[57] HQ Co, 6th Marines (?)
    Co B,[58] 2nd LAI Bn [MD USMCR]
    TF Breach Alpha[59] (Combat Engineers)
        Det,[60] 8th Tank Bn [M60A1] [USMCR]
    TF Vega[61]
        (1) Sec, 1st Plt, AT Co [TOW], 4th Tank Bn [OK USMCR]
        Co D,[62] 4th Recon Bn [NM USMCR]
        Det, 2nd LAAD Bn [Stinger] [Fr. MACG 28]
    Det, H&S Co, 2nd Recon Bn
    Det, 2nd Aslt Amphib Bn
    1st Plt(-), Btry B, 2nd LAAD Bn [Stinger] (?) [Fr. MACG 28]
        2nd Sec, 2nd Plt, Btry B, 2nd LAAD Bn [Stinger] (?) [Fr. MACG 28]

---

[56] Consisted of H&S Co, Co B, and AT Co(-) [TOW]. It appears that AT Co(-) consisted only of the Company HQ. Prior to its mobilization for Desert Storm, the 8th Tank Bn had a fourth tank company, Co D [SC USMCR]. This unit was dissolved before the battalion deployed to the Gulf because the MPS ships that provided the battalion's equipment only carried sufficient tanks for three companies. Company D's personnel were transferred to the battalion's other units. The 8th Tank Bn was supposed to execute an attack at 1000 hours on 27 Feb 91 and for this mission was to receive one company from the 2/2 Marines. This mission was never executed, however it appears the planned reorganization occurred, but possibly not until the morning of 28 Feb 91. Throughout the ground war, the 3rd Sec, 2nd Plt, AT Co was attached to CSSD-26, a logistics unit, to provide security. The 2nd Sec, 3rd Plt, AT Co provided security to the forward command group of the 2nd Mar Div on 25 Feb 91, but this was apparently a temporary assignment.

[57] Some or all of this platoon's sections were probably attached to the other units of the 6th Marines.

[58] Served primarily as the 6th Marines' reserve. This unit was actually Co B, 4th LAV Bn [MD USMCR]. See Footnote 83.

[59] Conducted the breach of the Iraqi front lines for the 6th Marines. Consisted of combat engineers mounted in 22 AAV7s, another 18 AAV7s with MICLICs, 2 M60A1 dozer tanks, 16 M60A1s w/track width mine plows, 4 M60A1s with mine rakes, 6 M1A1s w/mine plows, 4 AVLBs, and 15 M9 ACEs. This task force was sometimes referred to as "Task Force Alfa" or "Task Force Alfa(Breach)." There may have also been a TF Breach Bravo, but if this unit existed it does not appear to have played a major role in the breach. Task Force Breach Alfa was assisted by the General Eng Spt Unit, a provisional unit formed by the 2nd Aslt Amphib Bn.

[60] Consisted of 11 tanks. Apparently Cos A-C each contributed three tanks and two tanks came from H&S Co.

[61] Provided security at the breach site for the 6th Marines from early morning 23 Feb 91 until approximately noon, 26 Feb 91, when this task force was apparently disbanded. At that time, these units rejoined the 2nd Recon Bn(-).

[62] Served under TF Troy, 1st Mar Div, before the ground war, 5 Feb 91 to 22 Feb 91. See Footnote 45.

8th Marines[63]

2/4 Marines[64] [Fr. 22 MEU(SOC)]
  1st Plt,[65] Co C, 4th Tank Bn [M1A1] [ID/TX USMCR]
  (1) Sec,[66] AT Plt [TOW], HQ Co, 8th Marines
  Co B,[67] 2nd Recon Bn
  Co B, 4th Aslt Amphib Bn [FL/TX USMCR]
1/8 Marines(-)[68]
  Co B, 4th Tank Bn [M1A1] [WA USMCR]
  (1) Sec,[69] AT Plt [TOW], HQ Co, 8th Marines
  1st Sec, 2nd Plt, AT Co [TOW], 2nd Tank Bn
  Co C,[70] 2nd Recon Bn
  Co D(-),[71] 2nd Aslt Amphib Bn
3/23 Marines[72] [LA/TN/AL/AR USMCR]
  2nd Sec, __ Plt, AT Co [TOW], 4th Tank Bn [OK USMCR]
Co C,[73] 4th Tank Bn [M1A1] [ID/TX USMCR]
  AT Plt(-)[74] [TOW], HQ Co, 8th Marines
3rd Sec,[75] 2nd Plt, AT Co [TOW], 2nd Tank Bn
(1) Sec, __ Plt, AT Co [TOW], 4th Tank Bn [OK USMCR]
Co F,[76] 2nd LAI Bn [CA USMCR]
3rd Sec, 1st Plt, Btry B, 2nd LAAD Bn [Stinger] [Fr. MACG 28]

---

[63] See Footnote 84.

[64] See Footnote 75.

[65] Was attached to the 2/4 Marines, apparently beginning at 1000 hours on 26 Feb 91, although this may have occurred at 1000 hours on 25 Feb 91.

[66] The 2nd & 3rd Secs of the 8th Marines' AT Plt were with the 2/4 Marines & 1/8 Marines, but the sources disagree as to which section was with which battalion.

[67] May have been a company(-). See Footnote 84.

[68] Consisted of H&S Co, Cos A & C, and Wpns Co. Was attached to the 6th Marines for the breach of the Iraqi front lines on 24 Feb 91; returned to the 8th Marines at 1100 hours on 25 Feb 91.

[69] See Footnote 66.

[70] See Footnote 84.

[71] Consisted of Co HQ and the 1st & 4th Plts. See Footnote 82.

[72] See Footnote 73.

[73] Was the 8th Marines' reserve. The 1st Plt was attached to the 2/4 Marines for some portion of the ground war. See Footnote 65. One platoon conducted an operation with the 3/23 Marines on 27 Feb 91, but it is unclear which platoon this was and whether this platoon was formally attached to the 3/23 Marines.

[74] This platoon reportedly had at least six sections, three more than usual. In addition, it apparently had one section in the Mediterranean with the 24th MEU(SOC) and possibly a second section with the 26th MEU(SOC). See Chart 20, Footnotes 3 & 7.

[75] May have been attached to the 2/4 Marines for the entire ground war, or may have been attached to the 2/4 Marines 25-27 Feb 91.

[76] Returned to the 2nd LAI Bn on 25 Feb 91. This unit was actually Det, Co A, 4th LAV Bn [CA USMCR]. See Footnote 83.

1st Brigade, 2nd Armored Division "Tiger Brigade" [U.S. Army]

The Tiger Brigade was under the operational control of the 2nd Marine Division. See Chart 5 for subordinate units. Elements of the USMC's 2nd LAI Bn were attached to the 1st Bde, 2nd Armd Div:

  Co D,[77] 2nd LAI Bn [VA USMCR]
  2nd LAI Bn(Rein)[78]

2nd Tank Bn(-)[79] [M1A1]

  Co B, 1/8 Marines
    2nd Plt(-),[80] AT Co [TOW], 2nd Tank Bn
  AT Plt[81] [TOW], HQ Co, 24th Marines [MO USMCR]
  2nd Plt,[82] Co D, 2nd Aslt Amphib Bn

2nd LAI Bn(Rein)[83]

  1st Sec, 2nd Plt, Btry B, 2nd LAAD Bn [Stinger] [Fr. MACG 28]

---

[77] Company D (actually Wpns Co(-), 4th LAV Bn [VA USMCR]) was attached to the Tiger Bde from the beginning of the ground war until 1120 hours on 26 Feb 91. See Footnote 83.

[78] The 2nd LAI Bn(Rein) was attached to the Tiger Bde from noon on 26 Feb 91 until the end of the war. During this period the entire portion of the 2nd LAI Bn that was serving with the 2nd Mar Div, except for Co B (actually, Co B, 4th LAV Bn [MD USMCR]), was attached to the Tiger Bde. See Footnote 83.

[79] Served as the 2nd Mar Div's reserve. Consisted of H&S Co, Cos B-D, and AT Co(-) [TOW]. The AT Co(-) consisted of Co HQ and the 1st Plt. See Footnote 98. The 2nd & 3rd Secs, 3rd Plt, AT Co were attached to the H&S Co, 2nd Tank Bn. I have not been able to locate the 3rd Plt(-), AT Co. It may have been with the 4th MEB.

[80] See Footnote 98.

[81] Was probably attached to the AT Co, 2nd Tank Bn.

[82] This was a new unit that was created, apparently through cross-leveling of assets within the 2nd Aslt Amphib Bn, to replace the original 2nd Plt, which was supporting the 26th MEU(SOC). See Chart 20.

[83] Half of the 2nd LAI Bn served with the 4th MEB. See Footnote 101. The 2nd Mar Div's LAI unit was reinforced with the attachment of USMCR LAV and infantry units, and reorganized:

ODS Designation	Pre-ODS Unit
H&S Co	H&S Co(-), 2nd LAI Bn & H&S Co, 4th LAV Bn [CA USMCR]
Co A	Co A(-), 2nd LAI Bn
Co B	Co B, 4th LAV Bn [MD USMCR]
Co C	Co C, 2nd LAI Bn
Co D	Wpns Co(-), 4th LAV Bn [VA USMCR]
Co E	Co C, 4th LAV Bn [UT USMCR]
Co F	Det, Co A, 4th LAV Bn [CA USMCR]
AT Plt	AT Plt, Wpns Co, 4th LAV Bn [VA USMCR]

Unlike the active duty units, which were designated "LAI" battalions and had infantrymen who rode in the LAVs, the USMCR battalion was designated a "LAV" battalion and had no dismounts. Company F(-), 2/25 Marines [NY USMCR] provided dismounts to ride in the LAVs of the 4th LAV Bn. At the beginning of the ground war, the 2nd LAI Bn, with Cos A, C & E and the AT Plt, was assigned to the 2nd Mar Div. Companies D & F joined the battalion later, and the 2nd LAI Bn(Rein) was attached to the Army's 1st Bde, 2nd Armd Div at noon on 26 Feb 91. See Footnotes 58 & 76-78. Note: it is unclear if all, or only a part, of H&S Co, 4th LAV Bn, served with the 2nd LAI Bn, and it is unclear if Co C, 4th LAV Bn was a company or a company(-). See also Footnote 119 and page 19-20.

2nd Recon Bn(-)[84]
    1st Plt(-), AT Co [TOW], 4th Tank Bn [OK USMCR]

H&S Co, 2nd Aslt Amphib Bn[85]
    H&S Co(-), 4th Aslt Amphib Bn [FL USMCR]

General Eng Spt Unit(Prov),[86] 2nd Aslt Amphib Bn

<u>10th Marines</u> (Artillery)[87]

    2/10 Marines [155 T, 3 x 8] [DS 6 Marines]
        HQ Btry, 2/10 Marines
        Btry D, 2/10 Marines
        Btry E, 2/10 Marines
        Btry D, 2/14 Marines [IA USMCR]
    3/10 Marines [155 T, 3 x 8] [DS 8 Marines][88]
        HQ Btry, 3/10 Marines
        Btry I, 3/10 Marines [Fr. 22 MEU(SOC)]
        Btry H, 3/12 Marines [Fr. 3 Mar Div(-)]
        Btry F, 2/14 Marines [OK USMCR]

---

[84] Consisted of H&S Co(-) and Cos B & C, 2nd Recon Bn; Co D, 4th Recon Bn [NM USMCR]; and the "provisional platoon," which was formed in SWA to perform dismounted recon. The 2nd Recon Bn primarily used a "motorized approach" to perform its mission, with most of its personnel mounted in HMMWVs. From approximately noon on 26 Feb 91 until the end of the war, the 2nd Recon Bn(-) was DS to the 8th Marines, with Co B supporting the 2/4 Marines and Co C supporting the 1/8 Marines. (One source indicates Co B was attached to the 2/4 Marines 25-27 Feb 91.) See Footnotes 61 & 62. Companies B and C each had their 1st Plt detached to, respectively, the 26th MEU(SOC) and 24th MEU(SOC), see Chart 20, and it is unclear if one or both of these companies organized a new 1st Plt or was actually a company(-).

[85] Was GS to the 2nd Mar Div.

[86] See Footnote 59.

[87] The U.S. Army Tiger Bde's 1-3 FA(155 SP) was GS to the 2nd Mar Div from the beginning of the ground war until 1600 hours on 24 Feb 91.

[88] During the 2nd Mar Div's breach, was GS to the division. Became DS to the 8th Marines at 0924 hours on 25 Feb 91.

10th Marines (Artillery) (continued)

    5/10 Marines [155 SP/203 SP, 4 x 6][89] [GS][90]
        HQ Btry, 5/10 Marines
        Btry Q [155 SP], 5/10 Marines
        Btry R [203 SP], 5/10 Marines
        Btry K [155 SP], 4/14 Marines [AL USMCR]
        Btry M [155 SP], 4/14 Marines [TN USMCR]
    2/12 Marines [155 T, 4 x 6] [GS][91] [Fr. 3 Mar Div(-)]
        HQ Btry, 2/12 Marines [Fr. 3 Mar Div(-)]
        Btry S, 5/10 Marines
        Btry B, 1/12 Marines [Fr. 3 Mar Div(-)]
        Btry D, 2/12 Marines [Fr. 3 Mar Div(-)]
        Btry L, 4/12 Marines [Fr. 3 Mar Div(-)]
    Btry A(MLRS), 92nd FA [GS] [U.S. Army; Fr. 2 AD(-)]
    Det 1 [AN/TPQ-36], HQ Btry, 14th Marines [TX USMCR]
    4th Radar Sec, Btry A(TA), 26th FA [U.S. Army; Fr. 4 ID(M)(-)]
    1st Sec, 1st Plt, Btry B, 2nd LAAD Bn [Stinger] [Fr. MACG 28]

4th Marine Expeditionary Brigade

       The 4th Marine Expeditionary Brigade was afloat in the Gulf throughout the war.[92] The Marines did not execute an amphibious assault, however, and the 4th MEB did not see combat.[93]

---

[89] In the summer of 1990 the 5/10 Marines had just completed transitioning from a self-propelled GS battalion to a towed GS battalion. During Desert Shield this unit was converted back to a self-propelled GS battalion.

[90] At the beginning of the ground war was GSR to the 2/10 Marines, with an "on order" mission to reinforce the U.S. Army's 1-3 FA(155 SP), 1st Bde, 2nd Armd Div. Began reinforcing the 1-3 FA the morning of 25 Feb 91. At 1230 hours on 26 Feb 91 joined the advance of the Army's 1st Bde, 2nd Armd Div.

[91] Converted from a DS to a GS unit (with six howitzers per battery) in December 1990, shortly before deployment to SWA. Initially reinforced the 2/10 Marines, and then became GSR to the 2/10 Marines at 1920 hours on 25 Feb 91. Became GS to the 10th Marines at about 1930 hours on 26 Feb 91.

[92] See Chart 18 for information on the ships on which the 4th MEB was embarked.

[93] A small portion of the 4th MEB evacuated American and allied personnel from Somalia in early January 1991, however, just prior to ODS. This operation was called Eastern Exit. It involved elements of the 1/2 Marines (Co C and part of the Wpns Co), a detachment from the 2nd Force Recon Co, and the USS *Guam* (LPH 9) and USS *Trenton* (LPD 14) from PhibGru 2.

Organization of the 4th Marine Expeditionary Brigade

<u>Regimental Landing Team 2</u>[94] (Ground Combat Element)

    1/2 Marines[95] [Fr. 2 Mar Div]
    3/2 Marines[96] [Fr. 2 Mar Div]
        Co A,[97] 2nd Tank Bn [M60A1] [Fr. 2 Mar Div]
        2nd Plt,[98] AT Co [TOW], 2nd Tank Bn [Fr. 2 Mar Div]
        Co A,[99] 2nd Aslt Amphib Bn [Fr. 2 Mar Div]
        (1) LAAD Sec
    AT Plt [TOW],[100] HQ Co, 2nd Marines (?) [Fr. 2 Mar Div]
    Det,[101] 2nd LAI Bn [Fr. 2 Mar Div]
    Co A(-),[102] 2nd Recon Bn [Fr. 2 Mar Div]
    Det,[103] 2nd Force Recon Co [Fr. 2 SRI Gp]
    1/10 Marines (Artillery) [105 T/155 T][104] [Fr. 2 Mar Div]
        HQ Btry, 1/10 Marines [Fr. 2 Mar Div]
        Btry A, 1/10 Marines [Fr. 2 Mar Div]
        Btry C, 1/10 Marines [Fr. 2 Mar Div]
        Btry I, 3/12 Marines [Fr. 2 Mar Div ?]

<u>Marine Aircraft Group 40</u> (Aviation Combat Element)

    Btry A, 2nd LAAD Bn [Stinger] [Fr. MACG 28]

---

[94] RLT 2 was based upon the 2nd Marines. The 2nd Marines were assigned to the 2nd Mar Div before Desert Shield began.

[95] See Footnote 93.

[96] The 3/2 Marines, with attachments, comprised BLT 3/2, the mechanized element of RLT 2.

[97] Some sources state Co A was a reinforced company with 22 tanks, one platoon more than a normal company. The designation of this alleged extra platoon is unknown.

[98] It appears that the 3rd & 4th Squads, 2nd Sec, 2nd Plt, AT Co, with a total of four TOW HMMWVs, deployed with the 3/2 Marines and were later expanded into a full platoon (24 TOW HMMWVs) or a platoon(-) that called itself "2nd Plt, AT Co, 2nd Tank Bn." Two units with this designation served in Desert Storm. The "original" 2nd Plt(-), AT Co, 2nd Tank Bn served with the 2nd Mar Div: the platoon(-) was with the 2nd Tank Bn; the 1st Sec was with the 1/8 Marines; and the 3rd Sec was with the 8th Marines.

[99] May have been a company(-).

[100] Some or all of this platoon's sections were probably attached to the other units of RLT 2.

[101] Consisted of Det, H&S Co, and Cos B & D. Companies B and D each had 24 LAVs and Det, H&S Co had 4 LAVs.

[102] May have been a full-strength company.

[103] Part of the 5th MEB's command element. See Footnote 93.

[104] The 1/10 Marines had 24 M198 towed 155mm howitzers and 12 M101A1 towed 105mm howitzers. See Appendix E, page E-7 and Footnote 22.

5th Marine Expeditionary Brigade[105]

When the war began the 5th Marine Expeditionary Brigade was afloat in the Gulf, assigned to NAVCENT. In the afternoon of 24 Feb 91 the 5th MEB began landing in Saudi territory at Al Mish'ab and Al Jubayl and was, at that time, reassigned from NAVCENT to MARCENT as I MEF reserve.[106] The 5th MEB completed its offload by 27 Feb 91 and moved north to join I MEF and establish a blocking position at Kibrit. The ground combat elements of the 5th MEB screened I MEF's left flank and assisted with rear area security, the clearing of Kuwaiti territory seized from the Iraqis, and EPW processing.

Organization of the 5th Marine Expeditionary Brigade

Regimental Landing Team 5[107] (Ground Combat Element)

    3/1 Marines(-)[108] [Fr. 11 MEU][109]
        Det 11,[110] 1st LAI Bn
        1st Plt(?),[111] Co A, 1st Recon Bn
        (1) Aslt Amphib Plt[112]
    2/5 Marines[113] [Fr. 1 Mar Div]

---

[105] The 11th MEU(SOC) was "embedded" within the 5th MEB. The 11th MEU consisted of the 3/1 Marines; Btry G, 3/12 Marines (Artillery) with four M101A1 towed 105mm and six M198 towed 155mm howitzers; Det 11, 1st LAI Bn (see Footnote 110); 1st Plt(?), Co A, 1st Recon Bn (see Footnote 129); and a platoon of 12 assault amphibious vehicles (see Footnote 112).

[106] See Chart 18 for information on the ships on which the 5th MEB was embarked prior to its debarkation.

[107] RLT 5 was based upon the 5th Marines. The 5th Marines were assigned to the 1st Mar Div before Desert Shield began.

[108] The 3/1 Marines were the 5th MEB's heliborne assault element. After landing in Saudi Arabia via helicopter (the remainder of the 5th MEB landed via LCAC), the 3/1 Marines (with Btry E [155 T], 2/11 Marines (Artillery) in support replacing Btry G [105 T/155 T], 3/12 Marines, see Footnote 105, because Btry G lacked the necessary maps) left the 5th MEB and assisted the 2nd Mar Div with EPWs and Iraqi forces that had been bypassed. See Footnote 109.

[109] When Desert Shield began, the 3/1 Marines were assigned to the 11th MEU and were preparing for a forward deployment. This was cancelled and the 3/1 Marines shipped out with the 5th MEB, although the battalion remained associated with the 11th MEU, which was embedded within the 5th MEB.

[110] Consisted of six LAVs (one platoon), but the designation of this platoon is unknown. It probably came from Co B, 1st LAI Bn, or possibly Co D, 1st LAI Bn.

[111] See Footnote 129.

[112] The designation of this platoon is unknown. It probably came from either the 3rd Aslt Amphib Bn or Co A, 1st Armd Aslt Bn.

[113] The 2/5 Marines was the 5th MEB's motorized element. H&S Co, 2/5 Marines formed a provisional rifle company that supported naval mine clearing operations conducted by the Navy. See Chart 18, Footnote 7.

Regimental Landing Team 5 (continued)

    3/5 Marines[114] [Fr. 1 Mar Div]
        Co L, 3/1 Marines [Fr. 11 MEU]
        Co A, 4th Tank Bn [M60A1] [CA USMCR]
        3rd Sec, AT Plt [TOW],[115] HQ Co, 5th Marines
        Co A,[116] 4th Aslt Amphib Bn [VA/MS USMCR]
        (1) LAAD Sec
    AT Plt(-) [TOW],[117] HQ Co, 5th Marines
    AT Plt [TOW],[118] HQ Co, 23rd Marines [LA/CA USMCR]
    Co A(-),[119] 4th LAV Bn [CA USMCR]
        2nd Plt(Rein),[120] Co F, 2/25 Marines [NY USMCR]
    Co B, 1st Recon Bn [Fr. 1 Mar Div]
    2/11 Marines (Artillery) [105 T/155 T][121] [Fr. 1 Mar Div]
        HQ Btry, 2/11 Marines [Fr. 1 Mar Div]
        Btry E,[122] 2/11 Marines [Fr. 1 Mar Div]
        Btry F, 2/11 Marines [Fr. 1 Mar Div]
        Btry G, 3/12 Marines[123] [Fr. 1 Mar Div]

Marine Aircraft Group 50 (Aviation Combat Element)

    Btry A(-),[124] 3rd LAAD Bn [Fr. MACG 38]
    Btry A(?),[125] 4th LAAD Bn [Stinger] [CA USMCR] [Fr. MACG 48 ?]

---

[114] The 3/5 Marines, with attachments, comprised BLT 3/5, the 5th MEB's mechanized combined arms task force.

[115] See Footnote 117.

[116] May have been a company(-).

[117] Some or all of this platoon's sections were attached to the other units of RLT 5. The original AT Plt, HQ Co, 5th Marines, deployed with the 1st Tank Bn during the early stages of Desert Shield and was apparently then known as the 4th Plt, AT Co [TOW], 1st Tank Bn. The 5th Marines then recreated an AT Plt and deployed the AT Plt(-) in December 1990 as part of the 5th MEB. One source refers to this unit as the "2d (Composite) TOW Plt, 5th Marines."

[118] Some or all of this platoon's sections were probably attached to the other units of RLT 5.

[119] Two units designated Co A, 4th LAV Bn served in Desert Storm. Initially, Co A(-) shipped out with the 5th MEB, and then the remainder, a platoon-sized detachment, deployed with the 2nd LAI Bn. This remainder was beefed-up to company(-) strength through cross-leveling of LAVs within the 2nd LAI Bn(Rein), and this new unit was called Co F, 2nd LAI Bn(Rein). See Footnote 83.

[120] Included elements of Wpns Plt, Co F, 2/25 Marines [NY USMCR]. See Footnote 83.

[121] The 2/11 Marines had 22 M198 towed 155mm howitzers and four M101A1 towed 105mm howitzers. See Appendix E, page E-7 and Footnote 23.

[122] Battery E was attached to the 3/1 Marines for much of the ground war. See Footnote 108.

[123] When Desert Shield began, Btry G was preparing to ship out with the 11th MEU, but was apparently still assigned to the 1st Mar Div. See Footnotes 105 & 108.

[124] May have only been a platoon or a reinforced platoon. See Footnote 125.

[125] Most sources do not list this unit and it is doubtful it served with the 5th MEB. One source reports that only one platoon from this battery deployed with the 5th MEB. Other sources suggest that Btry A(-) deployed or that the elements of Btry A that deployed were augmented by personnel from H&S Btry, 4th LAAD Bn [__ USMCR] [Fr. MACG 48 ?]. One

SRI Spt Gp 5 (Part of Command Element)

    DRP/DA Plt, 1st Force Recon Co [Fr. 1 SRI Gp ?]
    Det, 4th Force Recon Co [NV USMCR]

13th Marine Expeditionary Unit(SOC)

    The 13th Marine Expeditionary Unit(SOC) was afloat in the Gulf throughout the war.[126] It raided Umm Al-Maradim Island, 12 miles off the coast of Kuwait, on 29 Jan 91. The Iraqis had hastily abandoned the island and the 13th MEU(SOC) did not encounter any resistance. The Marines withdrew after just over three hours, having captured enemy weapons, other equipment, and documents. It appears that two Armed OH-58Ds from the Army's 4th Sqdn(Air)(-), 17th Cavalry[127] supported this operation.

    The 13th MEU(SOC) later performed a feint simulating a landing in Kuwait near Ash Shuaybah in the early morning hours of 25 Feb 91. After the cease fire the 13th MEU(SOC) landed on Faylaka Island on 2-3 Mar 91 to accept the surrender of the Iraqi 440th Naval Infantry Brigade, capturing 1,400 EPWs.

Organization of the 13th Marine Expeditionary Unit(SOC)

1/4 Marines
    Co B(-),[128] 1st LAI Bn
    3rd Plt(?),[129] Co A, 1st Recon Bn
    1st Plt, Co A, 3rd Aslt Amphib Bn
    Btry B, 1/11 Marines (Artillery) [105 T/155 T][130]
Det, 1st Force Recon Co
Det, 3rd LAAD Bn

---

possibility is that personnel from Btry A, 4th LAAD Bn were used to flesh out Btry A, 3rd LAAD Bn, rather than deploying as a separate unit.

[126] See Chart 18 for information on the ships on which the 13th MEU(SOC) was embarked.

[127] See Chart 4, Footnote 84.

[128] May have been a full-strength company.

[129] It is uncertain if this platoon was the 3rd Plt, Co A. One source reports that it was the 1st Plt, Co A, but it appears that 1st Plt was with the 11th MEU(SOC).

[130] Had four M101A1 towed 105mm howitzers and four M198 towed 155mm howitzers. See Appendix E, page E-6.

3rd Marine Aircraft Wing (Aviation Combat Element, I MEF)

<u>Marine Air Control Group 38</u>

    2nd LAAD Bn(-) [Stinger] [Fr. MACG 28]
    3rd LAAD Bn(-) [Stinger]
    2nd LAAM Bn[131] [Hawk]
    3rd LAAM Bn [Hawk] [Fr. MACG 28]

Notes:

➤ Unit assignments prior to Desert Storm (shown as "[Fr. _____]") reflect assignments as of 6 Aug 90, just before the beginning of Operation Desert Shield. Some units changed assignments, pursuant to the Unit Deployment Program, in early August 1990. When Desert Shield began, the 22nd MEU(SOC) was forward deployed in the Atlantic Ocean off the coast of Liberia. The infantry battalion and artillery battery that were then assigned to the 22nd MEU are so noted; the 22nd MEU undoubtedly had other units, such as LAI, assault amphibian, and recon, but I have been unable to determine these units' designations.

➤ In many instances when a unit had detached one or more sub-elements to another command, and should have been listed as a unit(-), the documents did not list the unit as a unit(-). This could merely reflect sloppy record-keeping, or could indicate the unit was brought to full strength through cross-leveling of assets, etc. I have tried to indicate each instance where there is a question whether a unit should be listed as full strength or as a unit(-), but there may be additional instances I did not identify.

➤ It has been extremely difficult to track down the Marines' TOW antitank units, which were attached to the various Marine infantry units in a non-uniform and unpredictable manner. Each Marine infantry regiment was authorized a platoon of three sections (each with eight TOWs mounted on HMMWVs) for a total of 24 TOWs per platoon. Some platoons, however, acquired additional TOWs and used them to create additional sections. See Footnotes 24, 48 & 74. In addition, each Marine tank battalion was authorized an antitank company of three platoons, each with three sections, for a total of 72 TOWs in the company. Some tank battalions, however, created or obtained an additional AT platoon. See Footnotes 30, 98 & 117.

➤ Because many Marine artillery batteries served in battalions other than their parent battalion, I have listed each battery under the battalion with which it served. In addition, the entries for artillery battalions show the number of batteries and the number of howitzers authorized per battery in brackets, e.g., the 1st Bn, 11th Marines, 1st Marine Division, had three firing batteries each authorized eight towed 155mm howitzers [155 T, 3 x 8].

➤ Aviation units are not listed. Air defense artillery units (LAAD and LAAM units) assigned to aviation commands are listed; only those aviation commands that had ADA units assigned are shown. Unlike the Army's practice, the Marines do not generally attach their air defense artillery units to ground units such as divisions. Instead, these air defense units are integrated with, and controlled by, aviation units.

---

[131] Consisted of H&S Btry and Btrys A & B. Battery B, 1st LAAM Bn, which was assigned to the 2nd LAAM Bn when Desert Shield began, was inactivated on 28 Sep 90 without deploying to SWA.

➤ There were several instances where two Marine Corps units with the same designation served in Desert Storm with different commands. This typically occurred when all or most of the unit deployed with one command, and either the remainder left behind was brought to full strength or a new unit was created from scratch. In other situations, the parent unit that dispatched one of its elements (and should have been listed as a unit(-)) gained assets through cross-levelling, so that it was then referred to as a full strength unit, not a unit(-). This, of course, greatly complicates any attempt to track the Marine Corps' order of battle. I have identified three instances where this definitely occurred:

The AT Plt [TOW], HQ Co, 5th Marines. See Footnote 117.

Company A, 4th LAV Bn [CA USMCR]. See Footnotes 83 & 119.

The 2nd Plt, Co D, 2nd Aslt Amphib Bn. See Footnote 82.

I have identified one other instance where this probably occurred:

The 2nd Plt, AT Co [TOW], 2nd Tank Bn. See Footnote 98.

I have identified two other instances where this may have occurred:

The 1st Plt, Co B, 2nd Recon Bn. See Footnote 84.

The 1st Plt, Co C, 2nd Recon Bn. See Footnote 84.

Chart 20

U.S. Marine Corps Ground Combat Units That Were Afloat In The Mediterranean

The following Marine Corps units were deployed in the Mediterranean as the Landing Force, Sixth Fleet (LF6F), during the early stages of the air war:[1]

26th Marine Expeditionary Unit(SOC)[2]

3/8 Marines[3]
    Det 26, 2nd LAI Bn[4]
    1st Plt, Co B, 2nd Recon Bn
    2nd Plt,[5] Co D, 2nd Aslt Amphib Bn
    Btry G, 3/10 Marines (Artillery) [105 T/155 T][6]

The following Marine Corps units were deployed in the Mediterranean as LF6F during the later stages of the air war and during the ground war. These units assisted Kurdish refugees as part of "Operation Provide Comfort" in northern Iraq and southern Turkey after Desert Storm:

---

[1] The 26th MEU(SOC) departed CONUS in August 1990 and was relieved by the 24th MEU(SOC) as LF6F, on 16 Feb 91. The 26th MEU(SOC) departed Rota, Spain, for the United States on 20 Feb 91.

[2] Probably also had detachments from the 2nd Force Recon Co and the 2nd LAAD Bn.

[3] May have had an antitank section [TOW] attached from the AT Plt, 8th Marines.

[4] Consisted of a reinforced LAI platoon formed primarily from the 3rd Plt, Co A, 2nd LAI Bn.

[5] There were actually two platoons with this designation during Desert Storm. This is the original 2nd Plt. See Chart 19, Footnote 82 and page 19-20.

[6] Had four M101A1 towed 105mm howitzers and four M198 towed 155mm howitzers. See Appendix E, page E-6.

24th Marine Expeditionary Unit(SOC)

> 2/8 Marines
>> (1) AT Sec[7] [TOW]
>> Det 24, 2nd LAI Bn[8]
>> 1st Plt, Co C, 2nd Recon Bn
>> 3rd Plt, Co D, 2nd Aslt Amphib Bn
>> Btry H, 3/10 Marines (Artillery) [105 T/155 T][9]
> Det, 2nd Force Recon Co
> Det,[10] 2nd LAAD Bn [Stinger]

Notes:

➢ All of these units were assigned to these MEUs at the time Desert Shield began.

➢ These units were embarked upon the following Navy units:

   24th MEU(SOC)   Amphibious Squadron 8 (PhibRon 8)
   26th MEU(SOC)   Amphibious Squadron 2 (PhibRon 2)

➢ Amphibious Squadron 2, which carried the 26th MEU(SOC), consisted of five or six ships:[11]
   USS *Inchon* (LPH 12)
   USS *Whidbey Island* (LSD 41)
   USS *Nashville* (LPD 13)
   USS *Fairfax County* (LST 1193)
   USS *Newport* (LST 1179)
   USS *Barnstable County* (LST 1197)

➢ Amphibious Squadron 8, which carried the 24th MEU(SOC), consisted of three ships:
   USS *Guadalcanal* (LPH 7)
   USS *Austin* (LPD 4)
   USS *Charleston* (LKA 113)

   A shortage of shipping due to Desert Storm limited PhibRon 8 to only three ships, which forced the 24th MEU(SOC) to leave behind a substantial amount of its equipment.

➢ The Navy Amphibious Squadron deployed in the Mediterranean with a MEU embarked was known as the Mediterranean Amphibious Ready Group or "MARG."

---

[7] The designation of this unit is unknown, although it almost certainly was detached from the 8th Marines' AT Plt.

[8] This was a reinforced platoon that apparently consisted of 9 LAVs: 6 LAV-25s, 2 LAV-ATs, and 1 LAV-L. It is unclear which company provided this platoon.

[9] Had four M101A1 towed 105mm howitzers and four M198 towed 155mm howitzers. See Appendix E, page E-6.

[10] Was part of Marine Medium Helicopter Sqdn 264, which was the 24th MEU's Air Combat Element.

[11] The sources disagree as to whether the *Barnstable County* was assigned to PhibRon 2.

Chart 21

U.S. Marine Corps Ground Combat Units That Deployed To The Gulf Or The Mediterranean During Operation Desert Storm, By Unit Type

This chart lists all U.S. Marine Corps ground combat units that deployed to the KTO or the Mediterranean, and shows the major command to which they were assigned.

Infantry Units

1st Marines

HQ Co	1st Mar Div(Rein)
1st Bn	1st Mar Div(Rein)
3rd Bn	5th MEB (11th MEU(SOC))[1]

2nd Marines

HQ Co	4th MEB
1st Bn	4th MEB
2nd Bn	2nd Mar Div(Rein)
3rd Bn	4th MEB

---

[1] See Chart 19, Footnotes 105 & 109.

Infantry Units (continued)

3rd Marines

HQ Co	1st Mar Div(Rein)
1st Bn	1st Mar Div(Rein)
2nd Bn	1st Mar Div(Rein)
3rd Bn	1st Mar Div(Rein)

4th Marines

HQ Co	1st Mar Div(Rein)
1st Bn	13th MEU(SOC)
2nd Bn	2nd Mar Div(Rein)

5th Marines

HQ Co[2]	5th MEB
1st Bn	1st Mar Div(Rein)
2nd Bn	5th MEB
3rd Bn	5th MEB

6th Marines

HQ Co	2nd Mar Div(Rein)
1st Bn	2nd Mar Div(Rein)
3rd Bn	2nd Mar Div(Rein)

7th Marines

HQ Co	1st Mar Div(Rein)
1st Bn	1st Mar Div(Rein)
2nd Bn	1st Mar Div(Rein)
3rd Bn	1st Mar Div(Rein)

---

[2] Included within HQ Co was AT Plt(-). There were actually two platoons with this designation in Desert Storm; this was the second such platoon formed. See Chart 19, Footnote 117 and page 19-20. This "second" AT Plt, HQ Co, 5th Marines was a platoon(-) because its 2nd Sec remained at Camp Pendleton with the 15th MEU(SOC) when the AT Plt(-) deployed with the 5th MEB.

Infantry Units (continued)

8th Marines

HQ Co[3]	2nd Mar Div(Rein)
1st Bn	2nd Mar Div(Rein)
2nd Bn	24th MEU(SOC)
3rd Bn	26th MEU(SOC)

9th Marines[4]

3rd Bn	1st Mar Div(Rein)

23rd Marines [USMCR]

AT Plt, HQ Co	5th MEB
3rd Bn	2nd Mar Div(Rein)

24th Marines [USMCR]

HQ Co(-)	24th Marines(-)
AT Plt, HQ Co	2nd Mar Div(Rein)
2nd Bn	24th Marines(-)
3rd Bn	24th Marines(-)

25th Marines [USMCR]

1st Bn	1st Mar Div(Rein)
Wpns Plt, Co D, 2nd Bn	1st Mar Div(Rein)
Co F(-), 2nd Bn	2nd Mar Div(Rein)
2nd Plt & elements, Wpns Plt, Co F, 2nd Bn	5th MEB

Other Infantry Units

Co A, Marine Barracks, Washington, DC	2nd Mar Div(Rein)

---

[3] One section from the AT Plt was almost certainly attached to the 24th MEU(SOC), and another section may have been attached to the 26th MEU(SOC). See Chart 20, Footnotes 3 & 7.

[4] HQ Co, 9th Marines, and the 2/9 Marines remained on Okinawa with the 3rd Mar Div(-) during Desert Storm. The AT Plt [TOW], HQ Co, 9th Marines may have remained on Okinawa; I have seen no reference to it in any Desert Storm document. The 1/9 Marines remained at Camp Pendleton with the 15th MEU(SOC) during Desert Storm.

Tank Units

Co D, 1st Armd Aslt Bn[5]   1st Mar Div(Rein)
1st Tank Bn[6]   1st Mar Div(Rein)
2nd Tank Bn(-)[7]   2nd Mar Div(Rein)
Co A,[8] 2nd Tank Bn   4th MEB
2nd Plt,[9] AT Co, 2nd Tank Bn   4th MEB
3rd Tank Bn[10]   1st Mar Div(Rein)
3rd Plt(-), AT Co, 3rd Tank Bn   ?[11]
4th Plt, AT Co, 3rd Tank Bn   ?[12]
Co A, 4th Tank Bn [USMCR]   5th MEB
Cos B, C & AT Co, 4th Tank Bn[13] [USMCR]   2nd Mar Div(Rein)
8th Tank Bn[14] [USMCR]   2nd Mar Div(Rein)

Light Armored Infantry Units

1st LAI Bn(-)[15]   1st Mar Div(Rein)
Co B(-),[16] 1st LAI Bn   13th MEU(SOC)
Det 11,[17] 1st LAI Bn   5th MEB (11th MEU(SOC))[18]
2nd LAI Bn(-)[19]   2nd Mar Div(Rein)
Det,[20] 2nd LAI Bn   4th MEB

---

[5] See Appendix E, pages E-13 and E-14, for additional information on the 1st Armd Aslt Bn.

[6] Consisted of H&S Co, Cos A-D, and AT Co(Rein) [TOW]. See Chart 19, Footnotes 15 & 117.

[7] Consisted of H&S Co, Cos B-D, and AT Co [TOW]. See Chart 19, Footnotes 79, 97 & 98, and page 19-20.

[8] May have been a reinforced company with four platoons (22 tanks). See Chart 19, Footnote 97.

[9] There were apparently two platoons with this designation in Desert Storm. This is the second such platoon and may have been a platoon(-). See Chart 19, Footnote 98 and page 19-20.

[10] See Chart 19, Footnote 79.

[11] Consisted of H&S Co, Cos A-C, and AT Co [TOW]. The 3rd Tank Bn did not have a D Company.

[12] See Chart 19, Footnote 30.

[13] The 4th Tank Bn did not have a D Company.

[14] Consisted of H&S Co, Cos A-C, and AT Co [TOW]. See Chart 19, Footnote 56.

[15] Consisted of H&S Co and Cos A & C. Company D remained at Camp Pendleton during Desert Storm with the 15th MEU(SOC).

[16] May have been a full-strength company.

[17] Consisted of six LAVs (one platoon), but the designation of this platoon is unknown. It probably came from Co B, 1st LAI Bn, or possibly Co D, 1st LAI Bn.

[18] See Chart 19, Footnote 105.

[19] Consisted of H&S Co(-) and Cos A(-) & C. See Chart 19, Footnote 83.

[20] Consisted of Det, H&S Co, and Cos B & D.

Light Armored Infantry Units (continued)

Det 24,[21] 2nd LAI Bn	24th MEU(SOC)
Det 26,[22] 2nd LAI Bn	26th MEU(SOC)
Det,[23] 3rd LAI Bn	1st Mar Div(Rein)
4th LAV Bn(-)[24] [USMCR]	2nd Mar Div(Rein)
Co A(-),[25] 4th LAV Bn [USMCR]	5th MEB

Force Reconnaissance Units

1st Force Recon Co(-)[26]	1st SRI Gp
DRP/DA Plt, 1st Force Recon Co	5th MEB
Det, 1st Force Recon Co	13th MEU(SOC)
2nd Force Recon Co(-)	1st SRI Gp
Det, 2nd Force Recon Co	4th MEB
Det, 2nd Force Recon Co	24th MEU(SOC)
Det, 2nd Force Recon Co	26th MEU(SOC) (?)[27]
3rd Force Recon Co(-) [USMCR]	1st SRI Gp
4th Force Recon Co(-) [USMCR]	1st SRI Gp
Det, 4th Force Recon Co [USMCR]	5th MEB

---

[21] This was a reinforced platoon that apparently consisted of 9 LAVs: 6 LAV-25s, 2 LAV-ATs, and 1 LAV-L. It is unclear which company provided this platoon.

[22] This was a reinforced platoon formed primarily from the 3rd Plt, Co A, 2nd LAI Bn.

[23] Consisted of Det, H&S Co, and Cos B & D. H&S Co(-) and Co A remained on Okinawa with the 3rd Mar Div(-) during Desert Storm. Company C's status is unclear; it was apparently not active.

[24] Consisted of H&S Co; Det, Co A; Cos B & C; and Wpns Co. It is unclear if all, or only a part, of H&S Co deployed, and whether Co C was a full company or a company(-). Through cross-levelling, Det, Co A, was expanded to a company(-) or a full company and called "Company A," while the original Co A(-) served with the 5th MEB. Thus, two units with this designation served in Desert Storm. The unit that served with the 2nd LAI Bn(Rein) in the 2nd Mar Div(Rein) was the second such unit. See Chart 19, Footnotes 83 & 119 and page 19-20.

[25] There were actually two companies with this designation in Desert Storm. This is the original company. See Footnote 24.

[26] Consisted of Co HQ, the 5th-7th Plts, and probably other elements of the 1st Force Recon Co.

[27] Although it is not certain, the 26th MEU(SOC) probably had a platoon-sized detachment from the 2nd Force Recon Co.

Reconnaissance Units

1st Recon Bn(-)[28]	1st Mar Div(Rein)
1st Plt(?),[29] Co A, 1st Recon Bn	5th MEB (11th MEU(SOC))[30]
3rd Plt(?),[31] Co A, 1st Recon Bn	13th MEU(SOC)
Co B, 1st Recon Bn	5th MEB
2nd Recon Bn(-)[32]	2nd Mar Div(Rein)
Co A(-),[33] 2nd Recon Bn	4th MEB
1st Plt,[34] Co B, 2nd Recon Bn	26th MEU(SOC)
1st Plt,[35] Co C, 2nd Recon Bn	24th MEU(SOC)
Co A, 3rd Recon Bn[36]	1st Mar Div(Rein)
2nd Plt, Co C, 3rd Recon Bn	1st Mar Div(Rein)
Co D, 4th Recon Bn [USMCR]	2nd Mar Div(Rein)

Assault Amphibian Units

Co B, 1st Armd Aslt Bn[37]	2nd Mar Div(Rein)
2nd Aslt Amphib Bn(-)[38]	2nd Mar Div(Rein)
Co A,[39] 2nd Aslt Amphib Bn	4th MEB
2nd Plt, Co C, 2nd Aslt Amphib Bn	1st Mar Div(Rein)
2nd Plt,[40] Co D, 2nd Aslt Amphib Bn	26th MEU(SOC)

---

[28] Consisted of H&S Co and Cos A(-), C & D(-). Company D's 2nd Plt remained at Camp Pendleton with the 15th MEU(SOC) during Desert Storm.

[29] See Chart 19, Footnote 129.

[30] See Chart 19, Footnote 105.

[31] See Chart 19, Footnote 129.

[32] Consisted of H&S Co, Cos B & C, and "provisional platoon." See Chart 19, Footnote 84. Companies B and/or C may have been a company(-). Company D, 2nd Recon Bn did not participate in Desert Storm; it was apparently at cadre status and, unlike Co D, 1st Recon Bn, was not reactivated for the war.

[33] May have been a full-strength company.

[34] There may have been two platoons with this designation during Desert Storm. See Chart 19, Footnote 84 and page 19-20.

[35] There may have been two platoons with this designation during Desert Storm. See Chart 19, Footnote 84 and page 19-20.

[36] The 3rd Recon Bn(-), with H&S Co, Cos B & D, and (apparently) Co C(-), remained on Okinawa with the 3rd Mar Div(-) during Desert Storm. One source reports Co C(-) deployed and left one of its platoons on Okinawa, but this appears to be incorrect.

[37] May have been a company(-). See Appendix E, pages E-13 and E-14, for additional information on the 1st Armd Aslt Bn.

[38] Consisted of H&S Co, Cos B & D(-), and the General Eng Spt Unit(Prov). Company B may have been a company(-).

[39] May have been a company(-).

[40] There were actually two platoons with this designation during Desert Storm. This is the original platoon. See Chart 19, Footnote 82 and page 19-20.

Assault Amphibian Units (continued)

3rd Plt, Co D, 2nd Aslt Amphib Bn	24th MEU(SOC)
3rd Aslt Amphib Bn[41]	1st Mar Div(Rein)
1st Plt, Co A, 3rd Aslt Amphib Bn	13th MEU(SOC)
4th Aslt Amphib Bn(-)[42] [USMCR]	2nd Mar Div(Rein)
Co A,[43] 4th Aslt Amphib Bn [USMCR]	5th MEB
(1) Aslt Amphib Plt[44]	5th MEB (11th MEU(SOC))[45]

Artillery Units[46]

Unit	Battalion Assignment	Major Command
10th Marines (Artillery)		
HQ Btry	N/A	2nd Mar Div(Rein)
1st Bn [105T/155 T][47]		4th MEB
HQ Btry	1/10 Mar	4th MEB
Btry A	1/10 Mar	4th MEB
Btry B	3/12 Mar	1st Mar Div(Rein)
Btry C	1/10 Mar	4th MEB
2nd Bn [155 T]		2nd Mar Div(Rein)
HQ Btry	2/10 Mar	2nd Mar Div(Rein)
Btry D	2/10 Mar	2nd Mar Div(Rein)
Btry E	2/10 Mar	2nd Mar Div(Rein)
Btry F	3/12 Mar	1st Mar Div(Rein)

---

[41] Consisted of H&S Co, Cos A-D, and Det G. See Chart 19, Footnotes 27 & 46.

[42] Consisted of H&S Co(-) & Co B. Unlike the active duty assault amphibian battalions, which had four line companies, the 4th Aslt Amphib Bn had only two line companies.

[43] May have been a company(-).

[44] The designation of this platoon, which had 12 AAVs, is unknown. It probably came from either the 3rd Aslt Amphib Bn or Co A, 1st Armd Aslt Bn.

[45] See Chart 19, Footnote 105.

[46] Because many USMC artillery batteries served under a battalion other than their parent battalion, this portion of this chart addresses each individual battery. Only those batteries that deployed to SWA or the Mediterranean are listed.

[47] The 1/10 Marines had 24 M198 towed 155mm howitzers and 12 M101A1 towed 105mm howitzers. See Appendix E, page E-7.

Artillery Units

Unit	Battalion Assignment	Major Command
10th Marines (Artillery) (continued)		
3rd Bn [155 T]		2nd Mar Div(Rein)
HQ Btry	3/10 Mar	2nd Mar Div(Rein)
Btry G	None	26th MEU(SOC)
Btry H	None	24th MEU(SOC)
Btry I	3/10 Mar	2nd Mar Div(Rein)
5th Bn [155 T/155 SP/203 SP]		2nd Mar Div(Rein)
HQ Btry	5/10 Mar	2nd Mar Div(Rein)
Btry Q [155 SP]	5/10 Mar	2nd Mar Div(Rein)
Btry R [203 SP]	5/10 Mar	2nd Mar Div(Rein)
Btry S [155 T]	2/12 Mar	2nd Mar Div(Rein)
11th Marines (Artillery)		
HQ Btry	N/A	1st Mar Div(Rein)
1st Bn[48] [155 T]		1st Mar Div(Rein)
HQ Btry	1/11 Mar	1st Mar Div(Rein)
Btry A	1/11 Mar	1st Mar Div(Rein)
Btry B	None	13th MEU(SOC)
2nd Bn [105 T/155 T][49]		5th MEB
HQ Btry	2/11 Mar	5th MEB
Btry D	None	[50]
Btry E	2/11 Mar	5th MEB
Btry F	2/11 Mar	5th MEB
3rd Bn [155 T]		1st Mar Div(Rein)
HQ Btry	3/11 Mar	1st Mar Div(Rein)
Btry G	3/11 Mar	1st Mar Div(Rein)
Btry H	3/11 Mar	1st Mar Div(Rein)
Btry I	1/11 Mar	1st Mar Div(Rein)

---

[48] Battery C, 1/11 Marines (Artillery) [155 T] remained at Camp Pendleton with the 15th MEU(SOC) during Desert Storm.

[49] The 2/11 Marines had 22 M198 towed 155mm howitzers and four M101A1 towed 105mm howitzers. See Appendix E, page E-7.

[50] This battery deployed to the KTO in January 1991, but was disbanded shortly after arrival to provide filler personnel for other units. Accordingly, it is not listed on Chart 19. It was reformed after Desert Storm.

Artillery Units (continued)

Unit	Battalion Assignment	Major Command
<u>11th Marines</u> (Artillery) (continued)		
5th Bn [155 T/155 SP/203 SP]		1st Mar Div(Rein)
HQ Btry	5/11 Mar	1st Mar Div(Rein)
Btry Q [155 T]	5/11 Mar	1st Mar Div(Rein)
Btry R [155 T]	5/11 Mar	1st Mar Div(Rein)
Btry S [155 SP]	5/11 Mar	1st Mar Div(Rein)
Btry T [203 SP]	5/11 Mar	1st Mar Div(Rein)
<u>12th Marines</u>[51] (Artillery)		
1st Bn [155 T]		1st Mar Div(Rein)
HQ Btry	1/12 Mar	1st Mar Div(Rein)
Btry A	1/12 Mar	1st Mar Div(Rein)
Btry B	2/12 Mar	2nd Mar Div(Rein)
Btry C	1/12 Mar	1st Mar Div(Rein)
2nd Bn [155 T]		2nd Mar Div(Rein)
HQ Btry	2/12 Mar	2nd Mar Div(Rein)
Btry D	2/12 Mar	2nd Mar Div(Rein)
Btry E	3/11 Mar	1st Mar Div(Rein)
Btry F	1/12 Mar	1st Mar Div(Rein)
3rd Bn [155 T]		1st Mar Div(Rein)
HQ Btry	3/12 Mar	1st Mar Div(Rein)
Btry G	2/11 Mar	5th MEB (11th MEU(SOC))[52]
Btry H	3/10 Mar	2nd Mar Div(Rein)
Btry I	1/10 Mar	4th MEB
4th Bn[53]		
Btry L [155 T]	2/12 Mar	2nd Mar Div(Rein)

---

[51] The HQ Btry, 12th Marines, remained on Okinawa with the 3rd Mar Div(-) during Desert Storm.

[52] See Chart 19, Footnote 105.

[53] HQ Btry, 4/12 Marines remained on Okinawa with the 3rd Mar Div(-) during Desert Storm. It appears that Btrys K & M, 4/12 Marines remained on Okinawa with their parent battalion.

Artillery Units (continued)

Unit	Battalion Assignment	Major Command
<u>14th Marines</u> (Artillery) [USMCR]		
Det 1,[54] HQ Btry	N/A	2nd Mar Div(Rein)
Det 2,[55] HQ Btry	N/A	I MEF
2nd Bn [155 T]		
Btry D	2/10 Mar	2nd Mar Div(Rein)
Btry F	3/10 Mar	2nd Mar Div(Rein)
3rd Bn [155 T]		
Btry H	1/11 Mar	1st Mar Div(Rein)
Btry I	3/12 Mar	1st Mar Div(Rein)
4th Bn [155 SP]		
Btry K	5/10 Mar	2nd Mar Div(Rein)
Btry M	5/10 Mar	2nd Mar Div(Rein)

Low Altitude Air Defense Units[56] [Stinger]

Unit		Major Command
2nd LAAD Bn(-)		3rd MAW
Btry A, 2nd LAAD Bn		4th MEB
Btry B, 2nd LAAD Bn		2nd Mar Div(Rein)
Det, 2nd LAAD Bn		24th MEU(SOC)
Det, 2nd LAAD Bn		26th MEU(SOC) (?)[57]
Det, 2nd LAAD Bn		2nd Mar Div(Rein)
3rd LAAD Bn(-)		3rd MAW
Btry A(-),[58] 3rd LAAD Bn		5th MEB
1st Plt, Btry B, 3rd LAAD Bn		1st Mar Div(Rein)
Sec C, 3rd Plt, Btry B, 3rd LAAD Bn		1st Mar Div(Rein)
Sec A, 2nd Plt, Btry B, 3rd LAAD Bn		1st Mar Div(Rein)
Det, 3rd LAAD Bn		13th MEU(SOC)
Btry A, 4th LAAD Bn [USMCR]		5th MEB (?)[59]

---

[54] Equipped with the AN/TPQ-36 "Firefinder" Radar.

[55] Supplemented the I MEF Fire Spt Coordination Cell.

[56] Information on the pinpoint assignments of the Marine Corps' air defense artillery units has been difficult to locate. See Chart 19, page 19-20.

[57] See Chart 20, Footnote 2.

[58] May have only been a platoon or a reinforced platoon. See Chart 19, Footnote 125.

Light Anti-Aircraft Missile Units [Hawk]

2nd LAAM Bn	3rd MAW
3rd LAAM Bn	3rd MAW

Notes:

➤ The following Marine units were inactivated in the mid or late 1980s and were not available for Desert Storm:

 2/1 Marines
 3/4 Marines
 2/6 Marines
 4/10 Marines (Artillery)
 4/11 Marines (Artillery)

---

[59] See Chart 19, Footnote 125.

Chart 22

U.S. Marine Corps Reserve Ground Combat Units That Were Mobilized For Operation Desert Storm

This chart lists selected Marine Corps Reserve units that were mobilized for Operation Desert Storm.

| Units That Deployed To The Gulf |

Unit & State	Gaining Command
24th Marines(-)	I MEF
Hq Co(-) [KS USMCR]	" "
2/24 Marines [IL/WI/IA USMCR]	" "
3/24 Marines [MO/IL/IN/TN USMCR]	" "
3/23 Marines [LA/TN/AL/AR USMCR]	2nd Mar Div(Rein)
1/25 Marines [MA/NY/NH/CT/ME USMCR]	1st Mar Div(Rein)
Wpns Plt, Co D, 2/25 Marines [NJ USMCR]	1st Mar Div(Rein)
Co F(-),[1] 2/25 Marines [NY USMCR]	2nd Mar Div(Rein)
2nd Plt(Rein),[2] Co F, 2/25 Marines [NY USMCR]	5th MEB
AT Plt, HQ Co, 23rd Marines [LA/CA USMCR]	5th MEB
AT Plt, HQ Co, 24th Marines [MO USMCR]	2nd Mar Div(Rein)
Co A, 4th Tank Bn [CA USMCR]	5th MEB
Cos B, C & AT Co, 4th Tank Bn [WA/ID/TX/OK USMCR]	2nd Mar Div(Rein)
8th Tank Bn [NY/KY/FL/SC USMCR]	2nd Mar Div(Rein)

---

[1] See Chart 19, Footnote 83.
[2] See Chart 19, Footnotes 83 & 120.

Units That Deployed To The Gulf (continued)

Unit & State	Gaining Command
4th LAV Bn(-)[3] [CA/MD/UT/VA USMCR]	2nd Mar Div(Rein)
Co A(-),[4] 4th LAV Bn [CA USMCR]	5th MEB
3rd Force Recon Co(-) [AL USMCR]	1st SRI Gp
4th Force Recon Co(-) [HI USMCR]	1st SRI Gp
Det, 4th Force Recon Co [NV USMCR]	5th MEB
Co D, 4th Recon Bn [NM USMCR]	2nd Mar Div(Rein)
4th Aslt Amphib Bn(-) [FL/TX USMCR]	2nd Mar Div(Rein)
Co A,[5] 4th Aslt Amphib Bn [VA/MS USMCR]	5th MEB
Det 1, HQ Btry, 14th Marines (Arty) [TX USMCR]	2nd Mar Div(Rein)
Det 2, HQ Btry, 14th Marines (Arty) [TX USMCR]	I MEF
Btry D, 2/14 Marines (Arty) [155 T] [IA USMCR]	2nd Mar Div(Rein)
Btry F, 2/14 Marines (Arty) [155 T] [OK USMCR]	2nd Mar Div(Rein)
Btry H, 3/14 Marines (Arty) [155 T] [VA USMCR]	1st Mar Div(Rein)
Btry I, 3/14 Marines (Arty) [155 T] [PA USMCR]	1st Mar Div(Rein)
Btry K, 4/14 Marines (Arty) [155 SP] [AL USMCR]	2nd Mar Div(Rein)
Btry M, 4/14 Marines (Arty) [155 SP] [TN USMCR]	2nd Mar Div(Rein)
Btry A(?),[6] 4th LAAD Bn [Stinger] [CA USMCR]	5th MEB

Units That Deployed To Okinawa

Unit & State	Gaining Command
2/23 Marines [CA/UT USMCR]	3rd Mar Div(-)
1/24 Marines [MI/OH USMCR]	3rd Mar Div(-)
Btry C, 1/14 Marines (Arty) [155 T] [MS USMCR]	3rd Mar Div(-)
Btry G, 3/14 Marines (Arty) [155 T] [NJ USMCR]	3rd Mar Div(-)

---

[3] See Chart 19, Footnote 83.
[4] See Chart 19, Footnote 119.
[5] May have been a company(-).
[6] See Chart 19, Footnote 124.

Units That Deployed To Norway[7]

Unit	Mobilization Site
2nd MEB	Lejeune
25th Marines(-)(Rein) [MA/OH/WV USMCR]	" "
HQ Co, 25th Marines [MA USMCR]	" "
3/25 Marines [OH/WV USMCR]	" "
Co E, 4th Recon Bn [AK USMCR]	" "
1/14 Marines(-) (Arty) [155 T] [CA/WA USMCR]	" "
HQ Btry, 1/14 Marines [CA USMCR]	" "
Btry A, 1/14 Marines [WA USMCR]	" "
Btry B, 1/14 Marines [CA USMCR]	" "
Det 3, HQ Btry, 14th Marines [TX USMCR]	" "

Units That Were Mobilized But Not Deployed

Unit	Mobilization Site
Det, HQ, 4th Mar Div [NY USMCR]	?
23rd Marines(-)(Rein)[8] [CA/TX/LA USMCR]	Pendleton; 29 Palms
HQ Co(-), 23rd Marines [CA USMCR]	" "
1/23 Marines [TX/LA USMCR]	Pendleton; 29 Palms
Co B, 4th Recon Bn [MT USMCR]	" "
2/25 Marines(-)[9] [NY/NJ/PA USMCR]	" "
H&S Co, 4th Tank Bn [M60A1] [CA USMCR]	29 Palms
4th Recon Bn(-)[10] [TX USMCR	Pendleton

---

[7] In February and March 1991, the Marine Corps participated in Exercise Battle Griffin 91 in Norway. This exercise was the first test of the Norway Air-Landed MEB. Under this program the Marine Corps has prepositioned equipment and supplies for a MEB in Norway, and this allows the Marines to quickly deploy a MEB to Norway by air in time of emergency. This exercise was conducted entirely by the Marine Corps Reserve.

[8] Served as the Ground Combat Element of V MEF. See Chart 23, Footnote 1. Moved to Twentynine Palms after initially being stationed at Camp Pendleton.

[9] Consisted of H&S Co, Cos D & E, and Wpns Co. During mobilization, a new Weapons Plt, Co D, was organized to replace the platoon that had deployed to the KTO. In addition, this battalion organized a new unit, "Yankee Co," which apparently was intended to replace Co F, which had deployed to the KTO.

[10] Consisted of H&S Co(-) and Co C.

Units That Were Mobilized But Not Deployed (continued)

Unit	Mobilization Site
23rd Marines(-)(Rein) (continued)	
4/14 Marines(-) (Arty) [AL/IL USMCR]	29 Palms
HQ Btry, 4/14 Marines [AL USMCR]	" "
Btry E, 2/14 Marines [155 T] [IL USMCR]	" "
Btry L, 4/14 Marines [155 SP] [AL USMCR]	" "
4th Recon Bn(-)[11] [TX USMCR]	Lejeune
Det, H&S Co,[12] 4th LAV Bn [CA USMCR] (?)	?
Det 4, HQ Btry, 14th Marines (Arty) [TX USMCR]	29 Palms
Det A, H&S Btry, 4th LAAD Bn [Stinger] [GA USMCR]	?
Btry B, 4th LAAD Bn [Stinger] [GA USMCR]	?
H&S Btry(-), 4th LAAM Bn [Hawk] [__ USMCR]	Yuma
Det, H&S Btry, 4th LAAM Bn [Hawk] [__ USMCR]	?
Btry A, 4th LAAM Bn [Hawk] [__ USMCR]	Yuma
Btry C, 4th LAAM Bn [Hawk] [__ USMCR]	?

Notes:

➢ When a unit served at two mobilization sites at different times, the sites are separated by a semicolon and listed in chronological order.

---

[11] Consisted of H&S Co(-) and Co A. Company E may have rejoined the battalion after returning from Norway. See Footnote 7.

[12] See Chart 19, Footnote 83.

Chart 23

Major U.S. Marine Corps Ground Combat Units Stationed Outside the KTO At the Beginning Of Operation Desert Storm

In order to place the Gulf War in perspective it is necessary to consider the Marine Corps units that were active outside the Gulf during the war. This chart lists all of the major Marine Corps ground combat units that were active outside the KTO at the beginning of Operation Desert Storm, including the reserve component units that had been mobilized and were on active duty.

Unit	Location
HQ, II MEF	Lejeune
HQ, III MEF	Okinawa
HQ, V MEF[1]	Pendleton
3rd Mar Div(-)[2]	Okinawa
2nd MEB(-) [USMCR]	Lejeune & Norway[3]

---

[1] HQ, V MEF was activated on 15 Jan 91 to take the place of HQ, I MEF. HQ, V MEF was inactivated on 24 Apr 91 when HQ, I MEF returned to Camp Pendleton.

[2] The 3rd Mar Div(-) was substantially understrength during Desert Storm. For example, it had only three infantry battalions, while a Marine division was authorized nine infantry battalions. The 3rd Mar Div(-) shared these units with the 9th MEB, whose headquarters was embedded within III MEF.

[3] See Chart 22, Footnote 7.

Order of Battle

Unit	Location
HQ, 1st MEB[4]	Kaneohe Bay
HQ, 6th MEB	Lejeune
HQ, 9th MEB[5]	Okinawa
23rd Marines(-)(Rein)[6] [USMCR]	Pendleton & 29 Palms
15th MEU(SOC)[7]	Pendleton
HQ, 22nd MEU[8]	Lejeune

Notes:

➢ While HQ, 1st MEB and HQ, 6th MEB remained active at, respectively, Kaneohe Bay and Camp Lejeune, these headquarters were almost certainly stripped of personnel for other units. Thus, it is doubtful either of these headquarters could have commanded a MEB without a substantial infusion of new personnel.

➢ These units were organized as follows:

> II Marine Expeditionary Force [Lejeune]
> 2nd MEB(-) [USMCR]
> HQ, 6th MEB
> HQ, 22nd MEU
>
> III Marine Expeditionary Force [Okinawa]
> 3rd Mar Div(-)
> HQ, 9th MEB
>
> V Marine Expeditionary Force [Pendleton]
> HQ, 1st MEB [Kaneohe Bay]
> 23rd Marines(-)(Rein) [USMCR] [Pendleton & Twentynine Palms]
> 15th MEU(SOC)

---

[4] All of 1st MEB's units deployed to the Gulf, but HQ, 1st MEB, remained on Hawaii.

[5] See Footnote 2.

[6] The 23rd Marines were short an infantry battalion but were reinforced by tank, recon, and artillery units. See Chart 22, pages 22-3 and 22-4.

[7] See Chart 21, Footnotes 2, 4, 15, 28 & 48.

[8] Few if any units were assigned to the 22nd MEU, as substantially all of II MEF's units had deployed to the Gulf, or to the Mediterranean with the 24th or 26th MEU(SOC)s.

Chart 24

Selected U.S. Marine Corps
Ground Combat Equipment

Tanks

Virtually every Marine Corps tank unit, active and reserve, served in the Gulf.[1] When Desert Shield began, the total Marine Corps tank force consisted of five and a half battalions, with a total of five battalion headquarters & service companies and 20 tank companies. At that time, all Marine tank units, active and reserve, were equipped with the M60A1 Main Battle Tank,[2] which entered USMC service in the early 1970s as the replacement for the M48A3 Medium Tank and M103A2 Heavy Tank. A platoon of Marine Corps M60A1s saw combat in Grenada, and Marine Corps M60A1s served in Lebanon in 1982-83, but no Marine Corps M60A1s served in Panama. The Marine Corps had not adopted the M60A3 (the more advanced version of the M60A1), or the M1 series tank at the time Desert Shield began.

During Desert Shield the Marine Corps upgraded some of its tank units by re-equipping them with M1A1 series "Abrams" Main Battle Tanks. The Marines deployed

---

[1] No Marine tank units served in the Mediterranean with the 24th or 26th MEU(SOC)s.

[2] The 1st and 3rd Tank Bns had the M60A1(RISE Passive). It is unclear if the remaining M60A1 units had RISE Passives or basic M60A1s. The basic M60A1 used an active infrared (IR) system for night fighting. A searchlight provided the IR beam that was picked up by the tank's IR sight. The RISE Passive used a passive system that magnified available moon and/or star light and did not require an active IR source. "RISE" stood for "Reliability Improved Selected Equipment" and referred to a slight improvement that was achieved in the tank's reliability. In fact, the RISE Passive was only marginally more effective than the original M60A1 that had been fielded in the early 1960s. By contrast, the M60A3(TTS) represented a quantum leap in capability compared to the M60A1 RISE Passive.

a total of 76 M1A1 series tanks in SWA. Sixty of these were the M1A1HA version,[3] while the remaining 16 were the M1A1 "Common" version, which was a new version that included the characteristics the Army and Marine Corps desired in their tanks.

The remaining USMC tank units took their thirty-year old M60A1s into combat, supplemented by approximately ten M60A3s that the Marine Corps obtained from the Army.[4] Most or all Marine M60A1s had their armor protection upgraded through the attachment of reactive armor tiles to the outside of the tank.[5]

Of the 18 Marine tank companies in SWA, 13 were equipped with M60A1s/M60A3s, while five companies were equipped with the M1A1HA or M1A1 Common. Of the four H&S companies, three were equipped with M60A1s/M60A3s, while one was equipped with the M1A1HA.[6] Thus, just over 70 percent of the Marines' tank force in Desert Storm was equipped with M60 series tanks, and just under thirty percent was equipped with M1A1 series tanks.

M60A1/M60A3 Units

Unit	Assignment
H&S Co, 1st Tank Bn	1st Marine Div(Rein)
Co A, 1st Tank Bn	1st Marine Div(Rein)
Co B, 1st Tank Bn	1st Marine Div(Rein)
Co C, 1st Tank Bn	1st Marine Div(Rein)
Co D, 1st Tank Bn	1st Marine Div(Rein)
Co A, 2nd Tank Bn	4th MEB

---

[3] See Chart 13, page 13-2 for details concerning this version of the M1.

[4] The M60A3s were assigned to the 1st and 3rd Tank Bns. These were almost certainly the M60A3s that deployed to Saudi Arabia with Trp D, 4th Cav, 197th Inf Bde(M). See Chart 13, Footnote 7. The Marines also used the M60 AVLB, a derivative of the M60 series Main Battle Tank. The first U.S. main battle tanks to arrive in Saudi Arabia were M60A1s landed from MPS ships o/a 17 Aug 90 and issued to the Marines' 3rd Tank Bn, which had deployed its personnel by air as an element of the 7th MEB.

[5] The 1st, 3rd, and 8th Tank Bns had reactive armor. It is unclear if the two tank companies with the 4th and 5th MEBs (Co A, 2nd Tank Bn and Co A, 4th Tank Bn, respectively) had reactive armor. Reactive armor tiles were in short supply when the 8th Tank Bn arrived in the Gulf. As a result, the 8th's tanks received less than half the full allotment of reactive armor tiles. To protect the mounting brackets and deceive the Iraqis, the 8th Tank Bn mounted dummy tiles in all of the spaces that were missing real tiles.

[6] Six of the 18 tank companies were USMCR units, and one of the four H&S companies was a USMCR unit. Thus, the Marine Corps Reserve contributed about 30 percent of the Marine tank force in SWA.

M60A1/M60A3 Units (continued)

Unit	Assignment
H&S Co, 3rd Tank Bn	1st Marine Div(Rein)
Co A, 3rd Tank Bn	1st Marine Div(Rein)
Co B, 3rd Tank Bn	1st Marine Div(Rein)
Co C, 3rd Tank Bn	1st Marine Div(Rein)
Co A, 4th Tank Bn [CA USMCR]	5th MEB
H&S Co, 8th Tank Bn [NY USMCR]	2nd Marine Div(Rein)
Co A, 8th Tank Bn [KY USMCR]	2nd Marine Div(Rein)
Co B, 8th Tank Bn [SC USMCR]	2nd Marine Div(Rein)
Co C, 8th Tank Bn [FL USMCR	2nd Marine Div(Rein)
Co D, 1st Armd Aslt Bn	1st Marine Div(Rein)

M1A1 Series Units

All had the M1A1HA, except for Co C, 4th Tank Bn, which had the M1A1 Common:

Unit	Assignment
H&S Co, 2nd Tank Bn	2nd Marine Div(Rein)
Co B,[7] 2nd Tank Bn	2nd Marine Div(Rein)
Co C, 2nd Tank Bn	2nd Marine Div(Rein)
Co D, 2nd Tank Bn	2nd Marine Div(Rein)
Co B, 4th Tank Bn [WA USMCR]	2nd Marine Div(Rein)
Co C, 4th Tank Bn [ID/TX USMCR]	2nd Marine Div(Rein)

---

[7] Company B, 2nd Tank Bn was the first Marine Corps tank unit to complete M1A1 training (at Twentynine Palms on 19 Nov 90) and the first Marine Corps M1A1 unit to achieve operational readiness in SWA, which occurred on 12 Jan 91.

Not Present In the Gulf

Unit	Notes
H&S Co, 4th Tank Bn [CA USMCR]	Served at 29 Palms
Co D, 8th Tank Bn [SC USMCR]	Disbanded during Desert Storm because the MPS ships that provided tanks for the 8th Tank Bn lacked sufficient tanks to equip Co D. See Chart 19, Footnote 56.

Unit	Notes
Co C, 1st Armd Aslt Bn	Personnel remained at Camp Pendleton when 1st Tank Bn deployed to SWA to maintain the tanks that 1st Tank Bn left behind.

Marine tanks also served with the combat engineer units assigned to the 1st and 2nd Marine Divisions, although it is unclear if the tanks were actually assigned to the engineer units or if detachments from the tank battalions were attached to the engineer units.[8] Mine plows and rakes were mounted on these tanks and they were used to clear paths through the Iraqi minefields and obstacles.

After Desert Storm, the Marines re-equipped all of their tank units, active and reserve, with M1A1 series tanks.

THE LAV

The LAV, short for "Light Armored Vehicle," is a lightly-armored eight-wheeled armored car that is used exclusively by the Marine Corps.[9] The LAV is an adaptation of a family of vehicles that were built for the Canadian Army by General Motors of Canada. The LAV entered service with the Marine Corps in 1984.

---

[8] This latter approach is the more likely, as engineer personnel would not have known how to operate the tanks. See Chart 19, Footnotes 59 & 60.

[9] During Desert Storm, the Scout Plt of the Army's 3-73 Armor(Abn), 82nd Abn Div, used 14 LAV-25s and one LAV-R on loan from the Marine Corps to evaluate the LAV as a possible Army scout vehicle. To date, the Army has not adopted the LAV.

The basic version of the LAV is the LAV-25, which is armed with the same 25mm chain gun that is mounted on the Army's M2/M3 Bradley Fighting Vehicle. The LAV-AT is the antitank version and is armed with the same double-barrel TOW launcher that is mounted on the Army's M901 Improved TOW Vehicle. The LAV-M is armed with an M252 81mm mortar. The LAV-C2 is the command and control version, the LAV-R is the recovery variant, and the LAV-L is the logistics (cargo carrier) version.

A company of LAVs served in Operation Just Cause. During Desert Storm, the LAV equipped the Marines' light armored infantry and light armored vehicle battalions.[10] The LAVs that served on land achieved an operational readiness rate in excess of 94 percent, although those that were afloat experienced a somewhat lower rate. The LAV continues to serve in the Marine Corps in the same role today.

Assault Amphibious Vehicles

The Marine Corps' signature vehicle is the AAV7A1 Assault Amphibious Vehicle, a large, lightly-armored, fully-tracked amphibious vehicle that is able to land Marines on a beach through heavy surf and traverse normal terrain like any other tracked vehicle. The AAV7A1 exists in personnel carrier (AAVP7A1), command and control (AAVC7A1), and recovery (AAVR7A1) variants.

The AAV7A1 is an advanced version of the LVTP 7 (Landing Vehicle, Tracked, Personnel), which was fielded in 1972 as a replacement for the LVTP 5. The AAV7A1 began replacing the LVTP 7 in the mid-1980s. The LVTP 7 saw combat in Grenada, but the LVTP 7/AAV7A1 did not serve in Panama. In Desert Storm, the AAV7A1 served in Marine assault amphibian battalions.[11] Assault amphibious vehicles also served with the combat engineer units assigned to the 1st and 2nd Marine Divisions, although it is unclear if the AAVs were actually assigned to the engineer units or if detachments from the assault amphibian battalions were attached to the engineer units.[12] The AAV7A1 family achieved an operational readiness rate in excess of 93 percent. The AAV7A1 continues to serve in the same role today.

---

[10] Of the approximately 13 LAI/LAV companies that served in the Gulf, four-plus were USMCR units. Of the approximately three H&S companies that served in the Gulf, one (or part of one) company was a USMCR unit. Thus, the Marine Corps Reserve contributed about one-third of the LAI/LAV force in SWA.

[11] Of the approximately ten assault amphibian companies that served in the Gulf, two were USMCR units. Of the approximately three H&S companies that served in the Gulf, a company(-) was a USMCR unit. Thus, the Marine Corps Reserve contributed about twenty percent of the assault amphibian force in SWA.

[12] This latter approach is the more likely, as engineer personnel would not have been qualified to operate AAVs.

M1045/M1046 HMMWV With TOW Antitank Missile System

The High Mobility Multipurpose Wheeled Vehicle (HMMWV) was fielded as the replacement for the M151 quarter-ton truck, or "jeep," in the mid-1980s. The Marines use a variety of HMMWV versions for a wide range of missions. One of the most important functions the HMMWV serves in the Marine Corps is as a carrier for the TOW Antitank Missile System. This vehicle comes in two versions, the M1046 TOW Carrier, which has a winch to enable the vehicle to unditch itself, and the M1045 TOW Carrier, which lacks the winch.

The TOW HMMWV was the backbone of the Marines' antitank defense during Desert Storm. The antitank platoon in the headquarters company of each Marine infantry regiment was authorized 24 TOW HMMWVs, while the antitank company of each Marine tank battalion was authorized 72 TOW HMMWVs.[13] Many units obtained additional TOW HMMWVs from various sources, boosting the numbers of these weapon systems in SWA. TOW HMMWV continues to serve in the same role in the Marine Corps today.

Artillery

Marine artillery units that participated in Desert Storm were equipped with four weapon systems: (1) the M101A1 towed 105mm howitzer; (2) the M198 towed 155mm howitzer; (3) the M109A3 self-propelled 155mm howitzer; and (4) the M110A2 self-propelled 203mm (8 inch) howitzer. The Marines did not use the M102 towed 105mm howitzer, M270 MLRS, or Army Tactical Missile System (ATACMS), all of which were used by the Army in the Gulf.[14]

M101A1 Towed 105mm Howitzer

The M101 towed 105mm howitzer was a comparatively ancient system that entered service shortly after World War Two. Moreover, the M101 was closely related to the M2/M2A1 towed 105mm howitzer which was the standard U.S. direct support artillery piece in World War Two. The M101 served with the Marine Corps in Korea and Vietnam, but did not see combat in Grenada[15] or Panama.

---

[13] Of the approximately 11 regimental antitank platoons that served in the Gulf, two were USMCR units. Of the five antitank companies assigned to tank battalions that served in the Gulf, two were USMCR units. Thus, the Marine Corps Reserve contributed about 30 percent of the Marine TOW HMMWV force in SWA.

[14] See Chart 13, pages 13-9 through 13-11.

[15] The Marines deployed one artillery battery with their forces that invaded Grenada, but this unit served as a provisional

During Desert Storm, the M101A1 served only with artillery units that were afloat in the Gulf or the Mediterranean.[16] As a result, only a very limited number of M101A1s served in Desert Storm. These afloat units were equipped with a mix of M101A1s and M198 towed 155mm howitzers. These units had M101A1s because their light weight and small size when compared to the M198 made them easier to move by helicopter during an amphibious landing or raid. Today all Marine artillery units are equipped with the M198 towed 155mm howitzer, however some M101A1s are still held in storage for use during contingency operations.

M198 Towed 155mm Howitzer

The M198 towed 155mm howitzer was a relatively new system, having been fielded in 1982 to replace the M114 towed 155mm howitzer. No Marine M198s saw combat in Grenada[17] or Panama, however.

In Desert Storm, the M198 served as the Marines' standard direct support (DS) artillery piece, and also provided half of the Marines' general support (GS) artillery. Of the 37 firing batteries in SWA, 31 were equipped with the M198.[18] Thus, the M198 comprised almost 85 percent of the Marines' artillery force.[19] Today the M198 serves as the Marines' primary artillery piece, performing both the DS and GS roles.

M109A3 Self-Propelled 155mm Howitzer

The M109 series self-propelled 155mm howitzer was an old system that has seen substantial service with the Marine Corps. First fielded by the Marines in the 1960s, the M109 saw combat with the Marines in Vietnam but did not serve in Grenada or Panama.

---

rifle company and never took its howitzers ashore. This battery probably had some M101A1s.

[16] These were:

In the Gulf: (1) 1/10 Marines, 4th MEB; (2) 2/11 Marines, 5th MEB; and (3) Btry B, 1/11 Marines, 13th MEU(SOC).

In the Mediterranean: (1) Btry H, 3/10 Marines, 24th MEU(SOC); and (2) Btry G, 3/10 Marines, 26th MEU(SOC).

[17] The Marines deployed one M198 artillery battery with their forces that invaded Grenada, but this unit served as a provisional rifle company and never took its howitzers ashore.

[18] Four of these 31 batteries were USMCR units. Thus, the Marine Corps Reserve contributed 13 percent of the Marine M198s in SWA.

[19] These figures do not include the two MEUs afloat in the Mediterranean, each of which had an artillery battery with M198s and M101A1 towed 105mm howitzers. Although used by Army field artillery in the Gulf, the M198 was a relatively minor player, equipping only six percent of the Army field artillery units deployed to SWA.

In Desert Storm, the M109 served in the 1st and 2nd Marine Divisions as a GS artillery piece. Of the 37 firing batteries in SWA, only four were equipped with the M109.[20] Thus, the M109 comprised only ten percent of the Marines' artillery force.[21]

The M109s that served in the Gulf were the M109A3 version. The Marines were in the process of phasing out the M109 when Desert Shield began, and hastily reversed that decision as they began deploying to the desert to confront a mechanized opponent. Since Desert Storm, however, the M109 has been completely eliminated from both the Active Marine Corps and the Marine Corps Reserve.

M110A2 Self-Propelled 203mm Howitzer

The M110 series self-propelled 203mm (eight inch) howitzer was an old system that has seen substantial service with the Marine Corps. First fielded by the Marines in the 1960s, the M110 saw combat with the Marines in Vietnam but did not serve in Grenada or Panama.

In Desert Storm, the M110 served in the 1st and 2nd Marine Divisions as a GS artillery piece. Of the 37 firing batteries in SWA, only two were equipped with the M110.[22] Thus, the M110 comprised only five percent of the Marines' artillery force.[23]

The M110s that served in the Gulf were the M110A2 version. The Marines were in the process of phasing out the M110 when Desert Shield began and hastily reversed that decision as they began deploying to the desert to confront a mechanized opponent. Since Desert Storm, however, the M110 has been completely eliminated from both the Active Marine Corps and the Marine Corps Reserve.

AN/TPQ-36 "Firefinder" Radar

In addition to its howitzers, Marine artillery units employed the AN/TPQ-36 "Firefinder" Radar.[24] The AN/TPQ-36 was used to detect and track incoming mortar and artillery rounds so that friendly artillery could return fire and suppress or destroy the enemy's indirect fire assets. The AN/TPQ-36 was generally fielded in the Marine Corps in the mid-1980s, but saw service with the Marines in Lebanon in 1982-83. It did not serve with the Marines in Panama, however.

---

[20] Two of these batteries were USMCR units. Thus, the Marine Corps Reserve contributed 50 percent of the Marine M109s in SWA.

[21] The M109 provided over half of the Army's field artillery in the Gulf, however. See Chart 13, pages 13-9 and 13-10.

[22] Both of these batteries were active duty units.

[23] The M110 equipped 13 percent of Army field artillery units in SWA, however. See Chart 13, page 13-10.

[24] Unlike the Army, the Marines did not use the AN/TPQ-37 Radar.

In Desert Storm, the AN/TPQ-36 was assigned to the counter-battery radar platoon of the headquarters battery of Marine artillery regiments. An advanced version of the AN/TPQ-36, the AN/TPQ-46A, performs the same function for the Marine Corps today.

Air Defense Artillery

Marine air defense artillery units used two veteran weapon systems in the Gulf: (1) the "Stinger" manportable missile, and (2) the "Hawk" missile system. The Marines did not use any of the other air defense weapon systems that the Army used in Desert Storm, such as the "Avenger" or the "Patriot."[25]

"Stinger" Missile

Stinger was a manportable, shoulder-fired, heat-seeking air defense missile. Stinger entered service with the Marines in 1982 as a replacement for the "Redeye" missile, which was similar to Stinger but much less capable, as it could only be fired at the tail of enemy aircraft as they exited the area after completing their attack on friendly forces. The Marines may have deployed Stinger on Grenada, but did not use it in Panama. In Desert Storm, Stinger served in the Marines' two-plus low altitude air defense (LAAD) battalions.[26] Stinger continues to serve in the Marine Corps in the same role today.

"Hawk" Missile System[27]

Hawk is a medium-range missile designed to engage enemy aircraft. It entered service with the Marine Corps in 1962 and served in Vietnam in limited numbers. Hawk did not serve in Grenada or Panama. In Desert Storm, Hawk served in the Marines' two light antiaircraft missile (LAAM) battalions.[28] The Marines are now in the process of phasing out Hawk.

---

[25] See Chart 13, pages 13-10 through 13-16.

[26] Of the approximately five LAAD firing batteries in SWA, at most one was a USMCR unit. See Chart 19, Footnote 124. Thus, the Marine Corps Reserve contributed at most 20 percent of the Marine LAAD batteries in SWA.

[27] According to some sources, the correct name is "HAWK," an acronym for "Homing All the Way Killer." Most sources state the name as "Hawk," however, and I have used that spelling in this order of battle. The missiles deployed to SWA were actually an improved version of the Hawk, formerly known as the "I-Hawk," which had been fielded in the 1970s.

[28] These were both active duty units; no Marine Corps Reserve LAAM units served in SWA.

Helicopters

This chart does not address Marine Corps helicopters in any detail because the Marine Corps considers them to be part of its aviation community, rather than ground combat weapons. Marine helicopters differed from Army aviation in several significant ways. The Marines did not employ a scout helicopter like the Army's OH-58 "Kiowa." With regard to attack helicopters, the Marine Corps used its own versions of the AH-1 "Cobra," the AH-1J and AH-1T "Sea Cobra" and AH-1W "Super Cobra." Unlike the AH-1Fs flown by the Army, the AH-1W was able to fire the "Hellfire" antitank missile. The Marines began introducing the AH-1W in 1986. The Marines deployed to SWA 50 AH-1Ws and 26 of the less-advanced AH-1J version of the Cobra. The Marines also deployed approximately eight AH-1Ts to the Mediterranean during Desert Storm. The Marines did not use the AH-64 "Apache."

The Marines used limited numbers of UH-1N "Huey" Utility Helicopters for command and control, reconnaissance, and medical evacuation, but used other helicopters for most of their air assault and cargo missions. The Marines did not use the UH-60 "Black Hawk" Utility Helicopter.

For most of its air assault and cargo missions the Marines relied upon the CH-46E "Sea Knight" Medium-Lift Transport Helicopter, and the CH-53D "Sea Stallion" and CH-53E "Super Stallion" Heavy-Lift Cargo Helicopters. The Sea Knight was a version of the Army's CH-47 "Chinook," while the Sea Stallion and Super Stallion were large helicopters that were not used by the Army.

Notes:

➢ All information with regard to the current status of weapon systems is "as of" mid-1998.

Chart 25

U.S. Marine Corps
Service Streamers and Unit Awards
For Operation Desert Storm

Campaign and Service Streamers

The Marine Corps recognizes a unit's participation in combat by awarding it campaign or service streamers. Major wars, such as World War Two, are divided into numerous campaigns, each defined using geographic and chronological factors. Smaller conflicts, such as Grenada, constitute a single campaign.[1] Desert Shield/Storm was divided into three campaigns:

> Defense of Saudi Arabia (2 Aug 90 through 16 Jan 91)
> Liberation and Defense of Kuwait (17 Jan through 11 Apr 91)
> Southwest Asia Cease-Fire (12 Apr 91 through 30 Nov 95)[2]

Participation in Desert Storm is recognized by award of the "Southwest Asia Service Streamer." A Marine Corps unit that served in all three campaigns would be awarded the Southwest Asia Service Streamer with three bronze stars.

The Marine Corps awards campaign and service streamers through unit orders, and a unit's entitlement to campaign or service streamers is then memorialized in its

---

[1] Participation in small actions like Grenada are memorialized by award of the Armed Forces Expeditionary Streamer. Separate campaign or service streamers are not created for smaller actions like Grenada.

[2] These campaigns were established by the Department of Defense and apply to all of the Armed Services. In light of the fact that essentially no combat occurred during this time period it is difficult to understand why this third period of time qualifies as a campaign for streamer purposes.

honors certificate. Unlike the Army, the Marine Corps does not announce or memorialize the award of campaign or service streamers in widely-available documents such as orders issued by the Headquarters of the Marine Corps. Nor does the Marine Corps publish any sort of consolidated list of all units that have been awarded campaign or service streamers for a given conflict. Accordingly, determining all of the units that are officially credited with serving in a conflict such as Desert Storm can be quite difficult.

The Marine Corps Unit Award System

The Marine Corps recognizes superior unit performance through unit awards.[3] Marine Corps units were eligible for three such awards during Operation Desert Storm (listed in order of precedence, from highest to lowest):

(1) Presidential Unit Citation (Navy)
(2) Navy Unit Commendation
(3) Meritorious Unit Commendation (Navy-Marine Corps)

The Navy Presidential Unit Citation (PUC) is awarded to Navy and Marine Corps units for "extraordinary heroism in action against an armed enemy. The unit must have displayed such gallantry, determination, and esprit de corps in accomplishing its mission under extremely difficult and hazardous conditions to have set it apart and above other units participating in the same campaign."[4] The Navy PUC requires the level of heroism that would justify award of the Navy Cross to an individual.[5]

The Navy Unit Commendation (NUC) is the Navy's next highest unit award. The NUC is awarded to a Navy or Marine Corps unit that "has distinguished itself by outstanding heroism in action against the enemy, but not sufficient to justify the award of the Presidential Unit Citation." The NUC can also be awarded for superior noncombat service, to a unit "which has distinguished itself by extremely meritorious service not involving combat but in support of military operations, rendering the unit outstanding compared to other units performing similar service." The NUC requires the level of heroism that would justify award of the Silver Star for heroism, or award of the Legion of Merit for meritorious service, to an individual.[6] "Normal performance of duty

---

[3] The Marines also have a series of awards for individuals, some of which are limited to valor in combat (e.g., the Congressional Medal of Honor), while others can be awarded under other circumstances.

[4] All of the quotations in this chart are from SECNAVINST 1650.1F, *Navy And Marine Corps Awards Manual* (8 Aug 91) (with Change 1 (25 Feb 92)).

[5] The Navy Cross is the Navy's second-highest individual award for heroism. The Congressional Medal of Honor is the highest individual award for heroism.

[6] The Silver Star is the third-highest individual award for heroism. The Legion of Merit is the second-highest individual

or participation in a large number of combat missions does not in itself justify the award." Furthermore, the NUC will not be awarded to a Marine Corps unit "for actions of one or more of its component parts, unless the unit performed uniformly as a team in a manner justifying collective recognition."

The Navy-Marine Corps Meritorious Unit Commendation (MUC) is the final award for which Marine Corps units are eligible. The MUC is awarded to any unit "which has distinguished itself, under combat or noncombat conditions, by either valorous or meritorious achievement which renders the unit outstanding compared to other units performing similar service, but not sufficient to justify the award of the Navy Unit Commendation." The MUC requires the level of performance that would justify award of the Bronze Star, "or achievement of like caliber in a noncombat situation," to an individual.[7] As with the NUC, "[n]ormal performance of duty or participation in a large number of combat missions does not in itself justify" the MUC, and the MUC will not be awarded to a Marine Corps unit "for actions of one or more of its component parts, unless the unit performed uniformly as a team in a manner justifying collective recognition."

Marine Corps Unit Awards For Desert Storm

Unlike the Army, the Marine Corps has completed the unit award process for Desert Storm. The Navy Presidential Unit Citation has not been awarded to any unit for Desert Storm. The next highest unit award, the Navy Unit Commendation, however, was awarded to every — or virtually every — Marine Corps unit that served in SWA.

The entire I Marine Expeditionary Force received the NUC for the period 14 Aug 90 through 16 Apr 91. This included both combat arms and non-combat arms support units; ground and air units; and all of the headquarters units involved, all the way up to the headquarters of the I Marine Expeditionary Force. This award even included supporting units that did not deploy to Southwest Asia. Finally, included among the units awarded the NUC were the U.S. Navy's 3rd Naval Construction Regiment and the U.S. Army's 1st Brigade, 2nd Armored Division, both of which served with the I Marine Expeditionary Force.

The Marine units afloat in the Gulf during Desert Storm also received the NUC. The 4th and 5th Marine Expeditionary Brigades and the 13th Marine Expeditionary Unit(SOC) were awarded the NUC for the period 1 Aug 90 through 30 Apr 91.

---

award for meritorious service that does not involve heroism in combat.

[7] The Bronze Star can be awarded for heroism or non-heroic meritorious achievement. It is the fifth-highest individual award for heroism in combat and the fourth-highest individual award for non-heroic meritorious achievement.

It seems difficult to believe that every Marine unit in the Gulf deserved the Corps' second highest award for valor, the NUC. Each unit that served in the Gulf was automatically entitled to the Southwest Asia Service Streamer, and that should have been sufficient to commemorate the contribution made by the average unit. By awarding the NUC to every unit that was there — rather than selectively awarding it to those units whose performance set them apart from their comrades — the Marine Corps lost an opportunity to use the unit award system to differentiate between the average unit and the superior unit, and violated the spirit, if not the letter, of the *Navy and Marine Corps Awards Manual*.

The final Marine Corps unit award, the Meritorious Unit Commendation (Navy-Marine Corps), was awarded to numerous Marine Corps units that served outside the KTO during Desert Storm, including (1) the 2nd Bn, 9th Marines, the only active duty infantry battalion that remained on Okinawa with the 3rd Marine Division during Desert Storm; (2) the Marine Corps Reserve units that deployed to Okinawa to backfill the 3rd Marine Division after it deployed many of its units to the KTO; (3) the Marine Corps Reserve units that deployed to Norway pursuant to Exercise Battle Griffin 91; and (4) the Marine Corps Reserve units that were mobilized and served in CONUS as a strategic reserve. As with the blanket-award of the NUC, this generous approach to the MUC violated the spirit, if not the letter, of the *Navy and Marine Corps Awards Manual*.

Among those units that did not receive a unit award for Desert Storm were the 24th and 26th Marine Expeditionary Units, which were forward-deployed in the Mediterranean during the war. Why these units were left out of the unit award process is unclear. They certainly made a more significant contribution than did the Marine Corps Reserve units that remained in CONUS.

The Marine Corps announces/memorializes unit awards in "All Marine" messages (ALMAR) periodically issued by Headquarters, Marine Corps. The last such message with regard to Desert Storm, which lists all unit awards for ODS, is ALMAR 282/92, "Subject: MCBUL 1650, Awards Update" (6 Oct 92). In light of the fact that every unit in I MEF received the NUC, this document comes close to memorializing the Marine Corps' official position with regard to which units served in Operation Desert Storm. This information has now been incorporated into NAVMC 2922, *United States Marine Corps Unit Awards Manual*, which is periodically issued by the Marine Corps. The latest edition is dated 25 Feb 98.

Notes:

➢ There is also a Joint Meritorious Unit Award (JMUA) which can be awarded to joint activities of the DOD "for meritorious achievement or service, superior to that which is normally expected, under one of the following conditions: (1) During action in combat with an armed enemy of the United States, (2) For a declared national emergency situation, (3) Under extraordinary circumstances that involved the national interest." Thus, joint headquarters to which Marine Corps personnel are assigned are eligible for the JMUA, but normally Marine Corps units are not. The JMUA for Desert Storm was awarded to:

Headquarters, U.S. Central Command
Headquarters, SOCCENT
Headquarters, JTF Proven Force
Joint Special Operations Task Force, JTF Proven Force
U.S. Special Operations Command

Chart 26

Post-Desert Storm Developments, U.S. Marine Corps Ground Combat Units

With the end of the Gulf War on 28 Feb 91, the Marine Corps began the monumental task of standing down the large war machine that had deployed to Southwest Asia. The Marines had to move units, equipment, and supplies out of the Gulf, while ensuring the security of Saudi Arabia, Kuwait, and our other allies. Finally, notwithstanding our decisive victory, Saddam Hussein has continued to threaten our allies in the region, requiring periodic deployments of significant ground combat troops to Kuwait. This chart addresses the Marine Corps' drawdown in the KTO after the Gulf War, as well as the subsequent deployments in response to Saddam's continuing saber-rattling.

The Immediate Aftermath Of Desert Storm

➤ The last major Marine Corps maneuver unit to leave the KTO was the 2nd Marine Division's 8th Marines(-). For this mission, the 8th Marines were reorganized to consist of the 2nd Bn, 4th Marines; 3rd Bn, 23rd Marines; 3rd Bn, 10th Marines (Artillery), and probably other smaller attached units, such as tank, light armored infantry, reconnaissance, and assault amphibian units. The final element of the 2nd Marine Division departed the KTO on 10 Jun 91.

➤ From 18 Mar 91 to 7 May 91 the 5th MEB was afloat in the Gulf, embarked upon the Navy's Amphibious Group (PhibGru) 3, as a strategic reserve. In May 1991, the 5th MEB(-) and PhibGru 3(-) departed the Gulf. The 11th MEU(SOC), embarked upon the Navy's Amphibious Squadron (PhibRon) 1, remained behind in the Gulf as a strategic reserve until July 1991.[1] From the end of the war until the end of 1991, the Marine Corps maintained a Marine expeditionary unit afloat in the Gulf. Following the departure of the 11th MEU(SOC), this duty was performed by first the 15th MEU(SOC) and then the 22nd MEU(SOC).

Post-Desert Storm Training Exercises

➢ Since 1991, Marine units have participated in various exercises in the Gulf. The Marines typically have a Marine expeditionary unit forward-deployed in the Gulf and this unit frequently exercises with America's allies in the region.

Post-Desert Storm Redeployments To The KTO

➢ On numerous occasions since the Gulf War, Saddam Hussein has challenged United States forces in the KTO. The Marines have participated in these operations using the Marine expeditionary unit that is frequently forward-deployed in the Gulf. In addition, the Marine Corps has occasionally deployed additional forces to the region. The more significant deployments are discussed here.

➢ In October 1994, Marine units deployed to Kuwait in response to ominous Iraqi troop movements near the border. Although details are sketchy, it appears that at least one Marine expeditionary brigade deployed and that at least one Marine expeditionary unit remained in the Gulf for some significant period of time. The initial plan, which was reduced after Iraq pulled back from the border, envisioned deployment of the 1st Marine Division.

➢ In August 1995, Marines deployed to SWA pursuant to Operation Vigilant Sentinel, when Iraq threatened its neighbors after several high-ranking Iraqi officials defected. About 300 Marines from I Marine Expeditionary Force flew to the Gulf to be in position to unload prepositioning ships that sailed from their base at Diego Garcia. The Marines already had the 11th MEU(SOC), with the reinforced 2nd Bn, 1st Marines as its ground combat element, in the region when the crisis began. It does not appear that any other Marine units deployed during this crisis.

➢ In February 1998, the Marine Corps deployed forces to Kuwait pursuant to Operation Desert Thunder. These units included the 24th MEU(SOC), which arrived in Kuwait from the Mediterranean, and elements of I MEF, which flew in from the West Coast

---

[1] Prior to the departure of 5th MEB and PhibGru 3, the 11th MEU(SOC) had been embedded within 5th MEB and PhibRon 1 had been assigned to PhibGru 3. See Chart 18, page 18-3 and Chart 19, Footnote 105.

and linked up with equipment delivered by prepositioning ships. The 11th MEU(SOC) replaced the 24th MEU(SOC) in March 1998. This deployment was in response to increased tensions in the region as a result of Iraq's refusal to comply with a United Nations Security Council weapons inspection agreement. The ground troops were ordered to Kuwait as a deterrent in case airstrikes were ordered against Iraq. Iraq backed down, the airstrikes were never ordered, and the ground forces returned to the United States.

➤ In mid-November 1998, the Marine Corps deployed forces to the Persian Gulf in response to another round of Iraqi intransigence with regard to United Nations weapons inspectors. When the crisis broke the 15th MEU(SOC), with the 3rd Bn, 1st Marines as its ground combat element, was already in the region embarked upon PhibRon 5. The 15th MEU(SOC) was joined by the 31st MEU(SOC), with the 3rd Bn, 5th Marines as its ground combat element, embarked upon PhibRon 11, in late November. The United States was within one hour of launching an attack upon Iraq when Saddam appeared to back down. As a result, no additional Marine Corps units deployed to SWA.

➤ In December 1998, it became clear that Iraq's stated willingness to cooperate with United Nations weapon inspectors had been disingenuous. As a result, the United States and the United Kingdom launched Operation Desert Fox, an extensive aerial attack upon targets in Iraq. When the attack was launched the 31st MEU(SOC), with the 2nd Bn, 4th Marines as its ground combat element, was in the Persian Gulf embarked upon PhibRon 11. The Marines apparently did not deploy any additional forces to the region. No ground combat occurred during this operation. In addition to the forces in the Persian Gulf, the Marines had the 24th MEU(SOC), with the 1st Bn, 6th Marines as its ground combat element, in the eastern Mediterranean embarked upon PhibRon 4.

The Current Status of Marine Corps Units That Served In Desert Storm

➤ After Desert Storm, the U.S. military continued the downsizing process that had begun in the late 1980s with the end of the Cold War. As a result, some of the units that served in the Gulf War were inactivated, relocated, or reorganized. This chart summarizes some of the more significant developments.

➤ The Marine Corps has experienced the least down-sizing of any of the Armed Services, as its mission has changed the least since the end of the Cold War. Most of the major Marine Corps units that fought the Gulf War are still active at their pre-Desert Shield locations. The Marines have eliminated the Marine expeditionary brigade from their force structure, however, and hence the 4th and 5th MEBs are no longer active. In addition, the provisional units the Marines organized for Desert Storm — General Support Groups 1 and 2, the Direct Support Command (with its Direct Support Groups 1 and 2), and the Combat Replacement Regiment — were all inactivated shortly after Desert Storm's conclusion. Finally, the Marine Corps Reserve units that served in SWA have been released from active duty and returned to their status as reserve units.

➤ The Marines have only inactivated a handful of the ground combat units that fought in Desert Storm. The Marines have inactivated:

> 3rd Tank Bn
> 1st Recon Bn
> 2nd Recon Bn
> Co A, 3rd Recon Bn
> 2nd Plt, Co C, 3rd Recon Bn
> 2nd Bn, 12th Marines (Artillery)
> 2nd LAAM Bn
> 3rd LAAM Bn

In addition, the 3rd Bn, 9th Marines has received a new designation. It is now the 3rd Bn, 4th Marines.

Chart 27

British Ground Combat Units
That Participated In Operation Desert Storm

Only two of our European allies, the United Kingdom and France, deployed sizable ground combat units to the Gulf. The principal British unit was the 1st (UK) Armoured Division, which served with the U.S. VII Corps during the ground war. The British division was short a heavy maneuver brigade, but had extra artillery and a brigade of non-mechanized infantry for processing enemy prisoners of war.

The 1st (UK) Armoured Division entered Iraq through the breach created by the U.S. 1st Infantry Division(Mech), commencing at noon on 25 Feb 91. The 1st (UK) Armoured Division moved through the breach with the 7th Armoured Brigade in the lead, followed by the 4th Armoured Brigade, and completed passage through the breach by 0200 hours on 26 Feb 91. Shortly beyond the breach, the division pivoted to the right and attacked toward the east as the right-hand unit of the VII Corps. As the VII Corps attack came together, the 1st (UK) Armoured Division had the U.S. 2nd Armored Cavalry Regiment (later replaced by the U.S. 1st Infantry Division(Mech)) on its left, and the Joint Forces Command-North on its right.

The 1st (UK) Armoured Division attacked with the 7th Armoured Brigade on the left and the 4th Armoured Brigade on the right. The 7th Armoured Brigade crossed its line of departure at 1515 hours on 25 Feb 91 and the 4th Armoured Brigade crossed its line of departure at 1930 hours on 25 Feb 91. Rather than advance the two brigades simultaneously, the division used an alternating approach under which first one brigade, and then the other, was the division main effort. The 1st (UK) Armoured Division fought a series of fairly heavy engagements until 0730 hours on 28 Feb 91, when offensive operations ceased with the 7th Armoured Brigade astride the Kuwait City-Basrah road and the 4th Armoured Brigade approximately 50 kilometers short of that road.

Order of Battle

1st (UK) Armoured Division

A Co(+), 1st Bn, Queen's Own Highlanders[1]
B Co, 1st Bn, Queen's Own Highlanders[2]
C Co, 1st Bn, Queen's Own Highlanders[3]

4th Armoured Brigade[4]

14th/20th King's Hussars(-)[5] [Challenger MBT]
    The Queen's Co, 1st Bn, Grenadier Guards [Warrior IFV]
        (1) Sec, AT Plt [Milan], Fire Spt Co, 1st Bn, Queen's Own Highlanders
1st Bn, The Royal Scots(-)[6] [Warrior IFV]
    A Sqdn, The Life Guards[7] [Challenger MBT]
3rd Bn, The Royal Regt of Fusiliers(-)[8] [Warrior IFV]
    No. 2 Co, 1st Bn, Grenadier Guards[9] [Warrior IFV]
    B Sqdn, 14th/20th King's Hussars [Challenger MBT]
(1) Sqdn, 16th/5th The Queen's Royal Lancers [Scimitar]
2nd Field Regt, RA[10] [M109 155 SP, 3 x 8]
    46th Air Defense Btry, RA [Javelin SAM]

---

[1] Provided security to 1st (UK) Armd Div logistics units and division Main HQ.

[2] Provided security to division Rear HQ.

[3] Performed rear area security.

[4] HQ, 4th Armd Bde included an infantry platoon that was designated the Brigade Defence Plt and was staffed largely or entirely by the 1st Bn, Grenadier Guards.

[5] Consisted of HQ Sqdn and A & D Sqdns (C Sqdn was not in the Gulf and was apparently not active). Was reinforced by elements of the 4th RTR. D Sqdn was detached to the 3rd Bn, The Royal Regt of Fusiliers by approximately noon on 26 Feb 91. A Sqdn was detached to the 1st Bn, The Royal Scots late on 26 Feb 91. No. 2 Co,
1st Bn, Grenadier Guards was attached to 14th/20th King's Hussars from the evening of 26 Feb 91 to shortly after dawn on 27 Feb 91.

[6] Consisted of HQ Co, Cos A & B, and Fire Spt Co (Co C was disbanded before deployment to bring the battalion's other units up to strength). Was reinforced by elements of the 1st Bn, Queen's Own Highlanders. A Sqdn, 14th/20th King's Hussars joined the 1st Bn, The Royal Scots late on 26 Feb 91.

[7] This squadron deployed with the 14th/20th King's Hussars and was known in the Gulf as "The Life Guards Sqdn, 14th/20th King's Hussars."

[8] Consisted of HQ Co, Cos A & C, and Fire Spt Co (Co B was apparently not in the Gulf and was probably disbanded before deployment to bring the battalion's other units up to strength). Was reinforced by elements of the 1st Bn, Queen's Own Highlanders. D Sqdn, 14th/20th King's Hussars joined the 3rd Bn, The Royal Regt of Fusiliers by approximately noon on 26 Feb 91.

[9] Was attached to 14th/20th King's Hussars from the evening of 26 Feb 91 to shortly after dawn on 27 Feb 91.

[10] Consisted of "O," 23rd [Fr. 27 Field Regt, RA] & 127th Field Btrys [Fr. 49 Field Regt, RA], RA.

7th Armoured Brigade[11]

The Queen's Royal Irish Hussars(-)[12] [Challenger MBT]
    (3) Troops,[13] 17th/21st Lancers [Challenger MBT]
The Royal Scots Dragoon Guards(-)[14] [Challenger MBT]
    (1) Troop, 17th/21st Lancers [Challenger MBT]
    Co A, 1st Bn, The Staffordshire Regt [Warrior IFV]
1st Bn, The Staffordshire Regt(-)[15] [Warrior IFV]
    B Sqdn, The Royal Scots Dragoon Guards [Challenger MBT]
    C Sqdn, The Queen's Royal Irish Hussars [Challenger MBT]
        (1) Troop, 17th/21st Lancers [Challenger MBT]
40th Field Regt, RA[16] [M109 155 SP, 3 x 8]
    10th Air Defense Btry, RA [Javelin SAM]
664th Sqdn, Army Air Corps [Gazelle & Lynx Helicopters]

---

[11] See Footnote 20.

[12] Consisted of HQ Sqdn and A, B & D Sqdns. Company C, 1st Bn, The Staffordshire Regt was attached to The Queen's Royal Irish Hussars from the morning of 26 Feb 91 until 1645 hours.

[13] Although sources disagree, it appears that four troops from the 17th/21st Lancers served with The Queen's Royal Irish Hussars, one per sabre squadron. Thus, three 17th/21st Lancers troops served with The Queen's Royal Irish Hussars, and one 17th/21st Lancers troop served with C Sqdn, The Queen's Royal Irish Hussars in the 1st Bn, The Staffordshire Regt Battle Group. The 17th/21st Lancers deployed a total of five tank troops to SWA.

[14] Consisted of HQ Sqdn and A, C & D Sqdns. Was reinforced by elements of the 14th/20th King's Hussars and the 4th RTR.

[15] Consisted of HQ Co, Cos B & C, and Fire Spt Co. Company C was detached to The Queen's Royal Irish Hussars from the morning of 26 Feb 91 until 1645 hours. Was reinforced by elements of the 1st Bn, Grenadier Guards; 1st Bn, The Prince of Wales's Own Regt of Yorkshire; 2nd Bn, The Royal Anglian Regt; and 1st Bn, Royal Green Jackets.

[16] Consisted of the 38th, 129th & 137th Field Btrys, RA. May have had elements of the 21st & 43rd Air Defense Btrys, RA [Javelin SAM], attached.

Order of Battle

Divisional Artillery Group[17]

General Support/Recce Strike Group[18]
  16th/5th The Queen's Royal Lancers(-)[19] [Scimitar & Striker]
    A Sqdn, 1st The Queen's Dragoon Guards[20] [Scimitar & Striker]
    (1) Troop, 9th/12th Royal Lancers [Scimitar]
    49th Field Btry, RA[21]
    73rd (OP) Btry, RA[22] [Fr. 32 Hvy Regt, RA (?)]
  32nd Heavy Regt, RA[23] [M110A2 203 SP, 2 x 6]
  39th Heavy Regt, RA[24] [MLRS, 2 x 6]
26th Field Regt, RA[25] [M109 155 SP, 3 x 4]
  43rd Air Defense Btry, RA [Javelin SAM] [Fr. 94 Locating Regt]
  12th Air Defense Regt, RA[26] [Rapier SAM]
  4th Regt(-), Army Air Corps[27] [Gazelle & Lynx Helicopters]
    661st Sqdn, Army Air Corps [Gazelle & Lynx Helicopters] [Fr. 1st Regt, Army Air Corps]

---

[17] From 14 Feb 91 to 23 Feb 91, elements of the Divisional Artillery Group participated in artillery raids. In addition, all of the artillery units of the 1st (UK) Armd Div fired in support of the U.S. 1st Inf Div(M) when that division conducted its breach of the Iraqi front lines on 24 Feb 91.

[18] Also known as the "Depth Fire Group."

[19] Consisted of HQ Sqdn and A-C Sqdns. This unit was assigned to the Divisional Artillery Group so that it could identify long range targets for the 32nd and 39th Hvy Regts, RA. British recon units were assigned this role because they were unsuited for performing reconnaissance in front of the maneuver units, as they were too slow, lacked armor protection and fire power, and their night vision devices were inferior to those carried on British main battle tanks. At midday on 27 Feb 91, the 16th/5th The Queen's Royal Lancers was tasked with providing rear area security for the division's logistics units. The regiment departed the front lines for the rear area at 1800 hours on 27 Feb 91 and arrived in the divisional rear area in the very early hours of 28 Feb 91. A Sqdn was detached from the regiment to provide security to the PWGF on 28 Feb 91, some time after the 0800 ceasefire. A Sqdn rejoined the regiment on 3 Mar 91.

[20] Deployed with the 7th Armd Bde, but fought during the ground war as an element of 16th/5th The Queen's Royal Lancers until early on 27 Feb 91, when A Sqdn rejoined the 7th Armd Bde. It appears one troop may have been attached to HQ, Royal Engineers, 1st (UK) Armd Div.

[21] It is unclear if this was a firing unit (presumably equipped with M109 series self-propelled 155mm howitzers) or a FIST-type unit like the 73rd (OP) Btry, RA. See Footnote 22.

[22] Responsible for identifying targets and calling for artillery fire and tactical air support, as a U.S. Army FIST team would do.

[23] Consisted of the 18th & 74th Heavy Btrys, RA, and the 57th Locating Btry, RA (apparently a target acquisition unit).

[24] Consisted of the 132nd & 176th Heavy Btrys, RA.

[25] Consisted of the 16th, 17th & 159th Field Btrys, RA.

[26] Consisted of "T" & 58th Air Defense Btrys, RA.

[27] Consisted of the 654th & 659th Sqdns, Army Air Corps. One source reports that only two Army Air Corps squadrons deployed and that they were assigned to the 4th and 7th Armd Bdes. Another source shows the 4th Regt, AAC, as assigned directly to 1st (UK) Armd Div, rather than the Divisional Artillery Group.

Prisoner of War Guard Force "PWGF"[28]

    1st Bn(-), Coldstream Guards
    1st Bn(-), The Royal Highland Fusiliers
    1st Bn(-), The King's Own Scottish Borderers

Armoured Delivery Group "ADG"[29]

    HQ Co, 1st Bn, Queen's Own Highlanders
    The Life Guards(-) [Challenger MBT]
    1st Bn(-), Scots Guards [Warrior IFV]
    (1) Sqdn, 9th/12th Royal Lancers [Scimitar]
    (3) Troops, The Royal Hussars [Challenger MBT]
    (1) Artillery Btry(Composite)

Support Helicopter Unit

    (1) Squadron of Puma Helicopters (RAF)
    (1) Squadron of Chinook Helicopters (RAF)
    (1) Squadron of Sea King Helicopters (RN)

---

[28] The PWGF arrived in the Gulf in January 1991 and was assigned to the 1st (UK) Armd Div on 23 Feb 91. The PWGF consisted of three understrength infantry battalions (non-mechanized) organized as one collection battalion(-), one guard battalion(-), and one escort guard battalion(-). HQ, 1st Bn, Coldstream Guards was used to form a small brigade-level headquarters. One company of 1st Bn, The Royal Highland Fusiliers was apparently under the tactical control of the 1st (UK) Armd Div Admin Area. One company of 1st Bn, Coldstream Guards was under the tactical control of some other unit in 1st (UK) Armd Div.

[29] The ADG (also known as the Armd Delivery Battle Group) was formed on 4 Feb 91 to provide a source of replacement personnel and equipment in case the 1st (UK) Armd Div sustained significant losses, and to provide rear area security. The ADG was similar to the U.S. Army's WSRO program. See Text at pages 7 and 8, and Chart 12. The ADG's headquarters and logistics elements were provided by HQ Co, 1st Bn, Queen's Own Highlanders, while The Life Guards contributed three tank squadrons [equipped with Challenger] and a recon troop [equipped with Scorpion], and the 1st Bn, Scots Guards provided three armoured infantry companies [equipped with Warrior]. The ADG consisted of 1,200 soldiers and 250 vehicles. During the ground war, the ADG was split into two groups. One group advanced into Iraq on tank transporters, while the other group remained in Saudi Arabia. HQ and Co B, 1st Bn, Scots Guards were responsible for supervising the 1st (UK) Armd Div's Battle Casualty Replacements and ran Blackadder Lines, a tent camp where most of the ADG's personnel lived.

Order of Battle

Non-Divisional Units

Elements, 22nd SAS Regt[30]
Elements, Special Boat Service[31]

Forward Force Maintenance Area "FFMA"

RAC Armd Delivery Sqdn[32]
   (1) Sqdn, 9th/12th Royal Lancers[33] [Ferret Scout Car]
Ad Hoc Air Defence Btry

Ground Combat Forces Assigned to the Royal Air Force

Three RAF Rapier SAM squadrons deployed to the Gulf, No. 20 Squadron, No. 26 Squadron, and No. 66 Squadron. No. 66 Squadron served in Bahrain, while No. 26 Squadron provided air defense at an air base at Tabuk, Saudi Arabia. The location and assignment of No. 20 Squadron are unknown.

The RAF also has light armor units equipped with Scorpion light tanks that provide ground defense to air bases, and three of these squadrons deployed to the Gulf. No. 1 Squadron defended the RAF helicopters that supported 1st (UK) Armoured Division, No. 51 Squadron served in Dhahran and Tabuk, and No. 58 Squadron served in Bahrain.

---

[30] Although the 22nd SAS Regt operated in conjunction with the U.S. special operations units of the Joint Special Operations TF(Fwd) (see Chart 6), the SAS reported directly to General Sir Peter de la Billiere, commander of British Forces in the Gulf. The SAS hunted mobile Scud missile launchers in Western Iraq. Approximately 250 soldiers participated in this mission.

[31] The SBS conducted at least one direct action mission, but public details are very sketchy.

[32] This unit was formed primarily from 2nd RTR.

[33] Performed rear area security between the FFMA and the Divisional Maintenance Area. At one point, this unit reinforced other units at the British PW cage when it appeared the guard force was inadequate.

Ground Combat Forces Assigned to the Royal Navy

The British Army's 21st Air Defense Battery, RA [Javelin SAM] provided air defense on Royal Navy ships.

Notes:

➤ British Army units were under the command of the British government, but were under the tactical control of the U.S. VII Corps.

➤ Britain called its deployment to the Gulf "Operation Granby," the ground war "Operation Desert Sword," and the 1st (UK) Armd Div's role in the ground war "Operation Desert Sabre."

➤ The 5th Abn Bde was the British Army's quick reaction force in the summer of 1990. It was alerted for movement to Saudi Arabia shortly after Iraq invaded Kuwait, but did not deploy.

➤ Most units were understrength when Operation Desert Shield began and were brought up to full strength with individuals from other British Army units.

➤ The senior British headquarters in the Gulf was HQ, British Forces Middle East (BFME). BFME was commanded by General Sir Peter de la Billiere. The senior British logistics unit in the Gulf was the Force Maintenance Area (FMA). The FMA was responsible for providing support to the 1st (UK) Armd Div and was commanded by a brigadier. HQ, FMA was established in the Gulf on 7 Oct 90. The Forward Force Maintenance Area (FFMA) was responsible for providing forward logistics support to the 1st (UK) Armd Div.

➤ British Army regiments are typically the size of U.S. battalions. In British tank and cavalry units, a British regiment is the size of a U.S. battalion, a British squadron is the size of a U.S. company, and a British troop is the size of a U.S. platoon.[34] A British infantry battalion is the size of a U.S. battalion, however.

➤ Britain's initial contribution to the Coalition was the 7th Armd Bde, which began arriving in the KTO in mid-October 1990 and was declared operationally ready on 16 Nov 90. The 7th Armd Bde was initially attached to the U.S. Marine's I MEF, effective 16 Nov 90. On 22 Nov 90, Britain announced its intention to expand its contribution to a division. At Britain's request, its forces were reassigned to the Allies' main effort, the U.S. VII Corps. The U.S. Army's 1st Bde, 2nd Armd Div, which had been attached to the 1st Cav Div(-) during Desert Shield, was then attached to I MEF to provide additional armor to the Marines.

➤ It has been difficult to locate information on the pre-ODS assignments and locations of British units. The 7th Armd Bde deployed from Germany largely intact, but subsequent units were drawn from many different commands to create the 1st (UK) Armd Div in the KTO. Actually, the 1st (UK) Armd Div was active in Germany prior to ODS, and consisted of the 7th Armd Bde and other units. When the decision was made to increase Britain's commitment from a brigade to a division, HQ, 1st (UK) Armd Div and some of the division's support units deployed, while the division's remaining maneuver units (the 12th and 22nd Armd Bdes) were left behind and replaced by the 3rd Armd Div's 4th Armd Bde, which was task-organized for the deployment to include many

---

[34] The Royal Tank Regiment, however, consisted of several battalions, each approximately the size of a U.S. tank battalion. Note that the abbreviation "2nd RTR" stands for "2nd Bn, the Royal Tank Regt," not "2nd Royal Tank Regt."

units normally assigned to other brigades.[35] Other units were added from various sources to bring the 1st (UK) Armd Div up to the strength and configuration desired for the war. The 32nd Heavy Regt, RA; 39th Heavy Regt, RA; and 12th Air Defense Regt, RA, were all assigned to the corps artillery of the I (UK) Corps in Germany prior to deployment to the Gulf. The 664th Sqdn, Army Air Corps, was apparently assigned to I (UK) Corps prior to Desert Storm.

➤ The last combat element of 1st (UK) Armd Div to leave the Gulf was the 3rd Bn, The Royal Regt of Fusiliers, which departed on 13 Apr 91. It was replaced by the 2nd Bn, Royal Anglian Regt, which deployed from Germany and arrived in the Gulf o/a 11 Apr 91. It appears the last elements of this unit departed the Gulf by the end of July.

➤ Selected types of equipment are indicated in brackets [____]. Challenger is a main battle tank armed with a 120mm main gun that is equivalent to the U.S. M1A1 Abrams. All of the Challengers in SWA were the Challenger 1; Britain fielded an improved version, the Challenger 2, after Desert Storm. Prior to Desert Storm, the Challenger 1 had been fielded in three versions, the Mark 1, 2, and 3. All of the Challenger 1 tanks in SWA were the Mark 2 or 3, with the Mark 3 predominating. Most of the Mark 2 tanks were uparmored in-theater to Mark 3 standard and designated Mark 2(ACB), for "Armoured Charge Bins." Warrior is an infantry fighting vehicle armed with a 30mm automatic cannon that is equivalent to the U.S. Bradley. Scimitar, Scorpion, and Striker are small reconnaissance vehicles based on the same chassis for which there are no equivalent in the U.S. Army. Scimitar is armed with a 30mm automatic cannon, Scorpion is armed with a low-velocity 76mm cannon, and Striker is armed with the Swingfire antitank missile. This family of vehicles also includes Spartan, an APC; Sultan, a command vehicle; and Samaritan, a medic vehicle. The M109, M110, and MLRS are the same artillery systems used by the United States. The entries for field artillery firing units show the number of batteries per regiment and the number of tubes or MLRS launchers per battery, e.g., the 2nd Field Regt, RA, had three firing batteries each with eight howitzers (3 x 8). Javelin and Rapier are surface to air missiles used by ADA units; Javelin is similar to the U.S. "Stinger." The Gazelle is a scout helicopter that is equivalent to the U.S. OH-58 "Kiowa," while the Lynx is an attack helicopter similar to the U.S. AH-1 "Cobra."

➤ The British spell the word "armor" as "armour." Accordingly, I have used the British spelling when referring to British armoured units.

➤ Like the American Army, the British task organized combined arms units at the battalion level by trading armoured infantry companies and armoured squadrons. While the U.S. Army called such units "battalion task forces," the British Army called them "battle groups" and named them after their parent unit, e.g., "The Royal Scots Dragoon Guards Battle Group."

➤ The 1st (UK) Armd Div had three armoured regiments. British armoured regiments came in two types, the Type 57 and the Type 43, which refers to the number of main battle tanks in the regiment. The Queen's Royal Irish Hussars and The Royal Scots Dragoon Guards were Type 57 regiments. Each consisted of a headquarters squadron (with one tank for the commanding officer, and a reconnaissance troop with eight Scorpions) and four "sabre squadrons" (A-D Squadrons), each with 14 tanks. Each sabre squadron was organized into four tank

---

[35] For example, the 1st Bn, The Royal Scots and the 3rd Bn, The Royal Regiment of Fusiliers were normally assigned to the 6th Armd Bde. The 14th/20th King's Hussars was also previously assigned to some unit other than the 4th Armd Bde. This ad hoc approach was mandated by (1) the fact that the British Army was phasing-in the Challenger MBT and Warrior IFV and, with the exception of the 7th Armd Bde, no British brigade had been completely re-equipped with these new vehicles, and (2) numerous units had been stripped of personnel and equipment to bring the 7th Armd Bde to full wartime strength and thus were not available to deploy when the decision was made to expand the British commitment to a division.

troops, each with three tanks, and the squadron headquarters with two tanks. The 14th/20th King's Hussars was a Type 43 regiment, which used the same organization but had only three sabre squadrons (apparently A, B & D Squadrons). For Desert Storm, The 14th/20th King's Hussars was effectively upgraded to Type 57 standard by the attachment of A Squadron, The Life Guards. At the time of Desert Storm, the Royal Armoured Corps had 17 armoured regiments, seven of which were equipped with Challenger. (The remaining regiments used the older Chieftain main battle tank.) Thus, the United Kingdom had about half its Challenger tank force in the Gulf.

➢   The 1st (UK) Armd Div had three armoured infantry battalions. British armoured infantry battalions each consisted of a headquarters company, three rifle companies (Companies A-C), and a fire support company. The battalion was normally authorized 45 Warrior IFVs, one in the headquarters company, two in the fire support company, and 14 in each of the three rifle companies. Each rifle company consisted of three platoons, each with four Warriors, and company headquarters with another two Warriors. The battalion's fire support company had a reconnaissance platoon (with eight Scimitars), an antitank platoon (with 20 Milan antitank missile systems transported by 14 FV432 APCs, and four CVR(T) Spartan APCs each mounting a Milan launcher), and a mortar platoon (with eight FV432s carrying 81mm mortars, four Spartans carrying fire control parties, and two CVR(T) Sultan command vehicles). For Desert Storm, additional vehicles were issued to the armoured infantry battalions. Each battalion received 16 or 17 additional Warriors, which were used to replace the FV432s in the antitank platoon and the Spartans in the mortar platoon.

➢   The 1st (UK) Armd Div had a single reconnaissance regiment. This regiment had a headquarters squadron and three sabre squadrons (A-C Squadrons), with a fourth sabre squadron attached from the 1st The Queen's Dragoon Guards. Each reconnaissance squadron consisted of a squadron headquarters (with two Sultan command vehicles), three reconnaissance troops (each with four Scimitars), a guided weapons troop (with four Strikers), and a support troop (with infantry mounted in four Spartan APCs), for a total per squadron of 12 Scimitars, four Strikers, four Spartans, and two Sultans. This yielded a total, for the four sabre squadrons in the regiment, of 48 Scimitars, 16 Strikers, 16 Spartans, and eight Sultans.

➢   The 1st (UK) Armd Div had five field artillery regiments. These units varied with regard to the number of weapons per battery and regiment. The two regiments that provided direct support for the 4th and 7th Armd Bdes, the 2nd and 40th Field Regts, RA, each had three firing batteries each with eight M109 series self-propelled 155mm howitzers per battery, for a total of 24 howitzers per regiment. The third regiment that was equipped with the M109, the 26th Field Regt, RA, had only 12 howitzers, however. This regiment had three firing batteries, but each battery had only four howitzers. The 32nd Heavy Regt, RA, was equipped with 12 M110A2 203mm howitzers, six in each of the regiment's two firing batteries. The 32nd also had a target acquisition battery. Finally, the 39th Heavy Regt, RA, had 12 MLRS launchers, six in each of the regiment's two firing batteries.

➢   The only other Commonwealth country that deployed any ground combat units to the Gulf was Canada. Company C, 1st Bn, The Royal Canadian Regt, from Canadian Forces Base (CFB) London in Ontario, Canada, was attached to the 1st Canadian Field Hospital. The 1st Canadian Field Hospital supported 1st (UK) Armd Dv. Company C assisted 1st Canadian Field Hospital by providing security, guarding the many EPWs treated by the hospital, and providing manpower for basic tasks such as moving patients on stretchers. Canada also deployed an infantry company from the 4th Canadian Mechanized Brigade Group in Germany. This company provided security for Royal Canadian Air Force units stationed in Qatar. This mission was performed by Co M, 3rd Bn, The Royal Canadian Regt, until late December 1990 when Co C, 1st Bn, Royal 22e Regt, replaced Company M. Another platoon from the 3rd Bn, The Royal Canadian Regt, deployed to the Gulf to provide security for Canadian Joint Forces Headquarters Middle East (the senior Canadian headquarters in the region), which was located in Bahrain. Finally, 32 soldiers from the Canadian Army's 119th Air Defence Battery, Royal Artillery, stationed at CFB Chatham in New Brunswick, Canada, served on the three Royal Canadian Navy ships that deployed to the Gulf. This unit was equipped with the "Blowpipe" air defense missle, but upgraded to the Javelin missile during the Gulf crisis. None of these Canadian Army units entered Iraq or saw combat.

Official/Complete Designations of Certain British Army Units

Certain British Army units that deployed to the Gulf have long designations (resulting from amalgamations of old regiments) that are rarely used. These units (and their complete designations) are:

The Royal Scots Dragoon Guards (Carabiniers and Greys)
9th/12th Royal Lancers (Prince of Wales's)
Queen's Own Highlanders (Seaforth and Camerons)
2nd Bn(Lincolnshire, Leicestershire and Northamptonshire), The Royal Anglian Regt
The Royal Scots, (The Royal Regiment)
The Royal Highland Fusiliers (Princess Margaret's Own Glasgow and Ayrshire Regt)
The Royal Hussars (Prince of Wales's Own)
The Staffordshire Regt (The Prince of Wales's)

Chart 28

French Ground Combat Units That Participated In Operation Desert Storm

Only two of our European allies, the United Kingdom and France, deployed sizable ground combat units to the Gulf. The principal French unit was the 6th (French) Light Armored Division, which served with the U.S. XVIII Airborne Corps during the ground war. Compared to a U.S. Army division, the French division was rather small and lacked heavy firepower.

The 6th (French) Light Armored Division was the western most unit in the XVIII Airborne Corps. It attacked north into Iraq as two task forces, crossing the line of departure at 0400 hours on 24 Feb 91. The main effort was in the east, commanded by "PC Vert" (Command Post Green), while "PC Rouge" (Command Post Red) controlled the secondary effort in the west. The French encountered relatively light opposition and by the morning of 26 Feb 91 had secured their objectives, including the airfield at As-Salman in Iraq. For the remainder of the war, the 6th (French) Light Armored Division maintained a screen line protecting the Coalition's western flank.

At the beginning of the ground war the U.S. 2nd Brigade, 82nd Airborne Division and 18th Field Artillery Brigade(Abn)(-) supported PC Vert, while the 18th Field Artillery Brigade's 1st Bn(155 SP), 201st FA supported PC Rouge. The U.S. 12th Aviation Brigade and 937th Engineer Group also supported the 6th (French) Light Armored Division. These attachments ended on 26 Feb 91, after the French had secured their objectives and halted their attack. The artillery units were relieved from supporting the French at approximately noon and began moving east to support the U.S. 24th Infantry Division(Mech). The 12th Aviation Brigade ceased supporting the French around noon and became OPCON to the 101st Airborne Division(Air Aslt).

Order of Battle

The 2nd Brigade, 82nd Airborne Division left French control at approximately 1300 hours to become the 82nd Airborne Division reserve.

6th (French) Light Armored Division

Divisional Control

2nd Mar Inf Regt (2 RIMA)[1] [VAB APC] [Fr. 9 Mar Div]
   (1) Co, 21st Mar Inf Regt (21 RIMA) [VAB APC]
Commandos de Recherche et d'Action dans la Profondeur (CRAP)[2] [Fr. 11 Abn Div]
Elements, 13th Parachute Dragoon Regt[3] (13 RDP) [Fr. 1 Army]
Radar unit,[4] 35th Para Arty Regt (35 RAP) [Fr. 11 Abn Div]
(1) ADA Sec[5] [Crotale]

PC Vert

4th Dragoon Regt (4 RD) [AMX 30B2 MBT] [Fr. 10 AD]
3rd Mar Inf Regt (3 RIMA) [VAB APC] [Fr. 9 Mar Div]
   (1) Co, 21st Mar Inf Regt (21 RIMA) [VAB APC]
   (2) AT Secs [Milan],[6] 21st Mar Inf Regt (21 RIMA)
   (1) Co,[7] Mar Inf Tank Regt (RICM) [AMX 10RC] [Fr. 9 Mar Div]
1st Sqdn, 1st Para Hussars Regt[8] (1 RHP) [Panhard ERC 90] [Fr. 11 Abn Div]
1st Cbt Hel Regt (1 RHC) [Gazelle & Puma] [Fr. 4 Ambl Div]
   (1) Composite Inf Co[9]

---

[1] 2 RIMA was the division reserve.

[2] This was a deep operations commando unit of 120 personnel — despite the rather unfortunate acronym of "CRAP."

[3] This was a special operations "LRRP" type unit. It engaged in operations behind Iraqi lines. Probably only one squadron deployed.

[4] This was a TA unit.

[5] This unit's designation is unknown. It was presumably a French Air Force unit, as Crotale is strictly an Air Force weapon.

[6] One source reports this was three sections.

[7] One source indicates that this was a squadron rather than a company.

[8] Some sources indicate this regiment deployed a single company. One source reports this regiment deployed a company-sized unit to the United Arab Emirates and that it did not serve as part of the 6th (FR) Lt Armd Div.

[9] Formed from the 1st Inf Regt (1 RI) [Fr. 4 Ambl Div] and the 1st Foreign Legion Inf Regt (1 REI) [Fr. _____?]. The 1st Inf Regt was a specialized airmobile antitank unit that used the Milan AT missile.

6th (French) Light Armored Division (continued)

PC Rouge

1st Foreign Legion Cav Regt (1 REC) [AMX 10RC]
1st Regt de Spahis (1 RS) [AMX 10RC]
2nd Foreign Legion Inf Regt (2 REI) [VAB APC]
 (1) Co,[10] Mar Inf Tank Regt (RICM) [AMX 10RC] [Fr. 9 Mar Div]
3rd Sqdn, 1st Para Hussars Regt[11] (1 RHP) [Panhard ERC 90] [Fr. 11 Abn Div]
3rd Cbt Hel Regt (3 RHC) [Gazelle & Puma] [Fr. 4 Ambl Div]
 (1) Composite Inf Co[12]
11th Mar Arty Regt[13] (11 RAMA) [155 TR F1, 3 x 6] [Fr. 9 Mar Div]

6th Foreign Legion Engineer Regiment (6 REG)

6th Logistics Support Regiment (6 RCS)

(1) Composite Inf Co[14]
(1) ADA Btry[15] [Mistral SAM]
(1) ADA Btry[16] [Crotale SAM]

Additional Units

Elements, 503rd Cbt Tank Regt[17] (503 RCC) [AMX 30B2] [Fr. 10 AD]
Elements, 1st Mar Para Inf Regt[18] (1 RPIMA) [Fr. 11 Abn Div]
Elements, 5th Cbt Hel Regt (5 RHC) [Gazelle & Puma] [Fr.4 Ambl Div]

---

[10] See Footnote 7.

[11] See Footnote 8.

[12] See Footnote 9.

[13] This regiment's 3rd Btry [Mistral] did not deploy as a unit, but may have contributed personnel and equipment that went as part of another unit.

[14] See Footnote 9.

[15] This battery included elements of: 35th Para Arty Regt (35 RAP) [Fr. 11 Abn Div]; 68th Arty Regt (68 RA); and 11th Mar Arty Regt (11 RAMA) [Fr. 9 Mar Div].

[16] Some sources do not list this unit. One source states that this battery defended division headquarters. See Footnote 5.

[17] Deployed a reinforced squadron. Was attached to the 4th Dragoon Regt.

[18] A special operations "commando" type unit that conducted vehicular and airborne deep reconaissance.

Other Ground Combat Units

The French reportedly deployed an ADA battery to the United Arab Emirates. In addition, the French had two combined arms regiments with armor, infantry, and artillery elements, along with a support battalion, in Djibouti. These units were already stationed in Djibouti before the Gulf crisis began.

Notes:

➢ French Army units were under the command of the French government, but were under the tactical control of the U.S. XVIII Airborne Corps.

➢ The French called their participation in Operations Desert Shield/Storm, "Operation Daguet."

➢ French and other European sources indicate that the unit that France deployed to the Gulf was actually designated "The Daguet Division" and that the 6th (FR) Lt Armd Div merely provided some of the units for this provisional unit. I refer to the unit that France deployed to the Gulf as the 6th (FR) Lt Armd Div, however, because U.S. sources consistently use this designation.

➢ French "regiments" were, in reality, small battalions. Thus, the 6th (FR) Lt Armd Div was little more than a reinforced brigade and actually generated less combat power than the typical U.S. heavy brigade, as French equipment was generally old and not state of the art. For example, the entire French division had one battalion of 44 1970s-vintage AMX 30B2 Main Battle Tanks. By contrast, U.S. Army tank battalions fielded 58 tanks and U.S. armored divisions had six tank battalions, for a total of 348 tanks per division. In addition, the 6th (FR) Lt Armd Div had a single battalion of towed 155mm howitzers, whereas a U.S. heavy division had three battalions of self-propelled 155mm howitzers and an MLRS battery. Note also that a French squadron was the equivalent of a company and a French infantry platoon is called a "section."

➢ The alpha-numeric characters in parenthesis following most unit designations are the French acronym for the unit.

➢ All former assignments were to, of course, French units.

➢ Selected types of equipment are indicated in brackets [____]. The AMX 30B2 is an upgraded version of the venerable AMX 30 Main Battle Tank that is armed with a 105mm gun. The AMX 30B2 was clearly inferior to the M1, Challenger, and T-72 tanks used by (respectively) the United States, Great Britain, and Iraq. The AMX 30B2 is roughly equivalent to the U.S. M60A3. The Panhard ERC 90 is a six-wheeled armored car that is armed with a 90mm gun. The AMX 10RC is a six-wheeled armored car armed with a low-velocity 105mm gun. The VAB is a six-wheeled armored personnel carrier used by motorized infantry units. The Milan is a medium-range anti-tank missile that falls in between the U.S. "Dragon" and TOW. The 155 TR F1 is a 155mm towed howitzer that is equivalent to the U.S. M198 towed 155mm howitzer. The entry for this artillery unit shows the number of batteries in the regiment and the number of howitzers per battery: three batteries, each with six howitzers (3 x 6). Mistral and Crotale are surface to air missiles used by ADA units. Crotale is strictly a French Air Force weapon system that is used for airbase defense. The Gazelle was used in two roles, either as a scout helicopter with

Mistral air-to-air missiles and a 20mm cannon (similar to the U.S. OH-58 "Kiowa") or as a light attack helicopter with four HOT antitank missiles (similar to the U.S. AH-1 "Cobra"). The Puma was used as a utility helicopter, performing resupply or medical evacuation in the same role as the U.S. UH-1 "Huey" helicopter.

➢ The 4th Dragoon Regt (4 RD) consisted of a command and services squadron with five tanks, and three tank squadrons each with 13 tanks and an infantry platoon. This gave 4 RD a total of 44 AMX 30B2 Main Battle Tanks. One-plus squadron came from the 503rd Cbt Tank Regt (503 RCC).

➢ The 1st Foreign Legion Cavalry Regt (1 REC) and 1st Regt de Spahis (1 RS) were somewhat similar to U.S. armored cavalry units. Each consisted of a command and services squadron (with three VAB APCs), three line squadrons (each with 12 AMX 10RC Armored Cars organized into four platoons, each with three AMX 10RCs), and an antitank squadron with 12 VAB APCs mounting HOT antitank missiles. This gave each regiment 36 AMX 10RCs, 3 VAB APCs, and 12 VAB HOTs.

➢ The 6th (FR) Lt Armd Div had three motorized infantry units, the 2nd Marine Infantry Regt (2 RIMA), 3rd Marine Infantry Regt (3 RIMA), and 2nd Foreign Legion Infantry Regt (2 REI). Each of these regiments had a command and services company, and three (or in the case of 3 RIMA, possibly four) line companies. Each line company consisted of a headquarters (with two VAB APCs), three rifle platoons (each with three VABs), and heavy weapons elements equipped with Milan antitank missiles, 81mm mortars, and 20mm air defense guns.[19] In addition, the 3 RIMA and 2 REI each had an attached company or squadron of 12 AMX 10RC Armored Cars from the Marine Infantry Tank Regt (RICM). Finally, it appears that 2 RIMA, 3 RIMA, and 2 REI each had a total of 24 Milan antitank missile launchers and six 120mm towed mortars, although it appears that some of the Milans and some or all of the 120mm mortars were attached from other units.

➢ The 1st and 3rd Sqdns, 1st Parachute Hussars Regt (1 RHP) each consisted of a headquarters and four platoons. Each platoon had three Panhard ERC 90 Armored Cars and a light truck carrying a Milan antitank missile team, giving each squadron 12 Panhard ERC 90s and four Milan systems.

➢ The two aviation units, the 1st Combat Helicopter Regt (1 RHC) and 3rd Combat Helicopter Regt (3 RHC), were each authorized a command and services squadron, two scout squadrons (each with seven Gazelles configured for scouting), three antitank squadrons (each with ten Gazelles configured for antitank work), and two lift squadrons (each with seven (or possibly nine) Pumas). One or both regiments obtained additional assets, however. For example, 3 RHC had a total of 76 helicopters: the standard 14 Gazelles in the scout role, with 20mm cannon and Mistral air-to-air missiles; 40 Gazelles in the antitank role (ten more than normal), with HOT antitank missiles; and 22 Pumas in the lift role (eight or four more than normal). Each helicopter regiment also had an infantry company with 16 Milan antitank teams.

➢ The 11th Marine Artillery Regt (11 RAMA) consisted of a command and services battery, three firing batteries (each with six 155mm TR F1 Howitzers, for a total of 18 in the regiment), and an air defense battery equipped with Mistral surface to air missiles. However, the air defense battery did not deploy as a unit. See Footnotes 13 & 15.

---

[19] 2 RIMA had two organic companies and one company attached from the 21st Mar Inf Regt (21 RIMA). 3 RIMA had two or three organic companies, plus one attached from 21 RIMA. 2 REI had three organic companies.

Chart 29

Arab-Islamic Ground Combat Formations That Participated In Operation Desert Storm

Numerous Arab and Islamic countries contributed ground combat forces to the war effort. Egypt, Saudi Arabia, Kuwait, and Syria each contributed significant ground combat units of a division or more. All Arab and Islamic units were assigned to either Joint Forces Command-North or Joint Forces Command-East, both of which reported to the Arab-Islamic Joint Forces Command. See Chart 1.

Arab-Islamic Joint Forces Command

Joint Forces Command-North

Joint Forces Command-North was located in between the U.S. Army's VII Corps and I Marine Expeditionary Force. JFC-North initiated its attack at 1600 hours on 24 Feb 91. The Egyptian 3rd Mechanized Infantry Division, and Saudi and Kuwaiti units, led the attack. The Egyptian 4th Armored Division followed the 3rd Mechanized Infantry Division, with the Syrian 9th Armored Division as the JFC-North reserve. JFC-North advanced cautiously against light Iraqi resistance. During the morning of 27 Feb 91, elements of JFC-North moved east, past I Marine Expeditionary Force, and entered Kuwait City.

Order of Battle

Organization of Joint Forces Command-North

4th Abn Bn [RSLF]
(1) Inf Bn [Niger]
1st Avn Bn [RSLF]
15th FA Bn (Multiple Rocket Launcher) [RSLF]
7th TA Co [RSLF]

II Corps[1] [Egypt]

    4th Armd Div[2]
    3rd Mech Inf Div[3]
    Ranger Regt[4]
    Corps Arty

Task Force Khalid

Force Muthannah[5]

    20th Mech Bde [RSLF]
    35th Mech Inf Bde [Kuwait][6]

Force Saad

    4th Armd Bde [RSLF]
    15th Inf Bde [Kuwait][7]

---

[1] The 4th Armd Div and 3rd Mech Inf Div were normally assigned to the Egyptian 3rd Field Army.

[2] Consisted of the 2nd & 3rd Armd Bdes, 6th Mech Inf Bde, and other units, including a self-propelled artillery regiment and reconnaissance, antitank, and ADA battalions, plus supporting units.

[3] Consisted of three maneuver brigades, a self-propelled artillery regiment, and reconnaissance, antitank, and ADA battalions, plus supporting units. One source reports that the maneuver brigades were the 8th Tank Bde and the 11th and 12th Mech Inf Bdes, while another source states that the 3rd Mech Inf Div had the 10th, 22nd & 23rd Mech Inf Bdes, and that most of the units normally assigned to the 7th Mech Inf Div (8th, 11th & 12th Mech Inf Bdes) were attached to the 3rd Mech Inf Div.

[4] Some sources list this as the 20th SF Regt. One source speculates that this was the 5th Para Bde.

[5] One source spells this as "Muthena."

[6] Apparently also known as the "Shaheed" Bde, although some sources report it was known as the "Al-Tahrir" Bde. One source shows this unit in Force Muthannah and the 15th Inf Bde in Force Saad. Two sources state that the 35th was an armored brigade. Finally, one source states that there was only one Kuwaiti brigade in JFC North.

[7] Apparently also known as the "Al-Tahrir" Bde, although some sources report it was known as the "Shaheed" Bde. See Footnote 6.

Joint Forces Command-North (continued)

> 9th Armd Div[8] [Syria]
> 45th Commando Regt[9] [Syria]

Forward Forces Command Ar'ar[10]

> 7th Armd Bde [Pakistan]
> (1) Inf Bde [SANG][11]

Joint Forces Command-East

Joint Forces Command-East was the eastern-most element of the Coalition, with I Marine Expeditionary Force to its left and the Persian Gulf to its right. JFC-East initiated its attack at 0800 hours on 24 Feb 91 and made good progress against light Iraqi resistance, capturing many EPWs. JFC-East entered Kuwait City on 27 Feb 91 and linked up with elements of JFC-North.

Organization of Joint Forces Command-East

> 1st Inf Bn [East Bengal]
> 2nd AT Co [RSLF] (?)
> Cbt Avn Bn [Kuwait/UAE]
> 14th FA Bn (155 T) [RSLF]
> 18th FA Bn (Multiple Rocket Launcher) [RSLF]
> 6th TA Co [RSLF]

Task Force Omar

> 10th Mech Bde [RSLF]
> (1) Mtzd Inf Bn [UAE][12]
> (1) Recon Sqdn (?)

---

[8] Consisted of the 52nd & 53rd Tank Bdes, 43rd Mech Bde, and other units, including an artillery regiment, ADA regiment, reconnaissance company, and supporting units.

[9] Some sources list this as a "special forces regiment." Others list it as a brigade. One source lists it as the "4th Commando Gp."

[10] This unit was west of the XVIII Abn Corps sector (west of Rafha, Saudi Arabia) and served as a covering force in this area. It did not engage in any significant combat. It may have been assigned directly to Arab-Islamic Joint Forces Command, rather than being an element of JFC-North.

[11] This may have been the "King Faisal Bde." One source indicates that this brigade consisted of two infantry battalions and one airborne battalion.

[12] Some sources indicate this unit was part of TF Omar.

Joint Forces Command-East (continued)

Task Force Othman

8th Mech Bde [RSLF]
Al Fatah Bde [Kuwait][13]
(1) Mtzd Inf Bn [Oman][14]
(1) Inf Co [Bahrain]
(1) Recon Sqdn (?)

Task Force Abu Bakr

2nd Mtzd Inf Bde[15] [SANG]
Mech Inf Bn [Qatar][16]
(1) Recon Sqdn (?)
(1) FA Bn (?)

Task Force Tariq[17]

Marine Bn TF [RS Marines]
6th Mech Inf Regt [Morocco][18]
(1) Inf Bn [Senegal][19]
(1) Recon Sqdn (?)

Other Forces[20]

Al Haq Bde [Kuwait]
Khulud Bde [Kuwait]
Badr Bde [Kuwait]

---

[13] This may have been a light motorized brigade. One source lists this unit variously as the "Fath" Bde and the "Fatha" Bde.

[14] Some sources indicate this unit was part of TF Omar.

[15] Also known as the King Abdul Aziz Bde.

[16] One source indicates this unit was directly under the control of JFC East. Another source lists this unit as a brigade. One source indicates Qatar contributed two combined arms mechanized infantry battalions (which included tank and mechanized infantry units) and that one battalion served in TF Abu Bakr while the other was assigned to JFC East.

[17] One source lists this unit as the "Tario" Bde.

[18] One source indicates this unit was a mechanized infantry battalion. Another source indicates it was a motorized infantry battalion and that it served in TF Omar.

[19] This battalion may have been short one company.

[20] These units were apparently in the process of moving to the front at the time the war ended. It does not appear that any of these units saw combat, and it is unclear whether they had been fully trained and equipped, or whether they were brigade size. It is unclear where they fit into the chain of command.

The Battle of Khafji

The Coalition's Arab-Islamic forces experienced their baptism by fire from 30 Jan to 1 Feb 91, during the Battle of Khafji, when they attacked and destroyed elements of the Iraqi 5th Mechanized Division that had seized the Saudi Arabian town of Khafji.[21] The attack to retake Khafji was executed by the Saudi 5th, 7th, and 8th Combined Arms Battalions and elements of the 6th Combined Arms Battalion (all 2nd Motorized Infantry Brigade [SANG]); a tank battalion from the Saudi 8th Mechanized Brigade; and Qatari armored units. In addition, it appears that a Royal Saudi Marines battalion and the UAE motorized infantry battalion were in reserve during the battle.

Other Saudi Units

Various other Saudi units were stationed in other parts of Saudi Arabia performing internal security missions or guarding the border with Yemen, which was a supporter of Iraq. Presumably some or all of these units would have been available for the Gulf War if they had been needed. Information on these units is sketchy; they apparently included: Royal Guard Regt (three infantry battalions in Riyadh); 12th Armored Brigade (Tabuk); Parachute Brigade (Riyadh and Hafir al Batin); Hijaz Infantry Brigade (Western Saudi Arabia); one or more mechanized brigades on the border with Yemen; a marine regiment; and several Saudi Arabian National Guard brigades, including the 1st Motorized Infantry Brigade (also known as the Imam Mohammed Bin Saud Brigade), which remained in Riyadh during the war.[22]

Finally, the Royal Saudi Air Defense Forces included air defense artillery units equipped with the U.S. Redeye, Stinger, M163 self-propelled Vulcan, and Hawk, and the French-made AMX 30SA (twin 30mm guns on an AMX 30 tank chassis), and Crotale and Shahine missiles. Information on these units has been extremely difficult to locate, however one such unit was the 5th Air Defense Group. Marine ADA units performed coordination with this unit prior to the beginning of the war. Another such unit was the 6th Air Defense Group, which XVIII Airborne Corps coordinated with prior to the beginning of the war. The Royal Saudi Air Defense Forces reportedly had 33 firing batteries in August 1990.

---

[21] See Chart 19, Footnote 21.

[22] SANG reserve units apparently consisted of one motorized and two infantry brigades, in addition to the two SANG brigades listed in the text of the chart.

Order of Battle

Other Kuwaiti Units

One Kuwaiti special forces unit, the 1st Special Forces Battalion, served under U.S. command as an element of the 3rd Special Forces Group(Abn), which was part of SOCCENT. See Chart 6.

Other Units

The UAE had several Hawk batteries that were tied into the Coalition's air defense network.

Kuwait's Armed Forces in August 1990

The Kuwaiti Army apparently had four maneuver brigades and some separate units when Iraq invaded in August 1990. The brigades were the 35th Armored Brigade, the 6th and 15th Mechanized Brigades, and the 80th Infantry Brigade. The separate units included the Amiri Guard and a commando battalion. The Kuwaiti Air Force had an air defense artillery brigade with one battalion of Hawk II missiles, along with 35mm guns and Soviet-made Romb, Kub, and Strela 2 missiles. The Hawk battalion had enough equipment for four firing batteries, but was low on personnel. As a result, one battery was inactive, one was a training unit, and two firing batteries were actively engaged in air defense missions when Iraq invaded. These batteries were deployed south of Kuwait City, and there was also a single firing platoon on Faylaka Island in the Gulf. This platoon shot down seven Iraqi aircraft, and each of the two active firing batteries claimed eight Iraqi aircraft.

Selected Equipment

Egyptian units used American-made M60A3 Main Battle Tanks and M113A2 Armored Personnel Carriers, along with several M113 variants, including the M901 ITV, M106A2 self-propelled 4.2" mortar, M577A2 command post vehicle, and M730 Chaparral. Egyptian artillery units used the American-made M109 series self-propelled 155mm howitzer and the Soviet-made D-30 towed 122mm howitzer.

Saudi Arabia obtained most of its armored vehicles from the United States or France. Saudi units used American-made M60A3 and French-made AMX 30S Main Battle Tanks. The AMX 30S is a tropicalized version of the standard AMX 30. Saudi units also used American-made M113 series APCs and French-made AMX 10P IFVs. Saudi recon units used French-made AML-60 and AML-90 Armored Cars. Saudi artillery units used the French-made GCT 155mm self-propelled howitzer, which was based on the AMX 30 chassis; American-made M198 towed and M109 series self-propelled 155m howitzers; and the Brazilian-made ASTROS wheeled multiple rocket launcher. The Saudi Arabian National Guard was equipped with several versions of the American-made Cadillac Gage V-150 four-wheeled armored car, and with the M102 towed 105mm howitzer.

The Syrian 9th Armored Division used Soviet-made equipment, including T-55 and T-62 Main Battle Tanks, BMP-1 IFVs, BTR-60 APCs, BRDM-2 reconnaissance vehicles, and D-30 towed 122mm howitzers. The 9th Armored Division had few if any T-72 Main Battle Tanks.

Kuwaiti units used British-made Chieftain Main Battle Tanks and a Yugoslav-produced version of the T-72 that was designated the M84. Kuwaiti units also had American-made M113 series APCs and Soviet-made BMP-2 IFVs.

Qatari units used French-made equipment, including AMX 30 Main Battle Tanks, AMX 10P IFVs, and VAB APCs with HOT antitank missiles. The United Arab Emirates used French-made AMX 30 Main Battle Tanks and AMX 10P IFVs.

Notes:

➢ The Saudi Arabian National Guard is a lightly-armed organization that is recruited from Bedouin tribes. It is an active duty organization, not a reserve component like the U.S. National Guard.

➢ Information on these units remains sketchy. The information on this chart is the least reliable of all the information in this Order of Battle.

Chart 30

Comparison of
U.S. Ground Combat Forces Deployed,
Desert Storm, Just Cause(Panama),
Urgent Fury(Grenada), Vietnam, and Korea

Since World War Two, the United States has committed significant numbers of ground troops to combat on five occasions: Korea, Vietnam, Grenada (Operation Urgent Fury), Panama (Operation Just Cause), and Operation Desert Storm. This chart compares those five combat operations. These figures show that, measured by U.S. ground combat forces deployed, these five combat operations fall into three categories. Grenada and Panama were relatively small operations, Korea was a mid-size operation, and Vietnam and Desert Storm were major operations.

U.S. Army	Desert Storm	Just Cause	Urgent Fury	Vietnam	Korea
Active Army					
DEs Deployed	7.67	2.00	1.00	8.67	4.67
Reserve Components					
DEs Mobilized	1.00	- 0 -	- 0 -	.67	9.00
DEs Deployed	- 0 -	- 0 -	- 0 -	- 0 -	2.00
Total DEs Deployed	7.67	2.00	1.00	8.67	6.67

Order of Battle

U.S. Marine Corps	Desert Storm	Just Cause	Urgent Fury	Vietnam	Korea
Active USMC					
DEs Deployed	2.33	- 0 -	- 0 -	2.67	1.00
USMCR					
DEs Mobilized	1.00	- 0 -	- 0 -	- 0 -	- 0 -
DEs Deployed	.67	- 0 -	- 0 -	- 0 -	- 0 -
Total DEs Deployed	3.00	- 0 -	- 0 -	2.67	1.00

Total (USA & USMC)	Desert Storm	Just Cause	Urgent Fury	Vietnam	Korea
Active DEs Deployed	10.00	2.00	1.00	11.33	5.67
Reserve Components					
DEs Mobilized	2.00	- 0 -	- 0 -	.67	9.00
DEs Deployed	.67	- 0 -	- 0 -	- 0 -	2.00
Total DEs Deployed	10.67	2.00	1.00	11.33	7.67

Notes:

➤ "DE" stands for "Division Equivalents," i.e., a division's worth of combat troops, whether assigned to a division or to non-divisional units. I have recorded DEs in one-third increments. I ignored elements less than a third of a DE; thus, the Marine Corps is down for "zero" units for Panama and Grenada, notwithstanding that in both conflicts the USMC provided a battalion of combat troops.

➤ For the reserves, "DEs Mobilized" are the total reserves mobilized, without regard to whether they were deployed, while "DEs Deployed" are those reserves that were mobilized and deployed to the theater of operations. Thus, during the Korean War the Army mobilized the equivalent of nine reserve component divisions; two DEs were deployed to Korea, while the remaining seven were not.

➤ Desert Storm figures do not include Marine Corps units in the Mediterranean or Army units in Israel or Turkey.

➤ Figures for Vietnam are as of Summer 1968, the height of the U.S. war effort.

➤ Figures for Korea are as of Summer 1952, which was during the height of the U.S. war effort and after two National Guard divisions had replaced two Active Army divisions that had seen heavy combat during the opening stages of the war and had been placed in reserve in Japan.

➢ The Marines are credited with one active division in Korea and no reserve units, notwithstanding that many of the personnel of the 1st Mar Div were reservists called to active duty, because these reservists were mobilized on an individual basis and assigned to active Marine Corps units.

➢ This chart only addresses combat actions that involved significant numbers of ground troops. Not included are non-combat operations, such as the interventions in Lebanon (1958 and 1982-83), the Dominican Republic (1965-66), Somalia (1992-95), Haiti (1994-96), and Bosnia (1996-present), or combat actions that involved no ground troops (such as the raid on Libya in 1986) or very few ground troops (such as the Marines' recapture of the American merchant ship _Mayaguez_ after it had been seized by Cambodia in 1975).

➢ By contrast, at the end of World War II the U.S. Army consisted of 92 divisions and the U.S. Marine Corps consisted of six divisions. Neither figure includes nondivisional units.

Chart 31

Comparison Of Selected Active U.S. Army Units Deployed For Operation Desert Storm

This chart compares the major Active Army units that were deployed to the Gulf to those that were not deployed.

Unit	Total Active	Not Deployed To The Gulf	Deployed To The Gulf	Percentage Deployed
Corps HQ	5[1]	3	2	40%
Heavy Div HQ[2]	10	5	5	50%
Light Div HQ	6	4	2	33%
Heavy Bdes[3]	30	13	17	57%
Light Bdes[4]	21	15	6	29%
FA Bdes[5]	9	4	5	56%
SF Gps	5	2	3[6]	60%

[1] Does not include HQ, U.S. Army Japan/IX Corps, which was an administrative unit rather than a true tactical corps headquarters.

[2] Includes HQ, 2nd Inf Div because it included substantial numbers of heavy (tank, mechanized infantry, and self-propelled artillery) units. See Chart 11, Footnote 2.

[3] Includes all armored and mechanized brigades (divisional and nondivisional), two of the 2nd Inf Div's three brigades (see Chart 11, Footnote 2), and three armored cavalry regiments. Does not include the 177th Armd Bde(-) or the 3rd Bde, 1st Inf Div(M). As the OpFor at the NTC, the 177th was not available for deployment. The 3rd Bde(-), 1st Inf Div(M) had deployed to the Gulf, minus its equipment, to perform a support/logistics function and was, therefore, not available for combat. See Chart 4, page 4-28. Moreover, by early 1991 this brigade had begun the process of inactivation and was no longer combat ready.

[4] Includes all light infantry brigades (divisional and nondivisional), the Berlin Bde, the 199th Inf Bde(Mtzd), the 75th Rngr Regt(Abn), and one of the 2nd Inf Div's brigades, to take into account that this division had two air assault infantry battalions and one towed 155mm field artillery battalion. See Chart 11, Footnote 2.

[5] Assigned to corps artillery.

Thus, almost half of the Active Army's combat power was deployed in the Gulf for Operation Desert Storm.

Notes:

➤ By the time Desert Storm was initiated, the Army had inactivated the following units following its high-water mark during the height of the Cold War in the late 1980s:

HQ and 2nd Bde, 2nd Armd Div
HQ and 1st & 2nd Bdes, 9th Inf Div(Mtzd)[7]
2nd Bde, 4th Inf Div(M)
194th Armd Bde(-)[8]

In addition, some U.S. Army units in Germany were in the process of being inactivated and were, therefore, not available for combat operations in January 1991. Included among these was the 3rd Bde, 1st Inf Div(M). For this reason, and because part of this brigade deployed to the Gulf without its equipment to perform a support/logistics mission, see Chart 4, page 4-28, the 3rd Bde, 1st Inf Div(M) is not included in the totals depicted on this chart.

➤ This chart only addresses active duty Army units, not ARNG or USAR units.

---

[6] Includes the 10th SF Gp(Abn)(-), which deployed to Turkey.
[7] HQ, 9th Inf Div(Mtzd) is not included in the totals reflected in this chart. See Chart 11, Footnote 10.
[8] See Chart 11, Footnote 11.

Chart 32

Comparison Of Selected
Active U.S. Marine Corps Units
Deployed For Operation Desert Storm

This chart compares selected Active Marine Corps units that were deployed to the Gulf to those that were not deployed.

Unit	Total Active	Not Deployed To the Gulf	Deployed To the Gulf	Percentage Deployed
MEF HQ	3[1]	2	1	33%
Mar Div HQ	3	1	2	67%
MEB HQ	6	3[2]	3[3]	50%
Infantry Bns	24	4[4]	20	83%
Artillery Bns	12	1(+)	11(-)	90%
Tank Cos	13	1	12	92%
LAI Cos	11(?)[5]	1(?)[6]	9(-)	80%[7]

---

[1] Does not include HQ, V MEF, which was activated just before the beginning of Operation Desert Storm and was, therefore, not fully prepared to serve as a MEF headquarters during ODS.

[2] These were the 1st MEB, whose headquarters remained on Hawaii when its units deployed during the early days of Desert Shield; the 6th MEB at Camp Lejeune, whose headquarters remained behind when the 2nd Mar Div deployed; and the 9th MEB on Okinawa with the 3rd Mar Div(-).

[3] These were the 4th and 5th MEBs, which served with NAVCENT during Desert Storm; and the 7th MEB, whose headquarters was absorbed into HQ, I MEF when Marine units in Saudi Arabia were composited into I MEF in early August 1990. See Chart 17, "Notes."

[4] Includes two battalions afloat in the Mediterranean that could have reinforced Coalition forces in Turkey. See Chart 20. Also includes the 1/9 Marines, which remained at Camp Pendleton to provide the ground combat element of the 15th MEU(SOC), and the 2/9 Marines, which remained on Okinawa with the 3rd Mar Div(-).

[5] This assumes Co C, 3rd LAI Bn was not active. See Chart 21, Footnote 23.

Order of Battle

Thus, about 85 percent of the Active Marine Corps' ground combat power was deployed in the Gulf for Operation Desert Storm.

Notes:

➢ This chart only addresses active duty Marine Corps units, not USMCR units.

---

[6] See Footnote 5.
[7] See Footnote 5.

Chart 33

Analysis Of U.S. Army And Marine Corps Combat Arms Units That Participated In Operation Desert Storm

This chart covers all units deployed for Operation Desert Storm, including those deployed to the Gulf, Turkey, the Mediterranean, and Israel.

| U.S. Army |

Armor Units

Tank Bns [M1]:		2
Tank Bns [M1A1 series]:		26
M1A1 Bns:	6	
M1A1(Mod) Bns:	14	
M1A1HA Bns:	6	
Abn Armor Bn [M551A1(TTS)]:		1

TOTAL Tank Bns:		29
Armd Cav Sqdns (ACR):		6
Cav Sqdns (Heavy Div):		5(+)

TOTAL Cav Sqdns:		11(+)
TOTAL ARMOR BRANCH BNS:		40(+)

U.S. Army (continued)

Infantry Units

Mech Inf Bns [Bradley IFV]:	17
Mech Inf Bns [M113 APC]:	2

TOTAL Mech Inf Bns:	19

Abn Inf Bns:	9
Air Aslt Inf Bns:	9

TOTAL Light Inf Bns:	18

TOTAL INFANTRY BRANCH BNS:	37

Combat Aviation Units

Air Cav Sqdns (Light Div):	2
Avn Sqdns (ACR):	2
Air Cav Sqdn (Other):	1(-)[1]
-- Scout Cos (2 Cos):	0.5 BE[2]
Atk Hel Bn (Div) [AH-1]:	1
Atk Hel Bns [AH-64]:	15
Div Bns: 10(+)	
Corps Bns: 4	
EAC Bns: 1(-)[3]	

TOTAL COMBAT AVIATION BNS:	21

---

[1] This was the 4-17 Cav(Air)(-), which performed special missions for NAVCENT and the 3rd SF Gp(Abn). See Chart 4, Footnote 84 and Chart 6.

[2] These were the scout companies assigned to the 11th and 12th Avn Bdes.

[3] This was the 5-229 Avn(AH)(-). See Chart 4, Footnote 77.

U.S. Army (continued)

Field Artillery Units

105mm Towed Bns(Div):		6	
Abn Bns:	3		
AAslt Bns:	3		
155mm Towed Bns(FA Bde):		3	
Bns:	2^4		
Abn Bn:	1^5		
155mm SP Bns:		25 BE	[1 = ARNG]
Div Bns:	15		
ACR BEs:	3^6		
Bns(FA Bde):	7 [1 = ARNG]		
203mm SP Bns(FA Bde):		6	[4 = ARNG]
MLRS Bns:		6 BE	[1 = ARNG]
Bn(Div):	1(-)		
Bns(FA Bde):	$3(+)^7$ [1 = ARNG]		
Btrys(Div):	2 BE [6 Btrys]		
MLRS/ATACMS Bn(FA Bde):		1	

TOTAL FA Firing Bns:	47 BE	[6 = ARNG]
-- Target Acquisition Btrys:	8 Btrys	
-- Target Acquisition Dets:	2 Dets	

TOTAL FA TA BEs:	3 BE

TOTAL FA BRANCH BNS:	50 BE	[6 = ARNG]

---

[4] Includes the 5-8 FA, which initially had one battery attached to the 101st Abn Div(AAslt). Later the entire battalion was attached to the 101st.

[5] This was the 1-39 FA, which was attached to the 82nd Abn Div during the later stages of the war.

[6] Each armored cavalry regiment had a battalion's worth of self-propelled 155mm howitzers organic to its three armored cavalry squadrons (one battery per squadron). The "3" in the chart includes these two "hidden" battalions, plus the 3-18 FA, which was attached to the 3rd Armd Cav Regt.

[7] Includes the 1-158 FA(-), which was attached to the 1st Cav Div(-) at the end of the war.

U.S. Army (continued)

Air Defense Artillery Units

Gun/Missile Bns: 8
    Bns(Hvy Div) 5^8
    Bns(Lt Div): 2^9
    Bns(Non-Div): 1^{10}
Hawk Bns: 3
Patriot Bns: 6(-)   (1 = Israel,1(-) = Turkey)
-- Stinger/Avenger Secs/Plts:[11]   0.5 BE

TOTAL ADA BRANCH BNS: 17(+) BE (1 = Israel, 1(-) = Turkey)

Special Operations Forces Units

Special Forces Bns: 6(+)   (2 = Turkey)
"Delta Force" Sqdns: 2 (?)
Other units:[12]   2 BE

TOTAL SOF BNS: 10(+)(?)   (2 = Turkey)

---

[8] These battalions were armed with a mix of weapons, including self-propelled Vulcan, Chaparral, Stinger, and Avenger. See Chart 4 and Appendix D, pages D-18 and D-19, for the specific weapons used by each battalion.

[9] These battalions were armed with towed Vulcan and Stinger.

[10] This battalion was armed with self-propelled Vulcan and Stinger.

[11] Six platoons/sections. Counts stinger teams from the 3-5 ADA that were with the 3rd Armd Div and the ARCENT Avn Bde as one platoon.

[12] Consists of one airborne ranger company(+); two LRS companies; seven LRS detachments; and one pathfinder detachment. Technically, LRS and pathfinder units were not SOF units, but they perform a SOF-like mission rather than a traditional infantry mission.

U.S. Marine Corps

Infantry Units

Infantry Bns:	26(+)[13]	[4(+) = USMCR]
Regt'l AT Plts [TOW]:	1 BE[14]	[2 Plts = USMCR]
TOTAL INFANTRY BNS:	27(+) BE	[4(+) = USMCR]

Tank Units

Tank Bns [M1A1 Series]:[15]	1(+)	[2 Cos = USMCR]
Tank Bns [M60A1]:	4	[1(+) = USMCR]
TOTAL TANK BNS:	5(+)	[2 = USMCR]

Light Armored Infantry Units

LAI/LAV Bns:	3(+)[16]	[1 = USMCR]

Reconnaissance Units

Recon Bns:	2(+)[17]	[1 Co = USMCR]
-- Force Recon Cos (4 Cos):	1 BE	[2 Cos = USMCR][18]
TOTAL RECON BNS:	3(+)	[3 Cos = USMCR][19]

Assault Amphibian Units

Aslt Amphib Bns:	3(-)[20]	[1(-) = USMCR]

---

[13] Includes two infantry battalions afloat in the Mediterranean. See Chart 20.

[14] Consists of 11 antitank platoons. One was understrength (see Chart 21, Footnote 2) while others were overstrength (see Chart 19, Footnotes 24, 48 & 74).

[15] All were equipped with the M1A1HA, with the exception of one company that had the M1A1 Common. See Chart 24, page 24-3.

[16] Includes two reinforced LAI platoons afloat in the Mediterranean. See Chart 20.

[17] Includes two recon platoons afloat in the Mediterranean. See Chart 20.

[18] One of the USMCR companies was actually a company(-).

[19] See Footnote 18.

[20] Includes two assault amphibian platoons afloat in the Mediterranean. See Chart 20.

U.S. Marine Corps (continued)

Field Artillery Units

155mm Towed Bns:	9(+)[21]	[4 Btrys = USMCR]
155mm/203mm Bns:[22]	2(+)	[2 Btrys = USMCR]
-- 105 T/155 T Btrys (3 Btrys):	1 BE	(2 Btrys = Mediterranean)
--		
TOTAL FIELD ARTILLERY BNS:	13 BE	[6 Btrys = USMCR] (2 Btrys = Mediterranean)

Air Defense Artillery Units

LAAD Bns [Stinger]:	2(+)	[1 Btry[23] = USMCR]
LAAM Bns [Hawk]:	2	
--		
TOTAL AIR DEFENSE ARTY BNS:	4(+)	[1 Btry[24] = USMCR]

---

[21] Includes two battalions afloat in the Gulf (1/10 Marines, 4th MEB and 2/11 Marines, 5th MEB) that had a full, or nearly full, complement of 155mm towed howitzers plus some 105mm towed howitzers. See Appendix E, page E-7.

[22] The 5/10 Marines(Rein), 2nd Mar Div(Rein), had self-propelled 155mm and self-propelled 203mm howitzers, while the 5/11 Marines(Rein), 1st Mar Div(Rein), had towed 155mm, self-propelled 155mm, and self-propelled 203mm howitzers. The two USMCR batteries were self-propelled 155mm units.

[23] It is doubtful whether this unit served in SWA. See Chart 19, Footnote 124.

[24] See Footnote 23.

Recap – Selected Data

Unit	Total	U.S. Army	U.S. Marine Corps
Tank Bns:	34(+)	29	5(+)
Inf Bns:	64(+)	37	27(+)
Cav/LAI Bns:	14(+)	11(+)	3(+)
Cbt Avn Bns:	21	21	0
TOTAL MANEUVER BNS:	133(+)	98(+)	35(+)
Field Artillery Firing Bns:	60	47[25]	13
Air Defense Artillery Bns:	21(+)	17(+)	4(+)
SOF/USMC Recon Bns:	13(+)	10(+)	3(+)
TOTAL OTHER COMBAT BNS:	94(+)	74(+)	20(+)
TOTAL MANEUVER BNS:	133(+)	98(+)	35(+)
TOTAL OTHER COMBAT BNS:	94(+)	74(+)	20(+)
TOTAL COMBAT BNS:	227(+)	172(+)	55(+)

Notes:

➤ "BE" stands for "battalion equivalents," i.e., a battalion's worth of troops.

➤ U.S. Army combat arms units that served in a non-combat arms role (3-34 Armor; 4-16 Inf(M); and 3-2 ADA) are not included in any of these totals. See Chart 4, page 4-28.

➤ Because the Marines treat their attack helicopters as aircraft, not as ground maneuver weapons systems, the Marines' attack helicopter units are not covered here. For purposes of comparison, the Marines had the equivalent of three Army attack helicopter battalions.

➤ All units were located in Saudi Arabia unless indicated otherwise.

➤ All units were active duty (rather than reserve component) unless indicated otherwise.

---

[25] See Footnote 5.

Chart 34

Comparison of Selected
U.S. Ground Combat Units,
VII Corps, XVIII Airborne Corps, I MEF, and
NAVCENT

This chart depicts how selected U.S. ground combat units were allocated between the four major U.S. commands that included ground combat units. The entries for I MEF and NAVCENT reflect the situation at the beginning of the ground war, when the 5th MEB was still assigned to NAVCENT, before it was transferred to MARCENT and became I MEF reserve. The entries for the VII Corps, however, include the 1st Cavalry Division(-) even though that unit was not released to VII Corps until 26 Feb 91. This chart shows how decisive combat power was weighted to the VII Corps.

Brigades/Regts	Total	VII Corps	XVIII Abn Corps	I MEF	NAVCENT
Army Heavy Bdes	15	11	3	1	
Army ACRs	2	1	1		
Army Light Bdes	6		6		
USMC Inf Regts	9			7	2
TOTAL:	32	12	10	8	2

Order of Battle

Tank Battalions	Total	VII Corps	XVIII Abn Corps	I MEF	NAVCENT
M1A1[1]	27(+)	20	4	3(+)	
M1	2	2			
M60A1	4			3(+)	2(+) Cos
M551A1(TTS)	1		1		
TOTAL:	34(+)	22	5	6(+)	2(+) Cos

Cavalry Sqdns/LAI Bns	Total	VII Corps	XVIII Abn Corps	I MEF	NAVCENT
Armd Cav Sqdns(ACR)	6	3	3		
Hvy Div Cav Sqdns	5(+)	4(+)	1		
LAI Bns	3(+)			2(+)	1
TOTAL:	14(+)	7(+)	4	2(+)	1

Infantry Battalions	Total	VII Corps	XVIII Abn Corps	I MEF	NAVCENT
Mech Inf [Bradley]	17	13	3	1	
Mech Inf [M113]	2		2		
Light Infantry[2]	18		18		
Marine Infantry	24(+)			18(+)	6
TOTAL:	61(+)	13	23	19(+)	6

---

[1] Includes all versions of the M1A1: M1A1, M1A1(Mod), M1A1HA, and M1A1 Common.

[2] Includes U.S. Army airborne infantry and air assault infantry battalions.

Combat Aviation Units[3]	Total	VII Corps	XVIII Abn Corps	I MEF	NAVCENT
Air Cav Sqdns(Lt Div)	2		2		
Avn Sqdns(ACR)	2	1	1		
Atk Hel Bns [AH-64]	15[4]	8(+)	6		
Atk Hel Bns [AH-1]	1		1		
TOTAL:	20[5]	9(+)	10		

Field Artillery Units	Total	VII Corps	XVIII Abn Corps	I MEF	NAVCENT
105mm Towed Bns	6		6		
155mm Towed Bns[6]	12(+)		3	7(+)	2
-- 105 T/155 T Btrys	1				1
155mm/203mm Bns[7]	2(+)			2(+)	
155mm SP Bns	25[8]	17	7	1	
203mm SP Bns	6	3	3		
MLRS Bns	4	3	1		
MLRS/ATACMS Bns	1	1 Btry	1(-)		
-- MLRS Btrys(Div)	2 BE	4 Btrys	1 Btry	1 Btry	
TOTAL:	59[9]	24(+)	21	11	2(+)

---

[3] Because the Marines treat their attack helicopters as aircraft, rather than as ground maneuver weapons systems, the Marines' attack helicopter units are not included here. The Marines had the equivalent of three Army attack helicopter battalions in the Gulf.

[4] Includes the 5-229 Avn(AH)(-), which was an EAC unit assigned to the ARCENT Avn Bde and is, therefore, not included in the VII Corps or XVIII Abn Corps totals. See Chart 4, Footnote 77.

[5] See Footnote 4.

[6] See Chart 33, Footnote 20.

[7] See Chart 33, Footnote 21.

[8] Includes two battalions' worth of self-propelled 155mm howitzers "hidden" within the armored cavalry squadrons of the 2nd and 3rd Armd Cav Regts. See Chart 33, Footnote 5.

[9] See Footnote 8.

Notes:

➤ "BE" stands for "battalion equivalents," i.e., a battalion's worth of troops.

➤ This chart does not include those Marine Corps units afloat in the Mediterranean. As a result, the totals reflected here do not precisely match those on Chart 33, which includes the units that were in the Mediterranean.

➤ U.S. Army combat arms units that served in a non-combat arms role (3rd Bde(-), 1st Inf Div(M), with the 3-34 Armor and 4-16 Inf(M); and the 3-2 ADA) are not included in any of these totals. See Chart 4, page 4-28.

➤ This chart shows how decisive combat power was weighted to the VII Corps:

   ▪ Of the 17 Army heavy brigades and ACRs that served in the Gulf, 12 (more than 70 percent) served with the VII Corps.

   ▪ Of the 34-plus Army and Marine Corps tank battalions that served in the Gulf, 22 (almost two-thirds) served with the VII Corps. An even higher percentage of M1A1 series[10] tank units (the most capable U.S. tank units) served with the VII Corps: 20 of 27(+) battalions, almost 73 percent.

   ▪ Thirteen of the 17 Army mechanized infantry battalions that were equipped with the Bradley IFV (over 76 percent) served with the VII Corps.

   ▪ Of the 40(+) Army and Marine Corps field artillery battalion equivalents equipped with self-propelled 155mm and/or self-propelled 203mm howitzers, or the MLRS and/or ATACMS missile, 24(+) (more than 60 percent) served with the VII Corps.

   ▪ Of the 15 Army attack helicopter battalions equipped with the AH-64 Apache, 8(+) (just over 55 percent) served with the VII Corps.

➤ This chart does not take into account the British or French units that were assigned to, respectively, the VII and XVIII Abn Corps. However, the assignments of these units reflect the weighting of combat power toward the VII Corps, as the 1st (UK) Armd Div possessed much more combat power than did the 6th (FR) Lt Armd Div:

---

[10] Includes all versions of the M1A1: M1A1, M1A1(Mod), M1A1HA, and M1A1 Common.

	1st (UK) Armd Div (VII Corps)	6th (FR) Lt AD (XVIII Abn Corps)	Total
Armored/Recon Regiments			
Armd Regts	3	1	4
Armd Recon Regts	1(+)	2(+)	3(+)
TOTAL:	4(+)	3(+)	7(+)
Infantry Battalions			
Armd Inf Bns	3		3
Motorized Bns		3	3
Other Inf Bns	3[11]	1(-)	4(-)
TOTAL:	6	4(-)	10(-)
Field Artillery Regiments			
155mm Towed		1	1
155mm SP	3(-)		3(-)
203mm SP	1(-)		1(-)
MLRS	1(-)		1(-)
TOTAL:	5(-)	1	6(-)
Cbt Avn Sqdns:	4	2	6
TOTAL:	19	10	29

These figures do not include the British Armd Delivery Group or the RAC Armored Delivery Sqdn.

---

[11] These were primarily the non-mechanized infantry battalions that were deployed to handle EPWs. See Chart 27, Footnotes 1-3 & 28.

Chart 35

Comparison of Selected Marine Corps Ground Combat Units, I MEF Versus NAVCENT

This chart depicts how selected Marine Corps ground combat units were allocated between the two major commands that had Marine ground combat units in SWA, I Marine Expeditionary Force and NAVCENT. Marine units on the ground were assigned to I MEF, while those units afloat in the Gulf were assigned to NAVCENT. At the beginning of the ground war, NAVCENT had three Marine units assigned, the 4th MEB, 5th MEB, and 13th MEU(SOC). This chart shows that, at the beginning of the ground war, almost 80 percent of the Marines' ground combat units were on land with I MEF, while just over 20 percent were afloat in the Gulf with NAVCENT:

	Total	On Land (I MEF)	Afloat (NAVCENT)	Percent On Land	Percent Afloat
MEF HQs	1	1	0[1]	100%	0%
Marine Div HQs	2	2	0	100%	0%
Infantry Regt HQs	9	7	2	78%	22%
Infantry Bns	24(+)	18(+)	6	75%	25%
Artillery Bns	11(+)	9(+)	2(+)	79%	21%
Tank Cos	18	16	2	89%	11%
LAI/LAV Cos	14(-)	10(-)	4(-)	73%	27%

---

[1] Many sources state that Marine units afloat in the Gulf were assigned to II MEF. This is incorrect. HQ, II MEF did not deploy to the Gulf. The Marines afloat in the Gulf were under the command of MajGen Harry Jenkins, who was dual-hatted as Commander, Landing Force and Commanding General, 4th MEB.

On 24 Feb 91, shortly after the ground war began, the 5th MEB began landing in Saudi territory and was reassigned from NAVCENT to I MEF as the I MEF reserve. Once the 5th MEB landed almost 90 percent of the Marines' ground combat units were on land with I MEF, while just over 10 percent remained afloat in the Gulf with NAVCENT:

	Total	On Land (I MEF)	Afloat (NAVCENT)	Percent On Land	Percent Afloat
MEF HQs	1	1	0^2	100%	0%
Marine Div HQs	2	2	0	100%	0%
Infantry Regt HQs	9	8	1	89%	11%
Infantry Bns	24(+)	21(+)	3	88%	12%
Artillery Bns	11(+)	10(+)	1(+)	89%	11%
Tank Cos	18	17	1	94%	6%
LAI/LAV Cos	14(-)	11(-)	3(-)	78%	22%

Notes:

➢ This chart does not include those Marine Corps units afloat in the Mediterranean. As a result, the totals reflected here do not precisely match those on Chart 33, which includes the units that were in the Mediterranean.

[2] See Footnote 1.

Chart 36

Comparison Of Selected
Ground Combat Units By Country

This chart compares selected ground combat units that were contributed by the major Allied participants in Operation Desert Storm.

Country	Tank Bns	Cav Sqdns[1]	Inf Bns[2]	Cbt Avn Bns[3]	FA Bns[4]
USA	34(+)	14(+)	61(+)	21(-)	59(+)
UK	3	1(+)	6	4	5(-)
France	1	2(+)	4(-)	2	1

(continued on next page)

---

[1] Includes U.S. Army armored cavalry squadrons assigned to armored cavalry regiments; U.S. Army heavy division cavalry squadrons; USMC LAI/LAV battalions; and other countries' ground cavalry squadrons.

[2] Does not include special operations units.

[3] Includes U.S. Army air cavalry squadrons, aviation squadrons assigned to armored cavalry regiments, and attack helicopter battalions, along with other countries' attack helicopter units. Because the Marines treat their attack helicopters as aircraft, not as ground maneuver weapons systems, the Marines' attack helicopter units are not included here. For purposes of comparison, the Marines had the equivalent of three Army attack helicopter battalions in SWA.

[4] Includes all types of field artillery firing units; does not include TA units. Includes the two battalions of field artillery "hidden" in the Army's armored cavalry regiments (see Chart 33, Footnote 5), and counts the six U.S. Army divisional MLRS batteries as two battalions.

Order of Battle

Country	Tank Bns	Cav Sqdns	Inf Bns	Cbt Avn Bns	FA Bns
Egypt	9	2	9	?	14
Saudi Arabia	6	4	16[5]	1	8
Syria	7	1	5	?	4
Kuwait	2	?	8[6]	1	3
Pakistan	2	?	1	?	1
Other			7(+)		1
APPROX. TOTALS:	64(+)	24(+)	117	29(-)	96

	Tank Bns	Cav Sqdns	Inf Bns	Cbt Avn Bns	FA Bns
Approximate Percentage of Units Contributed by USA:	53%	59%	53%	71%	62%

Notes:

➤ Only includes units that were in the Gulf. Does not include units in Israel, Turkey, or the Mediterranean.

➤ British and French regiments that were the size of U.S. battalions are counted as battalions.

➤ The numbers of units for countries other than the United States, the United Kingdom, and France are approximate.

➤ The "Percentage of Units Contributed by USA" entry was calculated strictly on a numerical basis by unit, without taking into account the size of the units (i.e., one country's battalion with three line companies is treated as equivalent to another country's battalion with five line companies), the quality of the equipment, or the readiness of the units deployed. If these factors were considered, the percentage contributed by the United States would be much higher.

➤ U.S. Army combat arms units that served in a non-combat arms role (3-34 Armor; 4-16 Inf(M); and 3-2 ADA) are not included in any of these totals. See Chart 4, page 4-28.

➤ American and British WSRO/Armd Delivery Group units are not included. Also not included is Britain's RAC Armored Delivery Sqdn, which was part of the WSRO effort.

---

[5] Includes the combined arms battalions of SANG motorized brigades.

[6] Does not include any of the units assigned to the three Kuwaiti brigades listed under "Other Forces" on Chart 29.

Appendix A

Introduction To Military Ground Combat Units

This appendix provides basic information on how ground combat units are organized and other basic background information about ground combat units. For detailed information on how Army units were organized during Desert Storm, see Appendix D. For detailed information on how Marine Corps units were organized during Desert Storm, see Appendix E.[1]

A "Team Of Teams"

The military has frequently been described as "a team of teams," and this phrase accurately captures the military's nature. The military is a highly hierarchical organization. It consists of many levels, from individual private to the Commander-in-Chief. Every soldier is expected to know his chain of command, including the name and rank of the commanding officer at each level, all the way to the President. And at each level, a single individual — usually designated as "the commander" — is in charge. This individual has a clearly defined role: he or she is responsible for everything the unit does or fails to do.

---

[1] For information on selected equipment used by Army units during Desert Storm, see Chart 13. For information on selected equipment used by Marine Corps units during Desert Storm, see Chart 24. For information on how British Army units were organized and equipped during Desert Storm, see Chart 27. For information on how French Army units were organized and equipped during Desert Storm, see Chart 28. For information on how Arab-Islamic units were organized and equipped during Desert Storm, see Chart 29.

Order of Battle

The Hierarchy Of Army Units[2]

In most units, the smallest element is called a squad, and consists of approximately ten soldiers led by a sergeant, also known as a noncommissioned officer (NCO). In armored units, the vehicle crew is the smallest element, and the crew is led by a sergeant. The next level up from squad or crew is the platoon. The platoon is the lowest level that is authorized an officer as its leader; a senior NCO, known as the platoon sergeant, is the next highest ranking member. In infantry units, a platoon normally consists of three rifle squads, a weapons squad with heavy weapons, and the platoon headquarters. In armored or mechanized units, a platoon normally consists of from four to six vehicles.

Several platoons, plus a headquarters element, comprise a company. A company is commanded by a captain, with a senior lieutenant as the executive officer. Depending on the type of unit, a company typically is authorized 80 to 150 soldiers. In cavalry units a company-level unit is called a "troop," while in field artillery and air defense artillery units a company-level unit is called a "battery." Yet another company-level unit is the "detachment."[3] A detachment is generally smaller than a company — frequently the size of a large platoon — and is typically used when some specialty function is required in something less than full company strength.

The unit above company is battalion. A battalion is commanded by a lieutenant colonel and consists of several companies, plus a headquarters element. A major is the executive officer. In cavalry units, a battalion-level unit is called a "squadron."[4]

Above battalion level, things become problematic. In most units, the next echelon up is brigade. However, in a handful of units this echelon is designated "regiment," while in other units this level is known as "group." Whether this level of command is called a brigade, regiment, or group depends on the type of unit. Brigades, regiments, and groups are commanded by full colonels with a lieutenant colonel as the executive officer, with the exception of a handful of brigades that are commanded by brigadier (one-star) generals.

---

[2] This discussion is based on the Army. While the Marine Corps and allied armies are similar, they vary in some ways.

[3] Some detachments are commanded by more senior officers, however. For example, the Army has medical detachments that perform specialized functions such as preventive medicine or psychiatry, and are commanded by officers ranging from captains all the way up to full colonels.

[4] Some non-cavalry units, however, are designated as elements of cavalry regiments for historical reasons. These units are typically designated as battalions rather than squadrons, for example, "1st Bn, 8th Cavalry," which is a conventional tank battalion, not a cavalry unit that performs reconnaissance. The 5th, 6th, and 8th Cavalry were such units that served in Desert Storm. The 5th Cavalry consisted of mechanized infantry units, the 6th Cavalry consisted of attack helicopter units, and the 8th Cavalry consisted of tank units. See Chart 9.

Most of the Army's combat units are organized into divisions, the next echelon above brigade. A division is commanded by a major (two-star) general, with two brigadier generals as assistant division commanders, one focusing on maneuver and the other on support. Depending on the type, a division is authorized approximately 10,000 to 15,000 soldiers. In combat, other units are typically attached to the division and can easily swell its ranks past 20,000 soldiers. The division is the largest unit that, in theory, has a fixed, standardized organizational structure. In practice, however, each division varies from its brothers in some way.

Finally, the senior warfighting unit is the corps. A corps consists of two to five divisions, and a wide array of supporting units from every branch of the Army. A corps is commanded by a lieutenant (three-star) general, with a major general as the deputy commander.

At the theater level, the senior U.S. Army headquarters is typically a numbered army headquarters. While such headquarters played a major role in combat operations in World War Two, the army headquarters now typically plays more of a planning, coordination, and administrative role, and primary responsibility for warfighting has devolved to the next level down, the corps.

The Branches Of The Army

In addition to being organized into units, the Army also breaks down into branches. Every soldier in the Army has a military occupational specialty (MOS) — a trade, so to speak — that falls within the purview of one of the Army's branches. The Army's branches are:

> Armor
> Infantry
> Field Artillery
> Air Defense Artillery
> Engineers
> Aviation
> Special Forces
> Military Police Corps
> Signal Corps
> Medical Corps
> Medical Service Corps
> Medical Specialist Corps
> Nurse Corps
> Dental Corps
> Veterinary Corps

Transportation Corps
Ordnance Corps
Quartermaster Corps
Chemical Corps
Military Intelligence
Civil Affairs
Adjutant General Corps
Finance Corps
Inspector General
Judge Advocate General Corps
Chaplain Corps

Within the branches are various specialties. For example, the infantry includes mechanized infantry and light infantry.

"Heavy" Versus "Light" Versus Special Operations Forces

Combat forces are typically divided into three categories: heavy, light, and special operations. Heavy units are characterized by a large number of vehicles. Indeed, in a heavy unit, all soldiers are assigned to a vehicle; nobody walks into combat. The stereotypical heavy unit is an armored division. In a heavy unit, the combat elements are equipped with armored vehicles that are typically fully tracked, while the support elements, such as logistics units, possess large numbers of unarmored wheeled vehicles such as trucks. Heavy units also possess a large quantity of large-caliber, self-propelled field artillery. In light of these characteristics, heavy units possess substantial tactical mobility — they can move quickly and freely about the battlefield, even under enemy fire — and substantial fire power, but their strategic mobility is very limited. It is very difficult, and it requires a substantial amount of time, to move these units any substantial distance. In addition, once these units arrive in a theater of operations their logistic requirements are substantial, and the fuel, ammunition, and repair parts needed to keep these units operating must be transported to the theater of operations.

Light units, on the other hand, possess very few or no armored vehicles and far fewer wheeled vehicles than heavy units. The stereotypical light unit is a light infantry division. In light units, the vast majority of soldiers walk, and vehicles are limited to essential tasks such as moving heavy weapons, logistics, and medical evacuation. Light units have less field artillery than heavy units and their weapons are smaller caliber, which means they have less range and their shells deliver less explosive power. Thus, light units possess limited tactical mobility and firepower, but good strategic mobility. Whereas heavy units almost always deploy their equipment to a theater of operations by ship, light units typically deploy by air.

Special operations units engage in unconventional warfare. United States Army special operations forces include Special Forces, Rangers, special operations aviation, psychological operations, and civil affairs. Special Forces, frequently known as the "Green Berets," specialize in unconventional warfare, typically working in small, decentralized units (known as operational detachments A (ODA) or "A Teams") that interface with our allies and indigenous populations. Rangers, on the other hand, are the best light infantry in the Army and specialize in raids and other "direct action" missions. Rangers are properly considered both special operations and light forces.

Special operations aviation units fly specially-modified helicopters, primarily in support of the Green Berets and Rangers. Special operations aviation units are specially trained to perform extremely risky missions with an emphasis on night flying. Psychological operations units focus on using propaganda delivered by methods such as leaflets and loudspeakers to break the enemy's will to resist. Civil affairs units *liaise* with civilian governments and assist unit commanders with dealing with civilian populations.

Finally, in addition to these established categories, some units really fall in between heavy and light forces, and should be considered "medium-weight" units. The Army's 101st Airborne Division(Air Aslt) is such a unit. Like a light division, the 101st possesses no armored vehicles, fewer wheeled vehicles than a heavy division,[5] and less-capable, towed artillery.

Unlike a light division, however, the 101st possesses a large number of helicopters. The air assault division's many AH-64 "Apache" attack helicopters give it substantial firepower, greatly in excess of a light infantry division, and the division's UH-60 "Black Hawk" utility and CH-47 "Chinook" medium helicopters give the 101st the ability to move up to one-third of the division by air at a time, yielding far greater tactical mobility than a light infantry division. At the same time, all these helicopters are difficult to deploy and, once deployed, demand substantial logistical support to keep them in the air. Thus, the 101st falls in between a light and heavy division in terms of firepower, tactical mobility, strategic mobility, and logistical needs, and should be considered a medium-weight unit.

---

[5]The 101st Abn Div(AAslt) had more vehicles that a U.S. Army light infantry division, however.

Marine divisions should also be considered medium-weight units.[6] While the majority of the Marine division's combat power is provided by nine "footmobile" infantry battalions, during Desert Storm the Marine division was also authorized a tank battalion, a light armored infantry battalion equipped with an eight-wheeled armored car called the LAV, for "Light Armored Vehicle," and an assault amphibian battalion equipped with large, tracked armored amphibious landing vehicles that are peculiar to the Marines and that can operate on land or at sea. Finally, a Marine division's artillery falls in between Army light and heavy divisions, and the Marine division has more vehicles than the Army light division. Thus, the Marine division is really a medium-weight unit.

The U.S. Army Regimental System And Unit Designations

For most of its history, the majority of the Army's combat arms units have been organized into regiments. This rule had been largely eroded by World War II, however, as many combat arms units were then organized into battalions that were not part of any regiment. In the late 1950s the Army adopted a new system of unit designations in an attempt to improve unit cohesion and identity. This was the Combat Arms Regimental System (CARS). Under CARS, all Armor, Cavalry, Infantry, Field Artillery, and Air Defense Artillery units were designated as elements of regiments. These were, however, regiments in name only; there was no regimental commander, and the units bearing the regiment's designation did not necessarily serve together in the same division or other major command.

The Army revamped CARS in the 1980s and re-named the system the U.S. Army Regimental System (USARS). The number of regiments with active units was reduced, many units received new designations, and most regiments were restructured to consist of, for example, two battalions or squadrons in the continental United States (CONUS) and two battalions or squadrons outside of CONUS (OCONUS). Most importantly, an effort was made to create true regimental spirit and cohesion by assigning soldiers to successive tours in the same regiment. Thus, a soldier would typically move from an assignment in one of his regiment's CONUS units to one of its OCONUS units, and vice versa. Unfortunately, the Army's personnel bureaucracy never embraced this system — which made personnel assignments more difficult than when soldiers were just moved willy-nilly from one unit to another — and USARS has never lived up to its potential for improving unit cohesion and readiness.

---

[6] Another medium weight unit that was active in 1990 was the Army's 9th Inf Div(Motorized)(-), which was stationed at Fort Lewis. The 9th was an experimental unit that was an attempt to create a division that would have the strategic deployability of a light division and the firepower and tactical mobility of a heavy division. The 9th was mounted largely in "Fast Attack Vehicles," militarized dune buggies that were unarmored and relied on speed and small size for protection. The motorized division was not a success, and the Army was in the process of inactivating it when Desert Shield began. See Chart 11, Footnote 10.

A typical designation under USARS is "1st Bn, 37th Armor," which is frequently abbreviated as "1-37 Armor" or "1/37 Armor."[7] In this case, 37th Armor is the regiment. Some units use the colloquial — but inaccurate — designation, e.g., "1st Bn, 37th Armored Regiment."

A handful of the Army's regiments are true regiments, with a regimental commander who commands the units of the regiment. During ODS, the Army had five such regiments: the 2nd, 3rd, and 11th Armored Cavalry Regiments, the 75th Ranger Regiment(Abn), and the 160th Special Operations Aviation Regiment(Abn). The 2nd and 3rd ACRs, along with elements of the 75th Ranger Regiment and the 160th SOAR, fought in the Gulf. See Chart 6. In addition, elements of the 11th ACR served in the Gulf under the Weapon System Replacement Operations program (see Chart 12), and most of the 11th ACR served in the Gulf after the war was over. See Chart 15.

Organization Of The Department Of Defense

The United States Department of Defense (DOD) consists of three armed services: the Army, Navy, and Air Force. In addition, the DOD includes the Marine Corps, which is a separate military service within the Department of the Navy.[8] These services are responsible for organizing, equipping, and training our military units. When these units go to war, however, they typically do so under a joint command — an organization that includes units from all of the armed services, and that directs the actions of all military units that are participating in the conflict. History has demonstrated that this approach is essential in order to ensure that all of the units from the various services are working together toward a common goal and not off fighting their own individual, uncoordinated wars.

---

[7] For the vast majority of Army units, the correct abbreviation is, for example, "1-37 Armor," not "1/37." The slash ("/") is only correct for the Army's true regiments (the 2nd, 3rd, and 11th ACRs, 75th Ranger Regt(Abn), and 160th SOAR(Abn)) and the Special Forces groups. Thus, while "1-37 Armor" is the correct abbreviation for the 1st Bn, 37th Armor, the correct abbreviation for the 2nd Sqdn, 3rd Armd Cavalry Regt is "2/3 ACR". This rule is widely violated, however, and units that should be abbreviated with a dash ("-") are instead frequently abbreviated with a slash ("/").

[8] The United States Coast Guard is normally part of the Department of Transportation but serves under the Navy during war time.

The United States Central Command

The Department of Defense has divided the surface of the earth into geographic areas, with each area the responsibility of a different joint command. Southwest Asia, the area where the Gulf War was fought, was the responsibility of the United States Central Command, generally called "CENTCOM." CENTCOM had its headquarters at MacDill Air Force Base in Florida.

In August 1990 when Iraq invaded Kuwait, CENTCOM was commanded by General H. Norman Schwarzkopf, a full (four-star) Army general whose background was in the infantry. General Schwarzkopf had served in combat in Vietnam. He commanded the 24th Infantry Division(Mech) in 1983-86 and the I Corps in 1986-87. As the Commander-in-Chief or "CINC" of CENTCOM, General Schwarzkopf reported directly to the Chairman of the Joint Chiefs of Staff, GEN Colin Powell, and was responsible for everything CENTCOM did or failed to do.

Reporting to GEN Schwarzkopf were a number of senior officers who were responsible for their service's contributions to CENTCOM's overall effort. In each case, the service component commander was a three-star flag officer (lieutenant generals for the Army, Air Force, and Marine Corps, a vice admiral for the Navy). In addition to these service-specific commands, a small joint special operations command, which was a functional command consisting of special operations units from the Army, Navy, and Air Force and was commanded by an Army full colonel, was assigned to CENTCOM. During peace time, however, the units assigned to CENTCOM were extremely limited. For example, no Army units were assigned, other than HQ, Third Army (the Army component command headquarters), primarily because America's allies in the region would not allow the stationing of American forces on their soil. Thus, it was expected that Army units would be assigned to CENTCOM once an emergency arose, in response to the specific circumstances that existed at the time.

Appendix B

Officer Rank Structure

This appendix lists, in ascending order, the ranks held by Army and Marine Corps officers and the assignments typically held at each rank.

Rank	Typical Assignment
Second Lieutenant (O-1)	Platoon Leader
First Lieutenant (O-2)	Platoon Leader or Detachment Commander
Captain (O-3)	Company Commander
Major (O-4)	Staff Officer
Lieutenant Colonel (O-5)	Battalion Commander
Colonel[1] (O-6)	Brigade, Regiment, or Group Commander
Brigadier General (O-7)	Assistant Division Commander
Major General (O-8)	Division Commander
Lieutenant General (O-9)	Corps or Army Commander (U.S. Army)
	MEF Commander (U.S. Marine Corps)
General (O-10)	Commander-in-Chief, Regional Joint Command

---

[1] Also known as "Full Colonel" or "Bird Colonel."

Order of Battle

Notes:

➢ The U.S. Army and Marine Corps use different abbreviations for these ranks:

	U.S. Army	U.S. Marine Corps
Second Lieutenant (O-1)	2LT	2dLT
First Lieutenant (O-2)	1LT	1stLt
Captain (O-3)	CPT	Capt
Major (O-4)	MAJ	Maj
Lieutenant Colonel (O-5)	LTC	LtCol
Colonel (O-6)	COL	Col
Brigadier General (O-7)	BG	BGen
Major General (O-8)	MG	MajGen
Lieutenant General (O-9)	LTG	LtGen
General (O-10)	GEN	Gen

Note the lack of punctuation.

Appendix C

Hierarchy Of Ground Units

This appendix lists Army and Marine Corps units in ascending order, from squad to theater level. For information on how Army units were organized during Desert Storm, see Appendix D. For information on how Marine Corps units were organized during Desert Storm, see Appendix E.[1]

Squad

A squad consists of approximately ten soldiers, led by a non-commissioned officer (sergeant).

Section

In certain types of units several squads are organized into a section, and several sections comprise a platoon. A section is led by a senior sergeant.

Platoon

Two to four squads, led by a lieutenant. In armored units, typically consists of four to six vehicles.

---

[1] For information on selected equipment used by Army units during Desert Storm, see Chart 13. For information on selected equipment used by Marine Corps units during Desert Storm, see Chart 24. For information on how British Army units were organized and equipped during Desert Storm, see Chart 27. For information on how French Army units were organized and equipped during Desert Storm, see Chart 28. For information on how Arab-Islamic units were organized and equipped during Desert Storm, see Chart 29.

Order of Battle

Company

Two to four platoons, plus a headquarters element. Commanded by a captain. In U.S. Army cavalry units, company-sized units are called "troops." In field artillery and air defense artillery units, company-sized units are called "batteries."

Battalion

Two to five company-sized units, plus a headquarters company or, in some units detachment. Commanded by a lieutenant colonel. In U.S. Army cavalry units, battalions are called "squadrons."

Brigade

U.S. Army: Two to seven battalion-sized units, plus a headquarters company and other supporting companies and platoons. Commanded by a full colonel.

U.S. Marine Corps: A Marine expeditionary brigade is an air-ground task force consisting of a reinforced infantry regiment, a Marine aircraft group, and a brigade service support group. Commanded by a brigadier general or major general, it typically consists of 10,000 to 20,000 personnel.

Regiment

U.S. Army: The equivalent of a brigade. Used in lieu of brigade in certain specialized units (armored cavalry regiments, the 75th Ranger Regiment(Abn), and the 160th Special Operations Aviation Regiment(Abn)).

U.S. Marine Corps: Two to five battalions, plus a headquarters company. Commanded by a full colonel. The Marines use "regiment" in lieu of "brigade" in their infantry and artillery units.

Group

U.S. Army: The equivalent of a brigade. Used in lieu of brigade for special forces groups and for many non-divisional non-combat arms support units, such as corps support groups. Commanded by a full colonel.

U.S. Marine Corps: The equivalent of a regiment. The Marines use "group" in their aviation units and in specialty units such as the surveillance, reconnaissance, and intelligence group. Commanded by a full colonel or, in the case of the force service support group, a brigadier general.

Division

The standard unit by which ground combat strength is measured. Commanded by a major general, with typically around 15,000 personnel, not including attachments. An Army division consists of three maneuver brigades, an aviation brigade, division artillery (DIVARTY), division support command (DISCOM), other units and, in some divisions, an engineer brigade. A Marine division consists of three infantry regiments, an artillery regiment, and other units. See Appendices D and E for more detailed information on the composition of, respectively, U.S. Army and U.S. Marine Corps divisions.

Command

U.S. Army: A division-level unit, almost always of non-combat arms support troops. Commanded by a full colonel, brigadier general, or major general. May have one or more groups or brigades assigned. The Army typically has a command as the senior unit in a theater of operations in each of several functional areas, such as engineer, personnel, and medical.

U.S. Marine Corps: A non-standard unit that is rarely used. Typically commanded by a brigadier general.

Corps (U.S. Army Only)

Consists of two to five divisions, other combat units, and a host of non-combat arms support units. Commanded by a lieutenant general. During Desert Storm, the XVIII Airborne Corps reached a strength of 116,000 personnel and the VII Corps reached a strength of 142,000 personnel. A corps is designated using roman numerals. Although pronounced, for example, "Seventh Corps," the designation is always written "VII Corps" rather than "VIIth Corps."

Marine Expeditionary Force (U.S. Marine Corps Only)

The senior Marine headquarters in a theater of operations, roughly equivalent to a U.S. Army corps. The MEF is an air-ground task force that consists of one or more Marine divisions, a Marine air wing, a force service support group, and a surveillance, reconnaissance, and intelligence group. Commanded by a lieutenant general, a MEF typically has about 50,000 personnel. A MEF is designated using roman numerals and is pronounced, for example, "One MEF."

Order of Battle

Army (U.S. Army Only)

The senior U.S. Army headquarters in a theater of operations. Consists of one or more corps and numerous theater-level support units. Commanded by a lieutenant general. The numerical designation of an Army is typically spelled out: "Third Army" rather than "3rd Army."

Regional Unified Command

Above Army (U.S. Army) and MEF (U.S. Marine Corps) is a joint, theater level headquarters that reports directly to the National Command Authority in Washington, DC. The headquarters responsible for the mideast is the United States Central Command (CENTCOM). Joint theater-level commands are commanded by full (four star) generals or admirals. CENTCOM is always commanded by an Army general or Marine Corps general.

Appendix D

Organization Of U.S. Army Units

This appendix provides information on how U.S. Army units were organized during Operation Desert Storm (ODS). For information on selected equipment used by Army units during Desert Storm, see Chart 13. For basic information on how ground combat units are organized and other basic background information about ground combat units, see Appendix A. For information on how U.S. Marine Corps units were organized during Desert Storm, see Appendix E.[1]

I. The Organization Of An Army Corps

The **corps** is the Army's senior warfighting organization. A corps is commanded by a lieutenant (three star) general with a major (two star) general as the deputy corps commander. During Desert Storm, a corps typically consisted of two to five **divisions**, an **armored cavalry regiment** and perhaps other non-divisional maneuver units, an **aviation brigade, corps artillery**, an air defense artillery unit, a **corps support command** (COSCOM), an **engineer brigade**, a **signal brigade**, a **military intelligence brigade**, a **civil affairs brigade**, a **personnel group**, and a **finance group**. The organization of a corps was flexible, however, and each corps

---

[1] For information on selected equipment used by Marine Corps units during Desert Storm, see Chart 24. For information on how British Army units were organized and equipped during Desert Storm, see Chart 27. For information on how French Army units were organized and equipped during Desert Storm, see Chart 28. For information on how Arab-Islamic units were organized and equipped during Desert Storm, see Chart 29.

was task-organized for its mission.[2] During Desert Storm, the XVIII Airborne Corps had 116,000 personnel and the VII Corps had 142,000 personnel.

A corps-level **aviation brigade** consisted of several helicopter-equipped battalions and separate companies that provided lift for air assault, re-supply, and command and control missions. These units flew the OH-58 "Kiowa" Observation Helicopter, the UH-1 "Huey" and UH-60 "Black Hawk" Utility Helicopters, and the CH-47 "Chinook" Medium Lift Helicopter. In addition, the aviation brigade had an attack capability provided by two attack helicopter battalions equipped with AH-64 "Apache" Attack Helicopters and OH-58 Kiowas. As a corps asset, these attack helicopters were used for deep-strike missions and other priority operations at the direction of the corps commander.

Corps artillery was typically commanded by a brigadier (one star) general and consisted of those field artillery units that the corps commander could use to weight his main effort. Corps artillery typically consisted of one or more **field artillery brigades**, each commanded by a full colonel and consisting of three to four field artillery battalions. In a high-intensity conflict such as Desert Storm, corps artillery usually consisted of at least one field artillery brigade for each division.

The corps' air defense artillery unit could be either an **air defense artillery brigade** consisting of several battalions and commanded by a full colonel, or a smaller battalion-sized unit commanded by a lieutenant colonel. During Desert Storm, the VII and XVIII Airborne Corps each had a reinforced battalion task force in lieu of a brigade.

The **COSCOM** was a logistics unit that was commanded by a full colonel or brigadier general and that consisted of several **corps support groups** and a **medical brigade**. One **corps support group** was typically attached to each division, to provide logistic support (such as transportation of supplies and maintenance of equipment) in the forward part of the corps area, while one or more other support groups provided logistic support on an area basis to all units located in the rear of the corps area. Each of the support groups was commanded by a full colonel. The **medical brigade** was commanded by a full colonel or brigadier general and provided medical support to all of the units within the corps. The medical brigade consisted of several **medical groups**, each commanded by a full colonel. Assigned to these medical groups were various hospitals, medical battalions, and other medical units, such as helicopter medical evacuation units.

---

[2] For example, when the XVIII Airborne Corps went into Panama in 1989 pursuant to Operation Just Cause, it did not deploy any corps artillery or corps-level air defense artillery, as those capabilities were not needed in that operation.

The other support units assigned to the corps — the various functional-area brigades and groups — were each commanded by a full colonel. Most typically consisted of several battalions, all of the same branch as the brigade/group to which they were assigned. The **engineer brigade**, however, was noticeably larger than the other brigades, and consisted of several **engineer groups**. Each such group was commanded by a full colonel and consisted of several battalions. During Desert Storm, some engineer groups were attached to divisions, while others supported the corps' overall effort.

II. The Organization Of An Army Division

The premier war-fighting organization of the United States Army is the division. A division is authorized a major general as its commander, two assistant division commanders (both brigadier generals; one is responsible for maneuver, the other for support), and typically has around 15,000 soldiers assigned.[3] Attachments during wartime can greatly increase these numbers, however. The division is a combined-arms organization, which means it has a wide variety of arms (armor, infantry, field artillery, and air defense artillery) and services (such as maintenance, medical, and signal) necessary for combat operations on the modern battlefield.[4] The division is also the largest unit that has a fixed organization; the echelons above division are flexible, non-standard units that are task-organized for each operation.

During ODS, an Army division had six subordinate commands, each commanded by a full colonel: three maneuver brigades, an aviation brigade, division artillery (DIVARTY), and the division support command (DISCOM).[5] There were also several battalions and companies outside this framework that reported directly to division headquarters and that were frequently referred to as "division troops."

How the division's units task-organized for combat can be a little complex. While the maneuver brigades and aviation brigade typically operated as cohesive units under their respective commanders, the other commands typically did not, and instead farmed out most or all of their assets to the maneuver brigades and other divisional units. For example, the division's air defense artillery battalion never operated as a

---

[3] Army light infantry divisions only had about 10,000 soldiers. No light infantry divisions served in Desert Storm, however.

[4] Contrast this to, for example, the Civil War, when most divisions consisted almost solely of either infantry or cavalry units, with few artillery or logistics units.

[5] In addition, as explained below, some divisions had an engineer element commanded by a full colonel.

cohesive unit under the control of the battalion commander. Rather, the battalion detached a battery or a battery(-) to each of the division's maneuver brigades, with the remaining ADA units supporting the division's other units.[6] The packet of units that are attached to, for example, a maneuver brigade are that brigade's "slice" of divisional assets.

A. Maneuver Brigades

Most of the soldiers who actually closed with the enemy were assigned to the division's maneuver brigades, which were typically numbered as the 1st, 2nd, and 3rd Brigades. In light divisions, each maneuver brigade consisted of three infantry battalions, for a total of nine such battalions in the division. The 82nd Airborne Division, however, had an additional maneuver battalion, an airborne armor battalion equipped with the M551A1(TTS) "Sheridan" Armored Reconnaissance/Airborne Assault Vehicle.

In heavy divisions, each maneuver brigade consisted of a mix of three or four tank and mechanized infantry battalions, for a total of nine or ten maneuver battalions per division.[7] In theory, the difference between an armored division and a mechanized division was that an armored division had six tank battalions and four mechanized infantry battalions, whereas a mechanized division had five tank and five mechanized infantry battalions. This varied in practice, however.[8] In any event, the difference between an armored division and a mechanized division was pretty slim.

1. Maneuver Battalions

The division's maneuver battalions were the units that actually closed with the enemy. The divisions that deployed to the KTO included five such types of units: tank, airborne armor, mechanized infantry, airborne infantry, and air assault infantry.

---

[6] Other divisional units that were farmed out in this manner were the engineer battalion, signal battalion, military intelligence battalion, military police company, and chemical decontamination company.

[7] If the brigade had mostly tank battalions it was "tank heavy." If it had mostly mechanized infantry battalions it was "mech heavy." If it had equal numbers of tank and mechanized infantry units, it was "balanced." This terminology was also used for the combined arms units formed at battalion level (battalion task force) and company level (company team), as explained below.

[8] Four full strength heavy divisions served in Desert Storm. The 1st and 3rd Armd Divs each had six tank battalions and four mechanized infantry battalions, the 1st Inf Div(M) had six tank battalions and three mechanized infantry battalions, and the 24th Inf Div(M) had four tank battalions and five mechanized infantry battalions. The 1st Cav Div(-), which was short one brigade, had four tank battalions and two mechanized infantry battalions.

a. Tank Battalions

A tank battalion consisted of a headquarters & headquarters company, and four tank companies (Companies A-D). In addition to the commander and staff responsible for planning and directing the battalion's operations, the headquarters company included maintenance, support,[9] medical, and communications platoons that supported the battalion's operations. In addition, the headquarters company included three combat arms units: a tank section, a scout platoon, and a mortar platoon. The tank section consisted of two tanks, one for the battalion commander and one for the operations officer. Most scout platoons consisted of six M3 series CFVs,[10] and the mortar platoon consisted of six M106 series self-propelled 4.2" mortars. Each of the four tank companies was authorized 14 tanks, organized into a company headquarters of two tanks (one for the company commander and one for the executive officer) and three tank platoons, each with four tanks. Thus, each tank battalion was authorized 58 tanks.

b. Airborne Armor Battalion

The 3rd Bn(Abn), 73rd Armor, the 82nd Airborne Division's airborne armor battalion, used a somewhat different organization. Although the headquarters company had two M551A1 Sheridans, these vehicles were never deployed from Fort Bragg. As a result, the 3rd Bn, 73rd Armor went into combat with only 56 Sheridans, 14 in each tank company. The battalion commander used an M113A2 APC as a command track. In addition, the scout platoon had 14 LAV-25 armored vehicles (and one LAV-R recovery vehicle) that the Army borrowed from the Marines for evaluation purposes. It appears the 3rd Bn, 73rd Armor did not have a mortar platoon.

---

[9] The support platoon was a logistics unit that consisted of trucks that transported the ammunition, fuel, and other items needed to keep the battalion operating.

[10] In March 1990, the Army decided to convert the scout platoons of tank and mechanized infantry battalions from six M3 series Bradleys to ten HMMWVs. This approach increased the number of recon platforms in the platoon and facilitated a more stealthy approach to reconnaissance, but was not appropriate for desert operations in the Mid-East. In Desert Storm, about 70 percent of the scout platoons in tank and mechanized infantry battalions were equipped with M3 series Bradleys, another 15 percent used HMMWVs, and the remaining scout platoons used (1) a combination of Bradleys and HMMWVs; (2) M113 series APCs and M901A1 Improved TOW Vehicles; or (3) the LAV-25. Only one battalion, the 82nd Abn Div's 3-73 Armor(Abn), used LAV-25s.

c. Mechanized Infantry Battalions

A mechanized infantry battalion consisted of a headquarters & headquarters company, four mechanized infantry companies (Companies A-D) and, in some battalions, an antiarmor company (Company E). In addition to the commander and staff responsible for planning and directing the battalion's operations, the headquarters company included maintenance, support,[11] medical, and communications platoons that supported the battalion's operations. In addition, the headquarters company included several combat arms elements: a headquarters section, a scout platoon, and a mortar platoon. The headquarters section included two Bradleys, one for the battalion commander and one for the operations officer. The scout platoon typically consisted of six M3 series CFVs,[12] and the mortar platoon consisted of six M106 series self-propelled 4.2" mortars. Each of the four mechanized infantry companies was authorized 13 Bradleys, organized into a company headquarters with one Bradley for the company commander, and three mechanized infantry platoons, each with four Bradleys.[13] In addition to its four Bradleys, each platoon consisted of platoon headquarters and three small rifle squads (each included two M249 Squad Automatic Weapons and one M47 Dragon antitank missile launcher).[14] Thus, each mechanized infantry battalion was authorized 54 M2 series IFVs.[15]

Prior to Desert Storm, each mechanized infantry battalion had an antiarmor company equipped with 12 M901A1 Improved TOW Vehicles (ITV) organized into three platoons of four ITVs each. This unit was a holdover from the days when mechanized infantry battalions were equipped with M113 series APCs. Once the Bradley, with its double-barrel TOW launcher, was fielded there was little need for an antiarmor company, and the ITV's mobility and reliability left much to be desired. Nonetheless, the ITV soldiered on and the ten mechanized infantry battalions that deployed for Desert Shield from CONUS each brought an antiarmor company with ITVs.[16] The nine mechanized infantry battalions that deployed from Europe did not bring any ITVs, however, as their antiarmor companies were inactivated before these battalions deployed to SWA.

---

[11] See Footnote 9.

[12] See Footnote 10.

[13] During Desert Storm, however, at least some units, specifically from the 3rd Armd Div, obtained one additional Bradley for each mechanized infantry company and issued these vehicles to company executive officers.

[14] It appears that some mechanized infantry platoons went to a new organization shortly before Desert Storm, with four small fire teams (one in each Bradley) plus the platoon leadership.

[15] Two of the mechanized infantry battalions that served in ODS, the 197th Inf Bde(M)'s 1-18 Inf(M) and 2-18 Inf(M), were equipped with M113 series APCs in lieu of Bradleys.

[16] See Chart 13, Footnote 21.

d. Airborne And Air Assault Infantry Battalions

Airborne and air assault infantry battalions were organized differently from their mechanized brethren and consisted of a headquarters & headquarters company, three rifle companies (Companies A-C), and an antiarmor company (Company D). In addition to the commander and staff responsible for planning and directing the battalion's operations, the headquarters company included support,[17] medical, and communications platoons, and a maintenance section. In addition, the headquarters company included two combat arms units: a scout platoon mounted in HMMWVs and a mortar platoon equipped with four 81mm mortars. The antiarmor company was equipped with 20 HMMWVs mounting TOW missile launchers, organized into five platoons each with four TOW HMMWVs.

Each rifle company was authorized company headquarters, three rifle platoons, and a mortar section with two M224 60mm Mortars.[18] Each rifle platoon consisted of three rifle squads, a weapons squad, and the platoon leadership. Each rifle squad had nine soldiers: five armed with M16 Rifles, two with the M16 Rifle/M203 40mm Grenade Launcher combination, and two with the M249 5.56mm Squad Automatic Weapon. The weapons squad had two M60 7.62mm Machine Guns and two Dragon antitank missile systems.

2. Battalion Task Forces and Company Teams

Tank and mechanized infantry battalions existed during peace time as separate entities that were not combined arms units. During combat these battalions typically reorganized their assets to create combined arms units at the battalion or company level.

Tank and mechanized infantry battalions typically formed combined arms task forces by cross attaching one or more companies. For example, in a tank heavy brigade with two tank battalions and one mechanized infantry battalion, each tank battalion might trade one tank company to the mechanized infantry battalion, which would give up two of its mechanized infantry companies, one to each of the tank battalions. This would yield two tank heavy battalion task forces (each with three tank

---

[17] See Footnote 9.

[18] This is the organization used by airborne rifle companies. Air assault rifle companies may have used a slightly different approach, but the basic concept and the numbers and types of heavy weapons were the same.

companies and one mechanized infantry company) and one balanced task force with two tank companies and two mechanized infantry companies. This was the approach used by the 3rd Brigade, 1st Armored Division. See Chart 4A, page 4A-3.

Alternatively, during Desert Storm a significant number of tank battalions (but no mechanized infantry battalions) fought as pure battalions. In this situation, a tank heavy brigade would fight with one pure tank battalion (with four tank companies), and two balanced battalion task forces, each with two tank companies and two mechanized infantry companies. If the mechanized infantry battalion deployed with an antiarmor company, that company typically remained intact with its parent mechanized infantry battalion. This was the approach used by the 1st Brigade, 1st Infantry Division(Mech). See Chart 4A, pages 4A-6 and 4A-7.

Combined arms were also sometimes created at the company level using the same cross attachment process, with tank and mechanized infantry companies trading platoons. For information concerning how heavy units created combined arms battalion task forces and company teams, see Chart 4A. To avoid confusion, companies and company teams within a battalion task force were frequently referred to using their type and letter designation under the phonetic alphabet. Thus, a balanced task force such as TF 2-34 Armor, 1st Brigade, 1st Infantry Division(Mech) would refer to its company teams as "Alpha Mech," "Bravo Tank," "Charlie Tank," and "Delta Mech." See Chart 4A, page 4A-7.

B. Aviation Brigade

The aviation brigade[19] included a headquarters & headquarters company, the divisional cavalry squadron, one or more attack helicopter battalions, and lift and command aviation units. Each heavy division was supposed to have one assault helicopter company with 15 UH-60 Black Hawks and one command aviation company with six OH-58 Kiowas, six UH-1 Hueys, and three EH-60 "Quickfix" electronic warfare helicopters. However, most divisions combined these two companies into a provisional battalion.[20]

---

[19] The official designation of this organization was "Avn Bde, __ Division," however many divisions referred to their aviation brigade as the "4th Bde," and the 82nd and 101st Abn Divs sometimes referred to their aviation brigades as the 82nd and 101st Avn Bdes. See Chart 4, Footnotes 11, 16, 26, 49, 57.

[20] All of the heavy divisions that served in Desert Storm used this approach with the exception of the 1st Cav Div(-). The 82nd Abn Div was authorized an aviation battalion consisting of a headquarters & headquarters company, a command aviation company with 12 OH-58s and three EH-60s, two assault helicopter companies (each with 15 UH-60s), and an aviation maintenance company.

1. Attack Helicopter Battalions

All but one of the attack helicopter battalions deployed during Operation Desert Storm were equipped with the AH-64A Apache Attack Helicopter.[21] Each Apache attack helicopter battalion consisted of a headquarters & headquarters company[22] (with one OH-58C or D and three UH-60s), three attack helicopter companies (Companies A-C, each with a scout platoon of four OH-58Cs or Ds, and an attack, or "gun" platoon, of six AH-64As), and a maintenance company (Company D), for a total of 18 AH-64s, 13 OH-58s, and three UH-60s.

In keeping with its status as an air assault division, the 101st Airborne Division(Air Aslt)'s aviation brigade was much larger than other division's. The 101st's aviation brigade consisted of an air cavalry squadron, two attack helicopter battalions (one with AH-64A Apaches and one with AH-1F Cobras), three assault helicopter battalions, a command and control (C&C) aviation battalion, and a medium helicopter battalion. Each assault helicopter battalion had 30 UH-60s. The C&C battalion had 30 UH-1s. The medium helicopter battalion had 45 CH-47s and three UH-1s.

2. Divisional Cavalry Squadrons

In heavy divisions, the cavalry squadron was authorized a headquarters & headquarters troop, two (ground) cavalry troops (Troops A & B), and two air cavalry troops (Troops C & D). In addition to the commander and staff responsible for planning and directing the squadron's operations, the headquarters troop included maintenance, support,[23] medical, communications, and aircraft maintenance platoons[24] that supported the squadron's operations.[25] In addition, the headquarters troop had two M3

---

[21] The one exception was the 101st Abn Div(AAslt)'s 3-101 Avn(AH), which had seven AH-1Fs per attack company, for a total of 21 in the battalion. Some Apache battalions managed to field 19 AH-64s in the Gulf, rather than the 18 that were authorized. These were probably operational readiness float aircraft intended to replace unit aircraft that were down for one reason or another.

[22] Some units appear to have had a headquarters and service company, but this appears to be largely a semantic difference.

[23] As in maneuver battalions, the support platoon was a logistics unit that consisted of trucks that transported the ammunition, fuel, and other items needed to keep the squadron operating.

[24] At least two squadrons, the 1st Inf Div(M)'s 1-4 Cav and the 24th Inf Div(M)'s 2-4 Cav, had an aircraft maintenance troop (Trp E) in lieu of an aircraft maintenance platoon.

[25] As originally fielded in the mid-1980s, each cavalry squadron included a long range surveillance (LRS) detachment, a small unit of dismounted solders who provided intelligence through insertion deep into enemy territory. Prior to Desert Storm, however, the LRS detachments were transferred to the divisional military intelligence

series Cavalry Fighting Vehicles (one for the squadron commander and one for the operations officer) and one UH-60 Black Hawk. Each of the two cavalry troops was authorized 19 M3 series Bradleys and three M106 series self-propelled 4.2" mortars, organized into a troop headquarters with one Bradley for the troop commander, a mortar section with three M106s, and three scout platoons, each with six Bradleys. Each of the two air cavalry troops consisted of troop headquarters, a scout platoon with six OH-58C Kiowa Observation Helicopters, and an attack platoon with four AH-1F "Cobra" Attack Helicopters. This yielded a total for the squadron of 40 Bradleys, six M106 series self-propelled 4.2" mortars, 12 OH-58Cs, eight AH-1Fs, and one UH-60.

In Desert Storm, however, the actual organizations and equipment used by some heavy division cavalry squadrons varied substantially from the table of organization and equipment (TOE). These variations were fueled, in large measure, by the widely-held perception within the Armor community that divisional cavalry squadrons needed tanks in order to perform their missions.[26] Of the five heavy divisions in SWA, two substantially modified their cavalry squadrons by adding tanks (the 1st and 24th Infantry Divisions(Mech)), two left their squadrons pretty much as specified by the TOE (the 1st and 3rd Armored Divisions), and one expanded its cavalry squadron by adding two (ground) troops, but otherwise did not reorganize it (the 1st Cavalry Division(-)).

a. 1st Infantry Division(Mech)

The 1st Infantry Division(Mech)'s 1st Sqdn, 4th Cavalry obtained nine Modified M1A1 Main Battle Tanks and reorganized its two ground troops as follows.[27] Troop A consisted of troop headquarters, three scout platoons, a mortar section, and a specially-organized "Headquarters Reconnaissance/Security Platoon." Troop headquarters received two M3A2 CFVs,[28] one for the commanding officer and an extra (unauthorized) Bradley for the executive officer. Two of the three scout platoons adhered to the TOE, each receiving six M3A2 CFVs. The final scout platoon received two M3A2 CFVs and three Modified M1A1 MBTs. The mortar section had three M106A2 self-propelled 4.2" mortars. Finally, four M3A2s were used to from the "Headquarters Reconnaissance/Security Platoon," which was detached to the squadron combat trains.[29]

---

battalions. See Chart 9, page 9-7.

[26] The Army went through a substantial reorganization in the mid-1980s and, as a part of this reorganization, tanks were eliminated from the divisional cavalry squadron.

[27] This squadron otherwise used the standard organization of a heavy division cavalry squadron. Headquarters Troop had two M3A2 CFVs.

[28] These M3A2s replaced the earlier versions of the M3 that the division had deployed with. See Chart 13, pages 13-5 and 13-6.

[29] The squadron's logistics elements were split between the combat trains, which were closer to the front lines, and

Troop B used a similar approach, however it received six Modified M1A1s and did not form a headquarters reconnaissance/security platoon. As a result, it had one platoon with six M3A2s and no tanks, and two platoons each with six M3A2s and three tanks. Finally, the 1st Sqdn, 4th Cavalry's aviation elements, Troops C and D, adhered to the TOE. Each troop had a scout platoon with six OH-58Cs and a gun platoon with four AH-1Fs.

b. 24th Infantry Division(Mech)

The 24th Infantry Division(Mech) used another approach in its cavalry squadron, the 2nd Sqdn, 4th Cavalry. The squadron's two air cavalry troops (Troops C and D) and aviation maintenance troop (Troop E) were pulled from the squadron and organized into a separate battalion-level organization, "Task Force Air Cav," which operated under the division's aviation brigade. The ground elements served under the direct control of division headquarters as "Task Force 2-4 Cav."

Task Force 2-4 Cav included the squadron's sole organic ground unit, Troop A; Troop D, 4th Cavalry, formerly assigned to the 197th Infantry Brigade(Mech); Company D, 3rd Bn, 69th Armor, detached from the 2nd Brigade; and, for about half the war, Battery A, 13th FA, the 24th Infantry Division(Mech)'s MLRS battery. Troop A was organized as a standard divisional ground cavalry troop with 19 M3A1 CFVs and three M106 series self-propelled mortars. Troop D was organized as a regimental armored cavalry troop, but had M113 series vehicles in lieu of Bradleys as its parent unit, the 197th Infantry Brigade(Mech), had not been upgraded to Bradleys at the time Desert Shield began. Troop D consisted of two scout platoons (each with three M113 series APCs and three M901 series ITVs), two tank platoons (each with four Modified M1A1 MBTs), a mortar section with three M106 series self-propelled 4.2" mortars (one more than normal for a regimental troop), and a Modified M1A1 for the troop commander. Company D, 3rd Bn, 69th Armor was a standard tank company with 14 Modified M1A1 MBTs, and Battery A, 13th FA was a standard MLRS battery with nine MLRS launchers. During the night of February 24/25, 1991, however, the squadron reorganized Troop A and Company D, 3rd Bn, 69th Armor to give both units a mix of scout and tank platoons.[30]

---

the field trains, which were further to the rear.

[30] This was probably accomplished by each unit detaching to the other one platoon.

c. 82nd Airborne Division

The 82nd Airborne Division and 101st Airborne Division(Air Aslt) each used a different approach for their divisional cavalry squadrons. The 82nd Airborne Division's 1st Sqdn(Air), 17th Cavalry apparently consisted of a headquarters & headquarters troop, three air cavalry troops (Troops A-C), an assault helicopter troop (Troop D), and an aviation maintenance troop (probably designated Troop E). The air cavalry troops apparently used the standard organization, each consisting of a scout platoon with six OH-58s and an attack platoon with four AH-1Fs. The assault helicopter troop apparently had eight UH-60s. Thus, the squadron had a total of 18 OH-58s, 12 AH-1Fs, and eight UH-60s.

d. 101st Airborne Division(Air Aslt)

The 101st Airborne Division(Air Aslt)'s 2nd Sqdn(Air), 17th Cavalry, consisted of a headquarters & headquarters troop, three air cavalry troops (Troops A-C), an assault helicopter/command & control/CEWI troop (Troop D), and an aviation maintenance troop (Troop E).[31] The air cavalry troops used an unusual approach, called the "6 x 6 cav/attack organization." Under this approach, each troop had a scout platoon with six OH-58Cs and a gun platoon with six AH-1Fs. Finally, Troop D had ten UH-60 Black Hawks, giving the squadron a total of 18 OH-58Cs, 18 AH-1Fs, and ten UH-60s.

C. Division Artillery

Division artillery provided indirect fire support for the division's maneuver units. In heavy divisions, DIVARTY consisted of three direct support (DS) field artillery battalions, a general support (GS) battery, and a target acquisition battery. Each maneuver brigade was supported by a DS battalion with 24 M109 series self-propelled 155mm howitzers. The GS battery had nine M270 MLRS rocket launchers. The target acquisition battery was equipped with three AN/TPQ-36 Mortar Locating Radars, two AN/TPQ-37 Artillery Locating Radars, and one AN/TPS-25 Ground Surveillance Radar.[32] The Q-36 and Q-37 were used to detect and track incoming mortar and artillery fire so that friendly artillery could quickly return counter battery fire to destroy or suppress the enemy's artillery.[33]

---

[31] The 101st Abn Div(AAslt)'s LRS detachment and pathfinder detachment were apparently attached to the 2-17 Cav(Air).

[32] The AN/TPS-25 was an exceedingly old radar that was used to detect and track movement of enemy vehicles at night. It apparently played little or no role in Desert Storm.

[33] The three AN/TPQ-36s were typically attached, one each, to the division's three DS field artillery battalions, with the AN/TPQ-37s held as a GS asset.

In light divisions, the DS battalions were equipped with 18 M102 towed 105mm howitzers. The 82nd Airborne Division had no organic GS or TA artillery units, but GS M198 towed 155mm howitzers were attached for ODS. The 101st Airborne Division(Air Aslt) had an organic TA detachment, and GS M198 towed 155mm howitzers were attached for ODS.

D. Division Support Command

As with DIVARTY, the heavy division's division support command (DISCOM) consisted of DS and GS units. Each DISCOM included three DS forward support battalions, one per maneuver brigade. Each forward support battalion consisted of a headquarters & headquarters detachment, supply company (Company A), maintenance company (Company B), and medical company (Company C). General support units consisted of the DISCOM headquarters & headquarters company/material management center, a main support battalion, and an aviation intermediate maintenance (AVIM) company.[34] The main support battalion consisted of a headquarters & headquarters detachment, supply & service company (Company A), transportation company (Company B), light maintenance company (Company C), heavy maintenance company (Company D), missile support company (Company E), and medical support company (Company F).

The 82nd Airborne Division and 101st Airborne Division(Air Aslt) used a different approach, however. Instead of having multi-functional forward and main support battalions, in the 82nd and 101st the DISCOM consisted of a headquarters & headquarters company; a medical battalion consisting of a headquarters & headquarters company, and three line companies (Companies A-C)[35]; a supply and transportation (S&T) battalion consisting of a headquarters & headquarters detachment, three forward support companies (Companies A-C), and a transportation company (Company D)[36]; a maintenance battalion consisting of a headquarters and headquarters & light maintenance company, three forward support companies, and a heavy maintenance

---

[34] In some divisions, the AVIM company was assigned to the aviation brigade. The 1st and 3rd Armd Divs had reorganized their AVIM companies as provisional aviation support battalions which were then reassigned from DISCOM to the aviation brigade. These battalions apparently consisted of a headquarters element, Co A (fuel supply), Co B (vehicle repair), and Co C (AVIM).

[35] In addition, the 101st's medical battalion had an air ambulance (medevac) company equipped with helicopters (Co D).

[36] In addition, the 82nd's S&T battalion had an airdrop equipment support (parachute rigger) company (Co E).

company; and an aviation maintenance unit.[37] The 82nd had an aviation maintenance company, while the 101st had an aviation maintenance battalion (consisting of a headquarters and headquarters & supply company and two aviation maintenance companies) because of the large number of helicopters operated by that division.

E. Division Engineers

Prior to the late 1980s, each Army division had a single engineer battalion. Heavy divisions had a large battalion with a headquarters & headquarters company and five line companies (Companies A-E), while the 82nd Airborne Division and 101st Airborne Division(Air Aslt) had smaller battalions with a headquarters & headquarters company and three line companies (Companies A-C). Shortly before Desert Storm, the Army began reorganizing heavy divisions' engineer assets into an engineer brigade of three small battalions, one DS to each maneuver brigade. Some of the heavy divisions that fought in Desert Storm had begun to implement this initiative, and had a full colonel as the "Regimental Engineer," and two or more engineer battalions.[38] Under this new approach, the divisional engineer brigade was to have a headquarters & headquarters detachment and three engineer battalions, each with a headquarters & headquarters company, three combat engineer companies, and a support platoon.

F. Division Troops

Finally, each division had an assortment of other units that reported directly to division headquarters. These units are referred to collectively as "division troops," however, unlike the other subelements described above, there was no commander of division troops. Division troops included: an air defense artillery battalion; an engineer battalion, for those divisions that did not have an engineer brigade; a signal battalion; a military intelligence battalion(CEWI); a military police company; a chemical decontamination company; and a division band.[39]

---

[37] For field operations, however, the 82nd and 101st formed three multi-functional battalion-sized logistics task forces, each of which provided a complete spectrum of logistic support to the maneuver brigade it supported.

[38] It appears that the 1st Armd Div, 3rd Armd Div, and 1st Inf Div(M) had begun to implement this initiative by the time Desert Storm had begun. While these divisions each had a full colonel in command of its engineer units, the engineer brigade headquarters was not activated until after ODS.

[39] In some divisions, the chemical company and/or division band were assigned to the DISCOM, rather than being division troops. Each division also had an attached personal services company and finance support unit which were typically division troops, but were sometimes attached to the DISCOM.

The signal battalion was authorized a headquarters & headquarters company, and three line companies (Companies A-C). The military intelligence battalion was authorized a headquarters and headquarters & service company, three line companies (Companies A-C), and a long range surveillance detachment.[40]

III. The Organization Of An Armored Cavalry Regiment

Each armored cavalry regiment was authorized a headquarters & headquarters troop, three armored cavalry squadrons, an aviation squadron, a support squadron, and several other support units. The regimental headquarters troop included two Bradleys, one for the regimental commander and one for the operations officer, along with the commander and staff responsible for planning and directing the regiment's operations.

Each armored cavalry squadron consisted of a headquarters & headquarters troop, three armored cavalry troops, a tank company, and a howitzer battery.[41] In addition to the commander and staff responsible for planning and directing the squadron's operations, the headquarters troop included maintenance, support,[42] medical, and communications platoons. In addition, the headquarters troop included two Bradleys, one for the squadron commander and one for the operations officer.

Each armored cavalry troop consisted of a troop headquarters, with one M1A1 series tank for the troop commander; two scout platoons (1st & 3rd Platoons), each with six Bradleys; two tank platoons (2d & 4th Platoons), each with four M1A1 series tanks; a mortar section with two M106 series self-propelled 4.2" mortars; and a maintenance section with an M88A1 recovery vehicle and an M113 series APC. Although normally equipped with M3 series Cavalry Fighting Vehicles, the

---

[40] In some divisions the LRSD was known as "Company D," however this was an unofficial designation and all such units were detachment-sized.

[41] These company-level units were designated as follows:

	Armored Cavalry Troops	Tank Company
1st Sqdn	Troops A-C	Company D
2nd Sqdn	Troops E-G	Company H
3rd Sqdn	Troops I, K, L	Company M

In accordance with U.S. Army tradition, there was no Troop J. Howitzer batteries did not receive an alphabetical designation and were designated, _e.g._, "Howitzer Battery, 2nd Squadron."

[42] See Footnote 23.

2nd Armored Cavalry Regiment took M2A2 Infantry Fighting Vehicles into combat in Desert Storm.

The tank company represented the squadron's heavy punch. It was organized as a standard tank company, with 14 M1A1 series tanks organized into three tank platoons with four M1A1s each, and two M1A1s in the company headquarters. Finally, the squadron had an organic artillery capability in the form of its howitzer battery. This unit had eight M109 series self-propelled 155mm howitzers, organized into two platoons of four howitzers each.

Thus, each regimental armored cavalry squadron was authorized 38 M3 series CFVs, 41 M1A1 Main Battle Tanks, six M106 series self-propelled 4.2" mortars, and eight M109 series self-propelled 155mm howitzers. This gave each armored cavalry regiment 116 Bradleys, 123 M1A1s, 18 M106 series self-propelled 4.2" mortars, and 24 M109 series self-propelled 155mm howitzers.

Each armored cavalry regiment was also authorized an aviation squadron that consisted of a headquarters & headquarters troop, three air cavalry troops (Troops N, O & P), two attack helicopter troops (Troops Q & R), an assault helicopter troop (Troop S), and an aviation maintenance troop (Troop T). The headquarters troop had one OH-58, three UH-60s, and three EH-60 electronic warfare helicopters. The air cavalry troops used the same organization as the troops assigned to divisional cavalry squadrons. Each consisted of a troop headquarters, a scout platoon with six OH-58 Observation Helicopters, and an attack platoon with four AH-1F Attack Helicopters. The attack helicopter troops used the same organization as attack helicopter companies equipped with the AH-1F Cobra. Each attack troop consisted of troop headquarters, a scout platoon with four OH-58s, and an attack platoon with seven AH-1Fs. Finally, Troop S had 15 UH-60s.

The regiment's support units consisted of a support squadron and separate engineer, chemical, and military intelligence companies. The support squadron had a headquarters & headquarters troop, and supply & transportation, maintenance, and medical troops.

IV. Field Artillery

The direct support towed 105mm battalions that were assigned to the 82nd Airborne Division and 101st Airborne Division(Air Aslt) consisted of a headquarters and headquarters & service battery, and three firing batteries (Batteries A-C). All other field artillery battalions equipped with howitzers (155mm towed, 155mm self-propelled, and 203mm self-propelled) consisted of a headquarters & headquarters battery, three firing batteries (Batteries A-C), and a service battery. MLRS battalions consisted of a headquarters and headquarters & service battery, and three firing batteries (Batteries A-C).

As of the early 1980s, all U.S. Army 105mm and 155mm field artillery units were authorized six howitzers, or "tubes," per battery, while 203mm units were authorized only four tubes per battery.[43] Commencing in 1986, the Army began converting all of its 155mm and 203mm units to eight tubes per battery,[44] and the vast majority of Active Army units had been so upgraded by the time Desert Storm began.

All of the towed 155mm units that served in Desert Storm were authorized eight tubes per battery. All of the self-propelled 155mm units that served in Desert Storm were authorized eight tubes per battery, with the exception of three or four battalions that were still authorized six tubes per battery.[45] The two Active Army self-propelled 203mm battalions that served in Desert Storm were authorized eight tubes per battery,[46] while the four Army National Guard self-propelled 203mm battalions were still organized under the old TOE and only authorized four tubes per battery.[47] MLRS units were authorized nine MLRS launchers per battery, although at least three batteries had ten launchers each.[48]

Target acquisition batteries and detachments were organic to divisions and/or corps field artillery brigades. Each TA battery was authorized three AN/TPQ-36 radars and two AN/TPQ-37 radars. Each TA detachment was authorized two AN/TPQ-37 radars.

---

[43] U.S. Army field artillery battalions typically have three firing batteries per battalion. Thus, a battalion with three firing batteries, each with six howitzers, would be referred to as a "3 x 6" battalion.

[44] Some 203mm units had already converted to six howitzers per battery.

[45] These were: 1-17 FA, 75th FA Bde; 2-17 FA, 212th FA Bde; 1-201 FA [WV ARNG], 18th FA Bde(Abn); and possibly 3-18 FA, 3rd ACR.

[46] These were: 2-18 FA, 212th FA Bde; and 5-18 FA, initially 42nd FA Bde and later 75th FA Bde.

[47] These were: 1-142 FA and 2-142 FA, 142nd FA Bde [AR ARNG]; and 1-181 FA [TN ARNG] and 1-623 FA [KY ARNG], 196th FA Bde [TN ARNG].

[48] These were Btry A, 21st FA, 1st Cav Div(-); Btry A, 40th FA, 3rd Armd Div; and Btry A, 92nd FA, which was attached to the 2nd Marine Div.

Order of Battle

V. Air Defense Artillery

A. Divisional Air Defense Artillery

The standard divisional ADA battalion consisted of a headquarters & headquarters battery and three firing batteries (Batteries A-C). The headquarters battery included a "Stinger" missile element (15 Stinger teams in heavy divisions, 20 teams in the air assault and airborne division), while each firing battery had nine "Vulcans" (self-propelled M163s in heavy divisions, towed M167s in light divisions) and 20 Stinger teams, organized into three Vulcan platoons and one Stinger platoon.

These were the norms, but during ODS they were outnumbered by the exceptions. Four of the five heavy divisions varied materially from the standard TOE: the 1st Armored Division, 3rd Armored Division, 1st Cavalry Division(-), and 1st Infantry Division(Mech). The 1st Armored Division was one of only two divisions in SWA that had a battery (Battery D) of the venerable M730 series "Chaparral" self-propelled missile system in its ADA battalion, the 6th Bn(Vulc/Chap/Stinger), 3rd ADA. In addition, the 6th Bn, 3rd ADA used the forward area alerting radar crewmen in its headquarters battery to form 12 additional Stinger teams.

The 3rd Armored Division was the second division that had a battery of Chaparrals in its ADA battalion, the 5th Bn(Vulc/Chap/Stinger), 3rd ADA. In addition, the 3rd Armored Division had extra Stinger teams, some from the 3rd Bn, 5th ADA and others in a provisional Stinger Platoon formed by the 5th Bn, 3rd ADA.[49]

The 1st Cavalry Division(-) was unique in that it had the Army's first battery equipped with the "Avenger" air defense system. The 1st Cavalry Division(-) had six platoons of Avengers as Battery D of its ADA battalion, the 4th Bn(Vulc/Avenger/Stinger), 5th ADA. In addition, Battery B was detached from the division and served with the 1st Brigade, 2nd Armored Division in MARCENT.

The 1st Infantry Division(Mech) varied from the TOE by having additional Stinger teams. When the 3rd Brigade, 2nd Armored Division joined the 1st Infantry Division(Mech)(-), it brought its organic Stinger platoon (4th Plt(Stinger), Btry C, 2nd Bn, 5th ADA), which gave the 1st Infantry Division(Mech) 15 extra Stinger teams. As a result, the 1st Infantry Div(Mech) had 27 M163 series self-propelled Vulcans and 70 Stinger teams.

---

[49] The 3-5 ADA was the 3rd Armd Div's normally-assigned ADA battalion, which was being inactivated in the Fall of 1990 as part of the post-Cold War drawdown. As a result, most of the 3-5 ADA was unavailable for deployment, and the Army temporarily reassigned the 5-3 ADA, normally an element of the 8th Inf Div(M), to the 3rd Armd Div for Desert Storm. The similarity of the designations of these two battalions (3-5 versus 5-3) causes confusion.

Finally, the 82nd Airborne Division differed from the TOE during Desert Storm by reorganizing the assets of its ADA battalion, the 3rd Bn(Abn)(Vulc/Stinger), 4th ADA, to form a provisional fourth firing battery, Team D. Team D consisted of six Stinger sections (two each from Batteries A-C), and a Vulcan platoon from Battery C. Thus, of the seven Army divisions in SWA, only two (the 24th Infantry Division(Mech) and 101st Airborne Division(Air Aslt)) followed the TOE for their ADA battalions.

B. Corps And EAC Air Defense Artillery Units

It appears that the organization of Hawk battalions was in transition shortly before Desert Storm. At least some Hawk battalions consisted of a headquarters & headquarters battery, three firing batteries (Batteries A-C), and a DS maintenance battery. In these units, each firing battery had two firing platoons, each with four Hawk launchers, for a total of 24 Hawk launchers in the battalion.[50] In addition, each battalion was authorized 14 Stinger teams for local defense.

Patriot battalions consisted of a headquarters & headquarters battery and either four firing batteries (Batteries A-D) or six firing batteries (Batteries A-F). Each firing battery had two firing platoons, each with four Patriot launchers, for a total of eight launchers per battery. This yielded a total of 32 launchers in each four-firing-battery battalion, and 48 launchers in each six-firing-battery battalion. In addition, each Patriot battalion was authorized Stinger teams for local defense.

VI. The Organization Of A Special Forces Group

Each Special Forces group consisted of a headquarters & headquarters company, a group support company, and three Special Forces battalions. The group support company consisted of company headquarters, a military intelligence detachment, a signal detachment, and a service detachment.

Each Special Forces battalion consisted of a headquarters & headquarters detachment (a "Special Forces Operational Detachment-C," "ODC," or "C-Team"), three Special Forces companies, and a battalion support company. Each Special Forces company consisted of company headquarters (a "Special Forces Operational Detachment-B," "ODB" or "B-Team."), and six "Special Forces Operational Detachments-A," generally known as "ODA" or "A Teams." Each A Team was led by a

---

[50] This was the approach used by the 2-1 ADA(Hawk), XVIII Abn Corps, during Desert Storm.

captain and was authorized 12 soldiers: the captain, a warrant officer, and ten noncommissioned officers (sergeants). The battalion support company consisted of company headquarters, a military intelligence detachment, a signal detachment, and a service detachment.

VII. U.S. Army Hospitals

Above the divisional level, medical care is provided by a hierarchy of hospitals. Mobile army surgical hospitals (MASH),[51] combat support hospitals (CSH), and evacuation hospitals operate at corps level. MASHs are small (60 bed) hospitals that are typically the closest to the front lines. MASHs perform emergency, life-saving surgery so that patients can be evacuated to other hospitals further to the rear. MASHs are the only hospitals that can move without substantial assistance from outside units, thus their designation as "mobile" army surgical hospitals.

CSHs are larger (200 bed) hospitals that are, after the MASHs, closest to the front lines. CSHs specialize in performing surgery on patients whose condition is not life-threatening. CSHs also treat some patients with medical (non-surgical) conditions.

The hospitals that are the furthest from the front, but still within the corps zone, are the evacuation hospitals. Evacuation hospitals are medium-sized (400 bed) hospitals that perform surgery and provide short-term medical care. Evacuation hospitals also exist at the echelons above corps (EAC) level, along with field, station, and general hospitals. Field (400 bed), station (500 bed),[52] and general (1,000 bed) hospitals provide the final surgical care, and medium-term medical care, for many patients. Patients requiring even greater care are evacuated from the theater to hospitals in CONUS. During Desert Storm, the Army planned to use hospitals in Germany to provide some of this final level of medical care.

VIII. Echelons Above Corps Organizations

A numbered **army** headquarters is senior to the corps and is typically the most senior army headquarters in a theater of operations. Assigned directly to this army was a **support command** or **theater army area command** that was typically commanded by a major general and responsible for the overall logistics effort in the theater. This command typically had several **area support groups** that provided support on an area

---

[51] Technically, the correct designation for a MASH is "Surgical Hospital(Mobile Army)." However, I have used "MASH" throughout this order of battle because that colloquial designation is almost universally used by the Army and the correct designation is unwieldy.

[52] The one station hospital deployed for ODS only fielded 300 beds, however.

basis, and various functional area groups or brigades, depending on the size of the operation and the needs of the theater. For example, during Desert Storm the 22nd Support Command included an **ordnance group** that handled ammunition, a **military police brigade** that specialized in handling enemy prisoners of war, and an **explosive ordnance disposal group**.

Also assigned directly to the theater-level numbered army were various functional area commands and brigades, such as an **engineer command**, **signal command**, **medical command**, **personnel command**, **military police brigade**, and **military intelligence brigade**. Each of these was commanded by a full colonel or brigadier general. During Desert Storm, two theater-level functional area commands that were supposed to exist, a **transportation command** and a **finance command**, were never established. In both instances, the missions that would normally have been performed by these commands were performed by other units or personnel. See Chart 3, page 3-8 and Chart 10, page 10-10.

Almost all of the units at EAC level were non-combat arms support-type units. The only exceptions during Desert Storm were the 11th Air Defense Artillery Brigade, the senior air defense artillery unit in-theater, and the 5th Bn(AH)(-), 229th Aviation, ARCENT Aviation Brigade, which administered the weapon system replacement operations program for Third Army and apparently served as Third Army's reserve attack helicopter unit.[53]

Notes:

➢ Information with regard to the numbers of weapons authorized for the various types of units is based on the numbers authorized by the TOE. Some units, however, acquired extra weapons, typically from the operational readiness float stocks that were intended to replace vehicles and weapons that were not operationally ready, or "down," for various reasons. In addition, it is possible some units adopted different organizational approaches that were not approved by the Army as they prepared for war.

➢ Battalions and larger units have a headquarters unit that the Army typically designates a "headquarters and headquarters company." The TOE shows two distinct organizations, a small "headquarters" that consists of the commander, executive officer, and the staff, and a much larger "headquarters company" that consists of the support personnel necessary to sustain the unit's operations. In reality, the headquarters and the headquarters company are not distinct entities. Rather, they operate together to provide the command & control and support functions necessary for their parent unit to operate.

---

[53] For more information on the 5-229 Avn(AH), see Text at page 8 and Chart 4, Footnote 77.

Appendix E

Organization Of U.S. Marine Corps Units

This appendix provides information on how U.S. Marine Corps units were organized during Desert Storm. For information on selected equipment used by Marine Corps units during Desert Storm, see Chart 24. For basic information on how ground combat units are organized and other basic background information about ground combat units, see Appendix A. For information on how U.S. Army units were organized during Desert Storm, see Appendix D.[1]

Marine Air-Ground Task Forces

The Marine Corps is unique among the armed services in that it contains extensive ground and air units. As a result, the Marine Corps organizes for combat into MAGTFs, or Marine air-ground task forces. During Desert Storm, there were three standard MAGTFs (in order, from smallest to largest): the MEU,[2] or Marine expeditionary unit; the MEB, or Marine expeditionary brigade; and the MEF, or Marine expeditionary force. Each MAGTF consisted of four elements: a command element (CE), ground combat element (GCE), air combat element (ACE), and a logistics element known as the combat service support element (CSSE).[3]

---

[1] For information on selected equipment used by Army units during Desert Storm, see Chart 13. For information on how British Army units were organized and equipped during Desert Storm, see Chart 27. For information on how French Army units were organized and equipped during Desert Storm, see Chart 28. For information on how Arab-Islamic units were organized and equipped during Desert Storm, see Chart 29.

[2] Rhymes with "new."

[3] Each MAGTF was task-organized for its mission; as a result, no MAGTF "owned" any units except for its

Order of Battle

The Marine Expeditionary Unit

The MEU was the smallest MAGTF. It was commanded by a full colonel and normally consisted of approximately 2,000 personnel, although the 13th MEU(SOC) had about 2,600 personnel during its Desert Storm deployment in the Persian Gulf. The MEU's GCE was a battalion landing team (BLT) built around a Marine infantry battalion. Attached to this battalion was an artillery battery, and platoon-sized detachments of light armored infantry, reconnaissance and/or force reconnaissance, amphibious assault vehicles, combat engineers, and sometimes tanks. The MEU's ACE was a reinforced medium helicopter squadron with approximately two dozen rotary wing aircraft (helicopters),[4] sometimes several fixed wing aircraft,[5] and some Stinger air defense missile teams. Logistical support was provided by the MEU's CSSE, a MEU service support group (MSSG). The MEU's GCE, ACE, and CSSE were each commanded by a lieutenant colonel. While deployed, a MEU was embarked upon a Navy amphibious squadron (PhibRon), which typically consisted of four or five ships.

MEUs are used to project a forward presence into sensitive areas of the world. During the period prior to Desert Storm, the Marines operated six MEUs: the 11th, 13th, and 15th MEUs, which were resourced out of I MEF at Camp Pendleton, Twentynine Palms, and other bases on the West Coast; and the 22nd, 24th, and 26th MEUs out of II MEF at Camp Lejeune and other bases on the East Coast. At any given time, one of the east coast MEUs was on station, typically in the Mediterranean, while one of the other two Camp Lejeune MEUs was recovering from a deployment and the third was preparing to deploy. The 11th, 13th, and 15th MEUs went through the same cycle, with deployments into the Pacific or the Persian Gulf.

Since the mid 1980s, the Marine Corps has been providing its MEUs with specialized training during their pre-deployment work up to prepare the MEU to conduct raids, hostage rescues, and other special direct intervention missions. A unit that successfully completed this training was designated a "MEU(SOC)," for "Special Operations Capable."

---

headquarters elements. The units that comprised the MAGTF were detached from their normal units and served with their MAGTF only temporarily. The information provided here describes the "average" MEU, MEB, and MEF, and significant variations were commonplace. Moreover, in addition to MEUs, MEBs, and MEFs, the Marine Corps had contingency MAGTFs, which were typically smaller than MEUs and formed as needed for specific missions.

[4] These were primarily the CH-46 "Sea Knight" Medium-Lift Transport Helicopter, with some AH-1T "Sea Cobra" or AH-1W "Super Cobra" Attack Helicopters, UH-1N "Huey" Utility Helicopters, and CH-53D "Sea Stallion" or CH-53E "Super Stallion" Heavy-Lift Cargo Helicopters.

[5] These were typically four AV-8B "Harriers."

The Marine Expeditionary Brigade

The next largest MAGTF was a MEB. A MEB was commanded by a brigadier (one star) general or major (two star) general and had approximately 10,000 to 20,000 personnel.[6] The MEB's GCE was built around a Marine infantry regiment with three infantry battalions. Attached to that regiment was a direct support artillery battalion and possibly a second artillery battalion in the general support role, along with company-sized (or larger) detachments of tanks, light armored infantry, reconnaissance and/or force reconnaissance, amphibious assault vehicles, and combat engineers. The MEB's ACE was a Marine aircraft group (MAG), commanded by a full colonel, typically with between 50 and 100 rotary wing aircraft,[7] approximately 70 fixed wing aircraft,[8] a low altitude air defense battery or battery(-) with 30-45 Stinger air defense missile teams, and a light antiaircraft missile battery with eight Hawk air defense missile launchers. A brigade service support group (BSSG), normally commanded by a lieutenant colonel, provided logistical support as the MEB's CSSE. The MEB also had an intelligence analysis unit commanded by a lieutenant colonel. While deployed, a MEB was embarked upon a Navy amphibious group (PhibGru), which typically consisted of about a dozen ships.

The Marine Expeditionary Force

The largest MAGTF was the MEF. A MEF was commanded by a major general or lieutenant (three star) general and normally consisted of approximately 50,000 personnel, although I MEF expanded to over 90,000 personnel during Desert Storm. The MEF's GCE consisted of one or more Marine divisions. The MEF's ACE was a Marine aircraft wing (MAW) with approximately 140 fixed wing and 155 rotary wing aircraft, a LAAD battalion or battalion(-) with 75-90 Stinger missile teams, and a LAAM battalion with 24 Hawk missile launchers. The MAW was commanded by a major general. The MEF's CSSE was a force service support group commanded by a brigadier general. Finally, the MEF had a surveillance, reconnaissance, and intelligence group commanded by a full colonel.

---

[6] These figures appear to be somewhat optimistic and based upon the assumptions that ample shipping was available and that the Marine Corps' resources were focused on deploying one "deluxe" MEB, not an array of units that all had to be resourced simultaneously from limited assets. As a result, the reality of Desert Storm was very different from these theoretical numbers. When they shipped out during Desert Shield, the 4th MEB had just under 8,500 personnel and the 5th MEB had just under 7,500.

[7] These were CH-46 Sea Knight Medium-Lift Transport Helicopters, AH-1T Sea Cobra and/or AH-1W Super Cobra Attack Helicopters, UH-1N Huey Utility Helicopters, and CH-53D Sea Stallion and/or CH-53E Super Stallion Heavy-Lift Cargo Helicopters.

[8] These were primarily the F/A-18 "Hornet" and AV-8B Harrier.

Order of Battle

The Marine Division

A Marine division was commanded by a major general, with a brigadier general as the assistant division commander. The standard Marine division was authorized[9] a headquarters battalion, three infantry regiments, an artillery regiment, a tank battalion, a light armored infantry battalion, a reconnaissance battalion, an assault amphibian battalion, and a combat engineer battalion. The headquarters battalion consisted of the division's headquarters, the headquarters company, and military police, communications, truck, and service companies.

Unlike the Army and its USARS program,[10] Marine infantry and artillery units were organized as true regiments, with a regimental commander who led the regiment.[11] A Marine infantry regiment consisted of a headquarters company and three infantry battalions.[12] The regimental headquarters company had one combat arms unit, an antitank platoon equipped with 24 TOW missile systems mounted on HMMWVs. Each antitank platoon was organized into three sections, each with eight TOWs.[13] Each section was organized into two squads, each with four TOWs. Also included in the headquarters company was the regimental staff, a communications section, and company headquarters.

---

[9] Variations existed between the three active duty and one reserve Marine divisions.

[10] See Appendix A, pages A-6 and A-7.

[11] It was not unusual, however, for a Marine infantry or artillery regiment to control battalions other than its progeny. For example, during Desert Storm only two Marine regiments in SWA commanded all of their active, assigned battalions: the 3rd Marines, 1st Mar Div(Rein); and the 6th Marines, 2nd Mar Div(Rein). The 6th Marines only had two battalions active during Desert Storm, as the 2/6 Marines had been inactivated in the late 1980s.

[12] During Desert Storm the Marines had 12 infantry regiment headquarters companies (nine active duty and three USMCR) and 33 infantry battalions (24 active duty and nine USMCR). Eight of the active duty and one-plus USMCR regimental headquarters companies served in the Gulf. Twenty of the active duty and four-plus USMCR battalions served in the Gulf, while another two active duty battalions were forward deployed in the Mediterranean during Desert Storm.

[13] The antitank platoon rarely operated as a self-contained unit. Rather, its three sections were typically attached, one each, to the regiment's three infantry battalions. Marine infantry battalions frequently formed combined antiarmor teams (CAAT) by marrying their attached TOW HMMWVs to the HMMWV-mounted M2 .50 cal Machine Guns and MK-19 Automatic 40mm Grenade Launchers in their organic heavy machine gun platoon.

Each Marine infantry battalion consisted of a headquarters & service company, three or four rifle companies,[14] and a weapons company.[15] In addition to the battalion commander and staff, the headquarters & service company included communications, service, medical, and STA (surveillance & target acquisition) platoons. Each rifle company consisted of company headquarters, three rifle platoons, and a weapons platoon. The rifle platoon had three rifle squads, and each squad had 13 Marines: seven armed with M16 Rifles, three with the M16 Rifle/M203 40mm Grenade Launcher combination, and three with the M249 5.56mm Squad Automatic Weapon. The weapons platoon had a machine gun section with six M60 7.62mm Machine Guns, a mortar section with three M224 60mm Mortars, and an assault section with six MK-153 83mm Shoulder-Launched Multipurpose Assault Weapons. The battalion's weapons company consisted of company headquarters, an antiarmor platoon with 24 M47 "Dragon" antitank missile launchers organized into three sections of eight Dragons each, a heavy machine gun platoon with six M2 .50 cal Machine Guns and six MK-19 Automatic 40mm Grenade Launchers, and a mortar platoon with eight M29 or M252 81mm Mortars.

Marine artillery regiments consisted of a headquarters battery, which included a counterbattery radar platoon with the AN/TPQ-36 "Firefinder" target acquisition radar,[16] and four artillery battalions.[17] The 1st through 3rd Battalions were direct support (DS)

---

[14] The vast majority of infantry battalions had three rifle companies. Of the 26 Marine infantry battalions that deployed to SWA or the Mediterranean during Desert Storm, only five had four rifle companies: 1/1 Marines, 3/1 Marines, 1/4 Marines, 2/8 Marines, and 3/8 Marines. The Marines intended the four-rifle company battalions to serve in MEU(SOC)s.

[15] These units were designated as follows:

	3-Rifle Co Battalions	4-Rifle Co Battalions
1st Bn	Cos A-C	Cos A-D
2nd Bn	Cos E-G	Cos E-H
3rd Bn	Cos I, K, L	Cos I, K-M

In accordance with Marine Corps tradition, there was no Company J. Weapons companies did not receive an alphabetical designation and were designated, _e.g._, "Weapons Co, 1st Battalion." Three- and four-rifle company battalions were frequently mixed within the same regiment, however all of the Marine Corps Reserve's infantry battalions had three rifle companies. Company designations were assigned so that any battalion could be organized with four rifle companies. Thus, if a regiment's 1st Battalion had only three companies (Cos A-C), the 2nd Battalion's first company would be Company E, rather than Company D, so that Company D could be activated as the 1st Battalion's fourth rifle company.

[16] For example, the 11th Marines (1st Mar Div(Rein)) had five such radars in SWA, but two were inoperative during the ground war.

[17] During Desert Storm the Marines had four artillery regiment headquarters batteries (three active duty and one USMCR) and 17 artillery battalions (12 active duty and five USMCR), with a total of approximately 52 firing batteries

units, while normally the 5th Battalion was a general support (GS) unit.[18] Each battalion was authorized a headquarters battery and three firing batteries, however the GS battalions that served in Desert Storm each had four firing batteries.[19] Direct support units had eight howitzers per battery, while general support units had six howitzers per battery.[20] The M198 towed 155mm howitzer equipped all DS artillery units and half of the Marines' GS units in the Gulf.

Before Desert Storm, Marine GS artillery units included M109 series self-propelled 155mm howitzers and M110 series self-propelled 203mm howitzers. Shortly before Desert Shield, however, the Marines began eliminating their M109 and M110 howitzers and converting the affected units to the M198 towed 155mm howitzer. This decision was quickly reversed when Desert Shield began in August 1990, and Marine GS artillery units took M109A3 and M110A2 self-propelled howitzers to the Gulf.

Artillery units that were afloat with embarked Marine landing units used a different approach. In addition to their M198 towed 155mm howitzers, these units had M101A1 towed 105mm howitzers. These smaller weapons were kept in the inventory because they were easier to deploy in a fast-moving amphibious operation than the large, heavy M198. The artillery batteries assigned to MEUs consisted of two firing platoons, each with four howitzers. One platoon was equipped with the M101A1 while the other platoon was equipped with the M198.[21]

(37 active duty and approximately 15 USMCR). Two of the active duty regimental headquarters batteries served in the Gulf as did part of the one USMCR regimental headquarters battery. Eleven of the active duty battalion headquarters batteries served in the Gulf, but none of the five USMCR battalion headquarters batteries did. Thirty-one of the active duty firing batteries and six of the USMCR firing batteries served in the Gulf, while another two active duty firing batteries were forward deployed in the Mediterranean during Desert Storm.

[18] In the 12th Marines (3rd Mar Div(-)), the 4th Battalion was the GS battalion and the 5th Battalion was not active. In the 14th Marines (4th Mar Div [USMCR]), the 4th and 5th Battalions were both active as GS units.

[19] These units were designated as follows:

1st Bn	Batteries A-C
2nd Bn	Batteries D-F
3rd Bn	Batteries G-I
4th Bn	Batteries K-M
5th Bn	Batteries Q-T

In accordance with Marine Corps tradition, there was no Battery J.

[20] The Marines had 11 artillery battalions in the Gulf, eight DS battalions and three GS battalions. The 1st Mar Div(Rein) had five battalions (four DS and one GS), the 2nd Mar Div(Rein) had four battalions (two DS and two GS), and the 4th and 5th MEBs each had one DS battalion. The GS battalions, which had six howitzers per battery, were: 5/11 Marines (1st Mar Div), 5/10 Marines (2nd Mar Div), and 2/12 Marines (2nd Mar Div).

[21] There were three such units forward deployed during Desert Storm: Btry B, 1/11 Marines, 13th MEU(SOC), in the Persian Gulf with NAVCENT (see Chart 19, page 19-18); Btry H, 3/10 Marines, 24th MEU(SOC), in the Mediterranean with the Sixth Fleet (see Chart 20, page 20-2); and Btry G, 3/10 Marines, 26th MEU(SOC), in the

The two artillery battalions assigned to the 4th and 5th MEBs that were afloat in the Persian Gulf also had the M101A1 105mm howitzer. The 4th MEB's 1st Bn, 10th Marines had the full complement of 24 M198s, plus 12 M101A1s as contingency weapons.[22] The 5th MEB's 2nd Bn, 11th Marines had 22 M198s and four M101A1s.[23]

The Marine division's tank battalion consisted of a headquarters & service company, three or four tank companies (Companies A-C or A-D), and an antitank company.[24] In addition to the commander and staff responsible for planning and directing the battalion's operations, the headquarters & service company included communications, maintenance, and scout platoons, and possibly other units. The headquarters & service company had two tanks, one M88A1 Recovery Vehicle, and three or four M60 AVLBs. The scout platoon had eight HMMWVs mounting TOWs, M2 .50 cal Machine Guns, and MK-19 Automatic 40mm Grenade Launchers.

Each tank company consisted of a company headquarters with two tanks (one equipped with an M9 blade) and one M88A1, and three tank platoons. In units equipped with the M60A1, each platoon was authorized five tanks for a total of 17 in the company. The 3rd and 8th Tank Bns fielded fewer tanks in the Gulf, however, and had only four tanks per platoon, for a total of 14 per tank company.[25] This approach was also used in units equipped with the M1A1.[26]

The antitank company was equipped with 72 TOW missile systems mounted on HMMWVs, organized into three platoons with 24 TOW HMMWVs each. Each antitank platoon was organized into three sections, each with eight TOW HMMWVs. Each section was organized into two squads, each with four TOW HMMWVs.

Mediterranean with the Sixth Fleet (see Chart 20, page 20-1).

[22] Each firing battery had eight M198s. The distribution of the M101A1s is unclear.

[23] Batteries E & F, 2/11 Marines, each had eight M198s, while Btry G, 3/12 Marines, which was simultaneously assigned to the 2/11 Marines and the 11th MEU(SOC), had six M198s and four M101A1s. The 11th MEU(SOC) was embedded within the 5th MEB. See Chart 19, Footnote 105 and pages 19-16 and 19-17.

[24] The 1st, 2nd, and 8th Tank Bns each had four tank companies, while the 3rd and 4th Tank Bns each had only three tank companies. Company D, 8th Tank Bn was temporarily disbanded during Desert Storm, however. See Chart 19, Footnote 56. In addition to these tank units, the Marines had two tank companies in the 1st Armd Aslt Bn (Cos C & D), a special unit assigned to the 3rd Mar Div(-) on Okinawa. See pages E-13 and E-14 for more information on the 1st Armd Aslt Bn. Thus, during Desert Storm: (1) the Marines had 19 active tank companies (13 active duty and six USMCR, not counting the inactive Co D, 8th Tank Bn [USMCR]), and all but one active duty company served in the Gulf; (2) the Marines had five antitank companies (three active duty and two USMCR), and all five served in the Gulf; and (3) the Marines had five tank battalion H&S companies (three active duty and two USMCR), and all but one USMCR H&S company served in the Gulf. No Marine tank units served in the Mediterranean during Desert Storm.

[25] The 3rd Tank Bn also had five or six M60A3s, however.

[26] These were the 2nd Tank Bn(-), and Cos B & C, 4th Tank Bn [USMCR]. See Chart 19, pages 19-11 and 19-12 and Footnote 79, and Chart 24, page 24-3.

The light armored infantry (LAI) battalion consisted of a headquarters & service company, and four LAI companies (Companies A-D).[27] In addition to the commander and staff, the headquarters & service company included communications, service, maintenance, antitank, and mortar platoons. The antitank platoon had 16 LAV-ATs organized into four sections of four vehicles each. The mortar platoon had eight LAV-Ms organized into four sections of two vehicles each. In addition to these LAVs, the H&S company had four LAV-25s, four LAV-C2s, eight LAV-Ls, and two LAV-Rs. Each LAI company consisted of company headquarters (with one LAV-25, one LAV-C2, two LAV-Ls, and one LAV-R), and two LAI platoons, each with six LAV-25s.[28]

The LAI units in the Gulf did not use standard LAI tables of organization and equipment, however. The 1st Marine Division(Rein)'s LAI unit consisted of elements of the 1st and 3rd LAI Bns, while the 2nd Marine Division(Rein)'s LAI unit consisted of elements of the 2nd LAI Bn and the reserve 4th LAV Bn.[29] In addition, LAI units were deployed in the Gulf with the 4th and 5th MEBs and with the 13th MEU(SOC), as well as in the Mediterranean with the 24th and 26th MEU(SOC)s. For the organization of the 1st Marine Division(Rein)'s LAI units, see Chart 19, Footnotes 33-35. For the organization of the 2nd Marine Division(Rein)'s LAI units, see Chart 19, Footnote 83. Furthermore, each unit typically task-organized for combat by, for example, detaching the LAV-ATs of the antitank platoon and the LAV-Ms of the mortar platoon to the line LAI companies. As finally task-organized for combat, the 2nd LAI Bn(Rein) had the following equipment:

Unit	LAV-25	LAV-AT	LAV-M	LAV-C2	LAV-L	LAV-R
Co A	14	4	2	1	3	1
Co B	12	2	2	1	3	1
Co C	14	4	2	1	3	1
Co D	8	2	2	1	2	1
Co E	13	2	2	1	3	1
Co F	9	2	2	1	2	1
AT Plt	1	7	0	0	1	0

---

[27] During Desert Storm the Marines had four LAI/LAV battalions (three active duty and one USMCR). All of these units served in the Gulf or Mediterranean, with the exception of one active duty H&S company and two active duty line companies (or three, if Co C, 3rd LAI Bn was active, see Chart 21, Footnote 23). Two active duty reinforced platoons were forward deployed in the Mediterranean during Desert Storm.

[28] Some LAI units apparently reorganized their line companies to have three platoons, however. For example, Co A, 2nd LAI Bn had three platoons and its 3rd Plt served with the 26th MEU(SOC) in the Mediterranean during Desert Storm.

[29] The 4th LAV Bn was still organized under the previous tables of organization and equipment. As a result, it had no personnel assigned as dismounts in its LAVs. See Chart 19, Footnote 83. In addition, it consisted of three line companies with LAV-25s (Cos A-C) and a weapons company with the battalion's LAV-ATs and LAV-Ms.

Notwithstanding its designation as an infantry unit, the LAI battalion served a cavalry role, including performing reconnaissance, economy of force, and security missions for its division. Indeed, after the Gulf War the Marine Corps redesignated its LAI units as light armored reconnaissance (LAR) units.

The reconnaissance battalion was a fairly small unit that consisted of a headquarters & service company and three line companies (Companies A-C). A fourth line company, Company D, only existed at cadre strength at the time Desert Shield began.[30] Each line company consisted of a headquarters and three reconnaissance platoons. Marine reconnaissance battalions typically conducted dismounted reconnaissance using small patrols of foot soldiers that were frequently inserted behind enemy lines by helicopter. The reconnaissance battalion did not typically perform mounted reconnaissance, as U.S. Army cavalry units do.[31]

The assault amphibian battalion operated the Marines' signature vehicle, the AAV7A1 Amphibious Assault Vehicle (AAV). Each such battalion consisted of a headquarters & service company, and four line companies (Companies A-D).[32] The headquarters & service company apparently had 15 AAVP7A1 Amphibious Assault Vehicles, three AAVC7A1 command AAVs, and one AAVR7A1 recovery AAV. Each line company consisted of a headquarters and three to five platoons, although four platoons were specified by the tables of organization and equipment. Each platoon had ten AAVP7A1s, while company headquarters had three AAVP7A1 Amphibious Assault Vehicles, three AAVC7A1 command AAVs, and one AAVR7A1 recovery AAV.

---

[30] The USMCR's 4th Recon Bn, however, had five active line companies (Cos A-E). In addition, the 1st Recon Bn brought its Co D to full strength for Desert Storm. Thus, during Desert Storm the Marines had four recon battalion H&S companies (three active duty and one USMCR), and apparently 16 recon companies (11 active duty and five USMCR). One USMCR recon company and approximately eight active duty recon companies served in the Gulf, while another two active duty platoons were forward deployed in the Mediterranean during Desert Storm. Two of the active duty battalion H&S companies served in the Gulf; the one reserve H&S company did not.

[31] During Desert Storm, however, the 1st and 2nd Recon Bns employed a motorized approach using HMMWVs for some of their missions.

[32] The USMCR's 4th Aslt Amphib Bn, however, had only two line companies (Cos A & B). In addition to these AAV units, the Marines had two AAV companies in the 1st Armd Aslt Bn (Cos A & B), a special unit assigned to the 3rd Mar Div(-) on Okinawa. See pages E-13 and E-14 for more information on the 1st Armd Aslt Bn. Thus, during Desert Storm the Marines had three assault amphibian battalion H&S companies (two active duty and one USMCR), and 12 line assault amphibian companies (ten active duty and two USMCR). Approximately eight of the active duty and both USMCR AAV companies served in the Gulf, while another two active duty platoons were forward deployed in the Mediterranean during Desert Storm. All three battalion H&S companies served in the Gulf.

Order of Battle

During Desert Storm, the deployed assault amphibian units obtained extra vehicles and adopted new organizational approaches. For example, the 3rd Assault Amphibian Bn, 1st Marine Division(Rein), had a total of 285 amphibious assault vehicles under its command during the ground war:[33]

	AAVP7A1	AAVC7A1	AAVR7A1	Total
1st Mar Div "B" Cmd Gp[34]	3	2	0	5
TF Papa Bear (1st Mar)	111	8	3	122
TF Taro (3rd Mar)	2	0	0	2
TF Grizzly (4th Mar)	2	0	0	2
TF Ripper (7th Mar)	128	8	4	140
TF King (11th Mar)	10	0	0	10
TF Troy	0	2	0	2
3rd Aslt Amphib Bn	0	2	0	2
TOTAL:	256	22	7	285

Finally, the Marine division's combat engineer battalion consisted of a headquarters & service company, three combat engineer companies (Companies A-C), and one engineer support company.[35] For Desert Storm, however, the 1st and 2nd Marine Divisions(Rein) organized provisional combat engineer units to assist with breaching the Iraqi front lines. These provisional units were provided with tanks and amphibious assault vehicles.

One thing conspicuously absent from the Marine division, compared to its Army brethren, was extensive logistics and other support units. While an Army division had four-plus support battalions that provided transportation, maintenance, medical, and other support, plus a signal battalion, military police company, and chemical decontamination company, the Marine division merely had a single battalion's worth of such support troops: a truck company, a service company, a military police company,

---

[33] By contrast, the 2nd Mar Div(Rein)'s 2nd Aslt Amphib Bn, with attached units from the 4th Aslt Amphib Bn, had 248 AAVs.

[34] The B Command Group provided a back-up capability in case the primary "A" Command Group was unable to command the division.

[35] Except in the USMCR's 4th Cbt Eng Bn, which had four combat engineer companies (Companies A-D). During Desert Storm the Marines had four combat engineer battalions (three active duty and one USMCR), with a total of four battalion H&S companies (three active duty and one USMCR), 13 combat engineer companies (nine active duty and four USMCR), and four engineer support companies (three active duty and one USMCR). Eight active duty and three USMCR combat engineer companies served in the Gulf, while another two active duty platoons were forward deployed in the Mediterranean during Desert Storm. Two active duty engineer support companies served in the Gulf, but the one USMCR engineer support company did not. Two of the active duty battalion H&S companies served in the Gulf, but the one USMCR H&S company did not.

and a communications company. All remaining logistics units were assigned to a separate organization, the MEF's force service support group.

The Force Service Support Group

Marine logistics units were concentrated in the MEF's force service support group (FSSG). Each FSSG was commanded by a brigadier general and normally consisted of eight battalions:[36]

Headquarters & service battalion
Maintenance battalion
Supply battalion
Engineer support battalion
Landing support battalion
Motor transport battalion
Medical battalion
Dental battalion

The FSSG headquarters & service battalion consisted of a headquarters company, service company, communications company, and military police company. The maintenance battalion consisted of a headquarters & service company, ordnance maintenance company, engineer maintenance company, electronics maintenance company, motor transport maintenance company, and general support maintenance company. The supply battalion consisted of a headquarters & service company, supply company, ammunition company, and medical logistics company. The engineer support battalion consisted of a headquarters & service company, engineer support company, bridge company, bulk fuel company, and three engineer companies. The landing support battalion consisted of a headquarters & service company, landing support equipment company, beach and terminal operations company, and three landing support companies. The motor transport battalion consisted of a headquarters & service company, general support motor transport company, and two direct support motor transport companies. The medical battalion consisted of a headquarters & service company, two surgical support companies, and three collecting & clearing companies. The dental battalion consisted of a headquarters & service company, and three dental companies. During Desert Storm, the deployed FSSGs grew substantially in size as units from the 3rd FSSG on Okinawa and the Marine Corps Reserve's 4th FSSG were assigned to the 1st and 2nd FSSGs in SWA.

---

[36] Each FSSG also included the command elements for two MEB service support groups, and the 1st and 2nd FSSGs each included the command elements for three MEU service support groups.

Order of Battle

The Surveillance, Reconnaissance, and Intelligence Group

Each MEF also had a surveillance, reconnaissance, and intelligence group (SRIG). Each SRIG was commanded by a full colonel and normally consisted of:

Headquarters, and headquarters & service company
Radio battalion[37]
Communications battalion
Force reconnaissance company
Intelligence company
Air-naval gunfire liaison company (ANGLICO)
Remote piloted vehicle company

The SRIG's only combat arms unit was a force reconnaissance company that performed deep reconnaissance, inserting its personnel behind enemy lines using a variety of techniques, including parachute delivery.[38] This company consisted of company headquarters, four small direct action platoons, and four small reconnaissance platoons. During Desert Storm, the 1st SRIG in SWA grew in size as additional units were assigned from the 2nd and 3rd SRIGs.

Air Defense Artillery

The Marines' approach to air defense artillery was another area where they differed from the Army. The Marines had two types of air defense units: low altitude air defense (LAAD) battalions equipped with the Stinger air defense missile, and light antiaircraft missile (LAAM) battalions equipped with the Hawk air defense missile. Both types of units were assigned to the MEF's aircraft wing, rather than to the Marine division.

The LAAD battalion consisted of a headquarters & service battery, and two firing batteries (Batteries A & B).[39] Each firing battery consisted of battery headquarters and three firing platoons. Each platoon had three sections, each with five Stinger teams, for a total of 15 Stinger teams in the platoon. Thus, each LAAD battery had 45 Stinger teams, and each LAAD battalion had 90 Stinger teams.

---

[37] This was an electronic warfare unit rather than a communications unit.

[38] During Desert Storm the Marines had four force reconnaissance companies (two active duty and two USMCR). All or most of all four companies served in the Gulf, while two active duty platoons were apparently forward deployed in the Mediterranean during Desert Storm.

[39] During Desert Storm the Marines had three LAAD battalions (two active duty and one USMCR), with a total of three battalion H&S batteries and six firing batteries. All four of the active duty firing batteries served in the Gulf, minus two small detachments that were forward deployed in the Mediterranean. All or part of one USMCR firing battery served in the Gulf. Both active duty H&S batteries served in the Gulf; the one USMCR H&S battery did not.

The LAAM battalion consisted of a headquarters & service battery, and two firing batteries (Batteries A & B).[40] Each firing battery consisted of battery headquarters, two firing platoons, a support platoon, and a maintenance platoon. Each firing platoon had four Hawk launchers, for a total of eight launchers per firing battery and 16 Hawk launchers per LAAM battalion.

The 1st Armored Assault Battalion

A unique organization that did not serve as a unit in Desert Storm but contributed some of its assigned units was the 1st Armored Assault Bn. This was a composite unit stationed on Okinawa with the 3rd Marine Division(-). It consisted of a headquarters & service company, two assault amphibian companies (Companies A & B), and two tank companies (Companies C & D). The line companies rotated back and forth between Okinawa and CONUS, trading places with the line companies of the 1st and 3rd Tank Bns and the 2nd and 3rd Assault Amphibian Bns under the Unit Deployment Program (UDP).[41] When Desert Shield began, the 1st Armored Assault Bn controlled the following line units:

> Co D [M60A1], 1st Armd Aslt Bn
> Co D, 1st Tank Bn [M60A1]
> 3rd Plt, AT Co [TOW], 1st Tank Bn
> Co C, 2nd Aslt Amphib Bn
> Co A(-),[42] 3rd Aslt Amphib Bn

Company A [AAV7A1], 1st Armored Assault Bn was at Camp Pendleton with the 3rd Assault Amphibian Bn, 1st Marine Division. Company B [AAV7A1], 1st Armored Assault Bn was at Camp Lejeune with the 2nd Assault Amphibian Bn, 2nd Marine Division. Company C [M60A1], 1st Armored Assault Bn, was at Camp Pendleton with the 1st Tank Bn, 1st Marine Division.

---

[40] During Desert Storm the Marines had four LAAM battalions (three active duty and one USMCR), with a total of four battalion H&S batteries and about eight firing batteries. Two of the active duty battalions (two H&S batteries and four firing batteries) served in the Gulf; none served in the Mediterranean. No USMCR LAAM units served in the Gulf or Mediterranean.

[41] Very few 3rd Mar Div(-) units were permanently stationed on Okinawa. Most units serving with the 3rd Mar Div(-) did so pursuant to the UDP. Under this program, units served short tours with the 3rd Mar Div(-) of six months, rotating between Okinawa and their parent units in CONUS.

[42] See Chart 19, Footnote 27.

Order of Battle

During Desert Storm, H&S Company, 1st Armored Assault Bn and Company C(-), 2nd Assault Amphibian Bn remained on Okinawa with the 3rd Marine Division(-), while the remainder of the units that had been on Okinawa with the 1st Armored Assault Bn deployed to SWA. Company A(-), 1st Armored Assault Bn, an assault amphibian unit, did not deploy from Camp Pendleton and was stripped of personnel to bring the 3rd Assault Amphibian Bn to full strength before it deployed, while Company A's 1st Platoon(Rein) remained at Camp Pendleton as an element of the 15th MEU(SOC). Company C, 1st Armored Assault Bn, an M60A1 tank unit, remained at Camp Pendleton during Desert Storm to maintain the 1st Tank Bn's equipment, which was left behind when the personnel of the 1st Tank Bn deployed by air to SWA to meet up with equipment that had been delivered by maritime prepositioning ships.

Maritime Prepositioning Ships

One final factor that differentiated the Marine Corps from the Army was the Marines' reliance on floating forward-deployed collections of equipment and supplies to maximize their ability to quickly deploy relatively heavy units to world hot spots. This capability was provided by three maritime prepositioning squadrons (MPSRon), each with sufficient equipment and supplies to allow a MEB to deploy its personnel quickly by air, link up with the MPS ships in a friendly port, and be ready to conduct combat operations much more quickly than if the MEB's heavy equipment and supplies had to deploy from the United States via ship. At the time Desert Shield began, there were three such MPS squadrons. MPSRon 2 at Diego Garcia and MPSRon 3 at Guam played key roles in getting the first Marine Corps units to Saudi Arabia in August 1990 with enough heavy equipment and supplies to present a credible presence. This is one area where the difference between the Marine Corps and the Army has narrowed since Desert Storm, as the Army now has its own prepositioning ships to facilitate the rapid deployment of heavy units.

Appendix F

Unit Insignia

<u>Section I — U.S. Army Shoulder Patches, Desert Storm</u>

Major U.S. Army units are authorized shoulder patches (known officially as "shoulder sleeve insignia") which are worn on the left shoulder sleeve. Once a service member has served in the unit in combat, he can wear the patch on his right shoulder. This is referred to as a "combat patch." Each patch comes in full color and subdued versions. Section I.A. shows the color versions of the shoulder patches for the major units that served in Operation Desert Storm. Section I.B. shows the color versions of the patches worn by major Reserve Component units that were mobilized but did not deploy to Southwest Asia.[1]

---

[1] See Chart 10. These units were mobilized in their entirety, or had major portions mobilized.

Section I.A. — U.S. Army Shoulder Patches Worn By Units That Deployed To Southwest Asia

☐ U.S. Army personnel,[2]
U.S. Central Command

☐ U.S. Army personnel,
Special Operations Command,
Central Command[3]

☐ Third Army

☐ VII Corps

☐ XVIII Airborne Corps

☐ 1st Armored Division

☐ 2nd Armored Division[4]

☐ 3rd Armored Division

☐ 1st Cavalry Division

---

[2] The U.S. Central Command and the Special Operations Command, Central Command, are joint (multi-service) commands that include personnel from all four armed services. Only U.S. Army personnel wear shoulder patches, however. Accordingly, these first two patches are authorized for wear by Army personnel assigned to these two joint commands.

[3] This patch was designed by SOCCENT personnel and was manufactured, but was never approved by the Army. It is unclear if it was worn on the uniform.

[4] The 2nd Armored Division had been inactivated by the beginning of Operation Desert Storm, but three of its brigades served in Desert Storm and wore this patch. The 1st Brigade served with the 2nd Marine Division, the 3rd Brigade served with the 1st Infantry Division(Mech), and the Aviation Brigade was assigned to Third Army as the ARCENT Aviation Brigade.

☐ 1st Infantry
Division(Mech)

☐ 3rd Infantry
Division(Mech)⁵

☐ 24th Infantry
Division(Mech)

☐ 82nd Division Airborne

☐ 101st Airborne
Division(Air Aslt)

☐ 197th Infantry
Brigade(Mech)

☐ 2nd Armored
Cavalry Regiment

☐ 3rd Armored
Cavalry Regiment

☐ 11th Aviation Brigade

☐ 12th Aviation Brigade

☐ 18th Aviation
Brigade(Abn)

☐ 18th Field Artillery
Brigade(Abn)

⁵ Worn by the 3rd Brigade, 3rd Infantry Division(Mech), which served as the 1st Armored Division's 1st Brigade during Desert Storm.

☐ 42nd Field Artillery Brigade

☐ 75th Field Artillery Brigade

☐ 142nd Field Artillery Brigade

☐ 196th Field Artillery Brigade

☐ 210th Field Artillery Brigade

☐ 212th Field Artillery Brigade

☐ 11th Air Defense Artillery Brigade

☐ Special Forces[6]

☐ 416th Engineer Command

☐ 7th Engineer Brigade

☐ 20th Engineer Brigade(Abn)

☐ 411th Engineer Brigade

---

[6] This patch was worn by all of the personnel assigned to the Army's special forces groups. Each group had its own beret flash, however. These beret flashes are illustrated later in this appendix.

☐ 14th Military
Police Brigade

☐ 16th Military
Police Brigade(Abn)

☐ 89th Military
Police Brigade

☐ 800th Military
Police Brigade(EPW)

☐ 6th Theater Signal
Command(Army)

☐ 11th Signal Brigade

☐ 35th Signal Brigade(Abn)

☐ 93rd Signal Brigade

☐ 3rd Medial Command

☐ 44th Medical Brigade

☐ 332nd Medical Brigade

☐ 22nd Support Command

☐ 1st Corps
Support Command

☐ 2nd Corps
Support Command

☐ 7th Transportation
Group(Terminal)

☐ 207th Military
Intelligence Brigade

☐ 513th Military
Intelligence Brigade

☐ 525th Military
Intelligence Brigade(Abn)

☐ 352nd Civil Affairs
Command

☐ 354th Civil Affairs
Brigade

☐ 360th Civil Affairs
Brigade

☐ 10th Personnel Command

Section I.B. — Patches Worn By Major Reserve Component Units That Were Mobilized But Did Not Deploy to Southwest Asia[7]

☐ 48th Infantry Brigade(Mech)

☐ 256th Infantry Brigade(Mech)

☐ 155th Armored Brigade

☐ 70th Division(Training)

☐ 78th Division(Training)

☐ 84th Division(Training)

☐ 100th Division(Training)

☐ 353rd Civil Affairs Command

☐ 75th Maneuver Area Command

---

[7] See Chart 10. These units were mobilized in their entirety or had major portions mobilized.

Section II — Other Patches

Various other patches are shown in Section II. Depicted here are the pocket patch for Joint Task Force Proven Force, examples of standard subdued and desert subdued Army shoulder patches, and examples of Army and Marine Corps Desert Storm novelty patches.

☐ Joint Task Force Proven Force[8]

☐ Standard subdued shoulder patch: VII Corps

☐ "Desert subdued" shoulder patch: U.S. Army personnel, U.S. Central Command

☐ Desert Storm novelty patch: VII Corps[9]

☐ Desert Storm novelty patch: "Armor in Command"[10]

☐ Desert Storm novelty patch: 24th Infantry Division(Mech)

---

[8] JTF Proven force served in Turkey. See charts 1 & 7. This patch was locally approved and was worn during Operation Desert Storm.

[9] Desert Storm novelty patches were apparently never worn on the uniform, but were sold to collectors and may have been used by veterans on civilian clothing.

[10] Refers to the key role armor played in Desert Storm and is based on the shoulder patch for armored divisions.

☐ Desert Storm novelty patch: 101st Airborne Division(Air Aslt)

☐ Desert Storm novelty patch: 11th Air Defense Artillery Brigade

☐ Desert Storm novelty patch: Task Force Ripper, 1st Marine Division

☐ Desert Storm novelty patch: 6th Marines, 2nd Marine Division

☐ Desert Storm novelty patch: Apache Attack Helicopter

☐ Desert Storm novelty patch: U.S. Army

Section III — U.S. Army Beret Flashes, Desert Storm

U.S. Army airborne and special operations forces are authorized to wear a beret in lieu of the more conventional headgear worn by the rest of the Army. Enlisted men wear the unit's distinctive unit insignia (commonly but inaccurately known as a "crest") on the beret attached to a small shield-shaped patch known as a "beret flash."[11] Section III.A. shows the beret flashes worn by the major special operations forces units that served in Operation Desert Storm. Section III.B. shows the beret flash for the one major Reserve Component unit that was mobilized but did not deploy to Southwest Asia.

---

[11] Officers wear their rank insignia on the beret flash in lieu of the unit distinctive insignia worn by enlisted men.

Section III.A. — U.S. Army Beret Flashes Worn By Units That Deployed To Southwest Asia

☐ 3rd Special Forces
Group(Abn)

☐ 5th Special Forces
Group(Abn)

☐ 10th Special Forces
Group(Abn)

☐ 4th Psychological
Operations Group(Abn)

☐ 5th Special Operations
Support Command(Theater
Army) (Abn)[12]

☐ 7th Special Operations
Support Command (Theater
Army) (Abn)

Section III.B. — U.S. Army Beret Flashes Worn By Major Reserve Component Units That Were Mobilized But Did Not Deploy To Southwest Asia[13]

☐ 20th Special Forces
Group(Abn)

---

[12] This is a drawn representation of the flash's design, as this flash is very rare.

[13] See Chart 10.

Section IV — U.S. Marine Corps Unit Emblems

The Marine Corps has not used unit insignia that is worn on the uniform since shortly after World War II. Nonetheless, many (but not all) units have emblems that are used, for example, on signs, stationary, and coffee mugs. Illustrated here are the known emblems of some of the Marine Corps units that served in Operation Desert Storm.[14]

☐ I Marine Expeditionary Force

☐ 1st Marine Division

☐ 2nd Marine Division

☐ 24th Marines

☐ 1st Surveillance, Reconnaissance, and Intelligence Group

☐ 1st Service Support Group

---

[14] Because these emblems are not unit insignia, they are not considered official and the Marine Corps does not make any attempt to document these emblems. Accordingly, researching these emblems is difficult.

Section V — Selected Allied Unit Insignia

Illustrated here are unit insignia from selected allied units that served in Operation Desert Storm.[15]

☐ Emblem, 1st (UK)
Armoured Division

☐ Shoulder patch,
British 4th Armoured Brigade

☐ Shoulder patch,
British 7th Armoured Brigade

☐ Shoulder patch,
British Force
Maintenance Area

☐ Pocket badge,
French 6th Light
Armored Division

Section VI — Selected Desert Storm Medals

Illustrated here are the medals that are authorized for wear by U.S. military personnel for Operation Desert Storm.

☐ Southwest Asia
Service Medal

☐ Kuwait Liberation Medal
(Saudi Arabia)

☐ Kuwait Liberation Medal
(Kuwait)

---

[15] See Charts 27 & 28.

Selected Bibliography

Listed here are the most significant sources for order of battle information. Space limitations preclude listing every source I consulted.

Researching Desert Storm

The majority of the Army's Desert Storm material is archived at one of four locations: (1) The Center of Military History (CMH) at Fort McNair in Washington, DC;[1] (2) The Military History Institute (MHI), Carlisle Barracks, Pennsylvania; (3) The library of the U.S. Army War College (USAWC), Carlisle Barracks; or (4) The Combined Arms Research Library (CARL), Fort Leavenworth, Kansas. Information on special operations forces (SOF), however, is archived at Fort Bragg, North Carolina, with the U.S. Army Special Operations Command. The material at CMH, MHI, and USAWC is readily available to private researchers. The SOF material at Fort Bragg is available to private researchers if prior arrangements are made. The material at CARL is restricted and on-site research requires prior written application.

U.S. Army Center of Military History[2]
Building 35
102 Fourth Avenue
Fort Lesley J. McNair
Washington, DC
(202) 685-2194

---

[1] CMH moved to this location from downtown Washington, DC, in 1998.
[2] Mailing address is: 103 Third Avenue, Ft. Lesley J. McNair, Washington, DC 20319-5058.

Order of Battle

U.S. Army Military History Institute
22 Ashburn Drive
Carlisle Barracks
Carlisle, PA 17013-5008
(717) 245-3611

U.S. Army War College Library
122 Forbes Avenue
Carlisle Barracks
Carlisle, PA 17013-5220
(717) 245-4259

Combined Arms Research Library
250 Gibbon Avenue
Fort Leavenworth, KS 66027-2314
(913) 758-3053

Freedom of Information Act requests relating to Desert Storm should be submitted to:

Department of the Army
U.S. Armed Services Center for Research of Unit Records
7798 Cissna Road, Suite 101
Springfield, VA 22150-3197

      The majority of the Marine Corps' Desert Storm material is archived at the Marine Corps Historical Center in Washington, DC. These materials are readily available to private researchers.

Marine Corps Historical Center
Building 58
Washington Navy Yard
Washington, DC 20374

      Finally, each Army and Marine Corps installation presumably has some information on Desert Storm and the contribution made by the installation and its units.

The Internet

There is surprisingly little valuable material with regard to the Gulf War available on the Internet. The best such source is the web site of the Army's Center of Military History.[3] These materials include: (1) "Key Personnel Lists," which consist of detailed lists of the units that served in Desert Storm, organized by type, showing key personnel by name, rank, and duty position. In addition, for some units these lists address selected weapons systems, task organization, and other information; (2) selected oral history interviews conducted by XVIII Airborne Corps historians; (3) a detailed annotated chronology of XVIII Airborne Corps operations during Desert Shield and Desert Storm; (4) a bibliography compiled by CMH; (5) CMH's publication The Whirlwind War; (6) a selection of photographs; and (7) for the 1st Armored, 1st Cavalry, 1st Infantry, 82nd Airborne, and 101st Airborne Divisions, divisional orders of battle.[4] All of this material can be reached at: **http://www.army.mil/cmh-pg** In addition, lineage and honors certificates (which record the campaigns and awards credited to a unit), are available for some units that participated in Desert Storm at: **http://www.army.mil/cmh-pg/lineage/lindex.htm** Unlike many organizations, which establish a presence on the Web and then do nothing to update or expand their site, CMH is constantly improving its web site.

The Department of Defense (DOD) has established a web site called GulfLINK which is intended to assist veterans suffering from Gulf War Syndrome. As part of this effort, the DOD declassified thousands of documents from Desert Storm and has made them available for electronic searches at this site. Unfortunately, the system is about as user unfriendly as could be imagined, and finding useful documents among this collection is difficult, although perseverance (and luck) sometimes yields results. GulfLINK also has several fascinating reports on alleged chemical warfare incidents, some of which include detailed order of battle information. Finally, GulfLINK has several of the armed service's Desert Storm histories, and other materials such as illustrations of the medals the United States awarded for Desert Storm, on line. All of this material can be reached at: **http://www.gulflink.osd.mil**

Beyond this, there is very little of value. A handful of Gulf War veterans have written useful accounts of their Desert Storm service.[5] More (although not many) veterans have posted short accounts that have some limited historical value.[6] Many U.S. Army and Marine Corps units that served in Desert Storm have sites that mention their Gulf War service, but these accounts are typically painfully short and lack detail. Army units are reachable through

---

[3] The Army's Military History Institute also has a web site, however as of February 1999, it did not include any Gulf War material. MHI apparently intends to expand its presence on the World Wide Web, hence it may be worth visiting their site in the future: **http://carlisle-www.army.mil/usamhi/** MHI's collection includes substantial material on Desert Storm.

[4] This material is listed under the "Division Matrix" that provides detailed information on the ten Active Army divisions that are currently active. This material is available at: **http://www.army.mil/cmh-pg/matrix**

[5] See (1) Bo H. Friesen, Fratricide at Umm Hajul. n.p.: n.p., n.d. [3rd ACR] **Available on the Internet at: http://www.gulfweb.org/tracings/friesen.html** (2) Ronald A. Hoskinson, Gulf War Diary. n.p.: n.p., n.d. [3-82 FA & 2nd Bde, 1st Cav Div] **Available on the Internet at: http://users.aol.com/andyhosk/dstorm.html**

[6] Many of these can be accessed via: **http://www.gulfweb.org** and/or: **http://www.geocities.com/SoHo/9782/storm_sites.html**

the Army homepage at: **http://www.army.mil** while Marine Corps units are reachable through the Marines' homepage at: **http://www.usmc.mil** Unfortunately, as of February 1999, the Marine Corps Historical Center does not have a Web page, however this will presumably change in the future.

Items listed in this bibliography that are available on the Internet have that fact noted, and the Internet address, in bold. Web addresses are current as of June 1999.

Books

Barker, Geoffrey T. <u>A Concise History of U.S. Army Special Operations Forces</u>. 2nd ed. Tampa, FL: Anglo-American Publishing Co., 1993.

Benson, Nicholas. <u>Rats' Tales: The Staffordshire Regiment at War in the Gulf</u>. London: Brassey's, 1993.

Bergot, Erwan. <u>Operation Daguet: Les Francais dans la guerre du Golfe</u>. Paris: Presses de la Cite, 1991. [French forces; in French]

Blake, Thomas G. <u>The Shield And The Storm</u>. n.p.: The Commemorative Group, 1992(?).

Brown, LtCol Ronald J. <u>Humanitarian Operations in Northern Iraq, 1991: With Marines in Operation Provide Comfort</u>. Washington, DC: History and Museums Div, HQ, U.S. Marine Corps, 1995. [24th MEU(SOC)] **Available on the Internet at: http://www.gulflink.osd.mil/histories/**

Brown, LtCol Ronald J. <u>U.S. Marines in the Persian Gulf, 1990-1991: With Marine Forces Afloat In Desert Shield And Desert Storm</u>. Washington, DC: History and Museums Div, HQ, U.S. Marine Corps, 1998. [4th MEB, 5th MEB, and 13th MEU(SOC)] **Will presumably be available on the Internet at: http://www.gulflink.osd.mil/histories/**

Caraccilo, CPT Dominic J. <u>The Ready Brigade of the 82nd Airborne in Desert Storm</u>. Jefferson, NC: McFarland & Co., Inc., 1993. [2nd Bde, 82nd Abn Div; see especially pages 4-5]

Carhart, Tom. <u>Iron Soldiers</u>. NY: Pocket Books, 1994. [1st Armd Div]

Chadwick, Frank, et al. <u>Gulf War Factbook</u>. Bloomington, IL: GDW, Inc., 1991.

Clancy, Tom & Franks, GEN Fred, Jr. (Ret.). <u>Into The Storm: A Study In Command</u>. New York: G. P. Putnam's Sons, 1997. [VII Corps]

Cordingley, Maj Gen Patrick. <u>In The Eye Of The Storm: Commanding The Desert Rats In The Gulf War</u>. London: Hodder & Stoughton, 1996. [British 7th Armd Bde]

Crabtree, James D. On Air Defense. Westport, CT: Praeger Publishers, 1994.

Cureton, LtCol Charles H. U.S. Marines In The Persian Gulf, 1990-1991: With the 1st Marine Division in Desert Shield and Desert Storm. Washington, DC: History and Museums Div, HQ, U.S. Marine Corps, 1993. **Available on the Internet at: http://www.gulflink.osd.mil/histories/**

Currie, COL James T., et al. Twice The Citizen: A History of the United States Army Reserve, 1908-1995. 2nd revised and expanded ed. Washington, DC: Office of the Chief, Army Reserve, 1997.

Dufour, Pierre. La Legion Dans La Guerre Du Golfe. Paris: J. Grancher, 1991. [French forces; in French]

Dunnigan, James F., et al. From Shield To Storm: High-Tech Weapons, Military Strategy, and Coalition Warfare in the Persian Gulf. New York: William Morrow & Co., 1992.

Flanagan, LTG Edward M., Jr. (Ret.). Lightning: The 101st in the Gulf War. Washington, DC: Brassey's, Inc., 1994. [101st Abn Div(AAslt)]

Foss, Chris, et al. Scorpion Reconnaissance Vehicle, 1972-1994. London: Osprey, 1995. (New Vanguard No. 13) [16th/5th The Queen's Royal Lancers; A Sqdn, 1st The Queen's Dragoon Guards; & other British Army units]

Gehring, Stephen P. From The Fulda Gap To Kuwait: U.S. Army, Europe and the Gulf War. Washington, DC: Department of the Army, 1998.

Gill, CPT Kirk. 3rd Brigade, 101st Airborne Division(Air Assault) Rakkasans. Paducah, KY: Turner Publishing Co., 1992.

Hall, Margot C., ed. The Victory Book: A Desert Storm Chronicle. 2nd ed. n.p.: Josten's, 1992. [24th Inf Div(M), 197th Inf Bde(M), 212th FA Bde, 36th Eng Gp & other attached units]

Kamiya, MAJ Jason K. A History Of The 24th Mechanized Infantry Division Combat Team During Operation Desert Storm - "The Attack to Free Kuwait" (January through March 1991). Ft. Stewart, GA: 24th Inf Div(M)(?), 1991(?).

Kistler, Kent. Operation Desert Shield, Operation Desert Storm - Order Of Battle For United States Armed Forces. Naples, FL: H.J. Saunders U.S. Military Insignia, 1992.

McGrath, MAJ John J., et al. Theater Logistics And The Gulf War. Alexandria, VA: Historical Office, U.S. Army Material Cmd, 1994.

Order of Battle

Melson, Maj Charles D. U.S. Marines In The Persian Gulf, 1990-1991: Anthology And Annotated Bibliography. Washington, DC: History and Museums Div, HQ, U.S. Marine Corps, 1992. **Available on the Internet at: http://www.gulflink.osd.mil/histories/**

Milner, Laurie. Royal Scots In The Gulf: 1st Battalion, The Royal Scots, (The Royal Regiment) on Operation Granby 1990-1991. London: Leo Cooper, 1994.

Morrison, Bob. Operation Desert Sabre: The Desert Rat's Liberation Of Kuwait. Hongkong: Concord Publications Co., 1991. [British forces]

Mroczkowski, LtCol Dennis P. U.S. Marines In The Persian Gulf, 1990-1991: With the 2nd Marine Division in Desert Shield and Desert Storm. Washington, DC: History and Museums Div, HQ, U.S. Marine Corps, 1993. **Available on the Internet at: http://www.gulflink.osd.mil/histories/**

Pearce, Nigel. The Shield and the Sabre: The Desert Rats in the Gulf, 1990-91. London: Her Majesty's Stationary Office, 1992. [British forces]

Peck, SFC James F., et al. Stalwart Storm: The First Battalion Task Force, Forty-First Infantry Regiment (Straight and Stalwart) Second Armored Division(Forward) in Operations Desert Shield and Desert Storm. Germany: 1-41 Inf(M), 1991.

Phillips, MAJ Jeffrey E., et al. America's First Team In The Gulf. Dallas, TX: Taylor Publishing Co., 1992. [1st Cav Div(-) & 1st Bde, 2nd Armd Div]

Picard, Gilbert. Au Feu Avec La Division Daguet. [Suresnes]: Editions Aramon, 1991. [French forces; in French]

Quilter, Col Charles J., II. U.S. Marines In The Persian Gulf, 1990-1991: With the I Marine Expeditionary Force In Desert Shield And Desert Storm. Washington, DC: History and Museums Div, HQ, U.S. Marine Corps, 1993. **Available on the Internet at: http://www.gulflink.osd.mil/histories/**

Quinn, Maj John T. II. U.S. Marines In The Persian Gulf, 1990-1991: Marine Communications In Desert Shield And Desert Storm. Washington, DC: History and Museums Div, HQ, U.S. Marine Corps, 1996. **Available on the Internet at: http://www.gulflink.osd.mil/histories/**

Ripley, Tim. Desert Storm Special No. 1: Land Power, The Coalition And Iraqi Armies. London: Osprey Publishing Ltd., 1991.

Rottman, Gordon, et al. Armies of the Gulf War. London: Osprey Publishing Ltd., 1993. (Osprey Elite Series No. 45)

Scales, BG Robert H., Jr., et al. Certain Victory: The United States Army in the Gulf War. Washington, DC: Office of the Chief of Staff, U.S. Army, 1993.

Schubert, Frank N., et al. The Whirlwind War: The United States Army in Operations Desert Shield and Desert Storm. Washington, DC: Center of Military History, 1995.
Available on the Internet at: (1) http://www.gulflink.osd.mil/histories/
(2) http://www.army.mil/cmh-pg/online/SWA.htm

Stitt, Edgar A. 100-Days, 100-Hours: "Phantom Brigade" In The Gulf War. Hongkong: Concord Publications Co., 1991. [3rd Bde, 3rd Inf Div(M)]

Stokes, Dr. Carol E., et al. The US Army Signal Corps In Operation Desert Shield/Desert Storm. Fort Gordon, GA: Office of the Command Historian, U.S. Army Signal Ctr, 1994.

Swain, COL Richard M. "Lucky War" - Third Army in Desert Storm. Fort Leavenworth, KS: U.S. Army Command & General Staff College Press, 1994.

Taylor, Thomas. Lightning in the Storm: The 101st Air Assault Division in the Gulf War. New York: Hippocrene Books, 1994.

White, Maj Gen M.S., CBE, ed. Gulf Logistics: Blackadder's War. London: Brassey's, 1995. [British forces]

Zaloga, Steve, et al. M1 Abrams Main Battle Tank, 1982-1992. London: Osprey, 1993. (New Vanguard No. 2)

Zaloga, Steven J., et al. M2/M3 Bradley Infantry Fighting Vehicle, 1983-1995. London: Osprey, 1995. (New Vanguard No. 18)

Department of Defense. Conduct of the Persian Gulf War: Final Report To Congress. Washington, DC: Government Printing Office, 1992.

Department of the Army. Weapon Systems 1991 United States Army. Washington, DC: Government Printing Office, 1991.

Operation Desert Storm Sustainment. Washington, DC (?): Office of the Deputy Chief of Staff, Logistics, 1992.

Civil Affairs in the Persian Gulf War: A Symposium. Ft. Bragg, NC: U.S. Army JFK Special Warfare Ctr & School, 1991.

24th Mechanized Infantry Division Combat Team: Operation Desert Storm, Attack Plan OPLAN 91-3. Ft. Stewart, GA: 24th Inf Div(M), 1991(?).

North To The Euphrates: 101st Airborne Division, Operations Desert Shield and Desert Storm. n.p.: Tennessee-Kentucky Chapter, Association of the U.S. Army, 1991. **An excerpt from this book is available on the Internet at: http://www.campbell.army.mil/Euph.htm**

Order of Battle

Chapter XXXVIII, Special Forces Ass'n. Fifth Special Forces Group(Airborne) In Desert Shield And Desert Storm. n.p.: Jostens, 1991(?).

1st Battalion, 5th Cavalry "Black Knights" -- Knights In The Desert, Desert Shield And Desert Storm, 10 Aug 1990 - 16 Apr 1991. n.p.: n.p., n.d.

Periodical Articles

1-4 Cav Operations Staff. "Riders On The Storm." Armor. (May-Jun 1991), pp. 13-21. [1-4 Cav]

Anderson, COL Randall J., et al. "The Lightning of Desert Storm." Field Artillery. (Oct. 1991), pp. 57-63. [101st Abn Div(AAslt) DIVARTY]

Blackwell, James. "Georgia Punch: 24th Mech puts the squeeze on Iraq." Army Times. (Dec. 2, 1991), pp. 12-14, 20, 22, 61. [24th Inf Div(M)]

Bohannon, 2LT Richard M. "Dragon's Roar: 1-37 Armor in the Battle of 73 Easting." Armor. (May-Jun 1992), pp. 11-17.

Boyd, COL Morris J., et al. "Focusing Combat Power — The Role of the FA Brigade." Field Artillery. (Feb. 1992), pp. 46-52. [42nd FA Bde]

Brabham, BGen James A. "Training, Education Were the Keys." U.S. Naval Institute Proceedings. (Nov. 1991), pp. 51-54. [1st FSSG & Direct Spt Cmd]

Brown, COL Daniel G. "Lifeline to the Frontline." Transportation Corps Professional Bulletin. (July 1991), pp. 2-5. [7th Trans Gp]

Brown, LtCol Ronald J. "The Gulf War: Marine Forces Afloat in Southwest Asia, 1990-1991." Marine Corps Gazette. (Nov. 1992), pp. 60-63.

Cain, LTC F. Marion, III. "Building Desert Storm Force Structure." Military Review. (July 1993), pp. 21-30.

Carlton, Patrick W. "Civil Affairs Operations in Kuwait - A Case of Disparate Command Priorities." Army History. (Summer 1994), pp. 14-22.

Colucci, Frank. "Warriors At Sea." U.S. Army Aviation Digest. (Nov-Dec 1992), pp. 5-11. [4-17 Cav(Air)]

Cordingley, Maj Gen Patrick. "7th Armoured Brigade: Commander's Diary." Army Quarterly & Defence Journal.
   Part 1: (Apr. 1993), pp. 178-84.
   Part 2: (July 1993), pp. 287-95.

Dacus, SSgt Jeffrey R. "Bravo Company Goes to War." Armor. (Sep-Oct 1991), pp. 9-15. [Co B, 4th Tank Bn, USMC]

Dietrich, LTC Steven E. "In-Theater Armored Force Modernization." Military Review. (Oct. 1993), pp. 39-45.

Eldridge, Bo. "Desert Storm - Mother of All Battles." Command. (Nov-Dec 1991), pp. 12-43.
Fister, CPT George, et al. "Preparing and Organizing Medical Support to VII Corps: Operation Desert Shield and Storm." The Journal of the US Army Medical Department. (Mar-Apr 1992), pp. 16-19.

Fontenot, COL Gregory. "Fright Night: Task Force 2/34 Armor." Military Review. (Jan. 1993), pp. 38-52.

Frix, MG Robert S., et al. "Task Force Freedom and the Restoration of Kuwait." Military Review. (Oct. 1992), pp. 2-10.

Graves, MAJ Kenneth P. "Steel Rain -- XVIII Airborne Corps Artillery in Desert Storm." Field Artillery. (Oct. 1991), pp. 49-56.

Gray, Gen A.M. "Command Report: Doing What Must Be Done." Marine Corps Gazette. (Feb. 1991), p. 8. [V MEF]

Guss, Jack H. II. "Gulf War Formation Signs (Patches)." The Trading Post. (Apr-Jun 1993), pp. 39-41. [British units]

Harris, LTC G. Chesley. "Operation Desert Storm: Armored Brigade in Combat." Infantry. (May-Jun 1992), pp. 13-19. [3rd Bde, 1st Armd Div]

Hoffman, Larry. "How the 'Big Red One' Breached the Saddam Line." Command. (Mar-Apr 1992), p. 15. [2-16 Inf(M)]

Karegeannes, MG Harry G., et al. "Support Group Operations in Southwest Asia." Army Logistician. (Jan-Feb 1992), pp. 12-16. [U.S. Army Spt Gp]

Kershaw, LtCol Charles W. "Reconnaissance Battalion: Eyes and Ears in the Desert." Marine Corps Gazette. (Apr. 1992), pp. 95-96. [1st Recon Bn]

Keys, LtGen William M. "Rolling With the 2d Marine Division." U.S. Naval Institute Proceedings. (Nov. 1991), pp. 77-80.

Kimball, MAJ Charlotte E. "Maintenance during Gulf War: A piece of the story." Ordnance. (Feb. 1992), pp. 18-20. [2nd COSCOM]

Order of Battle

Kindsvatter, LTC Peter S. "VII Corps in the Gulf War: Deployment and Preparation for Desert Storm." Military Review. (Jan. 1992), pp. 2-16.

Kindsvatter, LTC Peter S. "VII Corps in the Gulf War: Ground Offensive." Military Review. (Feb. 1992), pp. 16-37.

Knight, LTC Kenneth R. "The Fire Support Dilemma: Location of the Fire Support Coordinator and the Task Force Fire Support Officer." Forward Observer. (June 1992). [2nd Bde, 1st Cav Div]

Ludvigsen, Eric C. "Rebuilding for 1980s With an Eye on 2000." Army. (Oct. 1982), pp. 248-403. [Army weapon systems]

Maggart, COL Lon E. "A Leap of Faith." Armor. (Jan-Feb 1992), pp. 24-32. [1st Bde, 1st Inf Div(M)]

McFarlin, BG Robert P. "Logistics Command and Control in Southwest Asia." Army Logistician. (Nov-Dec 1992), pp. 11-15.

McFarren, COL Freddy E., et al. "A Unique Challenge for the 18th FA Brigade(Airborne)." Field Artillery. (Oct. 1991), pp. 42-48.

McIntire, Katherine. "Speed Bumps: 82d Airborne's shaky line in the sand." Army Times. (Oct. 21, 1991), pp. 12-15, 76-77. [82nd Abn Div]

Morningstar, MAJ James K. "Points of Attack: Lessons From the Breach." Armor. (Jan-Feb 1998), pp. 7-13. [3-37 Armor & 2-16 Inf(M)]

Mulcahy, MG Terrence D. "Engineer Support in the COMMZ." Military Review. (Mar. 1992), pp. 14-21. [416th Eng Cmd & 411th Eng Bde]

Myatt, MajGen J. M. "The 1st Marine Division in the Attack." U.S. Naval Institute Proceedings. (Nov. 1991), pp. 71-76.

Naylor, Sean D. "Flight Of Eagles: 101st Airborne Division's raids into Iraq." Army Times. (July 22, 1991), pp. 8-14.

Naylor, Sean D. "Home Of The Brave." Army Times. (Jan. 27, 1992), pp. 8, 12-14, 16, 58. [3rd ACR]

O'Donovan, LtCol John A. "Combat Service Support During DESERT SHIELD and DESERT STORM: From Kibrit to Kuwait." Marine Corps Gazette. (Oct. 1991), pp. 26-31. [1st FSSG & Direct Spt Cmd]

Pagonis, LTG William G., et al. "Good Logistics is Combat Power: The Logistic Sustainment of Operation Desert Storm." Military Review. (Sep. 1991), pp. 28-39.

Petrosky, COL Daniel J., et al. "An Aviation Brigade Goes to War." U.S. Army Aviation Digest. (Sep-Oct 1991), pp. 44-65. [Avn Bde, 1st Armd Div]

Pierson, CPT David S. "Tuskers: Attack onto Battle Position 102." Army. (Dec. 1995), pp. 40-45. [4-64 Armor]

Rothwell, S.K. "Medium Reconnaissance in the Gulf." Army Quarterly & Defence Journal. [16th/5th Lancers, 1st (UK) Armd Div]
    Part 1: (Spring 1995), pp. 163-68.
    Part 2: (July 1995), pp. 308-13.

Scicchitano, J. Paul. "Eye Of The Tiger." Army Times. (June 10, 1991), pp. 12-13, 16, 18, 61. [1st Bde, 2nd Armd Div]

Scicchitano, J. Paul. "Night Strikes: The secret war of the 1st Cavalry Division." Army Times. (Sep. 23, 1991), pp. 8, 14-16.

Simmons, BGen Edwin H. "Getting Marines To the Gulf." U.S. Naval Institute Proceedings. (May 1991), pp. 50-64.

Spangler, MSG Chester G. "Army Air Traffic Services During Operations Desert Shield/Desert Storm." U.S. Army Aviation Digest. (May-Jun 1993), pp. 60-64. [29th Avn Gp(ATC)]

Stanton, LTC Martin N. "The Saudi Arabian National Guard Motorized Brigades." Armor. (Mar-Apr 1996), pp. 6-11.

Steiner, MAJ Lawrence M., Jr. "Rehearsal in War: Preparing to Breach." Armor. (Nov-Dec 1992), pp. 6-11. [2-34 Armor]

Stokes, Dr. Carol E., et al. "Getting the message through in the Persian Gulf War." Army Communicator. (Summer/Winter 1992), pp. 17-25. [Signal Corps units]

Summe, MAJ Jack N. "PSYOP Support to Operation Desert Storm." Special Warfare. (Oct. 1992), pp. 6-9.

Tice, Jim. "'Coming Through' -- The Big Red Raid." Army Times. (Aug. 26, 1991), pp. 12-13, 16, 18, 20. [1st Inf Div(M)]

Vogel, Steve. "A Swift Kick: 2d ACR's taming of the Guard." Army Times. (Aug. 5, 1991), pp. 10-13, 18, 28, 30, 61.

Vogel, Steve. "'Metal Rain' -- 'Old Ironsides' and the Iraqis who wouldn't back down." Army Times. (Sep. 16, 1991), pp. 8, 12-13, 16, 22, 61. [1st Armd Div]

Order of Battle

Vogel, Steve. "Hell Night -- For the 2d Armored Division(Forward), it was no clean war." Army Times. (Oct. 7, 1991), pp. 8, 14-16, 18, 24, 69. [3rd Bde, 2nd Armd Div]

Vogel, Steve. "Killer Brigade: 3d Infantry Division 'Phantoms' hunt the enemy." Army Times. (Nov. 11, 1991), pp. 10, 14-16, 22, 69. [3rd Bde, 3rd Inf Div(M)]

Vogel, Steve. "The Tip Of The Spear." Army Times. (Jan. 13, 1992), pp. 8, 10, 12-13, 16, 54. [3rd Armd Div]

Wilson, LTC Robert. "Tanks in the Division Cavalry Squadron." Armor. (Jul-Aug 1992), pp. 6-11. [1-4 Cav]

Yeosock, LTG John J. "Army Operations in the Gulf Theater." Military Review. (Sep. 1991), pp. 2-15, 80-81.

Yeosock, LTG John J. "H+100: An Army Comes of Age in the Persian Gulf." Army. (Oct. 1991), pp. 44-58.

Spearhead. Desert Blitzkrieg -- Desert Storm Issue (Spring 1991). [3rd Armd Div]

Logger News. Commemorative Edition (Nov. 1991). [22nd SUPCOM]

The Champion: 2nd Corps Support Command. (July 17, 1991).

The National Guard On Guard. Desert Storm Commemorative Issue (Dec. 1991).

Mississippi Guardsman. Special edition, "The Mississippi National Guard and Operation Desert Shield" (Winter 1990).

Marines. Almanac '90 Special Edition (Dec. 1990).

"Army Weaponry And Equipment." Army. (Oct. 1989), pp. 256-406.

"Redlegs in the Gulf." Field Artillery. (Apr. 1991), pp. 26-27. [U.S. Army and Marine Corps field artillery units]

"Silhouettes of Steel." Field Artillery. (Dec. 1991), pp. 8-29.

U.S. Army Unit After Action Reports

Barto, MAJ Joseph C., III. TF 2-4 Cav: "First In -- Last Out" The History of the 2nd Squadron, 4th Cavalry During Operation Desert Storm. Ft. Stewart, GA: HQ, 2-4 Cav, 1991(?).

Bennett, LTC James C. "Memorandum for Record, Subject: TF Jayhawk After Action Report." Saudi Arabia(?): HQ, TF Jayhawk, Mar. 14, 1991.

Bush, D. JULLS Long Report, "Mobilization/Demobilization." Fort Dix, NJ: n.p., Mar. 25, 1991. [78th Div(Tng) units]

Christian, LTC Dennis R. "Historical Summary Operation Desert Storm." Fairmont, WV: HQ, 1-201 FA, Aug. 29, 1991.

Foster, MAJ. JULLS Long Report, "Task Force 100 Participation in Operation Desert Storm." Fort Knox, KY: n.p., Oct. 25, 1996. [100th Div(Tng) units]

Garrett, COL Thomas W. "Memorandum For Commander, 101st Airborne Division (Air Assault), Subject: Executive Summary - OPERATION DESERT SHIELD/STORM." Ft. Campbell, KY: HQ, Avn Bde, 101st Abn Div(AAslt), June 10, 1991.

Goodwin, CW3 Mark G. "Historical Review: 2nd Squadron, 17th Cavalry Regiment, 1 October 1990 thru 1 April 1991 — 'Out Front'". Ft. Campbell, KY: HQ, 2-17 Cav(Air), July 18, 1991.

Hadad, CPT Mitchel E., II. "101st Aviation Brigade, 101st Airborne Division(Air Assault) 'Wings of Destiny' - Annual Historical Review, 1 October 1990 - 30 September 1991 FY 91." Ft. Campbell, KY: HQ, Avn Bde, 101st Abn Div(AAslt), Nov. 8, 1991.

Kropp, COL Anthony R. "Engineers Build For Victory In Operation Desert Storm." Saudi Arabia(?): HQ, 411th Eng Bde, 1991(?). [411th Eng Bde]

Pierson, LTC K. H. "After Action Report, Desert Storm/Shield." Saudi Arabia(?): HQ, 1st EOD Gp(Prov), June 14, 1991.

Scheider, CH (CPT) David M. 31st Combat Support Hospital Unit History Desert Shield/Storm. Saudi Arabia(?): 31st CSH, Mar. 25, 1991. [31st CSH, 115th MASH & 332nd Med Bde]

Schenck, LTC Philip K., Jr. The 173rd Medical Group And The Gulf War, 24 August 1990 - 24 May 1991. Dhahran, Saudi Arabia: HQ, 173rd Med Gp, 1991.

"Operation Desert Shield/Storm - 'Always First' 'We Were First.'" N.p.: HQ, Third Army, n.d. [Briefing slides]

FY 1991 Third U.S. Army Annual Historical Review. Ft. McPherson, GA: HQ, Third Army, June 10, 1992.

Chronicle of XVIII Airborne Corps Artillery Activity During Operation Desert Storm. Saudi Arabia: HQ, XVIII Abn Corps Arty, May 2, 1991.

Order of Battle

3 AD History of Operation Desert Storm And Operation Desert Spear. n.p.: HQ, 3rd Armd Div, 1991(?).

"Command Report: Executive Summary of Operations Desert Shield and Desert Storm by The First Team." Ft. Hood, TX: HQ, 1st Cav Div, Apr. 10, 1991.

"Annex E (Avn Bde) to 1st Cav Div After Action Report, Operation Desert Storm." Ft. Hood, TX(?): HQ, 1st Cav Div, 1991(?).

Operation Desert Shield and Desert Storm Command Report. Ft. Riley, KS: HQ, 1st Inf Div(M), Apr. 19, 1991.

197th Infantry Brigade(M): Operation Desert Storm, Summary of Operations, 17 January - 10 March 1991. Ft. Benning, GA: HQ, 197th Inf Bde(M), Apr. 24, 1991.

101st Airborne Division(Air Assault): History For Operation Desert Shield/Operation Desert Storm. Ft. Campbell, KY: HQ, 101st Abn Div(AAslt), July 1, 1991.

"Actions Of The 1st (Tiger) Brigade, 2nd Armored Division During Operation Desert Shield/Operation Desert Storm 10 Aug 90 - 1 Mar 91." n.p.: HQ, 1st Bde, 2nd Armd Div, 1991(?).

1st Inf Div(Fwd) Desert Shield/Desert Storm After Action Report. Germany: HQ, 1st Inf Div(Fwd), May 30, 1991.

"Second Armored Cavalry Regiment: Operation Desert Storm, 1990-1991." n.p.: HQ, 2nd Armd Cav Regt, 1991.

42nd Field Artillery Brigade Battle History. n.p.: HQ, 42nd FA Bde, n.d. [Includes after action reports from 3-20 FA, 1-27 FA & 2-29 FA]

"Operation Desert Shield/Storm After Action Report." Fayetteville, AR: HQ, 142nd FA Bde, Aug. 5, 1991.

After Action Report, 196th FA Brigade Operations during Desert Shield/ Storm. Chattanooga, TN: HQ, 196th FA Bde, Nov. 6, 1991. [Includes after action reports from 1-181 FA, 1-201 FA & 1-623 FA]

"210th Field Artillery Brigade Command Report." Saudi Arabia: HQ, 210th FA Bde, Apr. 1, 1991.

"Section I, Operations," of 212th FA Bde after action report(?). n.p.: HQ, 212th FA Bde(?), n.d.

Desert Shield & Desert Storm Task Organization Charts from 11th ADA Bde Desert Storm After Action Report. Ft. Bliss, TX(?), HQ, 11th ADA Bde.

Desert Shield, Desert Storm and Operation Urban Freedom After Action Review(U). Ft. Bragg, NC: HQ, 3rd SF Gp(Abn), May 9, 1991.

"Tab A - Operational Orders and Reports." Fort Campbell, KY: HQ, 5th SF Gp(Abn), 1991(?). [excerpt from after action report(?); includes excerpt from 5th SF Gp(Abn) Operation Order 02-91, ARSOTF Supporting Order for Offensive Operations, Desert Storm (declassified)]

22nd Support Command After Action Report. Saudi Arabia: HQ, 22nd SUPCOM, 1991. [16 volumes]

1st COSCOM Operation Desert Storm After Action Report. n.p.: HQ, 1st COSCOM, 1991.

1st Corps Support Command - Operation Desert Shield/Desert Storm After Action Review. n.p.: HQ, 1st COSCOM, n.d.

Desert Shield/Storm After Action Report. Saudi Arabia(?): HQ, 6th Sig Cmd, Apr. 20, 1991.

"After Action Review/Command Historical Report, 3rd Medical Command, 1 August 1990-26 April 1991." Saudi Arabia: HQ, 3rd Med Cmd, Apr. 27, 1991.

"36th Engineer Group (Combat) Operation Desert Shield/Storm Historical Summary 2 August 1990 - 29 March 1991." Ft. Benning, GA: HQ, 36th Eng Gp, 1991. [with attached Desert Storm history of 5th Eng Bn]

"Annual Historical Report for FY 1991." Ft. Campbell, KY: HQ, 3-101 Avn(AH), Nov. 18, 1991.

"After Action Report for Operation Desert Storm Deployment of Radar Section Four." Ft. Carson, CO: Btry A(TA), 26th FA, June 25, 1991.

"Operation Desert Shield/Desert Storm." Saudi Arabia: HQ, 4-27 FA, Mar. 18, 1991.

Army National Guard After Action Report, Operation Desert Shield, Operation Desert Storm, 2 August 1990 - 28 February 1991. Arlington, VA: National Guard Bureau, 1991.

North Carolina Army National Guard After Action Report, Operation Desert Shield/Storm. n.p.: Office of the Adjutant General, North Carolina, Dec. 1991.

U.S. Army Operations Orders

"OPLAN Desert Storm." Saudi Arabia: HQ, XVIII Abn Corps, Jan. 13, 1991. [Excerpt; declassified]

Order of Battle

"Deployment OPORD 1-91 (Operation Desert Storm)." Hunter Army Air Field, GA: HQ, 1/75 Rngr Regt(Abn), Feb. 16, 1991. [Excerpt; declassified, classified material redacted]

U.S. Army General/Permanent Orders[7]

General Orders No. 20. Washington, DC: HQ, Department of the Army, Aug. 30, 1991.

General Orders No. 22. Washington, DC: HQ, Department of the Army, Aug. 30, 1991.

General Orders No. 6. Washington, DC: HQ, Department of the Army, Jan. 31, 1992.

General Orders No. 17. Washington, DC: HQ, Department of the Army, June 19, 1992.

General Orders No. 34. Washington, DC: HQ, Department of the Army, Dec. 30, 1992.

General Orders No. 7. Washington, DC: HQ, Department of the Army, Apr. 2, 1993. [This is the general order that lists the units that are entitled to campaign participation credit for Desert Shield & Storm]

General Orders No. 14. Washington, DC: HQ, Department of the Army, June 25, 1993.

General Orders No. 12. Washington, DC: HQ, Department of the Army, May 13, 1994.

General Orders No. 27. Washington, DC: HQ, Department of the Army, Dec. 27, 1994.

General Orders No. 1. Washington, DC: HQ, Department of the Army, Mar 31, 1996.

Permanent Orders 3-17, "Temporary Change of Station for 5-229 Avn." Ft. Hood, TX: HQ, III Corps, Jan. 14, 1991.

Other U.S. Army Documents And Publications

Army Regulation 672-5-1, Military Awards. Washington, DC: HQ, Department of the Army, Oct. 1, 1990 (Updated reprint of a regulation originally issued Apr. 12, 1984; update includes Changes 1-15; update effective Nov. 1, 1990). [Unit awards and campaign participation credit]

Student Text 100-1, Navy And Marine Corps. Fort Leavenworth, KS: U.S. Army Command & General Staff College, June 30, 1993. [Organization and equipment of, and background on, Marine units]

---

[7] Listed here are all of the Department of the Army general orders that identify (1) the units that received campaign participation credit for Desert Storm, and (2) the units that received unit awards for Desert Storm.

Brinkerhoff, John R. United States Army Reserve In Operation Desert Storm: Civil Affairs in the War with Iraq. Washington, DC: Office of the Chief, Army Reserve, 1991.

Brinkerhoff, John R. United States Army Reserve In Operation Desert Storm: Countering the Terrorist Threat: The 3d Battalion, 87th Infantry. Washington, DC: Office of the Chief, Army Reserve, 1993.

Brinkerhoff, John R. United States Army Reserve In Operation Desert Storm: Enemy Prisoner of War Operations: The 800th Military Police Brigade. Washington, DC: Office of the Chief, Army Reserve, 1992.

Brinkerhoff, John R. United States Army Reserve In Operation Desert Storm: Engineer Support at Echelons Above Corps: The 416th Engineer Command. Washington, DC: Office of the Chief, Army Reserve, 1992.

Brinkerhoff, John R. United States Army Reserve In Operation Desert Storm: Port Operations. Washington, DC: Office of the Chief, Army Reserve, 1991.

Brinkerhoff, John R., et al. United States Army Reserve In Operation Desert Storm: Reservists of the Army Medical Department. Washington, DC: Office of the Chief, Army Reserve, 1993.

Brinkerhoff, John R. United States Army Reserve In Operation Desert Storm: The Signal Support Dilemma: The 335th Signal Command. Washington, DC: Office of the Chief, Army Reserve, 1992.

Brinkerhoff, John R. United States Army Reserve In Operation Desert Storm: Strategic Intelligence Support: Military Intelligence Detachments for the Defense Intelligence Agency. Washington, DC: Office of the Chief, Army Reserve, 1991.

Engelage, COL J.R., ed. Fourth Army, Operation Desert Shield: Mobilization and Deployment of Reserve Component Units to the Persian Gulf, 1990-91. Ft. Sheridan, IL: HQ, Fourth Army, 1991.

Fishel, John T. Liberation, Occupation, And Rescue: War Termination And Desert Storm. Carlisle, PA: Strategic Studies Institute, U.S. Army War College, 1992. [TF Freedom, Spt Cmd TF, CCATF, KTF & 352nd CA Cmd]

Floyd, LTC Arthur L. Echelons Above Corps Personnel Service Support In Operations Desert Shield And Desert Storm. Carlisle, PA: U.S. Army War College, 1993. (Army War College Class of 1993 Personal Experience Monograph) [3rd Pers Gp]

Henry, Lisa B., ed. Arabian Knights. Ft. Bliss, TX(?): U.S. Army ADA Ctr(?), 1991(?). [Army ADA units]

Reider, MAJ Bruce J. The Implications Of Weapon System Replacement Operations At The Operational Level Of War. Fort Leavenworth, KS: School of Advanced Military Studies, U.S. Army Command & General Staff College, 1995.

Sandler, Stanley, Ph.D. To Free From Oppression: A Concise History Of U.S. Army Special Forces, Civil Affairs, Psychological Operations And The John F. Kennedy Special Warfare Center And School. Fourth printing. Fort Bragg, NC: U.S. Army Special Operations Cmd, Directorate of History and Museums, 1997.

Sandler, Stanley, Ph.D. Cease Resistance: It's Good For You: A History of U.S. Army Combat Psychological Operations. Fort Bragg, NC: U.S. Army Special Operations Cmd, Directorate of History and Museums, 1995. [pages 308-30]

Schaefer, Mason. The Military Traffic Management Command's CONUS Port Operations During Operation Desert Shield/Desert Storm: 1990-91. Falls Church, VA: MTMC History Office, n.d.

Silva, Theodore S. United States Army Reserve In Operation Desert Storm: Augmenting The Training Base: The Army Reserve in Support of TRADOC. Washington, DC: Office of the Chief, Army Reserve, 1994. [USAR training units]

Silva, Theodore S., et al. United States Army Reserve In Operation Desert Storm: Ground Transportation Operations. Washington, DC: Office of the Chief, Army Reserve, 1994.

Silva, Theodore S., et al. United States Army Reserve In Operation Desert Storm: Personnel Services Support. Washington, DC: Office of the Chief, Army Reserve, 1995.

Stockmoe, CPT James L. Desert Shield/Storm History. Ft. Riley, KS(?): HQ, 1st Bde, 1st Inf Div(M)(?), 1992.

Tegtmeier, SFC Philip H., ed. The Desert Jayhawk. Stuttgart, Germany: VII Corps PAO, 1991(?). [VII Corps]

Webb, William Joe, et al. Department of the Army Historical Summary, Fiscal Years 1990 and 1991. Washington, DC: U.S. Army Center of Military History, 1997. [pages 16, 18-27, 74-77, 82-87, 93-96, 103-13, 150-52, 159]

Wright, Dr. Burton, III, ed. United States Army Aviation During Operations Desert Shield & Desert Storm. Ft. Rucker, AL: Office of the Aviation Branch Historian, 1993.

"Unit Awards, Operation Desert Shield/Storm." n.p.: n.p., Feb. 9, 1993.

List of Armor and Cavalry Units In Desert Shield/Storm. Ft. Knox, KY: U.S. Army Armor Ctr, 1992(?).

Desert Shield And Desert Storm Emerging Observations. Ft. Knox, KY: U.S. Army Armor Ctr, 1991.

"How USAARMC Went To War." Fort Knox, KY: HQ, U.S. Army Armor Ctr, n.d. [Briefing slides] [Army Reserve armor training units that served at Fort Knox]

List of Field Artillery units that deployed to Saudi Arabia from Fort Sill. Ft. Sill, OK: U.S. Army FA Ctr, 1991.

U.S. Army. Into The Storm. n.p.: n.p., n.d. [Army ADA units]

"Memorandum For Chairman, DMSPO, Subject: ADA Commander's Conference and Desert Shield/Storm After Action Review (AAR)." Germany (?): 32nd AADCOM, June 11, 1991.

Sine Pari — Without Equal: The Story of Army Special Operations. Fort Bragg, NC: U.S. Army Special Operations Cmd Directorate of History and Museums, 1995. **Available on the Internet at: http://www.usasoc.soc.mil**

List of "SOF Units in Desert Shield/Storm." Ft. Bragg, NC(?): HQ, U.S. Army Special Operations Cmd(?), 1991(?).

Handwritten list of engineer units that served in Operation Desert Storm. Ft. Leonard Wood, MO: U.S. Army Engineer Ctr, 1993(?).

Organizational charts showing Signal Corps units in Desert Storm: "EAC Signal Support in ODS/S," "Organizations Participating with 11th Signal Brigade," "XVIII Abn Corps Signal," and "VII Corps Signal." n.p.: U.S. Army Signal Ctr(?), n.d.

List of "Ord/Maint Units in SWA." n.p.: n.p., n.d. (Received from Ordnance Corps Historian, 1997)

List of "Chemical Corps Units In Operations Desert Shield And Desert Storm." Ft. McClellan, AL: U.S. Army Chemical Ctr, 1991.

"Deploying A Contingency PERSCOM — The Desert Experience." N.p.: HQ, 10th PERSCOM(?), n.d. [Briefing slides]

Finance Deployments Review - 1990-1996. Fort Jackson, SC: U.S. Army Finance School, 1996.

"U.S. Assistance For The Reconstruction Of Kuwait." n.p.: n.p., n.d. [Briefing slides]

First U.S. Army Historical Summary. Ft. Meade, MD: HQ, First Army, 1991.

Order of Battle

List of "First U.S. Army Reserve and National Guard Units Activated For Desert Shield/Storm." Ft. George G. Meade, MD: HQ, First Army, Mar. 20, 1991.

History of Reserve Component Mobilization, Second U.S. Army, Operation Desert Shield/Storm, August 1990-July 1991. Ft. Gillem, GA: HQ, Second Army, 1992.

List of Fourth U.S. Army National Guard and Army Reserve units activated for Operation Desert Storm. Ft. Sheridan, IL: HQ, Fourth Army, Aug. 2, 1991.

List of Fifth U.S. Army National Guard and Army Reserve units activated for Operation Desert Storm. Ft. Sam Houston, TX: HQ, Fifth Army, Feb. 22, 1991.

101st Mil Hist Det. Mobilization: Fifth Army Support For Desert Shield/Storm - A Historical Monograph. Ft. Sam Houston, TX: HQ, Fifth Army, 1991.

List of Sixth U.S. Army National Guard and Army Reserve units activated for Operation Desert Storm. Presidio of San Francisco, CA: HQ, Sixth Army, 1991(?).

"Mailing List For Ft. Lewis Units Deployed To Saudi Arabia." Ft. Lewis, WA: HQ, I Corps, 1991(?).

"XVIII Airborne Corps Desert Shield Chronology, 1-23 February 1991." Washington, DC: CMH, n.d. **Available on the Internet at:[8] http://www.army.mil/cmh-pg/online/SWA.htm**

"XVIII Airborne Corps Desert Storm Chronology, 24-28 February 1991, Ground Offensive Combat." Washington, DC: CMH, n.d. **Available on the Internet at: http://www.army.mil/cmh-pg/online/SWA.htm**

"Operation Desert Shield And Desert Storm Key Personnel Lists." Washington, DC: CMH, June 30, 1998. **Available on the Internet at: http://www.army.mil/cmh-pg/reference/dsds.htm**

Desert Storm Orders of battle prepared by the U.S. Army Center of Military History for:
    1st Armored Division
    1st Cavalry Division
    1st Infantry Division(Mech)
    82nd Airborne Division
    101st Airborne Division(Air Aslt)
Available on the Internet at: http://army.mil/cmh-pg/matrix

---

[8] This site has monthly chronologies for XVIII Abn Corps for August 1990 through June 1991.

Response to Freedom of Information Act Request on 3rd Armd Div. Fort Leavenworth, KS: U.S. Army Combined Arms Ctr, 1996. Includes document entitled "Task Organization to 1st Bde (Operation Desert Storm) As of 24 Feb 91"; document entitled "2d Bde Task Organization"; list of units entitled "VII Corps," dated Nov. 15, 1990; and information on the 3rd Armd Div extracted from Annex A (Task Organization) to VII Corps OPLAN 1990-2 (Operation Desert Saber).

List of Fort Drum Units that participated in Operation Desert Storm. Ft. Drum, NY: HQ, 10th Mtn Div(Lt Inf), 1992.

"2ACR Operation Desert Storm." Germany(?): HQ, 2nd Armd Cav Regt, 1991(?). [Briefing slides]

"Counterfire - The FA Bde Mission." n.p.: HQ, 75th FA Bde, n.d.

"Briefing For DA DCSLOG, 3 July 1991." Ft. Sill, OK(?); HQ, 75th FA Bde, 1991. [Briefing slides]

Untitled memorandum on the 142nd FA Bde. n.p., n.p., n.d.

210th Field Artillery Brigade Desert Storm Briefing Slides. n.p.: HQ, 210th FA Bde(?), n.d.

Organizational charts showing medical units in the KTO as of 29 Jan 91: "EAC Medical Support," "VII Corps Medical Support," and XVIII Abn Corps (unlabelled). n.p.: n.p., n.d.

"360th Civil Affairs Brigade Narrative Operation Desert Shield & Desert Storm." n.p.: HQ, 360th CA Bde, 1991.

The History of the Fourth United States Cavalry. Ft. Riley, KS: HQ, 1-4 Cav, 1992(?).

Unit Histories for HHC, Cos A-B & D, 3/160 Avn. n.p.: HQ, 3/160 Avn, 1991(?).

"Unit History, 3d Battalion, 160th Special Operations Aviation Regiment (Airborne)." n.p.: HQ, 3/160 Avn, 1992(?).

Unit History, 1-158 FA. n.p.: HQ, 1-158 FA(?), n.d.

List of U.S. Army Reserve Units Activated for Operation Desert Shield/Storm. Washington, DC: Office of the Chief, Army Reserve, May 22, 1991.

List of U.S. Army Reserve and National Guard Units Activated For Desert Shield/Storm. Washington, DC: U.S. Army, 1991.

"Reserve Component Active Duty Call-Ups As of 17 January 1991." Washington, DC: U.S. Army, 1991.

Order of Battle

"AMOPS Working Papers, Mobilization/Demobilization Report, 200K-13X, Work Order 91-4367, CONUS Units." n.p.: U.S. Army, June 13, 1991.

Desert Storm Briefing Slides. Fort Jackson, SC: n.p., n.d. [1-485 Regt, 2-485 Regt]

U.S. Army Oral History Interviews[9]

Interview of MAJ Stephen B. Finch, Air Defense Officer, XVIII Abn Corps. Oral Hist. Interview DSIT AE 009. Rafha, Saudi Arabia: Feb. 2, 1991.

Interview of COL Gerald R. Harkins, Commander, Dragon Bde. Oral Hist. Interview DSIT AE 112. Fort Bragg, NC: Aug. 26, 1991.

Interview of CPT Michael Johnson, S-4, 4th Regt of Dragoons, 6th (FR) Lt Armd Div. Oral Hist. Interview DSIT AE 072. As Salman, Iraq: Mar. 10, 1991.

Interview of LTC Walter F. Kilgore, Commander, 2nd Battalion, 1st Air Defense Artillery. Oral Hist. Interview DSIT AE 079. Logistical Base Charlie, Saudi Arabia: Mar. 21, 1991.

Interview of COL Hubert de Laroque Latour, Commander, 3rd Hel Regt, 6th (FR) Lt Armd Div. Oral Hist. Interview DSIT AE 073. As Salman, Iraq: Mar. 16, 1991.

Interview of MAJ(P) Philip X. Naven, Jr., S-3, 62nd Med Gp. Oral Hist. Interview DSIT AE 026. Logistical Base Charlie, Saudi Arabia: Feb. 28, 1991.

Interview of MG J. H. Binford Peay, III, Commanding General, 101st Abn Div(Air Aslt). Oral Hist. Interview DSIT AE 101. Fort Campbell, KY: June 5, 1991. [Includes a good background discussion of the 101st Abn Div(AAslt) in Desert Storm by an Army historian] **Available on the Internet at: http://www.army.mil/cmh-pg/documents/swa/dsit/peay.htm**

Interview of LTC Roger R. Sexton, Executive Officer, 62nd Med Gp. Oral Hist. Interview DSIT AE 025. Logistical Base Charlie, Saudi Arabia: Feb. 26, 1991.

Interview of COL Julian A. Sullivan, Jr., Commander, 507th Spt Gp(Corps). Oral Hist. Interview DSIT AE 019. Logistical Base Charlie, Saudi Arabia: Feb. 18, 1991.

Interview of MAJ Sam S. Walker, III, Executive Officer(Forward), 4th Sqdn(Air)(-), 17th Cav. Oral Hist. Interview DSIT AE 003. Manama, Bahrain: Feb. 13, 1991.

---

[9] These are all available on the Internet at: http://www.army.mil/cmh-pg/documents/swa/dsit/

U.S. Marine Corps Unit Command Chronologies[10]

I MEF (Dec. 1990)

2nd Mar Div (Jan-Apr 1991)

2nd MEB (Jan-Dec 1991)
4th MEB (Jan. 1991), (Mar. 1991)

11th MEU(SOC) (Jan-Jun 1991)
13th MEU(SOC) (16 Feb-15 Mar 1991)
24th MEU(SOC) (21 Jan-30 Jun 1991)

1st SRIG (Jan. 1991)
SRI Spt Gp 5 (Jan-Mar 1991)

1st Marines (Feb. 1991)
1/1 Marines (21 Dec 1990-31 Jan 1991), (Feb. 1991)
3/1 Marines (1 Jan-15 Feb 1991), (17 Mar-30 Jun 1991)
2nd Marines (Jan-Jun 1991)
1/2 Marines (Jan-Jun 1990), (16 Apr-30 Jun 1991)
2/2 Marines (Jan-Feb 1991)
3/2 Marines (Jul-Dec 1990), (Jan-Jun 1991)
3rd Marines (Feb. 1991)
1/3 Marines (Feb. 1991)
2/3 Marines (Jan-Jun 1990), (Jan-Feb 1991)
3/3 Marines (Jan. 1991), (Feb. 1991)
4th Marines (Jan-Feb 1991)
1/4 Marines (16 Feb-15 Mar 1991)
2/4 Marines (Feb. 1991)
5th Marines (Jul-Dec 1990)
1/5 Marines (Dec. 1990), (Jan-Mar 1991)
2/5 Marines (Jul-Dec 1990)
3/5 Marines (1 Jan-17 Mar 1991), (18 Mar-30 Jun 1991)
6th Marines (Jul-Dec 1990), (Jan-Feb 1991), (Mar 1991)
1/6 Marines (Sep. 1990), (Oct. 1990), (Jan-Feb 1991)
3/6 Marines (Jul-Dec 1990), (Jan-Feb 1991)
7th Marines (Jul-Sep 1990), (Jan-Feb 1991), (Mar. 1991)
1/7 Marines (Jul-Sep 1990), (Jan-Feb 1991)
2/7 Marines (Jan-Feb 1991), (Apr-Jun 1991)
3/7 Marines (Jan-Feb 1991)
8th Marines (Jul-Dec 1990), (Feb. 1991), (Mar. 1991)

---

[10] Command chronologies address each unit's organization, major items of equipment, and training or combat activities. Each unit prepares its command chronology shortly after the events it addresses. The time periods listed here are the time periods addressed in the command chronologies.

Order of Battle

1/8 Marines (Jul-Dec 1990), (Jan. 1991), (Feb. 1991)
2/8 Marines (Jan-Jun 1991)
3/8 Marines (Jan-Jun 1991)
9th Marines (Jul-Dec 1990)
1/9 Marines (Jan-Jun 1991)
3/9 Marines (Nov. 1990), (Feb. 1991), (Mar. 1991), (Apr-Jun 1991)
23rd Marines (Jan-Dec 1991)
1/23 Marines (Jan-Dec 1990), (Jan-Dec 1991)
3/23 Marines (Feb. 1991)[11]
24th Marines (Jan. 1991), (Feb. 1991)
25th Marines (Jan-Jun 1991)
1/25 Marines (Jan-Feb 1991)
Co A, 1/25 Marines (Jan-Jul 1991)
2/25 Marines (Jan-Dec 1991)
H&S Co, 2/25 Marines (Jan-Dec 1991)
Co E, 2/25 Marines (Jan-Dec 1991)
Co G, 2/25 Marines[12] (Jan-Dec 1991)
Wpns Co, 2/25 Marines (Jan-Dec 1991)

1st Tank Bn (Jul-Sep 1990), (Oct. 1990), (Nov. 1990), (Dec. 1990), (Jan-Feb 1991)
2nd Tank Bn (Jul-Dec 1990), (Jan-Feb 1991)
3rd Tank Bn (Jul-Sep 90), (Nov. 1990), (Dec. 1990), (Jan-Feb 1991)
4th Tank Bn (Jan-Dec 1991)
8th Tank Bn (26 Nov 1990-30 Apr 1991)
Co A, 8th Tank Bn (Jan-Dec 1991)

1st LAI Bn (Jul-Sep 1990), (Oct. 1990), (Nov. 1990), (Dec. 1990), (Jan-Feb 1991)
2nd LAI Bn (Jul-Dec 1990), (Jan-Mar 1991)
3rd LAI Bn (Jan-Jun 1991)

1st Recon Bn (Jul-Sep 1990), (Oct. 1990), (Dec. 1990), (Jan-Feb 1991)
2nd Recon Bn (Jan-Feb 1991), (28 Feb-30 Jun 1991)
3rd Recon Bn (Jan-Jun 1991)
Co A, 3rd Recon Bn (Jan-Feb 1991)
4th Recon Bn (Jan-Dec 1991)

1st Armd Aslt Bn (Jan-Jun 1991)

2nd Aslt Amphib Bn (Jul-Dec 1990), (Jan. 1991)
3rd Aslt Amphib Bn (Jul-Sep 1990), (Oct. 1990), (Nov. 1990), (Dec. 1990), (Jan-Feb 1991)

---

[11] **Available on the Internet at: http://www.marforres.usmc.mil/ Click on "4th Marine Division," then "23rd Marines," and then "3rd Bn, 23rd Marines"**

[12] This unit served in Desert Storm as Co D, 2/25 Marines. It was redesignated as Co G shortly after Desert Storm.

Co D, 3rd Aslt Amphib Bn (July 1990-June 1991)
4th Aslt Amphib Bn (Feb. 1991)

1/10 Marines (Jan-Jun 1990), (Apr-Jun 1991)
2/10 Marines (1 Jul-25 Nov 1990), (26 Nov 90-31 Jan 1991), (Feb. 1991), (Mar. 1991),
(Apr-Jun 1991)
3/10 Marines (Jul-Dec 1990), (Feb. 1991), (Apr-Jun 1991)
5/10 Marines (1 Jul-9 Dec 1990), (10 Dec 1990-10 Jan 1991), (10 Jan-10 Feb 1991),
(10 Feb-10 Mar 1991)
11th Marines (Jan-Feb 1991)
1/11 Marines (Jul-Dec 1990), (Jan-Feb 1991)
2/11 Marines (Jan-Jun 1990), (16 Feb-17 Mar 1991), (18 Mar-30 Jun 1991)
3/11 Marines (Jul-Sep 1990), (Jan-Feb 1991)
5/11 Marines (Jul-Sep 1990)
1/12 Marines (Jul-Sep 1990), (Mar-Jun 1991)
2/12 Marines (Jul-Dec 1990), (Jan. 1991), (Feb. 1991), (Apr-Jun 1991)
3/12 Marines (Jan-Dec 1990), (Jan-Jun 1991), (Feb. 1991)
14th Marines (Jan-Dec 1991)
4/14 Marines (Jan-Dec 1990), (Jan-Dec 1991)

3rd LAAD Bn (Sep. 1990), (Oct. 1990), (Nov. 1990)

2nd LAAM Bn (Jul-Sep 1990), (Oct. 1990), (Dec. 1990), (Jan. 1991), (Feb. 1991)

Co C, 1st Cbt Eng Bn (Jan-Jun 1991)
2nd Cbt Eng Bn (16 Dec 1990-15 Jan 1991)
Co C, 2nd Cbt Eng Bn (Mar. 1991)

MACG 38 (Sep. 1990), (Oct. 1990), (Nov. 1990)

U.S. Marine Corps Operations Orders[13]

Frag Order #001, Operation Desert Shield. Saudi Arabia: HQ, 2nd Mar Div, Dec. 20, 1990.

Frag Order 2-90 (Operation Desert Storm). Saudi Arabia: HQ, 2nd Mar Div, Dec. 31, 1990.

Frag Order 8-91 to Operation Order 1-91 (Operation Desert Storm). Saudi Arabia:
HQ, TF Taro, Feb. 19, 1991.

Operation Order 1-91 (Operation Desert Storm). Saudi Arabia: HQ, 6th Marines, Feb. 18, 1991.

Frag Order 11-91. Saudi Arabia: HQ, 8th Marines, Feb. 22, 1991.

---

[13] An operations order is a long and detailed written order issued before a battle. A frag (fragmentary) order is a very short written or verbal order issued during a battle to effectuate a change or execute a pre-planned contingency.

Order of Battle

Operation Order 1-91 (Operation Desert Storm). Saudi Arabia: HQ, 2/2 Marines, Feb. 18, 1991.

Operation Order __. Saudi Arabia: HQ, 2/4 Marines, Feb. 19, 1991.

Frag Order __. Saudi Arabia: HQ, 2/4 Marines, Feb. 24, 1991.

Operation Order 1-91 (Operation Desert Storm). Saudi Arabia: HQ, 1/6 Marines, Feb. __, 1991.

Operation Order 1-91 (Operation Desert Storm). Saudi Arabia: HQ, 3/6 Marines, Feb. 21, 1991.

Operation Order __ (Operation Desert Storm). Saudi Arabia: HQ, 2/7 Marines, date unknown.

Operation Order 6-91 (Operation Desert Storm). Saudi Arabia: HQ, 3/23 Marines, Feb. 18, 1991.

Operation Order __. Saudi Arabia: HQ, 2nd Tank Bn, Feb. 21, 1991.

Operation Order 1-91 (Operation Desert Storm). Saudi Arabia: HQ, 3rd Tank Bn, Feb. 3, 1991.

Operation Order 1-91. Persian Gulf: HQ, 2/11 Marines(Artillery), Feb. 21, 1991.

Other U.S. Marine Corps Documents And Publications

Fleet Marine Force Reference Publication 1-11, Fleet Marine Force Organization - 1992. Washington, DC: HQ, U.S. Marine Corps, 1992.

NAVMC 2922, United States Marine Corps Unit Awards Manual. Washington, DC: HQ, U.S. Marine Corps, Feb. 25, 1998.

ALMAR 282/92, "Subject: MCBUL 1650, Awards Update." Arlington, VA: HQ, U.S. Marine Corps, Oct. 6, 1992. [Unit awards for Desert Storm]

Hemleben, Maj J. "1st Tanks Combat Summary." n.p.: n.p., n.d. [1st Tank Bn]

"MARCENT - Operation Desert Storm: MARCENT Task Organization." n.p.: n.p., Aug. 13, 1991. [Briefing charts]

"USMC Forces That Served In SWA." n.p.: n.p., n.d. [Received from HQ, Marine Corps]

"List of Participating Units." n.p.: n.p., n.d. [Received from HQ, Marine Corps in December 1993]

Large packet of materials re 1st Mar Div received from Public Affairs Office, Camp Pendleton, in March 1992.

CO, Co C, 1st Recon Bn & CO, Co A, 3rd Recon Bn. Memorandum for CO, 1st Recon Bn, "Mission Capabilities For Operation Desert Storm." n.p.: n.p., n.d.

"Reserve Activations By State." n.p.: U.S. Marine Corps, Mar. 4, 1991.

Miscellaneous/Other

Investigation and Analysis Directorate, Office of the Special Assistant for Gulf War Illnesses, Office of the Secretary of Defense. Case Narrative: 11th Marines. n.p.: OSD, Oct. 30, 1998. [1st Mar Div] **Available on the Internet at: http://www.gulflink.osd.mil/11th_marines/**

Association of the United States Army. Special Report: The U.S. Army In Operation Desert Storm: An Overview. Arlington, VA: Institute of Land Warfare, AUSA, 1991.

Association of the United States Army. Special Report: Operations Desert Shield And Desert Storm: The Logistics Perspective. Arlington, VA: Institute of Land Warfare, AUSA, 1991.

Sawicki, James. Unit lineage & honors sheets for the following units: 3rd MP Gp; 400th MP POW Cp; 401st MP POW Cp; 403rd MP POW Cp; 6th Sig Cmd; 2nd Sig Bde; 30th Med Bde; 226th Spt Gp; 227th Spt Gp; 324th Spt Gp; 318th Trans Agency; HHC, 32nd Trans Gp; 111th Ord Gp; HHC, 304th CA Bde; HHC, 308th CA Bde; HHC, 10th PERSCOM; & HHD, 3rd Pers Gp.

Displays at the Royal Air Force Museum, London, England. Visited by the author, September 1997. [RAF Regiment]

Displays at the Royal Armoured Corps Tank Museum, Bovington Camp, England. Visited by the author, August 1993. [British and French units]

Correspondence & Telephone Conversations

Published Letters To the Editor

Letter to the editor from COL Peter D. Wells. Armor. (May-Jun 1991), p. 3. [1-7 Cav(-) and Trps A & B, 2-1 Cav]

Order of Battle

Letters To the Author

Letter to the author from HQ, 70th Div(Tng) re units mobilized for Operation Desert Storm (Oct. 14, 1995).

Letter to the author from HQ, Fort Bliss, TX, re USAR units that were mobilized and served at Fort Bliss during Operation Desert Storm (Nov. 4, 1996).

Letter to the author from LTC Larry D. Haub re the 1-158 FA in Operation Desert Storm (Sep. 27, 1995).

Letter to the author from COL Steve Speakes re the 2/11 ACR's participation in the WSRO program during Operation Desert Storm (Feb. 8, 1997).

Letter to the author from Naval Facilities Engineering Command Historian, Port Hueneme, CA, re Navy construction battalion units that participated in Operation Desert Storm (Mar. 4, 1999).

Telephone Conversations With the Author

Telephone conversation between the author and SSG Tom Baxter re the 2-68 Armor's participation in the WSRO program during Operation Desert Storm (June 27, 1996).

Telephone conversation between the author and CPT Burt, HQ, 3rd MP Gp(CID) re 3rd MP Gp's participation in Operation Desert Storm (Sep. 22, 1995).

Index

The entries in this index are organized by category and, within each category, generally in alphabetical order. The entries within "Military Equipment," however, are organized under a different approach. These entries are organized by category (e.g., tanks first, then infantry/cavalry vehicles, and so on) and, within each category, in a logical (rather than alphabetical or numeric) order. For example, the entries for U.S. Army tanks begin with the M60 series, followed by the M1 series, and then the M551 "Sheridan." The M60 preceded the M1 as America's main battle tank. The M551 is last because it served as a light tank and, in Desert Storm, played a very minor role.

[1] Many locations in the mideast have multiple spellings. I have tried to use those spellings used by the U.S. Department of Defense.

Military Equipment

U.S. Army Equipment

Tanks

Infantry/Cavalry Vehicles

---

[2] Listed here are all references to
the 105mm-armed M1.
[3] Listed here are all references to
the 120mm-armed M1A1.

Order of Battle

Field Artillery

M102 towed 105mm howitzer - 12-3, 13-8, 13-9, 13-20, 24-6, D-13

M119 towed 105mm howitzer - 13-9

M114 towed 155mm howitzer - 13-9

M198 towed 155mm howitzer - 12-3, 13-8, 13-9, 13-10, 13-20, 28-5, D-13

M109 series self-propelled 155mm howitzer – 4, 12-3, 13-8, 13-9, 13-10, 13-12, 13-20, D-12, D-16

M110 series self-propelled 203mm howitzer - 4, 12-3, 13-8, 13-10, 13-20

M270 Multiple Launch Rocket System (MLRS) - 4, 8, 4-7, 4-8, 4-11, 4-24, 4-25, 4-26, 4-29, 5-2, 9-10, 9-11, 10-1, 10-2, 12-3, 13-8, 13-9, 13-10, 13-11, 13-20, 15-3, 15-5, 19-14, 24-6, 33-3, 34-3, 34-4, 34-5, 36-2, D-11, D-12, D-17

Army Tactical Missile System (ATACMS) – 4, 4-25, 4-26, 4-29, 9-11, 9-12, 13-8, 13-11, 13-12, 24-6, 33-3, 34-3, 34-4

Lance Missile - 4-24, 4-26, 13-12

Pershing Missile - 11-2, 13-12

AN/TPQ-36 "Firefinder" Mortar Locating Radar - 4-11, 4-23, 4-25, 4-27, 13-11, 13-12, D-12, D-17

AN/TPQ-37 "Firefinder" Artillery Locating Radar - 4-15, 4-23, 4-25, 4-27, 13-11, 13-12, D-12, D-17

AN/TPS-25 Ground Surveillance Radar – D-12

M548 Tracked Cargo Carrier - 13-12, 13-14

M992 Field Artillery Ammunition Support Vehicle (FAASV) - 13-12

Air Defense Artillery

M163 series "Vulcan" self-propelled 20mm gatling gun - 4-3, 4-4, 4-5, 4-6, 4-7, 4-8, 4-10, 4-11, 4-13, 4-14, 4-15, 4-23, 4-26, 4-27, 5-1, 9-14, 9-15, 11-3, 13-13, 13-14, 13-15, 14-5, 33-4, D-18, D-19

M167 series "Vulcan" towed 20mm gatling gun - 4-15, 4-16, 4-17, 4-18, 4-19, 4-20, 4-21, 9-14, 9-15, 13-13, 13-15, 33-4, D-18, D-19

M730 series "Chaparral" self-propelled missile system - 4-3, 4-4, 4-5, 4-6, 4-27, 4-28, 9-14, 11-3, 13-13, 13-14, 33-4, D-18

"Redeye" missile - 13-15

"Stinger" missile - 4-2, 4-3, 4-4, 4-5, 4-6, 4-7, 4-8, 4-10, 4-11, 4-13, 4-14, 4-15, 4-16, 4-17, 4-18, 4-19, 4-20, 4-21, 4-22, 4-23, 4-24, 4-26, 4-27, 5-1, 9-14, 9-15, 9-16, 11-3, 13-13, 13-14, 13-15, 14-5, 27-8, 33-4, D-18, D-19

"Avenger" air defense system - 4-7, 4-8, 4-23, 4-27, 9-16, 13-13, 13-14, 13-15, 24-8, 33-4, D-18

Bradley Stinger Fighting Vehicle - 13-14

Bradley Stinger Fighting Vehicle-Enhanced (BSFV-E or Bradley Linebacker) - 13-14

"Hawk" missile system - 4-1, 4-2, 4-23, 4-27, 4-29, 7-1, 9-14, 9-15, 13-13, 13-16, 14-5, 33-4, D-19

"Nike-Hercules" missile - 13-16

"Patriot" missile system - 5, 4-1, 4-2, 4-27, 7-1, 7-2, 8-1, 8-2, 9-15, 13-13, 13-15, 13-16, 14-5, 15-4, 15-5, 15-6, 24-8, 33-4, D-19

"Patriot" PAC-2 missile - 4-27, 13-16

"Sidewinder" air-to-air missile - 13-14

Support Vehicles

M728 Combat Engineer Vehicle - 13-3

M60 Armored Vehicle Launching Bridge (AVLB) - 13-3

Armored Vehicle Launched MICLIC (AVLM) - 13-3

M9 Armored Combat Earthmover (ACE) - 3

M88A1 Armored Recovery Vehicle - D-15

High Mobility Multi-Purpose Wheeled Vehicle (HMMWV) - 13-8, 13-15, D-5, D-7

Weapons

M16 Rifle - D-7

M203 40mm Grenade Launcher - D-7

M249 5.56mm Squad Automatic Weapon (SAW) - D-6, D-7

M60 7.62mm Machine Gun - D-7

.50 cal machine gun - 4-24, 13-15

25mm automatic cannon - 3, 4

M47 "Dragon" antitank missile - 28-4, D-6, D-7

TOW antitank missile - 4, 13-7, 13-14, 28-4, D-6, D-7

Order of Battle

M151 quarter-ton truck (jeep) - 19-6, 24-5
High Mobility Multi-Purpose Wheeled
    Vehicle (HMMWV) - 19-13, 19-15,
    19-19, 24-5, 24-6, E-4, E-7, E-9
M1045 TOW Carrier - 24-5
M1046 TOW Carrier - 24-5

Weapons

M16 Rifle - E-5
M203 40mm Grenade Launcher - E-5
M249 5.56mm Squad Automatic Weapon
    (SAW) - E-5
M60 7.62mm Machine Gun - E-5
M2 .50 cal Machine Gun - E-4, E-5, E-7
MK-153 83mm Shoulder-Launched
    Multipurpose Assault Weapon (SMAW)
    E-5
MK-19 Automatic 40mm Grenade Launcher –
    E-4, E-5, E-7
M47 "Dragon" antitank missile - E-5
TOW antitank missile - 19-3, 19-4, 19-5,
    19-6, 19-9, 19-10, 19-11, 19-12, 19-13,
    19-15, 19-17, 19-19, 19-20, 20-1, 20-2,
    21-3, 21-4, 24-4, 24-5, 24-6, 33-5, E-4,
    E-7, E-13
"Hellfire" missile - 24-9
M224 60mm mortar - E-5
M29 81mm mortar - E-5
M252 81mm mortar - 24-4, E-5

Aircraft

AH-1 "Cobra" - 24-9
AH-1T "Sea Cobra" - E-2, E-3
AH-1W "Super Cobra" - E-2, E-3
UH-1N "Huey" Utility Helicopter - 24-10,
    E-2, E-3
CH-46 "Sea Knight" Medium-Lift Transport
    Helicopter - 24-10, E-2, E-3
CH-53D "Sea Stallion" Heavy-Lift Cargo
    Helicopter - 24-10, E-2, E-3
CH-53E "Super Stallion" Heavy-Lift Cargo
    Helicopter - 24-10, E-2, E-3
AV-8B "Harrier" - E-2, E-3
F/A-18 "Hornet" - E-3

Miscellaneous

Mine Clearing Line Charge (MICLIC) - 19-10
M9 Dozer Blade - E-7
Mine plow - 19-10, 24-4
Mine rake - 19-10, 24-4

British Equipment

Chieftain Main Battle Tank - 27-9
Challenger Main Battle Tank - 27-2, 27-3,
    27-5, 27-8, 27-9, 28-4
Scimitar reconnaissance vehicle - 27-2, 27-4,
    27-5, 27-8, 27-9
Scorpion reconnaissance vehicle - 27-5, 27-6,
    27-8, 27-9
Striker antitank vehicle - 27-4, 27-8, 27-9
Spartan Armored Personnel Carrier (APC) –
    27-8, 27-9
Sultan command vehicle - 27-8, 27-9
Samaritan medic vehicle - 27-8
FV432 Armored Personnel Carrier (APC) –
    27-9
Warrior Infantry Fighting Vehicle (IFV) - 27-2,
    27-3, 27-5, 27-8, 27-9
Ferret Scout Car - 27-6
M109 series self-propelled 155mm howitzer –
    27-2, 27-3, 27-4, 27-8, 27-9
M110 series self-propelled 203mm howitzer –
    27-4, 27-8, 27-9
M270 Multiple Launch Rocket System
    (MLRS) - 27-4, 27-8, 27-9
Milan antitank missile - 27-2, 27-9
Swingfire antitank missile - 27-8
81mm mortar - 27-9
Javelin surface-to-air missile (SAM) - 27-2,
    27-3, 27-4, 27-7, 27-8
Rapier surface-to-air missile (SAM) - 27-4,
    27-6, 27-8
Gazelle scout helicopter - 27-3, 27-4, 27-8
Lynx attack helicopter - 27-3, 27-4
Puma helicopter - 27-5
Chinook helicopter - 27-5
Sea King helicopter - 27-5
Tank transporters - 27-5

Order of Battle

Selected Military Units

Most military units are not listed here because the organization of this order of battle makes it easy to find the references to these units. See "How To Use This Book" at page xi. Listed here are (1) U.S. Army and Marine Corps named task forces, (2) the nicknames used by U.S. Army maneuver brigades, (3) U.S. Navy ships, and (4) Iraqi units.

U.S. Army

Named Task Forces

U.S. Army Maneuver Brigade Nicknames

Personnel

WELCOME TO

Hellgate Press

Hellgate Press is named after the historic and rugged Hellgate Canyon on southern Oregon's scenic Rogue River. The raging river that flows below the canyon's towering jagged cliffs has always attracted a special sort of individual — someone who seeks adventure. From the pioneers who bravely pursued the lush valleys beyond, to the anglers and rafters who take on its roaring challenges today — Hellgate Press publishes books that personify this adventurous spirit. Our books are about military history, adventure travel, and outdoor recreation. On the following pages, we would like to introduce you to some of our latest titles and encourage you to join in the celebration of this unique spirit.

Our books are in your favorite bookstore or you can order them direct at **1-800-228-2275** or visit our Website at **http://www.psi-research.com/hellgate.htm**

ARMY MUSEUMS

West of the Mississippi
by Fred L. Bell, SFC Retired

ISBN: 1-55571-395-5
Paperback: 17.95

A guide book for travelers to the army museums of the west, as well as a source of information about the history of the site where the museum is located. Contains detailed information about the contents of the museum and interesting information about famous soldiers stationed at the location or specific events associated with the facility. These twenty-three museums are in forts and military reservations which represent the colorful heritage in the settling of the American West.

BYRON'S WAR

I Never Will Be Young Again...
by Byron Lane

ISBN: 1-55571-402-1
Hardcover: 21.95

Based on letters that were mailed home and a personal journal written more than fifty years ago during World War II, *Byron's War* brings the war life through the eyes of a very young air crew officer. It depicts how the life of this young American changed through cadet training, the experiences as a crew member flying across the North Atlantic under wartime hazards to the awesome responsibility assigned to a nineteen year-old when leading hundreds of men and aircraft where success or failure could seriously impact the outcome of the war.

GULF WAR DEBRIEFING BOOK

An After Action Report
by Andrew Leyden

ISBN: 1-55571-396-3
Paperback: 18.95

Whereas most books on the Persian Gulf War tell an "inside story" based on someone else's opinion, this book lets you draw your own conclusions by providing you with a meticulous review of events and documentation all at your fingertips. Includes lists of all military units deployed, a detailed account of the primary weapons used during the war, and a look at the people and politics behind the military maneuvering.

FROM HIROSHIMA WITH LOVE

by Raymond A. Higgins

ISBN: 1-55571-404-8
Paperback: 18.95

This remarkable story is written from actual detailed notes and diary entries kept by Lieutenant Commander Wallace Higgins. Because of his industrial experience back in the United States and with the reserve commission in the Navy, he was an excellent choice for military governor of Hiroshima. Higgins was responsible for helping rebuild a ravaged nation of war. He developed an unforeseen respect for the Japanese, the culture, and one special woman.

NIGHT LANDING

A Short History of West Coast Smuggling
by David W. Heron

ISBN: 1-55571-449-8
Paperback: 13.95

Night Landing reveals the true stories of smuggling off the shores of California from the early 1800s to the present. It is a provocative account of the many attempts to illegally trade items such as freon, drugs, sea otters, and diamonds. This unusual chronicle also profiles each of these ingenious, but over-optimistic criminals and their eventual apprehension.

ORDER OF BATTLE

Allied Ground Forces of Operation Desert Storm
by Thomas D. Dinackus

ISBN: 1-55571-493-5
Paperback: 17.95

Based on extensive research, and containing information not previously available to the public, *Order of Battle* is a detailed study of the Allied ground combat units that served in Operation Desert Storm. In addition to showing unit assignments, it includes the insignia and equipment used by the various units in one of the largest military operations since the end of WWII.

PILOTS, MAN YOUR PLANES!

A History of Naval Aviation
by Wilbur H. Morrison

ISBN: 1-55571- 466-8
Hardbound: 33.95

An account of naval aviation from Kitty Hawk to the Gulf War, *Pilots, Man Your Planes! — A History of Naval Aviation* tells the story of naval air growth from a time when planes were launched from battleships to the major strategic element of naval warfare it is today. Full of detailed maps and photographs. Great for anyone with an interest in aviation.

REBIRTH OF FREEDOM

From Nazis and Communists to a New Life in America   ISBN: 1-55571-492-7
by Michael Sumichrast   Paperback: 16.95

"...a fascinating account of how the skill, ingenuity and work ethics of an individual, when freed from the yoke of tyranny and oppression, can make a lasting contribution to Western society. Michael Sumichrast's autobiography tells of his first loss of freedom to the Nazis, only to have his native country subjected to the tyranny of the Communists. He shares his experiences of life in a manner that makes us Americans, and others, thankful to live in a country where individual freedom is protected."

— *General Alexander M. Haig, Former Secretary of State*

THE WAR THAT WOULD NOT END

U.S. Marines in Vietnam, 1971-1973   ISBN: 1-55571-420-X
by Major Charles D. Melson, USMC (Ret)   Paperback: 19.95

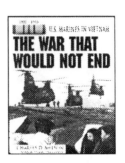

When South Vietnamese troops proved unable to "take over" the war from their American counterparts, the Marines had to resume responsibility. Covering the period 1971-1973, Major Charles D. Melson, who served in Vietnam, describes all the strategies, battles, and units that broke a huge 1972 enemy offensive. The book contains a detailed look at this often ignored period of America's longest war.

WORDS OF WAR

From Antiquity to Modern Times   ISBN: 1-55571-491-9
by Gerald Weland   Paperback: 13.95

Words of War is a delightful romp through military history. Lively writing leads the reader to an under- standing of a number of soldierly quotes. The result of years of haunting dusty dungeons in libraries, obscure journals and microfilm files, this unique approach promises to inspire many casual readers to delve further into the circumstances surrounding the birth of many quoted words.

WORLD TRAVEL GUIDE

                                         ISBN: 1-55571- 494-3
by Barry Mowell   Paperback: 19.95

The resource for the modern traveler, *World Travel Guide* is both informative and enlightening. It contains maps, social and economic information, concise information concerning entry requirements, availability of healthcare, transportation and crime. Numerous Website and embassy listings are provided for additional free information. A one-page summary contains general references to the history, culture and other characteristics of interest to the traveler or those needing a reference atlas.